Harnessing Omni-Channel Marketing Strategies for Fashion and Luxury Brands

GW00568430

Harnessing Omni–Channel Marketing Strategies for Fashion and Luxury Brands

Edited by

Wilson Ozuem, Elena Patten, and Yllka Azemi

BrownWalker Press
Irvine • Boca Raton

Harnessing Omni-Channel Marketing Strategies for Fashion and Luxury Brands

BrownWalker Press / Universal Publishers, Inc.
Irvine • Boca Raton
USA • 2020
www.BrownWalkerPress.com
2020

978-1-62734-740-2 (pbk.)
978-1-62734-741-9 (ebk.)

Typeset by Medlar Publishing Solutions Pvt Ltd, India
Cover design by Ivan Popov

Publisher's Cataloging-in-Publication Data

Names: Ozuem, Wilson, 1974- editor. | Patten, Elena, 1983- editor. | Azemi, Yllka, 1988- editor.
Title: Harnessing omni-channel marketing strategies for fashion and luxury brands / edited by Wilson Ozuem, Elena Patten, Yllka Azemi.
Description: Irvine : BrownWalker Press, 2019. | Includes bibliographical references.
Identifiers: LCCN 2019041390 (print) | LCCN 2019041391 (ebook) | ISBN 9781627347402 (paperback) | ISBN 9781627347419 (ebook)
Subjects: LCSH: Fashion merchandising. | Luxury goods--Marketing. | Luxury goods--Internet marketing.
Classification: LCC HD9940.A2 H367 2019 (print) | LCC HD9940.A2 (ebook) | DDC 658.8/7--dc23
LC record available at https://lccn.loc.gov/2019041390
LC ebook record available at https://lccn.loc.gov/2019041391

Table of Contents

Detailed Table of Contents

Chapter 1
Elena Patten, Macromedia University of Applied Sciences, Germany

The consumers' purchasing behaviour has changed tremendously with the development of E-Commerce. The so-called "omni-channel customers" tend to switch retail channels during their purchasing process. In order to address changing consumer behaviour, omni-channel fashion retailing companies still need to learn how to be able to provide an excellent service to these customers. This paper aims to investigate this phenomenon from the perspective of omni-channel customers.

Chapter 2
Guida Helal, American University of Beirut, Lebanon
Wilson Ozuem, University of Cumbria, United Kingdom

Brands can no longer survive without the intangible presence of a social media platform that allows a brand to travel beyond physical limitations in reaching consumers. Millennial markets have embodied social media as a central outlet of communication, going as far as deeming it a form of public identity consumers embody across global connections. Brand connections and perceptions are consequently developed based on the potential tangible and intangible values that a brand is perceived to offer. Social media acts as the bridge that furthers a brand's position in the market by providing Millennials with the platform to amplify social identity through brand association. This chapter examines the impact social media has had on brand perceptions in the fashion industry, from a social identity theory outlook. The following chapter considers the theoretical and managerial implications while offering insight into the significance of social media and social identity within marketing practices.

Within the fashion industry, managing the consumer-brand relationship is always challenging. Web 2.0-based brand communities and groups on social networking sites henceforth provide the solution to this problem and enable the marketers to create maximum brand awareness and engagement of consumers with the interactive promotional and informational content. This chapter explains the ubiquitous role of social media in strengthening the consumer-brand relationship which subsequently develops the purchase intentions. It further explains the explicit role of social networking sites (SNS) based fashion brand communities and groups which provide the essential platform for heterogeneous social interactions (information, social, hedonic and economic). Such social interactions develop brand awareness, brand loyalty, brand identification, eWOM and ultimately consumers' purchase intentions. Furthermore, the chapter also discusses the conclusion and potential managerial implications of this knowledge in the fashion industry.

This chapter investigates the case of Luisaviaroma, an emblematic company that pioneered online business in luxury fashion. Founded in Florence (Italy) as a physical retailer, it exploited its stores as a springboard to animate an e-commerce platform transforming itself over time into a digital enterprise. Today nearly all its turnover comes from online business. Nevertheless, the physical stores maintain a strategic role: they integrate the online business, acting as base for omni-channel strategies. Our aim is to investigate LVR's business integration and the related practices of omni-channel management.

It is widely recognised that an in-depth understanding of online brand communities and their implications is vitally important for enhancing online relationships. However, although various studies examine how online brand communities impact consumer behaviour, very few have examined how fashion brands can enhance online relationships with their consumers through online communities. The concept of online brand communities has been applied to a range of marketing studies on purchase experience, brand equity, customer participation and brand loyalty. Additionally, it has been applied to understand social behaviours of consumers including their individual motives, group intentions, social identity, and interactions between consumers. The various studies focus on different marketing characteristics concerning online brand communities; researchers provide mixed conclusions on how brands' online relationships with consumers are maintained; specifically, limited studies have focused on online brand communities in the fashion industry. The chapter offers insight into underpinning debates but also practical guidance and advice on the development and nurturing of sustainable online brand communities.

Organisations have veered communication to social media platforms in pursuit of the new-age vocal consumer. Social media means have allowed brands and customer to engage in real-time interchange, facilitating for the transposition of traditional brand communities to virtual communities.

Social media brand communities produce interactive spaces of variable extents across global consumers. Through social media platforms, brands are able to produce content that resonates with customers, expanding brand awareness, inducing brand impressions, and fostering brand-customer relationships that constitute the foundation for brand communities. Such social media brand communities have instigated a sense of belonging across worldwide consumers, allowing individuals to utilise overt brand associations through online brand communities as a means to further social identities. The following chapter examines the influence of social media brand communities on the Millennial generation in the fashion industry, from a social identity theory perspective. This chapter focuses on theoretical and managerial implications.

Chapter 7

In omni-channel retailing, the combination of different retail channels along the various customer touchpoints has become the predominant purchasing pattern for customers. The so-called "research shopper phenomenon" describes a common tendency amongst customers to use one channel to search and another to purchase. This paper suggests that four different types of German omni-channel fashion customers exist and therefore presents an omni-channel customer typology.

Chapter 8

This book chapter assesses the relationships between perceived justice and online service failure and recovery strategies in the fashion industry for customer retention. The existing literature has examined three-way and two-way interactions between procedural, distributive and interactional justice. The outcomes vary in terms of which combinations of justice create substantial interaction effects on customer recovery assessment. It recommends that for fashion brand providers to be competitive, they must combine both immersive technology and dimension metrics that comprise of subjective assessments. Both of these are critical to improve online service failure-recovery experiences which can have a significant impact on customer satisfaction and post-recovery behaviour. Furthermore, such a combination can mediate the relationship between satisfaction variables and justice dimensions.

Given the increasing focus on the practice of social media publicity in the context of fashion brands, this chapter discusses the key features associated with social media marketing approaches. The chapter reflects on varied approaches amongst the brands in terms of brand equity, value equity, affiliation equity, buyer equity, and buying behaviour. This study presents a critical review of the literature that overtly discusses the acceptance of practices associated with and influences of social media amongst the fashion brands. The literature review presents an assessment of recently published material on the context of social media standards amongst fashion brands. Various types of social networking sites are discussed along with the recognised advantages of using such sites from the perspective of public relations practitioners. Consumer power and the role of design are also discussed, and a literature gap is identified.

Online luxury brands are uniformly recognizing the practical advantages of electronic commerce. The existing literature provides conceptual elucidation that focuses on utilization of specific online marketing strategies. However, digital platforms invite holistic marketing applications—an all-embracing approach that nullifies the risk of potentially overlooked online marketing practices. This chapter provides conceptual insight into the overarching existing marketing literature, extending beyond the discourse of unconventional marketing utilization. The chapter also discerns insights fundamental to luxury customers with disabilities, as a customer group with increased potential to appraise a comprehensive marketing strategy. The chapter presents a model that provides four consequently driven marketing steps, which lead to customer attention grasp, customer zero-error perception, customer luxury brand online engagement, and monitoring of customers.

Chapter 11
> *Dominic Appiah, Arden University, United Kingdom*
> *Kerry Howell, University of Plymouth, United Kingdom*
> *Geoff Lancaster, London School of Commerce*

The smartphone is increasingly redefining our identities, and reshaping our perspectives about shopping, socialising, teaching and learning. With current developments and the shift towards luxury smartphones, the expectation of luxury smartphone manufacturers is ultimately to consolidate customer loyalty through improved user experiences. Nevertheless, luxury is considered as an experience that adds value to consumer-brand relationships, and emphasizes that luxury brands enable consumers to derive, to some extent, intangible benefits beyond their functional utility. Loyalty to a luxury smartphone brand occurs as a consequence of positive attitudes which motivate consumers to repeatedly demand a particular brand, or a limited number of brands within a suitably defined period of time. The management of these luxury smartphones is a key marketing function. A strong and healthy brand is instrumental in creating sustainable competitive advantage and the transition to a relationship marketing paradigm places brand loyalty at the heart of customer relational strength. It is widely accepted that brand loyalty has traditionally been perceived as a behavioural construct relating to intentions towards repeat purchases. This chapter aims to provide some insights into brand switching in the smartphone industry and offers opportunities for marketers and scholars in the development of related marketing plans.

Chapter 12
> *Jianqiong Xu, University of Gloucestershire, UK*
> *Wilson Ozuem, Arden University, UK*

Extant studies have illustrated that online brand communities (OBCs) are an important platform for customer participation in, and engagement with, brands. It is essential for OBC practitioners to focus on self-brand image congruity, and value congruity, to develop consumer engagement, which in turn, generates heightened brand loyalty. This chapter suggests that, in OBCs, consumer engagement is driven by OBC self-brand image congruity and value congruity. The current chapter makes a theoretical contribution in explaining brand loyalty through user engagement in OBCs. In addition, the chapter identifies that perceived benefits and perceived costs are key antecedents of user engagement, whilst user engagement influences brand loyalty both directly and indirectly through online community commitment. Therefore, the research results suggests that marketers are encouraged to demonstrate the benefits to their online brand community users to encourage customer participation and engagement.

Chapter 13

> *Samuel Ayertey, University of Plymouth, UK*
> *Gordon Bowen, Northumbria University, UK*
> *Maxwell Ayertey Banor, Lakeland University, USA*

By being able to fill the gap in product knowledge that is totally impossible to provide in a physical shop setting, fashion retailers are now able to merchandise an impressive variety of goods and products online. Yet, the phenomenal growth of online luxury fashion retailing has not occurred without a unique set of issues in terms of service delivery, product defects and website failure. Even though inexhaustible studies have been carried out in relation to service failure and recovery, the extent to which service recovery needs to be explored so that it is deciphered into a satisfactory state remains unresolved. Drawing on the constructivist perspective, this current chapter provides creative insights into failure-recovery strategies as competitive tools for marketing in the digital age. The closing section contributes to extant knowledge and provides some strategic implications and insights for fashion and luxury brands seeking accelerated success in the online marketplace.

Foreword

I was invited by the editors of this most welcomed volume to write a short preface to this book "Harnessing Omni-Channel Marketing Strategies for Fashion and Luxury Brands". The book with its thirteen chapters is a treatise of the power of emerging media and especially its use, application and driver for business applications and purposes. For those of us who have transitioned from the non-digital age to the digital age there has been significant un-learning and new learning required to not only keep abreast of technology and seek to master its potential for positive good to mankind. Social media is a multifaceted tool which society is only just learning how to use and dare we say master. It is however a tool which can easily be seen in partial and conflicting ways. Like all important discoveries in society the dilemma of what these new discoveries might bring to business let alone society, in both their positive and negative is enormous. This frequently poses challenges to fashion and luxury brands and the debate about the uses of emerging media can find themselves before a partisan jury.

When thinking about writing this foreword I was struck by a story from a business colleague back in 2008 on the rise of social media and its potential and power. The story went something like this: Social media has collected more personal information on citizens than what the CIA and the KGB together have collected on each other's citizens throughout the Cold War period. True or not true—the story is compelling and can make many to think about the power of social media—not always for positive purposes. Likewise Twitter around 2014 was on the verge of collapse as a social media company only to be salvaged by Republican Presidential running candidate Donald Trump who made it his policy tool platform to his audience. Let us not underestimate the power of social media. These two stories provide for us the power of social media in political spheres of historic kinds.

However in a more positive context, this book seeks to address the digital business applications that computer-mediated marketing environments can provide and how they can be of a positive nature to our consumers, businesses and economy overall. More specifically, as the editors have sought to point out, "The book takes a wider perspective of the application of social media so it is not just a marketing tool, but the societal benefits and implications are discussed from a millennial generation viewpoint". In the current climate of mass information in all avenues of life, this book has the remarkable coverage of covering a myriad of digital applications across a vast area of business and marketing activities. This is a book which eloquently describes and responds to the many, creative and innovative ways in which omni-channel retailing can be important to the enhancement but also the measurement of business activity. Most importantly the book does not shy away from the potential difficulties that arise and the need to not blindly rely solely on digital means. Business applications are always looking for ways to do things better, quicker and in ways that are more effective. I am thankful for this opportunity to write these few words of appreciation of this volume and recommend it to readers who will like myself, become convinced that this book theme will be a fundamental topic of our time.

Professor Bruno Mascitelli
Swinburne University of Technology, Melbourne, Australia

Foreword

Omni-channel is a term that represents more than 'just' a marketing strategy but something inevitable in today's marketing practice. As technology enables retailers to integrate all the information, marketers now have the opportunity to utilize their channel of distribution in every way possible (hence, omni). Harnessing the phenomenon requires an understanding of consumer behaviour and how to deliver a seamless experience, both in the physical and digital world. In the business of high luxury items, seamless experience is a crucial factor that contributes to value. Thus, best practices on how to approach omni-channel, specifically to this area, is something in high demand.

This book contains a selection of articles that discuss omni-channel as a popular topic, yet still able to provide a unique perspective to guide readers into the journey of understanding the phenomena. It starts the journey with customer purchasing behaviour and service quality from the customers' perspective. It set the base understanding of how consumers respond on various channels that are now presented in the market. The following chapters then narrow down on social media role in affecting purchase intention. Including in this topic is a fresh intake on omni-channel focusing on the millennial segment and typologies of omni-channels customers in the fashion industry.

The fashion and luxury branding industry are discussed, both from conceptual and practical evidence. The discussion laid out the understanding of the industry by an explanation on the communication and consumption trajectories of social media in the fashion industry and the ecosystem of luxury brands. On a more practical side, the topic delves on how to foster a relationship with customers, examine the drivers of brand loyalty and switching behaviour, including evidence of omni-channel practice from one of leading luxury fashion brand. Within the context of fashion luxury, the book has succeeded in compiling a well-known topic with an interesting twist—for example, the topic of brand communities in the light of social media. Towards the end of the book, readers will find a nice 'closure' in the area of service failure and recovery. The areas that are crucial in every industry yet sometimes overlook.

This book is an indispensable read for those who are interested to understand how omni-channel works related to consumer behaviour. I believe the book is a valuable addition to expand knowledge, not only within specific areas of fashion and luxury branding but also in novel marketing practices.

Professor (Dr) Nuri Wulandari
Dr Nuri Wulandari is Research Director of Indonesia Banking School.
Her expertise includes Service Marketing and Digital Customer Experience

Chapter 1

Omni–Channel Purchasing Behaviour and Service Quality

Elena Patten

Macromedia University of Applied Sciences, Germany

ABSTRACT

The consumers' purchasing behaviour has changed tremendously with the development of E-Commerce. The so-called "omni-channel customers" tend to switch retail channels during their purchasing process. In order to address changing consumer behaviour, omni-channel fashion retailing companies still need to learn how to be able to provide an excellent service to these customers. This paper aims to investigate this phenomenon from the perspective of omni-channel customers.

KEYWORDS

Channel Integration, Consumer Behaviour, Omni-channel Retailing, Retail-Mix Strategies, Shopping Experience

INTRODUCTION

Retailing has changed fundamentally during the last decade (Gensler, Neslin, & Verhoef, 2017; Heinemann, 2019; Hult, Tomas, & Zhang, 2019; Verhoef, Kannan, & Inman, 2015). This development was mainly driven by technological and societal factors (Emrich, 2011; Hsieh & Tseng, 2018). In this context, the commercialization of the Internet was probably the most important cornerstone (Cao, Liu, & Cao, 2018; Patten & Rashid, 2015; Ozuem, Howell and Lancaster, 2008).

Several different kinds of leisure activities nowadays take place in the Internet. The use of social media websites, such as Facebook, Twitter or Instagram, has become an important activity of everyday life (Stokinger & Ozuem, 2015). The permanent usage of mobile devices together with the dominance of Social Media has created the situation, that customers virtually bring their whole social network to a store (Piotrowicz & Cuthbertson, 2014). The borders between offline and online activities are blurred, and retailers use Social Media as an important instrument of communication (Stokinger & Ozuem, 2015).

The result is that retailers are continuing to develop their online shops. Over the past few years, several different online retailing business models have developed in the market (for a review, see Heinemann, 2019). During the initial phase, "pure online players", such as Amazon and eBay, launched their online shops. In the next phase, "shopping comparison" websites appeared on the market. These players allowed customers to compare products on a single page and to read recommendations and critiques written by previous users. The "optimization and scale-up" phase, which started from 2005, offered new system solutions and service providers. Since 2008, many brick-and-mortar retailers have been launching online shops as an addition to their offline channels and so have become multichannel retailers (Heinemann, 2013; Ozuem et al., 2017). Then, these retailers focussed on the integration of the different retail channels and offered "cross-channel"—services, such as "click and collect", the ability to order and return or exchange goods in-store, ordering while in-store, using own mobile device or self-service technology provided by the retailer (Piotrowicz & Cuthbertson, 2014; Reinartz, Wiegand, & Imschloss, 2019). Ultimately, "clicks and mortar" retailers aim to offer fully integrated channels to become omni-channel retailers (Saghiri, Wilding, Mena, & Bourlakis, 2017; Verhoef et al., 2015).

This chapter will focus on omni-channel retailing. It will, therefore, aim to investigate the concept of integration by considering the different elements of the retail mix. Furthermore, it will elaborate the key drivers of perceived omni-channel service quality.

THE CONCEPT OF INTEGRATION

Research about omni-channel retailing embraces the concept of "integration" of the different operated channels within an organization (Ailawadi

& Farris, 2017). Channel integration initially meant that a retailer should provide a seamless customer experience between stores and online shops; customers should be able to easily switch channels during their interaction with the retailer (Saghiri et al., 2017; Seck, 2013). However, important questions remain unanswered yet: Does a seamless customer experience automatically mean a full integration? In other words, does it mean the more integrated the better? For retailers, the level of integration is a difficult managerial decision. They face various challenges since channels might be different regarding purposes and features, cost structure and competitors (Berry et al., 2010). Studies have investigated the optimal level of integration in certain areas. Related literature has devoted to several aspects of the retail-mix. Mainly, a special focus has been set on integration of assortment (Emrich, Paul, & Rudolph, 2015; Mantrala et al., 2009), pricing and promotions (Vogel & Paul, 2015; Wolk & Ebling, 2010), fulfilment (Agatz, Fleischmann, & Van Nunen, 2008; Lang & Bressolles, 2013; Wolk & Ebling, 2010; Xing, Grant, McKinnon, & Fernie, 2010), and web- and store design integration (Emrich & Verhoef, 2015). However, none of the aforementioned areas have been completely resolved yet. Quite the contrary, there are still several areas for further investigation (Verhoef et al., 2015).

With regard to the assortment strategy of a retailer, it is deemed necessary to overcome the complex duty to offer an attractive assortment on the one hand side but avoid choice difficulty on the other hand side (Mantrala et al., 2009). There is a controversy in the reviewed literature about the degree of assortment integration in omni-channel retailing. Some researchers argue, that the assortment does not necessarily need to be integrated, when the target customer of the two channels is different (Berry et al., 2010; Neslin & Shankar, 2009). This is not the case for omni-channel customers, who switch retail channels during their purchases. However, other researchers argue that product consistency is crucial to provide a seamless shopping experience for the customer (Berman & Thelen, 2004). In practice, most of "clicks and mortar" retailers nowadays apply an asymmetrical assortment strategy, which means, that they offer a larger assortment online than offline (Emrich et al., 2015). Emrich et al. (2015) investigated the impact of assortment integration on underlying assortment relations. They classified three different assortment relations. Either, assortments are substitutive (for instance, when a retailer sells two different kinds of similar shoes), or complementary (shoes and shoe crème), or independent (shoes and sun lotion). Emrich et al. found out that in any of the three assortment structures no integration of assortment is detrimental. However, they argued, that for an omni-channel retailer with a substitutive assortment, the perceived variety is lower when the assortment strategy is asymmetrical, because customers tend to disesteem the decreased channel choice and autonomy.

Regarding pricing and promotions, "clicks and mortar" retailers often need to find a way out of a dilemma: Generally, customers expect products online to be equally or even less expensive than in-store (Zhang et al., 2010). But at the same time, customers expect integrated channels with a consistence pricing strategy among channels (Seck, 2013). How can retailers overcome this dilemma without loosing market share and unsatisfied customers? In practise, retailers mostly tend towards a partial integration of their pricing (Wolk & Ebling, 2010). They charge the same-posted prices among their different channels, because they fear that different prices might lead to customers' confusion and resentment. But, at the same time many retailers apply channel specific price promotions or charging handling and shipping costs (Neslin et al., 2006). In the reviewed literature, most of the researchers argue in favour of a consisting pricing strategy for all channels of a retailer (Berman & Thelen, 2004; Vogel & Paul, 2015; Wolk & Ebling, 2010).

Wolk and Ebling (2010) developed a conceptual framework on the factors, which might influence a pricing strategy across channels, namely competition, offline reach, online reach, number of distribution channels, size of company, product type, and brand power. They argued, that the lower the level of competition in one segment is, the higher the extent of price differentiation is. Thus, market power has an impact on price differentiation. For Wolk and Ebling, physical distance is a criterion, which determines if customers have an easy access to a product or if they need to spend high transaction costs to get access. For retailers that operate multiple channels this means, that if he operates just few stores and apart from that sells his products online, the retailer will be able to operate both channels more separable. As a consequence, this retailer is more in a position that he can apply price differentiation online and offline. The increasing number of customers who buy online and furthermore use different channels of one retailer during their purchase process leads customers to easily have access to a retailer's overall offer. This will lead retailers to offer the same prices among their different retail channels. Regarding the number of distribution channels, the two researchers argue, that a customized operation of each channel means an increase of transaction costs and effort for the retailer. Concluding, the more channels a retailer operates, the less channel-based price differentiation he will apply. The size of company is therefore pivotal, that retailers, which face lower cost when engaging in price differentiation, will apply it more often. Normally big companies can leverage on strategic advantages such as an efficient organization, cheaper purchases or superior technologies. Thus, bigger retailing companies will more likely apply channel-based price differentiation. For certain product types, customers prefer one channel over another. For instance, customers prefer to buy clothing in-store, since they want to try it on and physically see and touch the item. So, if one channel is superior for the customer than another, it is more likely that customers will accept channel-based price differentiation and pay a higher price in that channel, which they prefer. Generally, branding decreases the customer's price sensitivity. But channel-based price differentiation might lead also to confusion and in turn decreases brand power (Wolk & Ebling, 2010).

Wolk and Ebling's conceptual framework gives a valuable contribution to the debate of channel-based price differentiation. It is the first framework to conceptualize the different influencing factors considering customer (market), retailer and product characteristics.

However, channel-based price differentiation has certain positive and negative impacts on customer satisfaction: It positively affects their perceptions of value, increases relationship quality, and enhances repurchase intentions, but it also leads to perceptions of price unfairness and limits customer self-determination, which negatively affect retention outcomes (Vogel & Paul, 2015). It remains questionable, which of the mentioned criteria affect more the final choice of shopping location and furthermore the long-term relationship with the retailer: Would customers rather buy at a retailer with a higher perception of value or would they tend to buy at a competitor, where they find the pricing fairer?

A possible pricing strategy for omni-channel retailers, which embraces both- a high perception of value and price fairness, is considered as "self-matching pricing" (Kireyev, Kumar, & Ofek, 2015): Here, the retailer can set different prices across channels, but he will offer the lower price to the customer when he can supply evidence. Thus, 'self-matching policies, by design, offer retailers the flexibility of setting different prices across channels, while affording consumers the possibility of a consistent experience, presumably in line with the omni-channel philosophy' (Kireyev et al., 2015, p. 29).

Price promotions at omni-channel retailers have several within and across channel implications: Offline price promotions can reduce category sales online during the promotion period; furthermore, online promotions can reduce category sales offline during the promotion period; negative cross-channel effects are higher for loyal customers than for opportunists; and, the impact of online promotions on offline sales within the promoted category is higher than vice versa (Breugelmans & Campo, 2016).

One can conclude, that a successful management of pricing and promotions is a complex field in omni-channel retailing. It is deemed necessary to consider effects within and across channels and set a coherent pricing and promotion strategy.

Regarding fulfilment, a coherent omni-channel strategy should concern both the marketing mix and operations management (Agatz et al., 2008). In this respect fulfilment is an important component of a retailer's operations strategy. According to the reviewed fulfilment literature, omni-channel e-fulfilment can be considered as fulfilling online or in-store orders including warehousing, picking and order preparation, distribution, purchasing, delivery and returns (Agatz et al., 2008; Lang & Bressolles, 2013). For omni-channel customers, four dimensions of fulfilment can be considered as predominantly important, namely timeliness, availability, condition and return (Xing & Grant, 2006; Xing et al., 2010; Ozuem & Tan, 2014). Timeliness refers to several aspects, such as speed of delivery, choice of delivery date, or delivery within a certain time slot. Availability refers to the confirmation of availability, order tracking, or waiting time. Condition refers to order accuracy, order completeness, or order damage. Return refers to return policies, such as ease of return and return channel options, the promptness of collection and of replacement (Lang & Bressolles, 2013). For omni-channel retailers this means, that their supply chain management needs to be adapted to these specific customer needs. This has several impacts: (1) an online channel not only provides a physical product but also several related services, most notably delivery. The delivery service may range from making the product available for pick-up to time-specific home delivery. The management of this service component of e-fulfilment gives rise to novel planning issues. (2) The flexibility of an omni-channel retailer with respect to order promising and pricing, makes it necessary to imply an appropriate strategy. (3) The integration of different channels raises issues in inventory deployment, since different channels may require different service levels (Agatz et al., 2008). (4) E-fulfilment requirements are different across different product categories (Hu, Kumar, & Sumit, 2014).

PERCEIVED SERVICE QUALITY IN OMNI-CHANNEL RETAILING

In the context of omni-channel retailing, the evaluation and understanding of service quality has become a topic of major interest both for academics and practitioners (Badrinarayanan, Becerra, & Madhavaram, 2014; Banerjee, 2014; Patten, 2017; Seck & Philippe, 2013; Swaid & Wigand, 2012). "Owing to the intangible, heterogeneous and inseparable nature of services" (Martinez & Martinez, 2010, p. 30), several definitions of service quality have been built over the years. Zeithaml (1988), for instance, sees service quality as "... the consumer's judgment about a product's overall excellence or superiority" (Zeithaml, 1988, p. 3), Bitner and Hubbert (1994) view service quality as "... the consumer's overall impression of the relative inferiority/superiority of the organization and its services" (Bitner & Hubbert, 1994, p. 77). The academic debate about how to evaluate service quality has developed extensively since the 1980. In essence, the service quality literature can be divided into two streams: Some researchers use a performance-only approach to evaluate service quality (Boulding, Kalra, Staelin, & Zeithaml, 1993; Cronin & Taylor, 1992; Teas, 1993; Ozuem, Thomas & Lancaster, 2016). In contrast, the majority of researchers evaluate service quality based on the disconfirmation paradigm as a gap between expected service and perceived service (Carr, 2007; Dabholkar, Thorpe, & Rentz, 1996; Grönroos, 1984; Parasuraman, Zeithaml, & Berry, 1988). These studies draw extensively on the work of Oliver (1990). Oliver sees himself in the tradition of Sherif's and Hovland's "assimilation theory" (Sherif & Hovland, 1961) and Festinger's "dissonance theory" (Festinger, 1957), whereby "customers are posited to perceptually distort expectation- discrepant performance so as to coincide with their prior expectation level" and "post exposure ratings are primarily a function of the expectation level because the task of recognizing disconfirmation is believed to be psychologically uncomfortable" (Oliver, 1980, p. 460).

Several different service quality gap models, such as "The Service Quality Model" (Grönroos, 1984), "SERVQUAL" (Parasuraman et al., 1988), "E-SQUAL" (Parasuraman, Zeithaml, & Malhorta, 2005) or "WEBQUAL" (Loiacono, Watson, & Goodhue, 2002) have been developed to conceptualize service quality and consumers' perception of it. But most of the approaches tend to take a single-channel perspective and do not consider omni-channel settings (Seck & Philippe, 2013; Sousa & Voss, 2012). But, it is deemed necessary to view omni-channel service quality from a different perspective than traditional (for instance retail stores) and electronic (for instance the Internet) service settings, since perceived service quality results from all moments of contact between a retailer and its customers- across all channels (Sousa & Voss, 2006).

In examining omni-channel service quality conceptualizations, the current paper identifies five main elements as the five forces of service quality, as presented below:

Figure 1. Five forces of service quality

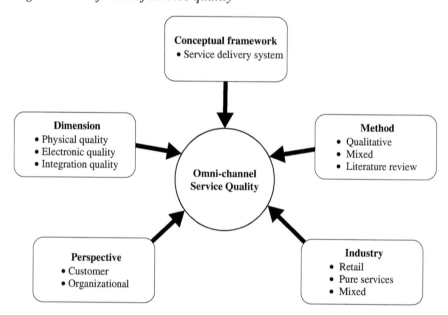

Regarding a **conceptual framework** for omni-channel service quality, Sousa and Voss (2006) were the first researchers to develop framework that did not take a single channel approach. In their "Service Delivery System (SDS)", they aim to consider all moments of contact between a firm and its customers. Sousa and Voss distinguish between a physical and a virtual component of service delivery. In the physical component non-automated operations take place and humans are directly involved. In the virtual component, operations are automated and humans do not play an active role. Sousa and Voss also distinguish between back office and front office operations. Back office operations are not directly visible to the customer whilst front office operations are visible. The researchers argue that existing service quality research has a single channel, which is a front office process. In their framework, the physical and the virtual service components (front office and back office) are linked with each other by integration mechanisms. These mechanisms function to integrate "the several service components and associated parts of the SDS" (Sousa & Voss, 2006, p. 359). According to Sousa and Voss, all front and back office physical and virtual operations enriched with integration mechanisms lead to overall perceived service quality. Sousa and Voss argue for a separate examination of physical, virtual and integration quality: First of all they emphasize the different nature of the three quality dimensions. Second, they forecast a rapid technological development for the virtual dimension and they see advantages in examining it separately from the other two, more constant dimensions of physical and integration quality.

Service quality attributes, the so-called **"dimensions"** play a predominant role in service quality research, as perceived service quality is a function of different dimensions (Zeithaml & Berry, 1990). In the reviewed literature there is agreement that the key distinction between omni-channel and single channel service quality conceptualizations is the "integration quality" dimension. The contribution of the reviewed studies to the concept of integration quality is illustrated below:

Figure 2. Sub-dimensions of integration quality

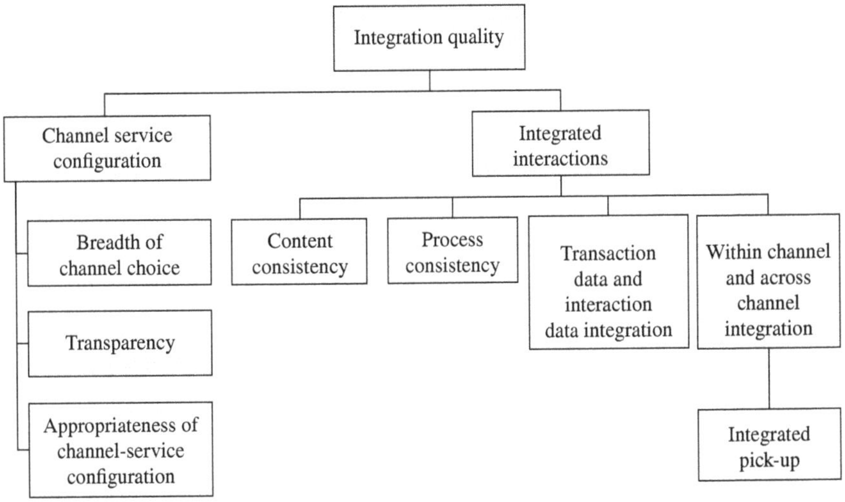

In their "Multichannel Service Delivery System (SDS)" framework Sousa and Voss established the integration quality dimension. They defined integration quality as providing a "seamless service experience across channels" (Sousa & Voss, 2006, p. 359). Sousa and Voss surmised that in a omni-channel service system, even when the service quality of each channel is very high, the overall perception of service could be very low when the integration quality is perceived as low. Sousa and Voss presented two sub dimensions for integration quality: "Channel-service configuration" and "integrated interactions": Channel-service configuration is the degree of choice a customer has regarding a service offer in each of the channel ("service breadth"). When introducing integrated interactions Sousa and Voss refer to "the consistency of interactions across channels" (Sousa & Voss, 2006, p. 366). The researchers emphasize two aspects of integrated interactions: Content and process consistency. Content consistency means that customers receive the same information from the company when communicating through different channels. Process consistency means that customers expect the same handling of comparable processes.

Banerjee (2014) built up on Sousa and Voss's framework and extended their findings about the integration quality dimensions into a new concept, consisting of three additional sub-dimensions. First, "the appropriateness of channel service configuration" refers to the degree to which a channel is suitable for different functions as a sub-dimension of channel-service configuration. Second, "transaction data and interaction data integration" refers to the degree to which customer transaction information and inbound and outbound interaction information are synthesized within and across channels. Third, "within channel and across channel integration" refers to the degree to which content and process information is integrated within parts of a channel and across channels (Sousa & Voss, 2006, p. 359).

Swaid and Wigand added "integrated pick-up" as another omni-channel service quality sub-dimenison, which means "the extend of smooth and easy pickup of products purchased online using a physical outlet/touchpoint" (Swaid & Wigand, 2012, p. 306). Swaid and Wigand concluded that integrated pick-up is one of the key dimensions of omni-channel service quality.

Next to integration quality, Sousa and Voss (2006) investigated virtual and physical quality as two other primary dimensions of omni-channel service quality (Sousa & Voss, 2006). The definition of virtual quality can be considered as the equivalent of electronic service quality based on single channel conceptualizations (for a review, see Ladhari, 2010). In an electronic setting, service quality means general perceived service in the virtual marketplace- with human intervention and without (Santos, 2003).

Furthermore, physical service quality can be considered as equivalent of traditional service quality based on single channel conceptualizations (for a review, see Martinez & Martinez, 2010).

Thus, from the reviewed literature, the extant knowledge about service quality dimensions can be synthesized as follows:

- Omni-channel service quality is a multidimensional construct, which consists of primary dimensions and corresponding sub dimensions.
- There is evidence in the reviewed literature that the existing dimensions have not fully grasped the customer's perception of omni-channel service quality yet since studies consistently investigate new dimensions.
- Omni-channel service quality consists of the quality that each channel can provide for the customer. However, omni-channel service quality is not a simple summation between service quality perceptions in each channel. Even when physical and electronic qualities are very high, the overall service quality perception from the customer can be very low when the integration of each service channel is missing. Thus, the service quality dimensions that are experienced in any channel during the purchase process should be congruent on and offline and should provide a seamless shopping experience for the customer.
- The key distinction between omni-channel and single channel service systems is the integration quality dimension. The integration quality dimension has the purpose to provide a "seamless service experience across channels" (Sousa & Voss, 2006, p. 359).

Regarding different **methods**, the research of service quality in omni-channel settings is still in its early stages and few studies have examined service quality in a omni-channel context. The reviewed omni-channel service quality studies applied different methods including a literature review (Sousa & Voss, 2006), qualitative methods (Banerjee, 2014) and mixed methods (Swaid & Wigand, 2012) (Seck & Philippe, 2013). There are several implications of method choices: With their literature review, Sousa and Voss set the foundation for developing a framework of service quality in omni-channel services. At the time of their research, there was an absence of a sound conceptual foundation for the research topic called omni-channel service quality. Sousa and Voss's study aimed to develop the theory (Sousa & Voss, 2006). Banerjee (2014) selected qualitative methods and conducted in-depth interviews in order to develop a service quality conceptualization and to gain an in-depth understanding of the omni-channel service quality phenomenon. Generally, the qualitative research method has a non-numeric manner and helps to observe a phenomenon in depth

(Saunders, Lewis, & Thornhill, 2009). It provides answers to "how" and "why" questions. In contrast, the quantitative method embraces a positivistic research paradigm and is applied either to analyse covariance or to test whether hypotheses are wrong or right (Guba & Lincoln, 1994). In the field of omni-channel service quality research, some researchers have applied mixed methods. They developed their theories applying a qualitative approach first before testing them in a quantitative manner.

Basically, there are two different **perspectives** regarding omni-channel service quality, namely the organizational and the customer ones. The perspective in the reviewed service quality literature is the customer's perspective. Grönroos argued that it is particularly important to understand how the customer evaluates service, because "if we know this and the components of service quality, we will be able to develop service-oriented concepts and models more successfully" (Grönroos, 1984, p. 36). Impacts related to high service quality can be considered as customer satisfaction (Bitner & Hubbert, 1994), customer loyalty (Grönroos, 1984, p. 37), purchase intention (Bolton & Drew, 1991; Bressolles, Durrieu, & Senecal, 2014; Cronin, Brady, & Hult, 2000; Cronin & Taylor, 1992; Spreng & Mackoy, 1996), profitability (Collier & Bienstock, 2006; Cox & Dale, 2001; Cristobal, Flavian, & Guinaliu, 2007; Gummerus, Liljander, Pura, & Van Riel, 2004), and purchase retention (Cai & Jun, 2003; Parasuraman et al., 1988; Zeithaml, 2000). One can conclude from this, that studies with a customer perspective help retailers improve their service strategy and the performance of their service offer (Cristobal et al., 2007; Fassnacht & Köse, 2007; Zeithaml, 2000).

In the reviewed literature, three different **industry** contexts of service quality can be identified: "pure" service industries (such as banking), the retail industry (such as clothing stores) and a mix of pure service and retail industries. The distinction between pure service and retail industries is that the pure service industry is an industry, where service is the actual "product", and the retail industry is an industry, in which stores offer a mix of merchandise and service (Dabholkar et al., 1996; Kaynama, Black, & Keesling, 2000). The early service quality models were researched in the pure service industry (Kaynama et al., 2000). Later, researchers argued for a distinction to be made between different industries as in, for instance, retail shopping which accounts for unique aspects of service. These aspects include store image (Thang & Tan, 2003), store environment (Baker, Grewal, & Parasuraman, 1994; Dabholkar et al., 1996), in-store experiences (Dabholkar et al., 1996) and experiences related to the merchandise (Dabholkar et al., 1996) (Bishop Gagliano & Hathcote, 1994). Mostly, these criteria can be translated to the online world (Kim & Stoel, 2004). Even though online and offline shopping provides for a different shopping experience: Online customers pay more attention to privacy/security; they appreciate some distinctive online capabilities such as interactivity, community, content, personalized experiences, increased product selection and information (Wolfinbarger & Gilly, 2003). Offline customers however value the personal contact with sales people in-store and the physical interaction with merchandise (Dabholkar et al., 1996).

AN OMNI-CHANNEL RETAILING SERVICE QUALITY CONCEPTUALIZATION

This paper builds on extant literature regarding omni-channel retailing and perceived service quality. Based on current literature perspective, this study proposes the following conceptualization as an approach towards omni-channel service quality, as presented in the figure below:

Figure 3. Conceptual framework of omni-channel service quality

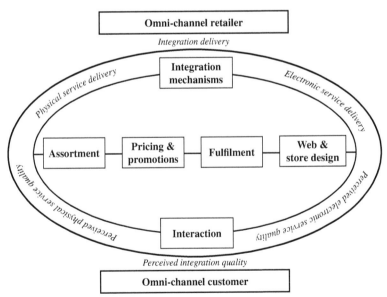

Omni-channel service quality conceptualization consists of different ingredients. It is an interplay between omni-channel customer interaction with the retailer and the omni-channel retailer's integration of assortment, pricing & promotions, fulfilment and web & store design. Ultimately, omni-channel service quality involves three dimensions, namely physical, electronic and integration quality. Or, as an equation: Omni-channel service quality = Integration quality – (physical channels quality + electronic channels service quality).

MANAGERIAL IMPLICATIONS
AND RECOMMENDATIONS

This chapter provides a number of managerial implications. Nowadays, customers use the Internet for many cultural activities everyday. The borders between activities like socializing, communicating and purchasing get blurred. That is why it is important for omni-channel retailers to set up coherent and integrated sales and communication strategies across channels. Omni-channel customers expect a seamless shopping experience. Against this background, it is a strategic managerial decision for omni-channel retailers to find the "right" level of integration regarding assortment, pricing and promotions, fulfilment, and web and store design. Omni-channel customers expect a high degree of product availability, immediate accessibility to information, products and service delivery. They will choose the channel and retailer who is able to provide him the best solutions.

Omni-channel retailers need to be aware of the fact that the customer's journey has changed fundamentally in the context of omni-channel retailing. Basically two different phenomena emerged, namely "web-rooming" and "show-rooming". It is crucial for omni-channel retailers to adequately respond to the new customer purchasing behaviour. First and foremost they need to train their sales force to be more competent than their customers in every respect. Otherwise they lose an important competitive advantage. Customers then rather stay online and buy on the Internet, or buy at someone else's store. Whichever journey customers choose, managers of omni-channel retailers should find ways to avoid "cross-channel free-riding" behaviour, which means that customers do not just switch the channel, but also the retailer. It might be necessary to install switching barriers. For instance, customers might find it costly when they need to provide their information again or when it is laborious to express their concerns every time they switch between retailers. Furthermore omni-channel retailers need to train the empathy of their sales force. Nowadays it is crucial that sales people have a feeling of what the each customer actually expects. Does this customer at all wish consultancy? Does this customer already have some knowledge about the product he requires? How can the sales person support customer loyalty at this client? Sales force is supposed to address to the various requests of an individualistic buyership.

Thus, the changed behaviour of omni-channel customers makes it necessary to elaborate a new approach towards service quality. At present, omni-channel retailers still take a single-channel approach, and do not consider the distinctive requirements of multiple-channel systems. Here, it is important to bear in mind that even when the service quality of each channel is very high, the overall perception of service could be very low when the integration quality is perceived as low. So, managers of omni-channel retailers should not only put their emphasis on enhancing and improving physical and/or electronic service quality, but also shift towards the integration of both channels` service offers. The overall purchasing experience needs to be consistent for the customer at all moments of contact between the retailer and him/her in order to receive a seamlessly perceived service quality. Then, omni-channel customers can take advantage of both online and offline channels and experience a congruent shopping experience across channels.

REFERENCES

Agatz, N., Fleischmann, M., & Van Nunen, J. (2008). E-fulfilment and multichannel distribution – a review. *European Journal of Operational Research, 187*, 339–356.

Ailawadi, K. L., & Farris, P. (2017). Managing multi- and omni-channel distribution: Metrics and research directions. *Journal of Retailing, 93*(1), 120–135.

Badrinarayanan, V., Becerra, E., & Madhavaram, S. (2014). Influence of congruity in store-attribute dimensions and self-image on purchase intentions in online stores of multichannel retailers. *Journal of Retailing and Consumer Services, 21*, 1013–1020.

Baker, J., Grewal, D., & Parasuraman, A. (1994). The influence of store environment on quality inferences and store image. *Journal of the Academy of Marketing Science, 22*(4), 328–339.

Banerjee, M. (2014). Misalignment and its influence on integration quality in multichannel services. *Journal of Service Research, 17*(4), 460–474.

Berman, B., & Thelen, S. (2004). A guide to developing and managing a well-integrated multi-channel retail strategy. *International Journal of Retail & Distribution Management, 32*(3), 147–156.

Berry, L., Bolton, R., Bridges, C., Meyer, J., Parasuraman, A., & Seiders, K. (2010). Opportunities for innovation in the delivery of interactive retail services. *Journal of Interactive Marketing, 24*(2), 155–167.

Bishop Gagliano, K., & Hathcote, J. (1994). Customer expectations and perceptions of service quality in retail apparel specialty stores. *Journal of Services Marketing, 8*(1), 60–69.

Bitner, M. J., & Hubbert, A. R. (1994). Encounter satisfaction versus overall satisfaction versus quality. In R. T. Rust & R. L. Oliver (Eds.), *Service Quality: New Directions in Theory and Practice* (pp. 72–94). London: Sage.

Bolton, R., & Drew, J. (1991). A multistage model of customers' assessments of service quality and value. *Journal of Consumer Research, 17*, 375–384.

Boulding, W., Kalra, A., Staelin, R., & Zeithaml, V. (1993). A dynamic process model of service quality: From expectations to behavioral intentions. *Journal of Marketing Research, 30*, 7–27.

Bressolles, G., Durrieu, F., & Senecal, S. (2014). A consumer typology based on e-service quality and e-satisfaction. *Journal of Retailing and Consumer Services, 21*, 889–896.

Breugelmans, E., & Campo, K. (2016). Cross-channel effects of price promotions: An empirical analysis of the multi-channel grocery retail sector. *Journal of Retailing, 92*(3), 333–351.

Cai, S., & Jun, M. (2003). Internet users' perceptions of online service quality: A comparison of online buyers and information searchers. *Managing Service Quality, 13*(6), 504–519.

Cao, L., Liu, X., & Cao, W. (2018). The effects of search-related and purchase-related mobile app additions on retailers' shareholder wealth: The roles of firm size, product category, and customer segment. *Journal of Retailing, 94*(4), 343–351.

Carr, C. (2007). The FAIRSERV model: Consumer reactions to services based on a multidimensional evaluation of service fairness. *Decision Science, 38*(1), 107–130.

Collier, J., & Bienstock, C. (2006). Measuring service quality in e-retailing. *Journal of Service Research, 8*(3), 260–275.

Cox, J., & Dale, B. G. (2001). Service quality and e-commerce: An explanatory analysis. *Managing Service Quality, 11*(2), 121–131.

Cristobal, E., Flavian, C., & Guinaliu, M. (2007). Perceived e-service quality: Measurement validity and effects on consumer satisfaction and web site loyalty. *Managing Service Quality, 17*(3), 317–340.

Cronin, J., Brady, M., & Hult, G. (2000). Assessing the effects of quality, value, and customer satisfaction on consumer behavioral intentions in service environments. *Journal of Retailing, 76*(2), 193–218.

Cronin, J., & Taylor, S. (1992). Measuring service quality: A reexamination and extension. *Journal of Marketing, 56*, 55–68.

Dabholkar, P., Thorpe, D., & Rentz, J. (1996). A measure of service quality for retail stores: Scale development and validation. *Journal of the Academy of Marketing Science, 24*(1), 3–16.

Emrich, O. (2011). *Cross Channel Management-Kompetenzen, Instrumente und Erfolgspotenziale* (Dissertation), University St. Gallen, St. Gallen.

Emrich, O., Paul, M., & Rudolph, T. (2015). Shopping benefits of multichannel assortment integration and the moderating role of retailer type. *Journal of Retailing, 91*(2), 326–342.

Emrich, O., & Verhoef, C. P. (2015). The impact of a homogenous versus a prototypical web design on online retail patronage for multichannel providers. *International Journal of Research in Marketing, 32*, 363–374.

Fassnacht, M., & Köse, I. (2007). Consequences of web-based service quality: Uncovering a multi-faceted chain of effects. *Journal of Interactive Marketing, 21*(3), 35–54.

Festinger, L. (1957). *A theory of cognitive dissonance.* New York: Harper & Row.

Gensler, S., Neslin, S. A., & Verhoef, P. C. (2017). The showrooming phenomenon. *Journal of Interactive Marketing, 38*, 29–43.

Grönroos, C. (1984). A service quality model and its marketing implications. *European Journal of Marketing, 18*(4), 36–44.

Guba, E. G., & Lincoln, Y. (Eds.). (1994). *Paradigmatic controversies, contradictions, and emerging confluences*. Thousand Oaks: SAGE.

Gummerus, J., Liljander, V., Pura, M., & Van Riel, A. (2004). Customer loyalty to content-based web sites: The case of an online health-care service. *Journal of Services Marketing, 18*(3), 175–186.

Heinemann, G. (2013). *No-Line-Handel*. Wiesbaden: Gabler Verlag.

Heinemann, G. (2019). *Handel mit Mehrwert*. Wiesbaden: Springer Gabler.

Hsieh, J., & Tseng, C. (2018). Exploring social influence on hedonic buying of digital goods-online games' virtual items. *Journal of Electronic Commerce Research, 19*(2), 164–185.

Hu, M., Kumar, R., & Sumit, C. (2014). Best pratices in strategic multi-channel fulfillment. *Ivey Business Journal, 2,* 1–6.

Hult, G., Tomas, M., & Zhang, Y. (2019). Antecedents and consequences of customer satisfaction: Do they differ across online and offline purchases? *Journal of Retailing, 95*(1), 10–23.

Kaynama, S., Black, C., & Keesling, G. (2000). Impact of the internet on internal service quality factors: The travel industry case. *The Journal of Applied Business Research, 19*, 135–146.

Kim, S., & Stoel, L. (2004). Apparel retailers: Website quality dimensions and satisfaction. *Journal of Retailing and Consumer Services, 11*, 109–117.

Kireyev, P., Kumar, V., & Ofek, E. (2015). *Match your own price? Self-matching as a multichannel retailer's pricing strategy*. Harvard Business Review: Watertown.

Ladhari, R. (2010). Developing e-service quality scales: A literature review. *Journal of Retailing and Consumer Services, 17*, 464–477.

Lang, G., & Bressolles, G. (2013). Economic performance and customer expectation in e-fulfillment systems: A multichannel retailer perspective. *Supply Chain Forum, 14*(1), 16–27.

Loiacono, E., Watson, R., & Goodhue, D. (2002). WEBQUAL: A measure of website quality. *Journal of Marketing, 60*, 432–438.

Mantrala, M., Levy, M., Kahn, B., Fox, E., Gaidarev, P., Dankworth, B., & Shah, D. (2009). Why is assortment planning so difficult for retailers? A framework and research agenda. *Journal of Retailing, 85*(1), 71–83.

Martinez, J., & Martinez, L. (2010). Some insights on conceptualizing and measuring service quality. *Journal of Retailing and Consumer Services, 17*, 29–42.

Neslin, S., Grewal, D., Leghorn, R., Shankar, V., Teerlin, M., Thomas, J., & Verhoef, P. (2006). Challenges and opportunities in multichannel customer management. *Journal of Service Research, 9*(2), 95–112.

Neslin, S., & Shankar, V. (2009). Key issues in multichannel customer management: Current knowledge and future directions. *Journal of Interactive Marketing, 23*, 70–82.

Oliver, R. L. (1980). A cognitive model of the antecedents and consequences of satisfaction decisions. *Journal of Marketing Research, 17*, 460–469.

Ozuem, W., Patel, A., Howell, K. E. & Lancaster, G. (2017). An exploration of consumers' response to online service recovery initiatives. *International Journal of Market Research, 59*(1), 97–115.

Ozuem, W., Howell, K., & Lancaster, G. (2008). Communicating in the new interactive marketspace. *European Journal of Marketing, 42*(9/10), 1059–1083.

Ozuem, W., Thomas, T., & Lancaster, G. (2016). The Influence of customer loyalty on small island economies: An empirical and exploratory study. *Journal of Strategic Marketing, 24*(6), 447–469.

Ozuem, W., & Tan, K. (2014). Reconciling Social Media with Luxury Fashion Brands: An exploratory study. In L. Aiello (Ed.), *Management of Cultural Products: E-Relationship Marketing and Accessibility Perspective*. Hershey: IGI Publications.

Parasuraman, A., Zeithaml, V., & Berry, L. (1988). SERVQUAL: A multiple-item scale for measuring consumer perceptions of service quality. *Journal of Retailing, 64*(1), 12–40.

Parasuraman, A., Zeithaml, V., & Malhorta, A. (2005). E-S-QUAL: A multiple-item scale for assessing electronic service quality. *Journal of Service Research, 7*(3), 213–233.

Patten, E. (2017). *Conceptualizing Service Quality in Multichannel Fashion Retailing*. (PhD), University of Gloucestershire, Cheltenham.

Patten, E., & Rashid, T. (2015). CRM in a German multichannel retailing company: Investigating and evaluating the sales peoples' role. *International Journal of Sales, Retailing and Marketing, 4*(2), 22–34.

Piotrowicz, W., & Cuthbertson, R. (2014). Introduction to the special issue: information technology in retail: Toward omnichannel retailing. *International Journal of Electronic Commerce, 18*(4), 5–16.

Reinartz, W., Wiegand, N., & Imschloss, M. (2019). The impact of digital transformation on the retailing value chain. *International Journal of Research in Marketing*. Forthcoming.

Saghiri, S., Wilding, R., Mena, C., & Bourlakis, M. (2017). Toward a three-dimensional framework for omni-channel. *Journal of Business Research, 77*, 53–67.

Santos, J. (2003). E-service quality: A model of virtual service quality dimensions. *Managing Service Quality, 13*(3), 233–246.

Saunders, M., Lewis, P., & Thornhill, A. (2009). *Research methods for business students* (5th ed., Vol. 5). Harlow: Pearson.

Seck, A. (2013). The issue of multichannel integration, a key challenge for service firms in a context of multichannel services distribution. *International Business Research, 6*(2), 160–169.

Seck, A., & Philippe, J. (2013). Service encounter in multi-channel distribution context: Virtual and face-to-face interactions and consumer satisfaction. *The Service Industries Journal, 33*(6), 565–579.

Sherif, M., & Hovland, C. I. (1961). Social judgment: Assimilation and contrast effects in communication and attitude change. *Yale University Press*.

Sousa, R., & Voss, C. (2006). Service quality in multichannel services employing virtual channels. *Journal of Service Research, 8*(4), 356–371.

Sousa, R., & Voss, C. (2012). The impacts of e-service quality on customer behavior in multi-channel services. *Total Quality Management & Business Excellence, 23*(7), 769–787.

Spreng, R., & Mackoy, R. (1996). An empirical examination of a model of perceived service quality and satisfaction. *Journal of Retailing, 72*(2), 201–214.

Stokinger, E., & Ozuem, W. (2015). Social media and customer retention: implications for the luxury beauty industry. In G. Bowen & W. Ozuem (Eds.), *Marketing strategies: Social media and online brand communities*. Hershey: IGI Global.

Swaid, S., & Wigand, R. (2012). The effective of perceived site-to-store service quality on perceived value and loyalty intentions in multichannel retailing. *International Journal of Management, 29*(3), 301–313.

Teas, K. (1993). Expectations, performance evaluation, and consumers' perceptions of quality. *Journal of Marketing, 57*, 18–34.

Thang, D., & Tan, B. (2003). Linking consumer perception to preference of retail stores: An empirical assessment of the multi-attributes of store image. *Journal of Retailing and Consumer Services, 10*, 193–200.

Verhoef, P., Kannan, P. K., & Inman, J. J. (2015). From multi-channel retailing to omni-channel retailing: Introduction to the special issue on multi-channel retailing. *Journal of Retailing, 91*(2), 174–181.

Vogel, J., & Paul, M. (2015). One firm, one product, two prices: channel-based price differentiation and customer retention. *Journal of Retailing and Consumer Services, 27*, 126–139.

Wolfinbarger, M., & Gilly, M. (2003). eTailQ: Dimensionalizing, measuring and predicting etail quality. *Journal of Retailing, 79*, 183–198.

Wolk, A., & Ebling, C. (2010). Multichannel price differentiation: An empirical investigation of existence and causes. *International Journal of Research in Marketing, 27*, 142–150.

Xing, Y., & Grant, D. (2006). Developing a framework for measuring physical distribution service quality of multichannel and 'pure player' Internet retailers. *International Journal of Retail & Distribution Management, 34*(4), 278–289.

Xing, Y., Grant, D., McKinnon, A., & Fernie, J. (2010). Physical distribution service quality in online retailing. *International Journal of Physical Distribution and Logistics Management, 40*(5), 415–432.

Zeithaml, V. (1988). Consumer perceptions of price, quality, and value: A means-end model and synthesis of evidence. *Journal of Marketing, 52*, 2–22.

Zeithaml, V. (2000). Service quality, profitability, and the economic worth of customers: What we know and what we need to learn. *Journal of the Academy of Marketing Science, 28*(1), 67–85.

Zeithaml, V., & Berry, L. (1990). *Delivering Quality Service.* New York: The Free Press.

Zhang, J., Farris, P., Irvin, J., Kushwaha, T., Steenburgh, T., & Weitz, B. (2010). Crafting integrated multichannel retailing strategies. *Journal of Interactive Marketing, 24*, 168–180.

KEYTERMS

Cross-channel free-riding: A customer first selects one retail channel to search for information about a product and then switches the retailer and the channel to purchase it.

Cross-channel retailing: A multichannel retailing system with a given degree of channel integration and customer interaction across different retail channels.

Integration quality: The distinctive dimension of service quality in a multichannel system, which provides a seamless service experience for multichannel customers.

Multichannel service quality: A construct, which consists of the three dimensions physical, electronic and integration quality.

Omni-channel retailing: A multichannel retailing system with full channel integration and/or customer interaction across different retail channels.

Show-rooming: Customers use an offline-mediated environment to gather information about a product, physically touch and see it, but then purchase it in an online-mediated environment.

Web-rooming: Customers use an online-mediated environment to gather information about products, but then purchase it in an offline-mediated environment.

Chapter 2

Social Media Ecosystems: The Millennial Brand Perceptions

Guida Helal
American University of Beirut, Lebanon

Wilson Ozuem
University of Cumbria, United Kingdom

ABSTRACT

Brands can no longer survive without the intangible presence of a social media platform that allows a brand to travel beyond physical limitations in reaching consumers. Millennial markets have embodied social media as a central outlet of communication, going as far as deeming it a form of public identity consumers embody across global connections. Brand connections and perceptions are consequently developed based on the potential tangible and intangible values that a brand is perceived to offer. Social media acts as the bridge that furthers a brand's position in the market by providing Millennials with the platform to amplify social identity through brand association. This chapter examines the impact social media has had on brand perceptions in the fashion industry, from a social identity theory outlook. The following chapter considers the theoretical and managerial implications while offering insight into the significance of social media and social identity within marketing practices.

INTRODUCTION

Internal brand marketing practices across industries continue to progress alongside external business environments (Kumar, 2018; Meyer, 2018).

Evolving realities, including economic and societal transformations, guide the market landscapes for businesses to follow suit (Kumar, 2015; Sheth, 2011). Marketing logics comparably advance to reflect the shifting nature of markets (Jayachandran, Gimeno, & Varadarajan, 1999; Vargo & Lusch, 2004). Technological innovations demonstrate one circumstance of a pivotal influencer that has markedly transformed society, notably the means of communication in modern society. The significance of the contemporary, Millennial approach to communication has permeated the corporate world as marketers employ the likes of Internet technologies along with their varied manifestations, such as social media, as a channel to reach consumers (Evans, 2012; Hoffman & Novak, 1996; Zarrella, 2009). Conventional marketing wanes in performance as one-way communication is relegated by dynamic two-way interchange (Houman Andersen, 2001; Ozuem, Howell, & Lancaster, 2008). As industries venture to adapt to prevailing communication instruments that appeal to today's customer, the fashion industry has recognised the potential social media brand presence is capable of exerting through online brand-customer exchange (Kim & Ko, 2012; Phan, Thomas, & Hein, 2011; Helal & Ozuem, 2019). The fashion market is fabricated on a foundation of progressive novelty and innovation, which accounts for the success in integration of dynamic technological advancements within this industry. There is ample literature investigating the progression of social media in varied facets of routine life (Fischer & Reuber, 2011; Hanna, Rohm, & Crittenden, 2011; Hoffman & Fodor, 2016; Huy & Shipilov, 2012; Kaplan & Haenlein, 2010; Kietzmann et al., 2011; Michaelidou et al., 2011). Additional research considers social media's professional function within an organisation's marketing practice (Luo, Zhang, & Duan, 2013; Naylor, Lamberton, & West, 2012; Simmons, 2008; Tuten & Solomon, 2014).

In a study investigating the application of social media marketing practices among luxury fashion brands, Kim and Ko (2012) demonstrated the potential social media brand presence may have on customer equity. The findings revealed that fashion brands employing social media marketing activities, such as interaction or word-of-mouth, experienced positive purchase intentions and customer equity among receiving audiences. However, this study allocated little attention to the leading demographic age using social media and able to yield definite and applicable feedback. Hughes, Bendoni and Pehlivan (2016) considered the significance of luxury fashion brands administering social media marketing in communicating with customers. A brand benefits from engaging consumers in a symbolic co-creation of that brand's image. This study also displays customers' interest in attaining and displaying a connection to a particular brand. This study can be used as a basis to further explore the motivations behind online customer interaction with a brand. However, this literature does not mention the demographic age of the customers in question, which produces general research results. An analysis on the use of social media by Pew Research Center demonstrated the highest use of social media sites in the U.S. to be among ages 18 to 29 years in 2018 (Pew Research, 2018). The statistic portal Statista likewise revealed that global social media use recorded the highest among users aged 25 to 34 years old in 2016 (Statista, 2016). A more recent study revealed the greatest use of social networking sites, such as Facebook and Instagram, by ages 18–34 years, while preceding generations demonstrated fewer percentages of average time spent on social media sites (Statista, 2017, 2018). The Millennial generation outruns other age groups as the leading social media user. There is extensive present literature exploring social media, yet few studies have investigated social media function within the fashion industry, particularly on the Millennial generation.

Social media is a development of the World Wide Web that began gaining ground between the late 1990s and early 2000s, establishing worldwide prominence by the late 2000s (Dewing, 2010). Yet before delving into the profound significance social media has exerted globally, the course of events leading up to its inception is considered. The initiation of the World Wide Web began in the early 1990s upon Tim Berners-Lee linking hypertext technology to the Internet. This allowed for one common worldwide foundation to be formed, whereby networked communication was born (Van Dijck, 2013). The consequent evolution of Web 2.0 brought about social media. Web 2.0 is described as consisting of two features that help define it, and these are *microcontent* and *social media. Microcontent* comprises pieces of content that express a primary idea. Such pieces cover much less information than websites and may take the form of blog posts, comments, or small images. These are designed for easy upload, reuse, and stimulating participation. The second feature of Web 2.0, *social media* or *social software*, consists of platforms organised around the framework of connecting people to one another. The *microcontent* produced by multiple users creates a page of shared interests different users can access to bond with one another (Alexander & Levine, 2008). In time, the growth of Web 2.0 prompted the birth of two-way communication platforms and the flow of user-generated content, which is today identified as social media (Arora, 2014; Fuchs, 2014; Gillies & Cailliau, 2000; O'Reilly, 2005).

Social media has prominently filtered into the fashion industry as active consumers seek to interact with brands throughout different phases of a product life cycle. Social media integration constitutes granting consumers a margin to receive and, above all, contribute to the communication of a brand. A study conducted by Statista asserts the magnitude social media has gained across the fashion industry, demonstrated by the immense response generated on social media by partakers during the bi-annual fashion-trading event, London Fashion Week in 2014 (Statista, 2016). Comparably, the 2018 Milan Fashion Week recorded customer interactions on Instagram in the millions, with high-end Gucci amassing over 7 million engagements across the platform (Statista, 2018). User access to fashion brands on social media platforms is projected to reach over one billion users by the year 2020 (Statista, 2016). Additional analyses identified social media as the most commonly used source by Millennials for updates on high-end fashion (Statista, 2017). The fashion industry is defined by innovation and originality (Bhardwaj & Fairhurst, 2010; Caniato, Caridi, & Moretto, 2013; Christopher, Lowson, & Peck, 2004), evoking brands to adapt to externalities such as modernisation of communication in maintaining a competitive edge. Fashion brands recognise the leverage of accumulating followers via social media channels that offer scope for content circulation among communities of Millennials. The social platform cultivates brand-customer relationships, as brands strive to publicly evoke customer loyalty, and customers, in turn, are receptive to demonstrating brand association and acquiring the promised relationship equity such brands are perceived to offer (Helal & Ozuem, 2018; Hughes, Bendoni, & Pehlivan, 2016; Lemon et al., 2001; Kim & Ko, 2012; Vogel et al., 2008).

By considering social identity, this study explores the employment of social media brand presence as a means of accentuating brand-customer relationship equity that consumers may exploit to invoke social identity. Social identity theory holds that individuals seek to allocate themselves or others according to social categories (Tajfel & Turner, 1985). Social groups elicit the promise of individual positive recognition and self-enhancement through group association (Ashforth & Mael, 1989; Hogg & Terry, 2000). A quantity of research has investigated consumers' motivations for affiliating with brands that advance social identity (Arnett, German, & Hunt, 2003; Bhattacharya & Sen, 2003; Lam et al., 2010). Individuals may choose to capitalise on material consumption as an aid to forming an identity (Elliot & Wattanasuwan, 1998; Kleine et al., 1993). Consumption of popular culture serves as a means for an individual in enforcing a desired social prominence or placement among a coalition. Fashion, a major segment of present pop culture, has manifested into a notable facilitator of social enhancement (Barron, 2012). Fashion brands are pursued by consumers with the intention of embracing individuality that, in fact, complies with a universal standard of social classification. People seek to individually speak, behave, or dress in a manner that is perceptible and significant, but that simultaneously resides within putative group norms. A consumer is placed amid two forces, the individual/psychological influence of personal opinions and preferences, and the public/social weight of uniform beliefs and attitudes (Burke, 2006; Carlson et al., 2008; Nowak et al., 1990).

Social media acts as an open platform accessible to brands and customers alike, facilitating relationship enrichment between the parties. The opportunity for the two to venture into first-hand interactions pilots a customer's chase for brand association, as brand perceptions are accordingly drawn based on that customer's notion of potential functional and symbolic profits. Consumer touchpoints have accordingly been reinvented to accommodate more than physical exchanges. Rather, brand-customer interaction has ensued beyond the point of sale and into a virtual realm of open interchange (Edelman, 2010; Fromm & Garton, 2013) that has become second nature to the Millennial generation. There is vast existing literature on the application of social media marketing practices to reach consumers, yet few current studies account for the leading Millennial user in demonstrating the impact of social media in the fashion industry. This study adds to the present exploration of social media. The investigation of social media as a marketing tool among Millennials provides an understanding of this cohort's motivation and reliance on online brand interaction in advancing social identity. This research offers groundwork for fashion brands to progress in future studies as a way of gaining insight into social media use among consumers. The results of this study expose the response social media has garnered on Millennial perceptions in the fashion world.

BACKGROUND

The fashion industry is one of few industries to attain growth among the global economic stagnancy and downfall over recent years (McKinsey &

Co., 2016). While sales growth may have reached a low amidst the most challenging period, some pockets of the industry have still managed to prosper such as luxury and fast-fashion (BOF & McKinsey & Co., 2017, 2018). Despite the trillion-dollar industry's caution heading into 2019, economic expansion is projected to shift into Asia with India achieving value of $59.8 billion by 2022, akin to $65 billion in the UK (BOF & McKinsey & Co., 2019). Alongside the transition from West to East, from matured to emerging markets China and India, women's apparel is foreseen to grow by 50 per cent over the coming decade (Remy et al., 2014). Emerging markets are expanding in number, sending the export value of clothing to a tremendous nearly $1.3 trillion figure (OEC, 2016). The global value of women's apparel is in the lead with over $600 billion, followed by menswear of over $400 billion and luxury goods of almost $350 billion (FashionUnited, 2016).

In a Deloitte study on the global fashion and luxury market from 2014–2017, most luxury brands revealed an increase in sales over the past years with major players attaining double-digit growth (Deloitte, 2018). Frontrunner LVMH (Moët Hennessy Louis Vuitton), house of numerous top player luxury brands, has especially enjoyed the elevated demand for luxury goods with a 13 per cent revenue growth in 2017 (LVMH, 2018). Another successful pocket of the industry, fast-fashion, has seen significant gains as consumers flock to disruptive retailers for replicated trends, fashion looks that have trickled down from luxury brand runways, offered at affordable prices. Fast-fashion groundbreakers such as Zara, H&M and Uniqlo have prevailed among competitors by offering consumers fashion-forward trends over a compressed fashion cycle of mere weeks rather than the traditional six-plus month cycle (Deloitte, 2018). Spanish brand Zara (Inditex) profitably managed net sales of €12 billion in the first half of 2018, 3 per cent higher sales than the previous year. Inditex remains shrewd in its winning tactic of flagship store investments across peak locations to offer brick-and-mortar stores in high foot traffic points. However, Inditex upholds its renowned pioneering approach amid the evolving industry by integrating its physical stores with worldwide online platforms. Zara (Inditex) has commenced its journey into omni-channel commerce by presenting customers with the ease of same-day or next-day delivery or click-and-collect. Inditex continues to develop global online platforms with the intention of acquiring online presence across all concept brands and all cities by the year 2020 (Inditex, 2018). Rival Swedish brand H&M has also enjoyed improved sales, attributing a 32 per cent increase in online sales. The company continues to acknowledge the merit of online and store integration in ensuring a smooth and appealing experience for customers (H&M, 2018).

An extensive annual forecast performed by leaders McKinsey & Co. and The Business of Fashion, *The State of Fashion 2019*, highlights key influences and transitions in the fashion industry to expect in 2019. While emerging markets are predicted to thrive over the coming years, the macroeconomic shift and sluggish growth in matured markets triggers the urgency for companies to shield themselves through buffers that sustain productivity. Companies realise the prominence of technology and with that, the call for speed in all aspects of production, distribution and responsiveness to meet consumer demands (The State of Fashion, 2019). Consumer interests continue to change as companies push to meet demands among high competition. The average consumer currently purchases 60 per cent more clothing than the average person did 15 years ago, yet only holds on to these goods for half the time (The State of Fashion, 2019). Fashion brands have respectively shortened lead times in supply chains and utilised social media platforms to monitor consumers. The former rigid fashion industry has transitioned to one of accessibility that values consumers' needs and curates accordingly. Social media brand-customer interaction allows brands to receive consumer opinion while working towards establishing an omni-channel experience that integrates the digital realm with the physical market.

Social media has empowered the fashion industry as a vital source for acquiring data, as well as an outlet for creative brand expression. Brands are given access to audiences through platforms such as Facebook, Instagram or Snap, among others, to share values, elaborate on creative processes and evidently establish a sense of community that stimulates interaction among consumers and potential customers alike. Brands are permitted a platform to share original relevant content while recipients digest and embody such content in expressing affiliation to those brands. Figures gathered on leading luxury brand presence on Instagram revealed Chanel amassed the highest quantity of followers with over 28 million, followed by Louis Vuitton of over 24 million followers (Statista, 2018). The exposure social media platforms are capable of achieving exceeds other promotional portals as worldwide users are delivered a consistent brand message communally. Social media employment travels beyond providing brands with optimum exposure; rather it delivers a multi-social brand experience whereby customers continue to communicate with a brand long after acquiring a product or service (BOF & McKinsey, 2019). The adoption of social media means within a brand's marketing approach has become a norm across industries, yet brands continue to be aware of the integration imperative in ensuring a consistent omni-channel experience across all offline and online channels involved.

As affirmed by Van Dijck (2013), upon the initial development of social media, 'participatory culture was the buzzword that connoted the Web's potential to nurture connections, build communities, and advance democracy' (Van Dijck, 2013, p. 4). This universal engagement has propelled the immense growth of social media into worldwide cultures. A study by Statista (2018) reveals the enormity social media holds as a defining phenomenon of the present time through a global infiltration of approximately 2 billion active social media users. Instagram, a photo-based application and social networking site, solely yielded a 21 per cent global reach merely one year after its launch in 2013, and reached a record in 2018 of over 800 million monthly active users (Statista, 2018). Social media has infiltrated a generation of devoted users comprising the Millennial age, as more than 85 per cent of 18–29 years olds use online social platforms (Smith & Anderson, 2018). Fashion leaders Zara and H&M have prevailed among the Millennial age group (Forbes, 2012), a technological age that has grown to embody social media as a key communication portal. By utilising social media as a major delivery approach, such brands are able to considerably impress their weight within the Millennial market. As the fashion world embraces digital integration, this study highlights the application of social media among the modern age of Millennials in the fashion industry.

Millennials

The Millennial Generation is defined as a demographic cohort born between the early 1980s and the early 2000s. This generation differs remarkably from previous groups, as the Millennial perception of communication is that it is conveniently available and instant, therefore obstacles such as time or geography do not impinge upon the presence of technology (Strauss & Howe, 1991; Lingelbach et al., 2012; Rainer & Rainer, 2011). Global boundaries are non-existent with the presence of the Internet, extending to Millennials a common ground that elicits homogeneous consumer behaviour (Moore, 2012). Despite geographical or cultural disparity, worldwide networks of mass media bond Millennials through comparable consumption and behaviours. Millennial interaction has evolved parallel to the Internet, characterising this generation as *digital natives* (Hershatter & Epstein, 2010; Prensky, 2001). This cohort is unique among other generations in its virtual method of communication and ensuing reverence for public and conspicuous behaviour (Bennett, Matson, & Kervin, 2008; Bakewell & Mitchell, 2003; Paulin et al., 2014). Twenge (2006) and Twenge et al. (2012) dissect this generation into a cohort of communistic interests, 'Generation We', responsive to societal and environmental duties, as well as individualistic 'Generation Me', with qualities of materialism and ostentatious behaviour that feed into a public image. Millennials desire to convey consumption, activity and lifestyle practices that assert the '*me*' through a global medium, social media.

This age group has grown accustomed to the reach this medium provides, including instant and direct access to brands (Moore, 2012; Nowak et al., 2006). The Millennial age has surpassed technology adaptation; rather technology is profoundly entwined as an essential daily occurrence (Hershatter & Epstein, 2010). Brand marketers are not oblivious of the interdependence Millennials have garnered in engaging social media as a gateway to real-time information (Eastman et al., 2012; Eastman & Liu, 2012; Hewlett et al., 2009). The notion of remaining connected to real-time occurrences is an underlying motivation for Millennials to seek social media, and brands to consequently use interactive technologies to directly reach Millennials (Engel et al., 2011; Fiore et al., 2005; Helal & Ozuem, 2018; Valentine & Powers, 2013). Recurring brand-customer contact bears the potential to evolve into emotional interaction through trust, loyalty and commitment that advances brand equity (Nowak et al., 2006), symbolically influencing Millennial perceptions of brands. Moreover, Bergman et al. (2011) demonstrated potential inclinations of Millennial social media usage that looked past mere network connection to consider social networking site use fuelled by personal motives such as self-promotion. The relevance of social media is only expected to grow with continuing consumer dependence on the network to which it caters, and newfound proficiency amongst brands in delivering a unified message worldwide is also set to evolve (Stephen & Galak, 2010; Mangold & Faulds, 2009; Prensky, 2001). Such characteristics justify the worth of social media as a phenomenon that merits exploration.

CONTEXT

From inception, social media has upheld its abiding intrusion into habitual, routine life, emerging as a focal gateway in societal interplay. Its success lay in the simplicity it originally offered any participating user to virtually connect to networks of users, before shattering conventionalities as a phenomenon responsible for connecting individuals, organisations, markets and industries globally. Thorough, comprehensive literature developed through vast research on the nature of social media has produced numerous definitions, all reiterating an underlying interpretation that social media comprises Internet-centred platforms that facilitate and stimulate a free flow of user-generated information (Kaplan & Haenlein, 2010; Safko, 2012; Kietzmann et al., 2011; Hanna, Rohm, & Crittenden, 2011; Luo, Zhang, & Duan, 2013; Ngai, Tao, & Moon, 2015; Stokinger & Ozuem, 2015).

Kaplan and Haenlein (2010) define social media as a 'group of Internet-based applications that build on the ideological and technological foundations of Web 2.0, and allow the creation and exchange of user generated content' (Kaplan & Haenlein, 2010, p. 61). The pair's description has succeeded in identifying the paramount function social media embodies in allowing free circulation of content across a shared platform. Dahl (2018) comparably accentuates the central facets of social media as universally spread, computer-mediated and user-generated content in virtual communities. Obar and Wildman (2015) summarise social media into Web 2.0 applications allowing individual or group-based profiles to share user-generated content across a vine of networks. Social media's survival is fuelled by user-produced content that facilitates a growth of interactions to cultivate an environment of open exchange. Ngai, Tao, and Moon (2015) identify the potential social media holds in establishing and advancing relationships within career prospects. Social media is further defined as part of an organisational paradigm that creates internal and external contact portals used among departments of the organisation or as an outward gateway to external stakeholders, respectively (McAfee, 2009; Piskorski, 2011). Considering the ongoing progression of definitions, social media is viewed as a maturing phenomenon continuing to unfold across different areas of society.

Agarwal and Yiliyasi (2010) refer to social media as a *participatory web* defined by five characteristics: 1) *accessibility* encouraged through its free and public platforms, 2) *permanence* as social media sites and user profiles allow for easy edits to any liking, 3) *reach* provided by the global audience it is capable of retrieving, 4) *recency*, a key feature of new age communication that eliminates time lag and promotes immediacy, and 5) *usability*, which considers the ease with which social media can be adopted by users. Panahi et al. (2012) characterise social media through user-centric features including *user-generated content, peer to peer communication, networking, multimedia oriented, and user friendly*. Kietzmann et al. (2011) use a framework of seven functional building blocks to reveal and progress different levels of user experience on social media: 1) *identity*, which considers the degree to which a user is willing to reveal his/her identity, 2) *conversation*, which considers the level of communication between users, 3) *sharing*, which is the amount of content circulating between users, 4) *presence*, which refers to the access given to display available users, 5) *relationships*, which reflect the extent of users relating to one another, 6) *reputation*, which considers the degree to which users can identify their stance within settings, and finally 7) *groups*, which refers to the ability to form or belong to a community. The functional blocks social media are built on create its flexibility in producing an open environment that consolidates worldwide users and advances relationships.

A misperception arises of the connotations of social media and social networking sites. While the two may be regularly used interchangeably, it is important to recognise that the terms differ in meaning. Social media embodies applications and services on a larger scale, involving a collective assembly and circulation of media. Such applications and services may include social networking sites, podcasts, or wikis, among others (Collin et al., 2011; Dewing, 2010; Weinberg & Pehlivan, 2011). Social networking sites are web-based services that are a form of social media and primarily involve distributing media between networks of participants (Collin et al., 2011). Boyd and Ellison (2008) define social network sites as 'web-based services that allow individuals to: 1) construct a public or semi-public profile within a bounded system, 2) articulate a list of other users with whom they share a connection, and 3) view and traverse their list of connections and those made by others within the system' (Boyd & Ellison, 2008, p. 211). User profiles created on social networking sites allow individual users to publicly share and retrieve information through networks they choose to connect with (Rains & Brunner, 2014; Zhang & Leung, 2015). Social networking sites include well-known websites such as Facebook, Instagram, Twitter, and Snap, among others, that initially engage users through a registration and profile creation process that opens the way for users to connect and share content with one another. Such groundbreaking websites have created a virtual social world allowing participating users to connect in a people-driven community that encourages the free flow of content (Berthon et al., 2012; O'Reilly & Battelle, 2009; Smith, 2009). User profiles are allowed the opportunity to send and receive messages across global networks within the shortest time. This fluency of open interchange triggers a communal environment supportive of individual self-expression (Ifinedo, 2016; Susarla et al., 2012). The following research aims to explore the administration of social media marketing methods and its influence on Millennial brand perceptions.

SOCIAL MEDIA—A MARKETING INSTRUMENT

Companies have been confronted with untouched territory amidst this transitional phase of virtual adoption across societies. While social media remains largely embraced as a superior communication tool among Millennials, marketers have grown to realise survival lies in their own receptivity to an ever-changing landscape now manipulated by the consumer (Mangold & Faulds, 2009; Michaelidou et al., 2011). Social media is regarded as an essential component of marketing agendas to access and reach customers (Chang, Yu, & Lu, 2014; Fischer & Reuber, 2011; Helal & Ozuem, 2016; Luo, Zhang, & Duan, 2013). Organisations are compelled to modernise their approach by merging conventional outbound marketing with interactive inbound marketing (consumer response through social media), to appeal to the new consumer type (Smith & Zook, 2011). Traditional marketing means no longer suffice as brands have progressed to applying informal-like social media promotions in kick-starting and supporting more conservative offline marketing methods. Social media allows for real-time news to travel at a faster rate on a larger scope (Chu & Kim, 2018; Tirunillai & Tellis, 2017). Brands profit from the circulation social media instigates as initial brand awareness and interaction hold the potential to form brand-customer relationships as part of brand communities (Chiu et al., 2006; Enders et al., 2008). Marketers unfold a new spin on customer relationship as contact exceeds physical touchpoints into a global virtual platform that encourages the exchange of resources, information, trust and vision between brands and customers (Ngai, Tao, & Moon, 2015; Heinonen, 2011; Tsai & Ghoshal, 1998).

Viral Marketing/EWOM

Social media's uninhibited free-flow nature empowers the web circulation of user-generated knowledge on abundant matters. Before social media offered a global reach for any user to employ, marketers trusted in word-of-mouth to circulate and deliver brand information. Such indirect promotional means permit brands to infuse markets by subtly fomenting chatter among target audiences (Huang et al., 2011; Trusov, Bucklin, & Pauwels, 2009; Vazquez-Casielles et al., 2013). Word-of-mouth (WOM), an offline depiction of today's frequently used viral marketing, has long assumed a notable function in generating brand buzz (Godes & Mayzlin, 2009; Katz & Lazarsfeld, 1955). WOM is defined as the transfer of product or brand information among consumers (Arndt, 1967; Kaplan & Haenlein, 2011; Stern, 1994).

WOM has been used as a complement to marketing and advertising campaigns (Herr et al., 1991). A promotional strategy is initially implemented by a brand in hopes of generating WOM that can successfully escalate that information to a broad sphere of receivers. Marketing messages create prime awareness among consumers, who in turn relegate their own experience to their own networks. WOM is subsequently regarded through a ripple effect that is evaluated by the extent that a brand advertisement is multiplied by WOM (Hogan et al., 2004). According to Huang et al. (2011), while organisations may not have complete regulation over word-of-mouth, marketers must heed the significance of the ripple effect. As such, marketers are responsible for producing a build-up and experience that encourages receiving individuals to become *resenders* and share feedback with others, thus widening the effect of WOM. Marketers are also expected to lengthen the WOM chain by providing experiences and settings that encourage even passive receivers to re-communicate brand information. Shared brand interactions generate chains of conversations that are strewn on to widespread recipients (Anderson, 1998; Bone, 1995; Herr, Kardes, & Kim, 1991; v. Wangenheim & Bayon, 2004). However, accepting and consequently contributing to the distribution of WOM may depend on certain aspects of this information. Huang et al. (2011) and Rieh (2002) suggest four dimensions that impel acceptance and in turn intent to re-distribute information received. *Quality*, the most important dimension, considers the nature of the information in accuracy or usefulness. *Authenticity* reflects on the trustworthiness and reliability of the information. The source of the information represents the standard of *authority* and its credibility.

Finally, *interestingness* plays the role of capturing a receiver's attention and inclination to echo the information.

The utterance of an informed and vocal customer has carried traditional WOM on to virtual channels as electronic word-of-mouth (eWOM), provoking the surge of user input and feedback (Cheung & Thadani, 2012; Chu & Kim, 2011; Trusov, Bucklin, & Pauwels, 2009). The development of consumer behaviour drives companies to extend products/services that spawn online conversations and propel sales (Reichelt, Sievert, & Jacob, 2013; Babić Rosario et al., 2016). In a study on the transition of WOM to online channels, Kozients (2010) highlights the evolution WOM has undergone throughout market changes. The three models consist of *the organic interconsumer influence model*, which involves direct consumer-to-consumer communication without disruptive marketer influences. *The linear marketer influence model* considers the impact marketers incite among opinion leaders, and the consequent indirect influence such leaders stimulate among receiving consumers. The third model, *the network coproduction model* concurs with the development of the Internet and reflects on the circulation of WOM that the presence of networks allows for. While all three models may co-exist, marketers hold the responsibility for alternating influence to oversee consensus among offline and online outlets in representing a brand (Kozinets et al., 2010). As companies are aware of the global range eWOM is capable of attaining through social media channels, maintaining the circulation of appropriate brand buzz is important to brand image.

Baker, Donthu and Kumar (2016) undertook a study on the properties of word-of-mouth in measuring purchase intentions and retransmission intentions among consumers. Purchase intentions are defined by the incentive to purchase a brand and are viewed from a practical advantage of physical brand consumption. Contrarily, retransmission intentions are described as the motivation to communicate WOM depending on the social benefits it is perceived to offer. Certain findings of this study demonstrated the significance of negative WOM in impacting consumer purchase intentions, while underscoring the inclination to re-communicate positive WOM as part of consumers' retransmission intentions (Baker, Donthu, & Kumar, 2016). As companies gain intelligence in understanding personal motivations that incline consumers to produce brand buzz, brands can excel in this to keep WOM alive. You, Vadakkepatt, and Joshi (2015) draw on varied factors that may affect the reception of eWOM. The study underlines the potency of eWOM to be dependent on the motivation of the sender.

EWOM is accordingly categorised into *organic*, material that an eWOM sender innately chooses to share, or *incentivised eWOM*, material that is induced by the promise of company incentives (You, Vadakkepatt, & Joshi, 2015). The latter may not be perceived as genuine or trustworthy. Social media's communal nature ensures any one post has broad reach, placing significance on the personal motivations behind consumers' willingness to share or re-distribute eWOM. Hartman et al. (2008) discuss the existence of social interactions within marketing communications. The study considers the *social spillover effect*, described as the impress a marketing action toward one individual may have on that individual's network through social interactions. EWOM is considered one form of modern social interaction that holds great potential for marketing agents to access targeted individuals while infiltrating subsequent networks of users on a global scale. WOM has long been a marketing phenomenon recognised by industries worldwide; however, eWOM revives the magnitude that consumer interaction is capable of achieving by highlighting brand influence from WOM and eWOM alike, and by acknowledging the social gains behind consumers sharing eWOM that reinforce individual motives.

Brand Communities

The transparent circulation of eWOM enriches online communication among Millennials into social interactions that power the rise of online communities and ensuing relationships (Gruen et al., 2006; Taken Smith, 2012; Van Doorn et al., 2010; Veloutsou & McAlonan, 2012). Initial social contact may begin with purchase review intentions before maturing into rooted motives of asserting community affiliations. Social media permits the development of contact from mere brand-customer interchange to a broader scope of customer-customer brand communities (Baldus, Voorhees, & Calantone, 2015; Rossman et al., 2016). Brands foster communities that engage consumers in experiences and relationships, providing consumers with a platform to symbolically unite through knowledge and alliance (de Valck et al., 2009; Helal, 2019; Robards & Bennett, 2011). The commonality cultivated between community members produces a tribe of supporters devoted to a particular brand (Cova & Cova, 2001).

Muniz and O'Guinn (2001) define brand community as 'a specialized, non-geographically bound community, based on a structured set of social relationships among admirers of a brand' (Muniz & O'Guinn, 2001, p. 412).

Brand communities are housed on the basis of mutuality of admiration to the brand and arising social ties among engaging members, irrespective of geographic distances.

Muniz and O'Guinn (2001) deduce brand communities over three components:

1. A mutual consciousness defined by a connection community members hold on a deep-seated parallel. This nurtures a feeling of intimacy among supporters while creating an aggregate notion of distance to those not part of the community.
2. Practices, culture, attitudes, beliefs, and ethics that found the nature of the community and impart on the emblematic behaviours and values adopted by the brand and its followers.
3. The group coherence instituted by the obligations and responsibilities held towards the community and community members.

The transposition of brand communities to social media has prolonged the interaction a brand retains with a customer, as accessibility is no longer a deterrent via the Internet. An online society is forged between the brand and a multitude of consumers, perpetuating an inviting setting of unending interaction, engagement, relationship advancement and, ultimately, customer trust and loyalty (Fischer, Bristor, & Gainer, 1996; Luo, Zhang, & Duan, 2013; Sheth & Parvatiyar, 1995; Zaglia, 2013). Social media's immediacy intensifies brand-customer interactions, driving forces such as gratification, trust and commitment to be cultivated among community members (Jang et al., 2008; Kim et al., 2008; Wirtz et al., 2013). The communal culture that arises from consistent brand and member interchange within a community reinforces brand image, birthing an authentic brand environment that encourages purchase intentions (Adjei, Noble, & Noble, 2009; Lipsman et al., 2012).

In an exploration of the use of online brand communities from both a consumer and company perspective, Wirtz et al. (2013) identify key criteria that outline an online brand community:

1. *Brand orientation* considers the focus the community has on the brand itself. The brand inhabits the complete heart upon which the entirety of the community places significance. The stronger the brand identity

among followers, the more committed members may be toward the community.

2. *Internet use* involves brand communities located both online and offline. Wirtz et al. (2013) highlight the advantages and disadvantages of falling on either continuum, rather contributing the most success to a brand that utilises both offline and online means in structuring a community.

3. *Funding and governance* considers the input the brand employs in community involvement. This may take the form of monetary funding, such as budgetary schemes assigned to push agendas within the brand community. Further, this may involve the degree of immersion a brand chooses to exercise in guiding community interactions.

Online brand communities are particularly characterised by the open nature they possess, leaving brands to administer rigorous thought to sustaining positive customer management among viewers (Dessart et al., 2015; Gu & Ye, 2014; Ozuem, Howell, & Lancaster, 2016a). In a research study deliberating consumer response to online brand communities, Simon and Tossan (2018) draw on the impressions brand-hosted communities expend on consumers and brands. Among the findings, the study features four gratification dimensions: *brand intimacy, brand individual recognition, brand influence,* and *brand community belonging.* Social media derives two-way conversations that produce an enriched understanding of community members, eliciting intimacy between parties. Brand-customer interchange develops into a give-and-take relationship of consumers contributing feedback, and brands, in return, acknowledging consumer involvement. This propels the development of interdependent relationships as groundwork to further the sense of belonging in communities (Simon & Tossan, 2018). Such online platforms assist brands in producing successions consumers can advance through, from an initial place of brand encounters up to a progressed point of pre-eminent affinity.

Community engagement allows brands to benefit from the employment of social networks as consumers engage social media to seek and contribute content (Clark, Black, & Judson, 2017). Brand mentions, which travel through the numerous vines of consumers' social networks, produce bands of admirers who further support the brand (Fournier & Lee, 2009). Community members advance their own brand associations through their networks, allowing brands to gain a competitive edge as content circulation is multiplied via copious webs of connections. Online interactions supersede physical boundaries, allowing any individual to mimic the guise of a brand ambassador in expressing commitment past the point of purchase into vaster realms (Dobele et al., 2007; McAlexander et al., 2002; Rosenthal & Brito, 2017). The global stretch available through social media signifies the diverse demographics any one message can reach; thus social integration within a community serves as the binding factor whereby diverse customers unite over the devotion to a brand (Brown, Broderick, & Lee, 2007; Jones, 1998). Prolonged interaction intensifies consumer response to a brand, as the longer a customer engages in a community, the stronger the involvement and resulting purchase intentions (Beukeboom, Kerkhof, & de Vries, 2015; Wang et al., 2017).

Reference Groups

Brand communities attribute their own continuity to a premise of rooting environments for ample consumer participation (Kamboj & Rahman, 2017; Nambisan & Baron, 2010). Online communities bear the dynamic tendencies for continual turnover of members, allowing for high rates of newcomers to depart the community within the very first participation (Ren et al., 2012). This calls upon the implementation of forces to ensure stability in online brand community flow by perpetuating consumer stimulation (Liao, Huang, & Xiao, 2016; Kozinets, 2002). Influence expended within brand societies may be contingent to a number of catalysts, one of which is the credibility and expertise of the content contributor (Gilly et al., 1998; Sweeney, Soutar, & Mazzarol, 2008). Consumers display a greater inclination of appeal towards content dispensed by opinion leaders or reference groups (Flynn et al., 1996; Senecal & Nantel, 2004). A reference group is defined as 'that group in which the actor aspires to gain or maintain acceptance: hence, a group whose claims are paramount in situations requiring choice' (Shibutani, 1955, p. 563). Shibutani (1955) depicts reference groups as the product of mass societies being divided and subdivided into segregated social groups governed by isolated principles. The integrity held by members towards a chosen reference group allows marketers to progress past functional and practical promotions of a product into advancing symbolical gains of consumption (Ekinci et al., 2011; Englis & Solomon, 1995; Escalas & Bettman, 2005; Levy, 1959). Symbolic consumption defies the notion of necessity; rather it regards individual identification with brands that conform to personal motives (Helal, Ozuem & Lancaster,

2018; O'Cass & Frost, 2002), possibly instituted by admiration of an opinion leader or adherence to a reference group. Social environments carry implications for brand preferences as consumers are allured by brands they deduce as favourable within their social groups, while deferring from those interpreted as ill-favoured (Hogg et al., 2009; Pronay & Hetesi, 2014). Consumption choices significantly reflect on the symbolic gain a brand is perceived to offer.

Reference groups may fall under a normative category, pertaining to direct influence from factions of family members and/or peers, or a comparative category, involving individual aspiration to principles reinforced by public personalities (Carmeli & Schaubroeck, 2007; Childers & Rao, 1992; Kelley, 1952; Li & Su, 2007). Archetypal classifications of icons, such as the likes of demographic or cultural factors, have been widely manipulated by marketers as means to impinge on followers of social groups (McCracken, 1989; Escalas & Bettman, 2003; Amaldoss & Jain, 2008; Choi & Rifon, 2012; Seno & Lukas, 2007; Ozuem & Tan, 2014). Consumer response to glorification of prominent figures is fuelled by the personal aspiration to embody the idolised celebrity persona that the desired social group responds to (Amos, Holmes, & Strutton, 2008; Atkin & Block, 1983; Choi & Rifon, 2012). Individuals seek to establish association with figures that further their presence within their social community. Yuan et al. (2016) demonstrate the potential influence public personalities may have on consumers in a study on the correlation of parasocial relationships and customer equity. Parasocial relationships involve illusory relations admirers develop with media personalities (Horton & Wohl, 1956). Consumers foment a sense of familiarity and trust with celebrities from recurring encounters or interactions via media outlets. The findings of the research revealed a direct influence of parasocial relationships on customer equity drivers, consisting of brand, value and relationship equity (Yuan et al., 2016). Consumers use social media's reach to connect with brands and individuals that convey the views of the lionised reference group. Virtual communities may excel in attracting participants with brand information or product feedback, however attachment is formed to societies that extend a pertinent environment to advance social needs (Dholakia, Bagozzi, & Pearo, 2004; Pentina, Prybutok, & Zhang, 2008).

Brands gain value from the presence of brand communities, offering consumers an outlet for expression. Brand possession gains symbolic significance as it allows for social gratification among the community

(Cova, 1997). Consumers form sentimental attachments to brands that evoke self-identification and group association. Brand-customer relationships gain depth as sentiment becomes more rooted in consumers' brand perception (Hwang & Kandampully, 2012). Brand communities formed on social media platforms accentuate a customer-centric approach of active, real-time engagements that generate value among community members (Huy & Shipilov, 2012; Sashi, 2012).

SOCIAL IDENTITY THEORY AND SOCIAL MEDIA

Social media has granted individuals a large platform in relaying identities (Bagozzi & Dholakia, 2002; Bargh & McKenna, 2004; Dholakia, Bagozzi, & Pearo, 2004; Hogg & Reid, 2006; Pentina, Prybutok, & Zhang, 2008; Hennig-Thurau et al., 2004; Kane et al., 2014; Schivinski & Dabrowski, 2016; Veletsianos, 2013). The ease of accessibility to social media and online brand communities has conceived a dynamic of unrestricted expression, allowing customers to openly affiliate with brands in building the self. Consumers recognise the advantage of associating with brands, via social networking sites, in advancing self-presentation. Brand communities assume a valuable role in affording an outlet for active engagement, consequently intensifying member relationships as consumers seek the promise of such interchanges in securing social placement (Algesheimer et al., 2005; Helal, 2019; Ma & Agarwal, 2007; Ren et al., 2012; Zhu & Chen, 2015). The pursuit of self-identification impels individuals to readily voice affiliation to brands that facilitate the climb to social enhancement.

Identification of the self consists of personal and social identity. While personal identity centres on recognition of individual characteristics, social identity is concerned with a communal identification of the society the individual ascribes to (Luhtanen & Crocker, 1992; Nowak et al., 1990; Onorato & Turner, 2004). In evolving the self, an individual fosters personal identity by adopting a demeanour that is inherent of its own individuality, albeit individualism pertaining to a socially approved identity. As such, customers are attentive to brands that attest to personal apperception whilst preserving societal appreciation. Drawing on Vernuccio et al.'s (2015) study on the influence of social identity on brand love within online social-interactive engagements, the findings revealed the shift in significance from personal to social identity within online (salient) settings. This research emphasises consumers' self-definition drawn from the social group of a brand and the added emotional bond consumers foster with a brand as a result of acquiring social belonging. The structure of social media, consisting of integrated webs of worldwide users, emboldens users to share personal stances, bearing in mind that these stances are congruent to the prevailing attitude held by the favoured community (Clement & Krueger, 2002; Haslem et al., 1999; Hogg & Turner, 1987; Kietzmann et al., 2011). Social media serves as an outlet that individuals can utilise to advocate an idolised social group's mannerisms in favour of asserting social inclusion.

Turner et al. (1994) describe social identity theory as 'self-categories that define the individual in terms of his or her shared similarities with members of certain social categories in contrast to other social categories' (Turner et al., 1994, p. 454). Social categories reflect the classifications used in forming social identification. An individual aspires to depict his/her identity alongside that of the sought group (Hogg & Abrams, 1988; Hogg, Terry, & White, 1995). The social categories that characterise pursued social communities consequently shape followers' self-definition. Individuals seek to identify with the social categories held by a group in the interest of acquiring social consensus by way of group affiliation (Jenkins, 2008; Tajfel & Turner, 1985; Trepte, 2008). This social consensus feeds back into an individual's self-definition by reinforcing social identity. Social identification is imperative in obtaining group admittance that is socially acknowledged (Ashforth & Mael, 1989; Hogg & Terry, 2000). Such social identification incites value through group affiliation, as overt recognition serves to augment individual identity.

Correia, Kozak, and Reis (2014) demonstrate the role of social influence in a study that highlights the significance of social identity in settings of conspicuous consumption. The findings indicated that maintaining social status was a major theme within settings of public consumption. Among the incentives of brand consumption, consumers concede the influence of non-economic gains, such as social recognition, from capitalising on particular brands (Arnett et al., 2003; Kleine et al., 1993; Laverie et al., 2002). Each brand embodies its own presence and image, representative of the capability its brand equity holds in the market (Aaker, 1996; Keller, 2012). As brand image is aligned with the entirety of the brand, a brand community is formed in correspondence with what that brand personifies. Such social collectives offer consumers the prospect of advancing self-image and ultimately social identity based on what the brand equity is perceived to offer (Argo et al., 2005; Gurău, 2012; O'Cass & McEwen, 2004;

Bearden & Etzel, 1982). In the world of fashion consumerism, a customer may opt for a luxury fashion brand to portray a standard of socio-economic success. Another instance may involve an individual's pronounced adoption of a sustainable fashion brand in depicting a conscious social identity.

Social media serves as a driver for individuals to deploy in expressing brand association to gain social consensus. Virtual brand communities facilitate platforms of interaction that consumers use to retain affiliation. Brands profit from consumers' pursuit of social identity as consumers' need to interact with a brand for personal motives evidently strengthens brand-consumer relationships (Bhattacharya & Sen, 2003; Escalas & Bettman, 2005; Helal, Ozuem, & Lancaster, 2018). Brand-customer relationships evolve along a spectrum to comprise affection, trust and loyalty as customers rely on brands to attain the desired social identity.

SOCIAL MEDIA PLATFORMS

Social media comprises different Internet-based services, including blogs, wikis, and social networking sites, among others, that empower communication interchange between users (Campbell et al., 2011, Dewing, 2010; Weinberg & Pehlivan, 2011). Interactive social networking sites have prevailed in instituting an environment of free-flow exchange within formerly restricted markets (Bernoff & Li, 2008; Bolton et al., 2013; Dutta, 2010; Hansen et al., 2010). Social media sites including Facebook, Instagram, and Twitter have developed into primary connective outlets among consumers, and more notably between customers and brands. Each social networking site has thrived in offering users a unique experience, allowing brands to capitalise within platforms that appeal to their target markets. This study focuses on the visual social media sites, Instagram, Snap and lifestyle blogs, which have excelled in translating the fashion industry's aesthetics to the virtual realm.

Instagram

As Millennials' adoption of social media has transformed the dynamic of brand-customer communication, marketers are adjusting to the shift in consumer power. Instagram, a multi-billion dollar social networking site, has thrived with consumers and brands alike (Holmes, 2015; Miles, 2014;

Kerpen, 2015; Richards, 2015; Macarthy, 2013), particularly within the visually immersive fashion industry. Instagram was launched in 2012 as a photo-sharing application connecting global users around the founding notion of circulating real-time images. The application, turned social media website, was immediately acquired by Facebook, attaining over six million users within a six-month period (Holmes, 2015; Miles, 2014). Instagram has excelled in its use of a *hashtag* that groups photos into categories to be easily accessed, allowing an image to be shared across a wider scope of followers (Miles, 2014). The extent of exposure one post is capable of acquiring exhibits the influential leverage marketers require in remaining relevant among new age consumers (Kerpen, 2015; Richards, 2015; Macarthy, 2013). De Veriman et al. (2017) demonstrate the influence marketers can project on social media in a study that reveals considerable impressions exerted on consumers by brand-led Instagram accounts. Fashion brands have significantly flourished on Instagram by using posts, stories, and live feeds to relay real-time brand messages involving the latest campaigns and collections. Companies are granted a platform to draw consumers by utilising Instagram's biography to include direct links to brand websites or post photos of brand items with embedded links to brand shopping pages.

Snap

A fast-growing social network, Snap, similarly uses visuals as the foundation of its communication structure. However, Snap employs ephemeral photos and videos featured within a timeframe of mere seconds to 24 hours after posting (Snap Inc., 2018). This notion allows the social networking site to filter outdated content in time for new posts, thus exclusively immersing its users in real-time interaction. The fashion industry has thrived on this social media website by applying Snap's immediacy and relentless turnover of trending topics to its own unceasing progression. This functions as an advantage to fashion brands that operate the moment-driven marketing instrument, as it accommodates the ever-transitioning industry of fleeting fashion fads (Kim & Ko, 2012; Sashittal et al., 2016; Wolny & Mueller, 2013). The likes of Instagram and Snap represent outlets of expression that brands may apply in preserving relevancy amid prevalent pop culture instances. Sashittal et al. (2016) present the correlation between Snap brand use and corresponding brand perception among college students in a research on the influence of Snap brand presence on college pupils.

The outcome determined a direct link between active brands on Snap and higher subjected influence on recipients, as further exposure accounted for a sense of familiarity that instigated intimacy and emotional attachment among brand-customer relationships. Greater intimacy earned the brand superior brand perception with consumers.

The fourth quarter of 2017 saw Snap amass a substantial 185+ million active users on its platform on a day-to-day basis (Statista, 2018). Interestingly, the social networking site began losing popularity in 2018 upon introducing an update that included a separation of actual users' friends from *influencers* or celebrities (Forbes, 2018). After becoming accustomed to a platform whereby public figures carried the same level of accessibility as any real-life friend, Snap users rejected the new layout that sought to personalise a user's profile to his/her close network, rather preferring to group friends and celebrities within the same category. This demonstrates the significance social media holds in connecting global users to any person or big personality and the reach the Millennial generation has become adapted to.

Blogs

The typical Millennial consumer has proclaimed the emphasis of remaining globally interconnected on a large scale, alluding to links with public figures and brands being just as vital as connections with peers. Brands have embodied promotional liaisons of third parties, including reference groups, lifestyle bloggers, and celebrity figures, as persuasive tools in reaching customers (Colliander & Dahlen, 2011). Weblogs or blogs, once acknowledged as virtual transpositions of traditional diary/journal inputs, have universally expanded as extensions of social networking site profiles belonging to prominent online influencers. Bloggers run successful social media profiles alongside personal blogs to share views, opinions and lifestyle mannerisms with an audience they develop affinity to (Hsu & Lin, 2008; Kumar et al., 2004; Nardi et al., 2004; McKenna & Pole, 2008; Singh et al., 2008). This advances the underlying intention of social identity as influencers seek to portray a personality that is admired across society, and receivers correspondingly reciprocate interaction in forming their own identity and social placement within that community (Dholakia, Bagozzi, & Pearo, 2004; Farrell & Drezner, 2008). As blogs further abate a brand's power over its own publicity, marketers find value in pairing with influencers to subtly push brand promotions through the authentic setting blogs are perceived to portray (Simmons, 2008). The production of content via multiple platforms augments visibility triggering additional dispersion of eWOM (Weinberg, 2009; Huang et al., 2007). Brand eminence is distributed through bloggers' circles to widespread followers, as such power personalities mature into an instrumental portrait of groundbreakers consumers chase to emulate (Colliander & Dahlen, 2011; Rettberg, 2008). Consumers are drawn to opinion leaders, who depict a fantasy living viable for the regular individual, in order to propel social identification and ultimately achieve social identity based on values exercised in the ideal group (Langner, Hennigs, & Wiedmann, 2013; Liu & Hu, 2012; Van Knippenberg et al., 2004).

SOCIAL MEDIA INFLUENCE ON BRANDS

Social media offers exposure at a scope and speed that is unparalleled to conventional marketing instruments. Online brand communities embody the potential to sustain global consumer engagement and first-hand interchange that feeds into brand-customer loyalty (Chaudhuri & Holbrook, 2001; Chauhun & Pillai, 2013). Adapting to a customer-centric environment has become a fundamentally imperative external operation to be managed comparably to other business operations (Blattberg, Getz, & Thomas, 2001; Da Silva & Alwi, 2008; Hollebeek, Glynn, & Brodie, 2014; Malthouse et al., 2013; Sashi, 2012). The informal interplay social media promises allows companies to enact unified brand messages, instituting a coherent brand perception to be conveyed across all platforms alike (Keller, 2009; Naylor, Lamberton, & West, 2012). Multinational brands can ensure consistent brand images communicated worldwide in building brand equity.

Brand equity describes the added value a recognised brand name emits among consumers (Feldwick, 1996; Park & Srinivasan, 1994; Rangaswamy, Burke, & Oliva, 1993). The presence of solid brand equity empowers a brand to elicit prominent influence that a comparable marketing approach from inferior brand equities would fail to educe in the market. Keller (2001) divides customer-based brand equity into four building blocks, attained in sequential order:

- *Brand identity*, which is accentuated by *brand salience. Brand salience* involves consumers' awareness and ability to recognise a brand. Establishing initial recognition in the market paves the way for a brand to move on to the next block.

- *Brand meaning* comprises the outlook customers carry of a brand image. *Brand meaning* is divided into *brand performance*, the practicality of a brand or a brand's product line, and *brand imagery*, the symbolism the consumption of a brand subjectively or psychologically evinces. Brand image encompasses demographic and psychographic personifications that set the brand apart from others in the mind of the customer.
- *Brand responses*, developed as the third block, involve *judgements*, the value or quality a brand carries, and *feelings*, the emotional resignation from acquiring a brand.
- The final block to building customer-based brand equity involves *brand relationships*, which considers the level of *brand resonance* a brand has attained among customers. Resonance is further divided into *loyalty, attachment, community* and *engagement.*

Brand equity sets one brand apart from another in a consumer's mind. A consumer begins to draw awareness to a brand from initial exposure, whereby this awareness evolves into a perception of the functional and symbolic value of that brand (Aaker, 1991; Biel, 1993; Kirmani & Zeithaml, 2013; Bong et al., 1999; Ozuem, Howell, & Lancaster, 2016b). Perception is further advanced as brand-customer interaction foments relationships of trust between both parties.

Aaker (1996) considered a comparable evaluation of brand equity labelled The Brand Equity Ten. This model suggests five categories, four of which convey customer brand perception, and the fifth considers market behaviour. The classifications are as follows:

- *Loyalty* views the monetary value a consumer is willing to forgo for a brand, and the ensuing experience of acquiring that brand.
- *Perceived quality/leadership* considers the practical and emblematic value associated with consumption of a brand.
- *Association/differentiation* are determinants that differentiate one brand from another within the same market.
- *Value* measures the price of the brand for what it is capable of offering. This classification includes *brand personality*, which is personified by the target customer, and *organisational association*, which is concerned with the integrity of the brand.
- *Awareness* demonstrates the recognition and perception a brand has in the market.

Customer-based brand equity has been investigated and revised within numerous literatures (Aaker, 1991, 1996; Keller, 2001; Lemon et al., 2001; Gurhan-Canli et al., 2016; Chae & Ko, 2016; Chatzipanagiotou et al., 2018; Davcik et al., 2015; Datta et al., 2017). While a brand may be conceptualised through an illustration of the archetypal customer or personified through brand personality (Hoeffler & Keller, 2002; Brakus et al., 2009; Valette-Florence et al., 2011), the inclusive brand image a customer deduces represents the interpretation of brand perception in this study.

Within a new age of technology, social media plays a vital role in enforcing brand equity by extending webs of networks to imbue awareness. Social media platforms possess a range that surpasses the vicinity of current followers and stretches to potential customers. The capability of inducing exposure and propagating brand insight (Barwise & Meehan, 2010; Hoffman & Fodor, 2010; Weinberg & Pehlivan, 2011) is not lost on marketers as brands embrace virtual outlets as essential preliminaries in imparting brand messages (Tiago & Verissimo, 2014) and ensuring customer reassurance through powerful brand recognition (Huang et al., 2004). Brand awareness is the foundation of brand equity; thus a brand lacking in awareness is absent of equity, as it holds no value among consumers (Hakala, Svensson, & Vincze, 2012; Kumar & Mirchandani, 2012). A brand succeeds in its industry upon relaying an identity that resonates with an audience. Cho et al. (2015) draw on the conceptualisation of brand image in a study that measures brand image associations within the fashion industry. The study demonstrates brand image against cognitive, sensory and affective dimensions that consider tangible and intangible values of a brand. Cognitive dimensions focus on consumers' impression of the quality, performance and symbolic value of a brand (Keller, 1993; Park & Rabolt, 2009). The second dimension, sensory, considers a consumer's view of a brand's appearance, texture, or scent (Chang & Chieng, 2006; Low & Lamb, 2000; Roberts, 2006). Cho et al. (2015) discuss the third dimension, affective, as the emotional derivatives of brand-customer interactions. This includes the response consumers emit in the form of trust, loyalty, and commitment (Esch et al., 2006; Faircloth et al., 2001; Roberts, 2006). Companies have long prospered in refining a brand's image through tangible outlets such as the branding of stores or product design; however, the incorporation of social media has compelled brands to translate this identity via intangible, online channels.

Brand identity is defined as 'a set of brand associations that the brand strategist aspires to create or maintain. These associations imply a promise to customers from the organization members' (Aaker & Joachimsthaler, 2000, p. 45). It is a depiction of the very essence that consolidates a brand into a consistent identity which is sustained throughout internal or external changes, promising consumers a degree of dependability that serves as the connection between brand and customer (Aaker, 2004; Ghodeswar, 2008). Brand identity comprises brand associations, ingrained in consumers' memories and initiated as brand nodes from the early point of brand awareness. As recurrent exposure cultivates, consumers are given the opportunity to accumulate more experiences of a brand (Keller, 1993), evidently forging an interpretation or perception of the brand.

Social media's transparent nature produces an accessible, welcoming climate for any user to partake in, cueing marketers to perpetuate brand associations that depict and preserve positive conceptions of the brand (Aaker & Keller, 1990; Pitta & Katsanis, 1995; Andzulis et al., 2012; Bolton et al., 2013; Huang & Sarigollu, 2012; Kaplan & Haenlein, 2011; Vermeulen & Seegers, 2008). In view of brand presence being exerted over social media's extensive scale (Kozinets et al., 2010; Singh & Sonnenburg, 2012), the projection of fastidious brand impressions is imperative to those foreign to the brand. Continuous virtual appearances set the tone for affluent brand assertions that evidently contribute to heightened purchase intentions (Naylor, Lamberton, & West, 2012), thus encouraging an enactment of brand-mapping techniques in furthering brand association impact on consumers (John et al., 2006). Companies may implement comparable methods in weighing brand positioning in consumers' minds and proceeding accordingly.

Brand perceptions can be further shaped through the clout of prominent third-party individuals in the form of spokespeople, influential bloggers, or celebrity endorsers (Cornwell, Roy, & Steinard, 2001; Cornwell, Weeks, & Roy, 2005). A brand's affiliation to a public personality constructs an anthropological rendering of that brand within a consumer's discernment. Each reference group or opinion leader personifies a demographic and psychographic identity that a consumer aspires to socially convey, and will seek to do so through the consumption of brands that that opinion leader is associated with. Brands develop brand personalities, 'the set of human characteristics associated with a brand' (Aaker, 1997, p. 347), that enable audiences to relate to a brand on a human standard. On account of such symbolism, labels are appreciated as prestige enhancers providing an entry into sought social communities (Maehle, Otner, & Supphellen, 2011;

Plummer, 2000; Wee, 2004). A brand's personality compels customers to exalt a brand from a market of comparable competitors on account of what that label represents (Biel, 1993; Freling & Forbes, 2005). By obtaining a degree of prevalence in the industry, brands amass consumer preference that triggers emotion toward the brand before evolving into sentiments of loyalty and trust. Brands seek to stimulate emotive interactions that relay transactional contacts into consequential grounds of brand-customer bonding (Malär et al., 2011; Whan Park et al., 2010; Gobe, 2010). Fashion labels have thrived on visual platforms, such as the likes of Instagram, in offering audiences insight into the fabric of a brand. Consumers have grown past the practicality of a product into a dimension that focuses on the authenticity of the embodiment of a brand. This familiarity sheds an intimate light on brand perception, allowing for valuable interchanges that mature into deep-seated brand-customer relationships (Thompson et al., 2006; Roberts, 2006). Loyalty is only projected to grow through recurring emotionally impelling involvements (Brakus et al., 2009; Sung & Kim, 2010). According to a study performed on potential influencers of brand equity, the method with which a brand communicates itself coupled with consumer interference, through their own input and promotion, enhances brand equity (Valette-Florence et al., 2011). Social media is thus applied as a complement to a brand's strategy in building a presence and image among viewers.

MANAGERIAL IMPLICATIONS AND RECOMMENDATIONS

This chapter seeks to touch on an unexplored area of the influence social media exerts on brand perceptions in the fashion industry, in the case of the Millennial generation (Colliander & Dahlen, 2011; Gensler et al., 2013; Kim & Ko, 2012; Moore, 2012; Singh & Sonnenburg, 2012; Taken Smith, 2012). The fashion industry can find immense success in adopting social media platforms as primary outlets of communication with consumers, as this literature demonstrates an underlying link between social media and social identity that sways brand perceptions. Millennials pursue a desired social identity by accruing brand affiliations that embody the social status to further this identity through the public platform social media provide.

The likes of Instagram and Snap lend brands a powerful outlet to preserve relevance in real-time events and exert a consistent presence that resonates among consumers. Social media extends a virtual reach that complements a brand's overall marketing strategy (Godey et al., 2016). Instagram demonstrates this in the manner it extends a medium for brands to connect with customers, progress relationships and evoke an impression that invites those customers to seek more, perhaps by visiting the website or physical store. Snap has regularly been an avenue for lifestyle influencers to detail genuine daily affiliations to trending brands through promotional events or endorsements that assemble a social image for both blogger and brand. Consumers congregate an image of a brand that is anthropomorphised by third-party bloggers, who advertently add symbolism to a brand's relevance in the social world. The fashion industry would profit from utilising social media as a functional and symbolic connection to worldwide consumers. Finally, the findings from this study can be used to initiate future research based on a larger sample.

Marketers have recognised the shift in brand-customer dynamic that has unfurled along with the conception of social media (Hanna et al., 2011; Kaplan & Haenlein, 2010; Ngai, Tao, & Moon, 2015; Ozuem, Howell, & Lancaster, 2008), as labels flock to social networking sites to chase a new-age active consumer. This study draws on the development of social media in the fashion industry, considering the incessant pace at which global industries are evolving. The fashion sector has especially boomed as a frontrunner in adapting to a market of brisk turnover of short-lived fads in response to the unyielding demand of consumerism. This research draws attention to the importance of employing social media in marketing approaches as a modern instrument fit to sustain in the contemporary world. This chapter adds to existing literature on the evolution of marketing techniques among the tech-savvy era of Millennials (Kilian et al., 2012; Moore, 2012; Taken Smith, 2011). It is imperative to recognise that while Millennials have resorted to social media for reliable day-to-day interactions, this generation does not segregate the online world from reality; rather it holds virtual means as an extension to the physical realm. Social media is merely a complement to traditional outlets, inciting brands to be mindful of portraying a communication pattern that is aligned over all spectrums. Any brand content should embody a representation of the core brand DNA that can be conveyed over any medium. This research seeks to underline the integrity of merging online channels into business operations in marketing to Millennials using social media.

This study adds to the literature on the consideration of social identity theory in online outlets (Bagozzi & Dholakia, 2002; Ozuem, Thomas, &

Lancaster, 2016; Dholakia, Bagozzi, & Pearo, 2004; Helal & Ozuem, 2019; Hogg & Reid, 2006; Pentina, Prybutok, & Zhang, 2008). This research recognises the existing, underlying motives guiding the adoption of social media in pursuing social benefits. Social media is considered an intermediary for contact between brand and customer, yet it also carries the responsibility of elevating such relationships into brand communities of belonging and trust. This chapter illustrates individuals' pursuit of a social identity that is facilitated through brand affiliation on social media platforms. The belonging that a customer establishes among a brand society paves the way for self-advancement as it fulfils a personal need of social inclusion while providing the necessary association for social enhancement. Social media is the inclusive podium that advances brand perceptions through the functional and symbolic motivations affiliated with the interaction and consumption of that brand.

REFERENCES

Aaker, D. (2004). Leveraging the corporate brand. *California Management Review, 46*(3), 6–18.

Aaker, D. (1991). *Managing brand equity: Capitalizing on the value of a brand name*. New York: Free Press.

Aaker, D. (1996). Measuring brand equity across products and markets. *California Management Review, 38*(3), 102–120.

Aaker, D., & Joachimsthaler, E. (2000). *Brand leadership* (p. 45). New York: Free Press.

Aaker, D., & Keller, K. (1990). Consumer evaluations of brand extensions. *Journal of Marketing, 54*(1), 27–41.

Adjei, M., Noble, S., & Noble, C. (2009). The influence of C2C communications in online brand communities on customer purchase behavior. *Journal of the Academy of Marketing Science, 38*(5), 634–653.

Alexander, B., & Levine, A. (2008). *Web 2.0 storytelling emergence of a new game* (pp. 40–48). Texas: EDUCAUSE Review.

Algesheimer, R., Dholakia, U., & Herrmann, A. (2005). The social influence of brand community: Evidence from European car clubs. *Journal of Marketing, 69*(3), 19–34.

Amaldoss, W., & Jain, S. (2008). Research note—trading up: A strategic analysis of reference group effects. *Marketing Science, 27*(5), 932–942.

Amos, C., Holmes, G., & Strutton, D. (2008). Exploring the relationship between celebrity endorser effects and advertising effectiveness. *International Journal of Advertising, 27*(2), 209–234. doi:10.1080/02650487. 2008.11073052

Anderson, E. (1998). Customer satisfaction and word of mouth. *Journal of Service Research, 1*(1), 5–17.

Andzulis, J., Panagopoulos, N., & Rapp, A. (2012). A review of social media and implications for the sales process. *Journal of Personal Selling and Sales Management, 32*(3), 305–316.

Argo, J., Dahl, D., & Manchanda, R. (2005). The influence of a mere social presence in a retail context. *Journal of Consumer Research, 32*(2), 207–212.

Arndt, J. (1967). Role of product-related conversations in the diffusion of a new product. *Journal of Marketing Research, 4*(3), 291–297.

Arnett, D., German, S., & Hunt, S. (2003). The identity salience model of relationship marketing success: The case of nonprofit marketing. *Journal of Marketing, 67*(2), 89–105.

Arora, P. (2014). *The Leisure commons*. New York: Routledge.

Ashforth, B., & Mael, F. (1989). Social identity theory and the organization. *The Academy of Management Review, 14*(1), 20–39.

Atkin, C., & Block, M. (1983). Effectiveness of celebrity endorsers. *Journal of Advertising Research, 23*(1), 57–61.

Babić Rosario, A., Sotgiu, F., De Valck, K., & Bijmolt, T. (2016). The effect of electronic word of mouth on sales: A meta-analytic review of platform, product, and metric factors. *Journal of Marketing Research, 53*(3), 297–318.

Bagozzi, R., & Dholakia, U. (2002). Intentional social action in virtual communities. *Journal of Interactive Marketing, 16*(2), 2–21.

Baker, A., Donthu, N., & Kumar, V. (2016). Investigating how word-of-mouth conversations about brands influence purchase and retransmission intentions. *Journal of Marketing Research, 53*(2), 225–239.

Bakewell, C., & Mitchell, V. (2003). Generation Y female consumer decision-making styles. *International Journal of Retail & Distribution Management, 31*(2), 95–106.

Baldus, B., Voorhees, C., & Calantone, R. (2015). Online brand community engagement: Scale development and validation. *Journal of Business Research, 68*(5), 978–985. doi:10.1016/j.jbusres.2014.09.035

Bargh, J., & McKenna, K. (2004). The internet and social life. *Annual Review of Psychology, 55*(1), 573–590.

Barron, L. (2012). *Social theory in popular culture*. Basingstoke: Palgrave Macmillan.

Barwise, P., & Meehan, S. (2010). The one thing you must get right when building a brand. *Harvard Business Review*, December 2010.

Bearden, W., & Etzel, M. (1982). Reference group influence on product and brand purchase decisions. *Journal of Consumer Research, 9*(2), 183–194.

Bennett, S., Maton, K., & Kervin, L. (2008). The 'digital natives' debate: A critical review of the evidence. *British Journal of Educational Technology, 39*(5), 775–786.

Bergman, S., Fearrington, M., Davenport, S., & Bergman, J. (2011). Millennials, narcissism, and social networking: What narcissists do on social networking sites and why. *Personality and Individual Differences, 50*(5), 706–711. doi:10.1016/j.paid.2010.12.022

Bernoff, J., & Li, C. (2008). Harnessing the power of the oh-so-social web. *Sloan Management Review, 49*(3), 36–42.

Berthon, P., Pitt, L., Plangger, K., & Shapiro, D. (2012). Marketing meets Web 2.0, social media, and creative consumers: Implications for international marketing strategy. *Business Horizons, 55*(3), 261–271.

Beukeboom, C., Kerkhof, P., & de Vries, M. (2015). Does a virtual like cause actual liking? How following a brand's facebook updates enhances brand evaluations and purchase intention. *Journal of Interactive Marketing, 32*, 26–36. doi:10.1016/j.intmar.2015.09.003

Bhattacharya, C., & Sen, S. (2003). Consumer-company identification: A framework for understanding consumers' relationships with companies. *Journal of Marketing, 67*(2), 76–88.

Bhardwaj, V., & Fairhurst, A. (2010). Fast fashion: Response to changes in the fashion industry. *The International Review of Retail, Distribution and Consumer Research, 20*(1), 165–173.

Biel, A. (1993). Converting image into equity in the book. In D. Aaker & A. Biel (Eds.), *Brand Equity and Advertising: Advertising's Role in Building Strong Brands* (1st ed., pp. 67–82). New York: Psychology Press.

Blattberg, R., Getz, G., & Thomas, J. (2001). *Customer equity: Building and managing relationships as valuable assets* (pp. 3–32). Boston, Mass.: Harvard Business School Press.

BOF, & McKinsey & Co. (2017). *The state of fashion 2017*. Retrieved from https://www.mckinsey.com/~/media/McKinsey/Industries/Retail/Our per cent20Insights/The per cent20state per cent20of per cent20fashion/The-state-of-fashion-2017-McK-BoF-report.ashx

BOF & McKinsey & Co. (2018). *The state of fashion 2018* (pp. 1–83). Retrieved from https://cdn.businessoffashion.com/reports/The_State_of_Fashion_2018_v2.pdf

BOF, & McKinsey & Co. (2019). *The state of fashion 2019*. Retrieved from https://www.mckinsey.com/~/media/McKinsey/Industries/Retail/Our per cent20Insights/The per cent20State per cent20of per cent20Fashion per cent202019 per cent20A per cent20year per cent20of per cent20awakening/The-State-of-Fashion-2019-vF.ashx

Bolton, R., Parasuraman, A., Hoefnagels, A., Migchels, N., Kabadayi, S., & Gruber, T., et al. (2013). Understanding generation Y and their use of social media: A review and research agenda. *Journal of Service Management, 24*(3), 245–267.

Bone, P. (1995). Word-of-mouth effects on short-term and long-term product judgments. *Journal of Business Research, 32*(3), 213–223.

Bong Na, W., Marshall, R., & Lane Keller, K. (1999). Measuring brand power: Validating a model for optimizing brand equity. *Journal of Product & Brand Management, 8*(3), 170–184.

Boyd, D., & Ellison, N. (2008). Social network sites: Definition, history, and scholarship. *Journal of Computer-Mediated Communication, 13*(1), 211.

Brakus, J., Schmitt, B., & Zarantonello, L. (2009). Brand experience: What is it? How is it measured? Does it affect loyalty? *Journal of Marketing, 73*(3), 52–68.

Brown, J., Broderick, A., & Lee, N. (2007). Word of mouth communication within online communities: Conceptualizing the online social network. *Journal of Interactive Marketing, 21*(3), 2–20.

Burke, P. (2006). *Contemporary social psychological theories.* Stanford, Calif.: Stanford Social Sciences.

Campbell, C., Pitt, L., Parent, M., & Berthon, P. (2011). Understanding consumer conversations around ads in a web 2.0 World. *Journal of Advertising, 40*(1), 87–102.

Caniato, F., Moretto, A., & Caridi, M. (2013). Dynamic capabilities for fashion-luxury supply chain innovation. *International Journal of Retail & Distribution Management, 41*(11/12), 940–960.

Carlson, B., Suter, T., & Brown, T. (2008). Social versus psychological brand community: The role of psychological sense of brand community. *Journal of Business Research, 61*(4), 284–291.

Carmeli, A., & Schaubroeck, J. (2007). The influence of leaders' and other referents' normative expectations on individual involvement in creative work. *The Leadership Quarterly, 18*(1), 35–48.

Chae, H., & Ko, E. (2016). Customer social participation in the social net-working services and its impact upon the customer equity of global fashion brands. *Journal of Business Research, 69*(9), 3804–3812. doi:10.1016/j.jbusres.2015.12.072

Chang, Y., Yu, H., & Lu, H. (2015). Persuasive messages, popularity cohesion, and message diffusion in social media marketing. *Journal of Business Research*, 68(4), 777–782.

Chatzipanagiotou, K., Christodoulides, G., & Veloutsou, C. (2018). Managing the consumer-based brand equity process: A cross-cultural perspective. *International Business Review, 28*(2), 328–343. doi:10.1016/j.ibusrev.2018.10.005

Chaudhuri, A., & Holbrook, M. (2001). The chain of effects from brand trust and brand affect to brand performance: The role of brand loyalty. *Journal of Marketing, 65*(2), 81–93.

Chauhan, K., & Pillai, A. (2013). Role of content strategy in social media brand communities: A case of higher education institutes in India. *Journal of Product & Brand Management, 22*(1), 40–51.

Cheung, C., & Thadani, D. (2012). The impact of electronic word-of-mouth communication: A literature analysis and integrative model. *Decision Support Systems, 54*(1), 461–470.

Childers, T., & Rao, A. (1992). The influence of familial and peer-based reference groups on consumer decisions. *Journal of Consumer Research, 19*(2), 198–211.

Chiu, C., Hsu, M., & Wang, E. (2006). Understanding knowledge sharing in virtual communities: An integration of social capital and social cognitive theories. *Decision Support Systems, 42*(3), 1872–1888.

Cho, E., Fiore, A., & Russell, D. (2015). Validation of a fashion brand image scale capturing cognitive, sensory, and affective associations: Testing its role in an extended brand equity model. *Psychology & Marketing, 32*(1), 28–48. doi:10.1002/mar.20762

Choi, S., & Rifon, N. (2012). It is a match: The impact of congruence between celebrity image and consumer ideal self on endorsement effectiveness. *Psychology & Marketing, 29*(9), 639–650.

Christopher, M., Lowson, R., & Peck, H. (2004). Creating agile supply chains in the fashion industry. *International Journal of Retail & Distribution Management, 32*(8), 367–376.

Chu, S., & Kim, Y. (2011). Determinants of consumer engagement in electronic word-of-mouth (eWOM) in social networking sites. *International Journal of Advertising, 30*(1), 47–75.

Chu, S., & Kim, J. (2018). The current state of knowledge on electronic word-of-mouth in advertising research. *International Journal of Advertising, 37*(1), 1–13.

Clement, R., & Krueger, J. (2002). Social categorization moderates social projection. *Journal of Experimental Social Psychology, 38*(3), 219–231.

Colliander, J., & Dahlén, M. (2011). Following the fashionable friend: The power of social media. *Journal of Advertising Research, 51*(1), 313–320.

Collin, P., Rahilly, K., Richardson, I., & Third, A. (2011). *The Benefits of Social Networking Services*. Research Report. Melbourne: Cooperative Research Centre for Young People, pp. 8–27.

Cornwell, T., Roy, D., & Steinard, E. (2001). Exploring managers' perceptions of the impact of sponsorship on brand equity. *Journal of Advertising, 30*(2), 41–51.

Cornwell, T., Weeks, C., & Roy, D. (2005). Sponsorship-linked marketing: Opening the black box. *Journal of Advertising, 34*(2), 21–42.

Correia, A., Kozak, M., & Reis, H. (2014). Conspicuous consumption of the elite. *Journal of Travel Research, 55*(6), 738–750. doi:10.1177/0047287514563337

Cova, B. (1997). Community and consumption. *European Journal of Marketing, 31*(3/4), 297–316.

Cova, B., & Cova, V. (2001). Tribal aspects of postmodern consumption research: The case of French in-line roller skaters. *Journal of Consumer Behaviour, 1*(1), 67–76.

Da Silva, R., & Alwi, S. (2008). Online brand attributes and online corporate brand images. *European Journal of Marketing, 42*(9/10), 1039–1058.

Dahl, S. (2018). *Social media marketing: Theories and applications* (1st ed.). SAGE.

Datta, H., Ailawadi, K., & van Heerde, H. (2017). How well does consumer-based brand equity align with sales-based brand equity and marketing-mix response? *Journal of Marketing, 81*(3), 1–20. doi:10.1509/jm.15.0340

Davcik, N., Vinhas da Silva, R., & Hair, J. (2015). Towards a unified theory of brand equity: Conceptualizations, taxonomy and avenues for future research. *Journal of Product & Brand Management, 24*(1), 3–17. doi:10.1108/jpbm-06-2014-0639

de Valck, K., van Bruggen, G., & Wierenga, B. (2009). Virtual communities: A marketing perspective. *Decision Support Systems, 47*(3), 185–203.

De Veirman, M., Cauberghe, V., & Hudders, L. (2017). Marketing through Instagram influencers: The impact of number of followers and product divergence on brand attitude. *International Journal of Advertising, 36*(5), 798–828. doi:10.1080/02650487.2017.1348035

Deloitte. (2018). *Global powers of retailing 2018*. Retrieved from https://www2.deloitte.com/content/dam/Deloitte/at/Documents/about-deloitte/global-powers-of-retailing-2018.pdf

Deloitte. (2018). *Global powers of luxury goods 2018*. Retrieved from https://www2.deloitte.com/content/dam/Deloitte/de/Documents/consumer-industrial-products/Deloitte_CIP_Report_GPLG2018.PDF

Dessart, L., Veloutsou, C., & Thomas, A. (2015). Consumer engagement in online brand communities: A social media perspective. *Journal of Product & Brand Management, 24*(1), 28–42.

Dewing, M. (2010). *Social media: An introduction*. Ottawa: Library of Parliament.

Dholakia, U., Bagozzi, R., & Pearo, L. (2004). A social influence model of consumer participation in network- and small-group-based virtual communities. *International Journal of Research in Marketing, 21*(3), 241–263.

Dobele, A., Lindgreen, A., Beverland, M., Vanhamme, J., & van Wijk, R. (2007). Why pass on viral messages? Because they connect emotionally. *Business Horizons, 50*(4), 291–304.

Dutta, S. (2010, November). What's your personal social media strategy? *Harvard Business Review*, 1–5.

Eastman, J., & Liu, J. (2012). The impact of generational cohorts on status consumption: An exploratory look at generational cohort and demographics on status consumption. *Journal of Consumer Marketing, 29*(2), 93–102.

Eastman, J., Iyer, R., & Thomas, S. (2013). The impact of status consumption on shopping style: An exploratory look at the millennial generation. *The Marketing Management Journal, 23*(1), 57–73.

Edelman, D. (2010, December). Branding in the digital age: You're spending your money in all the wrong places. *Harvard Business Review, 88*, 62–69.

Ekinci, Y., Sirakaya-Turk, E., & Preciado, S. (2011). Symbolic consumption of tourism destination brands. *Journal of Business Research, 66*(6), 711–718.

Elliott, R., & Wattanasuwan, K. (1998). Brands as symbolic resources for the construction of identity. *International Journal of Advertising, 17*(2), 131–144.

Enders, A., Hungenberg, H., Denker, H., & Mauch, S. (2008). The long tail of social networking. *European Management Journal, 26*(3), 199–211.

Engel, C., Bell, R., Meier, R., & Rumpel, J. (2011). Young consumers in the new marketing ecosystem: An analysis of their usage of interactive technologies. *Academy of Marketing Studies Journal, 15*(2), 23–44.

Englis, B., & Solomon, M. (1995). To be and not to be: Lifestyle imagery, reference groups, and the clustering of America. *Journal of Advertising, 24*(1), 13–28.

Escalas, J., & Bettman, J. (2003). You are what they eat: The influence of reference groups on consumers' connections to brands. *Journal of Consumer Psychology, 13*(3), 339–348.

Escalas, J., & Bettman, J. (2005). Self-construal, reference groups, and brand meaning. *Journal of Consumer Research, 32*(3), 378–389.

Evans, D. (2012). *Social media marketing: An hour a day* (2nd ed.). Indianapolis, Ind.: John Wiley & Sons Publishing, Inc.

FashionUnited. (2016). *Global fashion industry statistics*. Retrieved from https://fashionunited.com/global-fashion-industry-statistics/

Farrell, H., & Drezner, D. (2008). The power and politics of blogs. *Public Choice, 134*(1–2), 15–30.

Feldwick, P. (1996). Do we really need 'Brand Equity'? *Journal of Brand Management, 4*(1), 9–28.

Fiore, A., Kim, J., & Lee, H. (2005). Effect of image interactivity technology on consumer responses toward the online retailer. *Journal of Interactive Marketing, 19*(3), 38–53.

Fischer, E., Bristor, J., & Gainer, B. (1996). Creating or escaping community? An exploratory study of Internet consumers' behaviors. *Advances in Consumer Research, 23*, 178–182.

Fischer, E., & Reuber, A. (2011). Social interaction via new social media: (How) can interactions on Twitter affect effectual thinking and behavior? *Journal of Business Venturing, 26*(1), 1–18.

Flynn, L., Goldsmith, R., & Eastman, J. (1996). Opinion leaders and opinion seekers: Two new measurement scales. *Journal of the Academy of Marketing Science, 24*(2), 137–147.

Forbes. (2012). *The future of fashion retailing—The H&M approach (Part 3 of 3)*. Retrieved from http://www.forbes.com/sites/gregpetro/2012/11/05/the-future-of-fashion-retailing-the-hm-approach-part-3-of-3/#49f3d33d6dbf

Forbes. (2018). *Snap had a tough 2018, will next year be better?* Retrieved from https://www.forbes.com/sites/greatspeculations/2018/12/05/snap-had-a-tough-2018-will-next-year-be-better/#340ad914c283

Fournier, S., & Lee, L. (2009, April). Getting brand communities right. *Harvard Business Review*, 2–8.

Freling, T., & Forbes, L. (2005). An empirical analysis of the brand personality effect. *Journal of Product & Brand Management, 14*(7), 404–413.

Fromm, J., & Garton, C. (2013). *Marketing to millennials* (pp. 60–87). United States of America: Barkley, Inc.

Fuchs, C. (2014). *Social media: A critical introduction*. London: Sage Publications, Ltd.

Gensler, S., Völckner, F., Liu-Thompkins, Y., & Wiertz, C. (2013). Managing brands in the social media environment. *Journal of Interactive Marketing, 27*(4), 242–256.

Ghodeswar, B. (2008). Building brand identity in competitive markets: A conceptual model. *Journal of Product & Brand Management, 17*(1), 4–12.

Gillies, J., & Cailliau, R. (2000). *How the web was born*. Oxford: Oxford University Press.

Gilly, M., Graham, J., Wolfinbarger, M., & Yale, L. (1998). A dyadic study of interpersonal information search. *Journal of The Academy of Marketing Science, 26*(2), 83–100.

Godes, D., & Mayzlin, D. (2009). Firm-created word-of-mouth communication: Evidence from a field test. *Marketing Science, 28*(4), 721–739.

Godey, B., Manthiou, A., Pederzoli, D., Rokka, J., Aiello, G., Donvito, R., & Singh, R. (2016). Social media marketing efforts of luxury brands: Influence on brand equity and consumer behavior. *Journal of Business Research, 69*(12), 5833–5841.

Gruen, T., Osmonbekov, T., & Czaplewski, A. (2006). EWOM: The impact of customer-to-customer online know-how exchange on customer value and loyalty. *Journal of Business Research, 59*(4), 449–456.

Gu, B., & Ye, Q. (2014). First step in social media: Measuring the influence of online management responses on customer satisfaction. *Production and Operations Management, 23*(4), 570–582.

Gurău, C. (2012). A life-stage analysis of consumer loyalty profile: Comparing Generation X and Millennial consumers. *Journal of Consumer Marketing, 29*(2), 103–113.

Gürhan-Canli, Z., Hayran, C., & Sarial-Abi, G. (2016). Customer-based brand equity in a technologically fast-paced, connected, and constrained environment. *Academy of Marketing Science, 6*(1–2), 23–32. doi:10.1007/s13162-016-0079-y

H & M. (2018). *Nine month report*. Retrieved from https://about.hm.com/content/dam/hmgroup/groupsite/documents/masterlanguage/cision/2018/09/2281603.pdf

Hakala, U., Svensson, J., & Vincze, Z. (2012). Consumer-based brand equity and top-of-mind awareness: A cross-country analysis. *Journal of Product & Brand Management, 21*(6), 439–451.

Hanna, R., Rohm, A., & Crittenden, V. (2011). We're all connected: The power of the social media ecosystem. *Business Horizons, 54*(3), 265–273.

Hansen, D., Dunne, C., & Shneiderman, B. (2010). *Analyzing social media networks with NodeXL*. Maryland: HCIL University of Maryland.

Hartmann, W., Manchanda, P., Nair, H., Bothner, M., Dodds, P., Godes, D., Hosanagar, K., & Tucker, C. (2008). Modeling social interactions: Identification, empirical methods and policy implications. *Marketing Letters, 19*(3–4), 287–304.

Haslam, S., Oakes, P., Reynolds, K., & Turner, J. (1999). Social identity salience and the emergence of stereotype consensus. *Personality and Social Psychology Bulletin, 25*(7), 809–818. doi:10.1177/0146167299025007004

Heinonen, K. (2011). Consumer activity in social media: Managerial approaches to consumers' social media behavior. *Journal of Consumer Behaviour, 10*(6), 356–364.

Helal, G. (2019). The influence of social media brand communities on millennial brand perceptions in the fashion industry: A social identity outlook. In G. Bowen & W. Ozuem (Eds.), *Leveraging Computer-Mediated Marketing Environments* (pp. 143–172).

Helal, G., & Ozuem, W. (2018). Social identity matters: Social media and brand perceptions in the fashion apparel and accessories industries. In W. Ozuem & Y. Azemi (Eds.), *Digital Marketing Strategies for Fashion and Luxury Brands* (pp. 326–361). Hershey, U.S.A: IGI Global.

Helal, G., & Ozuem, W. (2019). Social media and social identity in the fashion industry: Among the millennial generation. In G. Bowen & W. Ozuem (Eds.), *Leveraging Computer-Mediated Marketing Environments* (1st ed., pp. 43–82). Hershey, U.S.A: IGI Global.

Helal, G., & Ozuem, W. (2016). The dynamics of social media in the fashion industry: The case of the millennial generation. In *Exceeding the Vision: Innovate, Integrate and Motivate* (pp. 194–202). United States of America: The Global Business and Technology Association.

Helal, G., & Ozuem, W. (2018). The emerging, evolving social media platforms and social identity: Implications for the fashion industry. In *Shaping the Next Wave of Globalization: Using Current Trends to Reconnect with Markets and Create Value* (pp. 204–211). United States of America: The Global Business and Technology Association.

Helal, G., Ozuem, W., & Lancaster, G. (2018). Social media brand perceptions of millennials. *International Journal of Retail & Distribution Management, 46*(10), 977–998.

Hennig-Thurau, T., Gwinner, K., Walsh, G., & Gremler, D. (2004). Electronic word-of-mouth via consumer-opinion platforms: What motivates consumers to articulate themselves on the Internet? *Journal of Interactive Marketing, 18*(1), 38–52.

Herr, P., Kardes, F., & Kim, J. (1991). Effects of word-of-mouth and product-attribute information on persuasion: An accessibility-diagnosticity perspective. *Journal of Consumer Research, 17*(4), 454–462.

Hershatter, A., & Epstein, M. (2010). Millennials and the world of work: An organization and management perspective. *Journal of Business and Psychology, 25*(2), 211–223.

Hewlet, S., Sherbin, L., & Sumberg, K. (2009). How geny & boomers will reshape your agenda. *Harvard Business Review*, (July–August 2009).

Hoeffler, S., & Keller, K. (2002). Building brand equity through corporate societal marketing. *Journal of Public Policy & Marketing, 21*(1), 78–89.

Hoffman, D., & Fodor, M. (2016). Can you measure the ROI of your social media marketing? *Sloan Management Review, 52*(1), 41–49.

Hoffman, D., & Novak, T. (1996). Marketing in hypermedia computer-mediated environments: Conceptual foundations. *Journal of Marketing, 60*(3), 50–68.

Hogan, J., Lemon, K., & Libai, B. (2004). Quantifying the ripple: Word-of-mouth and advertising effectiveness. *Journal of Advertising Research, 44*(3), 271–280.

Hogg, M., & Abrams, D. (1988). *Social identifications*. London: Routledge.

Hogg, M., Banister, E., & Stephenson, C. (2009). Mapping symbolic (anti-) consumption. *Journal of Business Research, 62*(2), 148–159.

Hogg, M., & Reid, S. (2006). Social identity, self-categorization, and the communication of group norms. *Communication Theory, 16*(1), 7–30.

Hogg, M., & Terry, D. (2000). Social identity and self-categorization processes in organizational contexts. *The Academy of Management Review, 25*(1), 121–140.

Hogg, M., Terry, D., & White, K. (1995). A tale of two theories: A critical comparison of identity theory with social identity theory. *Social Psychology Quarterly, 58*(4), 255–269.

Hogg, M., & Turner, J. (1987). Intergroup behaviour, self-stereotyping and the salience of social categories. *British Journal of Social Psychology, 26*(4), 325–340.

Hollebeek, L., Glynn, M., & Brodie, R. (2014). Consumer brand engagement in social media: Conceptualization, scale development and validation. *Journal of Interactive Marketing, 28*(2), 149–165.

Holmes, J. (2015). *Instagram black book*. Lexington, Kentucky.

Horton, D., & Wohl, R. (1956). Mass communication and parasocial interaction: Observations on intimacy at a distance. *Psychiatry, 19*(3), 215–229.

Houman Andersen, P. (2001). Relationship development and marketing communication: An integrative model. *Journal of Business & Industrial Marketing, 16*(3), 167–183.

Hsu, C., & Lin, J. (2008). Acceptance of blog usage: The roles of technology acceptance, social influence and knowledge sharing motivation. *Information & Management, 45*(1), 65–74.

Hwang, J., & Kandampully, J. (2012). The role of emotional aspects in younger consumer-brand relationships. *Journal of Product & Brand Management, 21*(2), 98–108.

Huang, M., Cai, F., Tsang, A., & Zhou, N. (2011). Making your online voice loud: The critical role of WOM information. *European Journal of Marketing*, 45(7/8), 1277–1297.

Huang, R., & Sarigöllü, E. (2012). How brand awareness relates to market outcome, brand equity, and the marketing mix. *Journal of Business Research, 65*(1), 92–99.

Huang, W., Schrank, H., & Dubinsky, A. (2004). Effect of brand name on consumers' risk perceptions of online shopping. *Journal of Consumer Behaviour, 4*(1), 40–50.

Huang, C., Shen, Y., Lin, H., & Chang, S. (2007). Bloggers' motivations and behaviors: A model. *Journal of Advertising Research, 47*(4), 472–484.

Hughes, M., Bendoni, W., & Pehlivan, E. (2016). Storygiving as a co-creation tool for luxury brands in the age of the internet: A love story by Tiffany and thousands of lovers. *Journal of Product & Brand Management, 25*(4), 357–364.

Huy, Q., & Shipilov, A. (2012). The key to social media success within organisations. *Sloan Management Review, 54*(1), 73–81.

Ifinedo, P. (2016). Applying uses and gratifications theory and social influence processes to understand students' pervasive adoption of social networking sites: Perspectives from the Americas. *International Journal of Information Management, 36*(2), 192–206.

Inditex. (2018). *Interim half year 2018 results.* Retrieved from https://www.inditex.com/documents/10279/588138/INDITEX+ 1H2018+Results.pdf/89063f93-3c40-f38c-8e0d-9bc6eb53de3b

Jang, H., Olfman, L., Ko, I., Koh, J., & Kim, K. (2008). The influence of on-line brand community characteristics on community commitment and brand loyalty. *International Journal of Electronic Commerce, 12*(3), 57–80.

Jayachandran, S., Gimeno, J., & Varadarajan, P. (1999). The theory of multimarket competition: A synthesis and implications for marketing strategy. *Journal of Marketing, 63*(3), 49–66.

Jenkins, R. (2008). *Social identity* (Key Ideas) (3rd ed.). London: Routledge.

John, D., Loken, B., Kim, K., & Monga, A. (2006). Brand concept maps: A methodology for identifying brand association networks. *Journal of Marketing Research, 43*(4), 549–563.

Jones, S. (1998). Information, internet and community: Notes toward an understanding of community in the information age. In S. Jones (Ed.), *Cybersocierty 2.0: Revisiting Computer-Mediated Communication and Community* (2nd ed., pp. 1–34). London: Sage Publications.

Kamboj, S., & Rahman, Z. (2017). Understanding customer participation in online brand communities. *Qualitative Market Research: An International Journal, 20*(3), 306–334. doi:10.1108/qmr-08-2016-0069

Kane, G., Alavi, M., Labianca, G., & Borgatti, S. (2014). What's different about social media networks? A framework and research agenda. *MIS Quarterly, 38*(1), 274–304.

Kaplan, A., & Haenlein, M. (2011). Two hearts in three-quarter time: How to waltz the social media/viral marketing dance. *Business Horizons, 54*(3), 253–263.

Kaplan, A., & Haenlein, M. (2010). Users of the world, unite! The challenges and opportunities of Social Media. *Business Horizons, 53*(1), 59–68.

Kaplan, A., & Haenlein, M. (2010). Users of the world, unite! The challenges and opportunities of social media. *Business Horizons, 53*(1), 61.

Katz, E., & Lazarsfeld, P. (1955). *Personal influence.* Glencoe, Ill.: Free Press.

Keller, K. (2001). *Building a customer-based brand equity: A blueprint for creating strong brands* (pp. 3–30). Massachusetts: Marketing Science Institute.

Keller, K. (2009). Building strong brands in a modern marketing communications environment. *Journal of Marketing Communications, 15*(2–3), 139–155.

Keller, K. (1993). Conceptualizing, measuring, and managing customer-based brand equity. *Journal of Marketing, 57*(1), 1. doi:10.2307/1252054

Keller, K. (2012). *Strategic brand management* (4th ed., pp. 30–35). Upper Saddle River, N.J.: Prentice Hall.

Kelley, H. (1952). Two functions of reference groups. In G. Swanson, T. Newcomb & E. Hartley (Eds.), *Society for the Psychological Study of Social Issues, Readings in Social Psychology* (1st ed., pp. 410–414). New York: Holt.

Kerpen, D. (2015). *Likeable social media*. New York: McGraw-Hill.

Kietzmann, J., Hermkens, K., McCarthy, I., & Silvestre, B. (2011). Social media? Get serious! Understanding the functional building blocks of social media. *Business Horizons, 54*(3), 241–251.

Kilian, T., Hennigs, N., & Langner, S. (2012). Do Millennials read books or blogs? Introducing a media usage typology of the Internet generation. *Journal of Consumer Marketing, 29*(2), 114–124.

Kim, J., Choi, J., Qualls, W., & Han, K. (2008). It takes a marketplace community to raise brand commitment: The role of online communities. *Journal of Marketing Management, 24*(3–4), 409–431.

Kim, A., & Ko, E. (2012). Do social media marketing activities enhance customer equity? An empirical study of luxury fashion brand. *Journal of Business Research, 65*(10), 1480–1486.

Kirmani, A., & Zeithaml, V. (1993). Advertising, perceived quality, and brand image. In D. Aaker & A. Biel (Eds.), *Brand Equity & Advertising: Advertising's Role in Building Strong Brands* (1st ed., pp. 143–162). Hilldale, NJ: Lawrence Erlbaum Associates.

Kleine, R., Kleine, S., & Kernan, J. (1993). Mundane consumption and the self: A social-identity perspective. *Journal of Consumer Psychology, 2*(3), 209–235.

Kozinets, R. (2002). The field behind the screen: Using netnography for marketing research in online communities. *Journal of Marketing Research, 39*(1), 61–72. doi:10.1509/jmkr.39.1.61.18935

Kozinets, R., de Valck, K., Wojnicki, A., & Wilner, S. (2010). Networked narratives: Understanding word-of-mouth marketing in online communities. *Journal of Marketing, 74*(2), 71–89.

Kumar, R., Novak, J., Raghavan, P., & Tomkins, A. (2004). Structure and evolution of blogspace. *Communications of The ACM, 47*(12), 35–39.

Kumar, V. (2015). Evolution of marketing as a discipline: What has happened and what to look out for. *Journal of Marketing, 79*(1), 1–9.

Kumar, V. (2018). Transformative marketing: The next 20 years. *Journal of Marketing, 82*(4), 1–12.

Kumar, V., & Mirchandani, R. (2012). Increasing the ROI of social media marketing. *Sloan Management Review, 54*(1), 55–61.

Lam, S., Ahearne, M., Hu, Y., & Schillewaert, N. (2010). Resistance to brand switching when a radically new brand is introduced: A social identity theory perspective. *Journal of Marketing, 74*(6), 128–146.

Langner, S., Hennigs, N., & Wiedmann, K. (2013). Social persuasion: Targeting social identities through social influencers. *Journal of Consumer Marketing, 30*(1), 31–49.

Laverie, D., Kleine III, R., & Kleine, S. (2002). Reexamination and extension of kleine, kleine, and kernan's social identity model of mundane consumption: The mediating role of the appraisal process. *Journal of Consumer Research, 28*(4), 659–669.

Lemon, K., Rust, R., & Zeithaml, V. (2001). What drives customer equity. *Marketing Management, 10*(1), 20–25.

Levy, S. (1959). Symbols for Sale. (2016). *Harvard Business Review*, July-August 1959(37), 117–124.

Li, J., & Su, C. (2007). How face influences consumption. *International Journal of Market Research, 49*(2), 237–246.

Liao, J., Huang, M., & Xiao, B. (2017). Promoting continual member participation in firm-hosted online brand communities: An organizational socialization approach. *Journal of Business Research, 71*, 92–101. doi:10.1016/j.jbusres.2016.10.013

Lingelbach, D., Patino, A., & Pitta, D. (2012). The emergence of marketing in Millennial new ventures. *Journal of Consumer Marketing, 29*(2), 136–145.

Lipsman, A., Mudd, G., Rich, M., & Bruich, S. (2012). The power of "like": How brands reach (and Influence) fans through Social-Media marketing. *Journal of Advertising Research, 52*(1), 40–52.

Liu, X., & Hu, J. (2012). Adolescent evaluations of brand extensions: The influence of reference group. *Psychology and Marketing, 29*(2), 98–106.

Luhtanen, R., & Crocker, J. (1992). A collective self-esteem scale: Self-evaluation of one's social identity. *Personality and Social Psychology Bulletin, 18*(3), 302–318.

Luo, X., Zhang, J., & Duan, W. (2013). Social media and firm equity value. *Information Systems Research, 24*(1), 146–163.

LVMH. (2018). *LVMH 2017*. Retrieved from https://r.lvmh-static.com/uploads/2018/03/lvmh_ra_2017-va.pdf

Ma, M., & Agarwal, R. (2007). Through a glass darkly: Information technology design, identity verification, and knowledge contribution in online communities. *Information Systems Research, 18*(1), 42–67.

Macarthy, A. (2013). *500 Social media marketing tips: Essential advice, hints and strategy for business*. Charlotte, NC: CreateSpace Independent Publishing Platform.

Maehle, N., Otnes, C., & Supphellen, M. (2011). Consumers' perceptions of the dimensions of brand personality. *Journal of Consumer Behaviour, 10*(5), 290–303.

Malär, L., Krohmer, H., Hoyer, W., & Nyffenegger, B. (2011). Emotional brand attachment and brand personality: The relative importance of the actual and the ideal self. *Journal of Marketing, 75*(4), 35–52.

Malthouse, E., Haenlein, M., Skiera, B., Wege, E., & Zhang, M. (2013). Managing customer relationships in the social media era: Introducing the social crm house. *Journal of Interactive Marketing, 27*(4), 270–280.

Mangold, W., & Faulds, D. (2009). Social media: The new hybrid element of the promotion mix. *Business Horizons, 52*(4), 357–365.

McAfee, A. (2008). Shattering the myths about enterprise 2.0. *Harvard Business Review*, (November 2009).

McAlexander, J., Schouten, J., & Koenig, H. (2002). Building brand community. *Journal of Marketing, 66*(1), 38–54.

McCracken, G. (1989). Who is the celebrity endorser? Cultural foundations of the endorsement process. *Journal of Consumer Research, 16*(3), 310–321.

McKenna, L., & Pole, A. (2008). What do bloggers do: An average day on an average political blog. *Public Choice, 134*(1–2), 97–108.

McKinsey & Co. (2016). *The state of fashion.* Retrieved from https://www.mckinsey.com/industries/retail/our-insights/the-state-of-fashion

Meyer, R. (2018). Reflections on "Transformative marketing: The next 20 years". *Journal of Marketing, 82*(4), 13–14.

Michaelidou, N., Siamagka, N., & Christodoulides, G. (2011). Usage, barriers and measurement of social media marketing: An exploratory investigation of small and medium B2B brands. *Industrial Marketing Management, 40*(7), 1153–1159.

Moore, M. (2012). Interactive media usage among millennial consumers. *Journal of Consumer Marketing, 29*(6), 436–444.

Miles, J. (2014). *Instagram power.* Nueva York: McGraw Hill.

Muniz, A., & O'Guinn, T. (2001). Brand community. *Journal of Consumer Research, 27*(4), 412–432.

Nambisan, S., & Baron, R. (2010). Different roles, different strokes: Organizing virtual customer environments to promote two types of customer contributions. *Organization Science, 21*(2), 554–572. doi:10.1287/orsc.1090.0460

Nardi, B., Schiano, D., Gumbrecht, M., & Swartz, L. (2004). Why we blog. *Communications of The ACM, 47*(12), 41–46.

Naylor, R., Lamberton, C., & West, P. (2012). Beyond the "Like" button: The impact of mere virtual presence on brand evaluations and purchase intentions in social media settings. *Journal of Marketing, 76*(6), 105–120.

Ngai, E., Tao, S., & Moon, K. (2015). Social media research: Theories, constructs, and conceptual frameworks. *International Journal of Information Management, 35*(1), 33–44.

Nowak, A., Szamrej, J., & Latané, B. (1990). From private attitude to public opinion: A dynamic theory of social impact. *Psychological Review, 97*(3), 362–376.

Nowak, L., Thach, L., & Olsen, J. (2006). Wowing the millennials: Creating brand equity·in the wine industry. *Journal of Product & Brand Management, 15*(5), 316–323.

Park, C., & Srinivasan, V. (1994). A survey-based method for measuring and understanding brand equity and its extendibility. *Journal of Marketing Research, 31*(2), 271–278.

Paulin, M. J., Ferguson, R., Jost, N., & Fallu, J. (2014). Motivating millennials to engage in charitable causes through social media. *Journal of Service Management, 25*(3), 334–348.

Pentina, I., Prybutok, V., & Zhang, X. (2008). The role of virtual communities as shopping reference groups. *Journal of Electronic Commerce Research, 9*(2), 114–136.

Pew Research. (2018). *Social Media Use 2018*: Demographics and Statistics. Retrieved from http://www.pewinternet.org/2018/03/01/social-media-use-in-2018/

Phan, M., Thomas, R., & Heine, K. (2011). Social media and luxury brand management: The case of burberry. *Journal of Global Fashion Marketing, 2*(4), 213–222.

Pitta, D., & Katsanis, L. (1995). Understanding brand equity for successful brand extension. *Journal of Consumer Marketing, 12*(4), 51–64.

Plummer, J. (2000). How personality makes a difference. *Journal of Advertising Research, 40*(6), 79–83.

Prensky, M. (2001). *Digital Natives, Digital Immigrants Part 1*. On The Horizon, *9*(5), 1–6.

Prónay, S., & Hetesi, E. (2014). *Symbolic Consumption in the Case of Brand Communities*. Vietnam: The international conference on finance and economics.

O'Cass, A., & McEwen, H. (2004). Exploring consumer status and conspicuous consumption. *Journal of Consumer Behaviour, 4*(1), 25–39.

O'Reilly, T. (2005). *Web 2.0: Compact Definition?*—O'Reilly Radar. Radar.oreilly.com. Retrieved from http://radar.oreilly.com/2005/10/web-20-compact-definition.html

O'Reilly, T., & Battelle, J. (2009). *Web Squared: Web 2.0 Five Years On* (pp. 1–12). California: O'Reilly Media, Inc.

Obar, J., & Wildman, S. (2015). Social media definition and the governance challenge—an introduction to the special issue. *Telecommunications Policy, 39*(9), 745–750. doi:10.2139/ssrn.2663153

OEC. (2016). *OEC*: The Observatory of Economic Complexity. Retrieved from https://atlas.media.mit.edu/en/

Onorato, R., & Turner, J. (2004). Fluidity in the self-concept: The shift from personal to social identity. *European Journal of Social Psychology, 34*(3), 257–278.

Ozuem, W., Howell, K., & Lancaster, G. (2008). Communicating in the new interactive marketspace. *European Journal of Marketing, 42*(9/10), 1059–1083.

Ozuem, W., Howell, K., & Lancaster, G. (2017). An exploration of consumers' response to online service recovery initiatives. *International Journal of Market Research, 59*(1), 97–115.

Ozuem, W., Howell, K., & Lancaster, G. (2016). Understanding technologically induced customer services in the Nigerian banking sector: The Internet as a post-modern phenomenon, *International Journal of Information Technology and Management, 15*(3), 272–290.

Ozuem, W., Thomas, T., & Lancaster, G. (2016). The influence of customer loyalty on small island economies: An empirical and exploratory study, *Journal of Strategic Marketing, 24*(6), 447–469.

Ozuem, W., & Tan, K. (2014). Reconciling social media with luxury fashion brands: An exploratory study. In L. Aiello (Ed.), *Management of Cultural Products: E-Relationship Marketing and Accessibility Perspective*. Hershey: IGI Publications.

Rainer, T., & Rainer, J. (2011). *The millennials: Connecting to America's largest generation*. Nashville, Tennessee: B & H Pub. Group.

Rains, S., & Brunner, S. (2014). What can we learn about social network sites by studying Facebook? A call and recommendations for research on social network sites. *New Media & Society, 17*(1), 114–131.

Rangaswamy, A., Burke, R., & Oliva, T. (1993). Brand equity and the extendibility of brand names. *International Journal of Research in Marketing, 10*(1), 61–75.

Reichelt, J., Sievert, J., & Jacob, F. (2013). How credibility affects eWOM reading: The influences of expertise, trustworthiness, and similarity on utilitarian and social functions. *Journal of Marketing Communications, 20*(1–2), 65–81. doi:10.1080/13527266.2013.797758

Remy, N., Schmidt, J., Werner, C., & Lu, M. (2014). *Unleashing fashion growth city by city*. Retrieved from https://www.mckinsey.com/~/media/mckinsey/dotcom/client_service/marketing per cent20and per cent20sales/pdfs/unleashing_fashion_growth.ashx

Ren, Y., Harper, M., Drenner, S., Terveen, L., Kiesler, S., Riedl, J., & Kraut, R. (2012). Building member attachment in online communities: Applying theories of group identity and interpersonal bonds. *MIS Quarterly, 36*(3), 841–864.

Rettberg, J. (2008). *Blogging: Digital media and society series*. Cambridge, UK: Polity.

Rieh, S. (2002). Judgment of information quality and cognitive authority in the Web. *Journal of the American Society for Information Science and Technology, 53*(2), 145. doi:10.1002/asi.10017.abs

Richards, M. (2015). *Social Media: Dominating strategies for social media marketing*. CreateSpace Independent Publishing Platform.

Robards, B., & Bennett, A. (2011). Mytribe: Post-subcultural manifestations of belonging on social network sites. *Sociology, 45*(2), 303–317.

Roberts, K. (2006). *Lovemarks: The future beyond brands* (2nd ed.). New York: Powerhouse Books.

Rosenthal, B., & Brito, E. (2017). How virtual brand community traces may increase fan engagement in brand pages. *Business Horizons, 60*(3), 375–384. doi:10.1016/j.bushor.2017.01.009

Rossmann, A., Ranjan, K., & Sugathan, P. (2016). Drivers of user engagement in eWOM communication. *Journal of Services Marketing, 30*(5), 541–553. doi:10.1108/jsm-01-2015-0013

Safko, L. (2012). *The social media bible: Tactics, tools, and strategies for business success* (pp. 4–30). Hoboken, N.J.: John Wiley & Sons.

Sashi, C. (2012). Customer engagement, buyer-seller relationships, and social media. *Management Decision, 50*(2), 253–272.

Sashittal, H., DeMar, M., & Jassawalla, A. (2016). Building acquaintance brands via Snap for the college student market. *Business Horizons, 59*(2), 193–204.

Schivinski, B., & Dabrowski, D. (2016). The effect of social media communication on consumer perceptions of brands. *Journal of Marketing Communications, 22*(2), 189–214.

Senecal, S., & Nantel, J. (2004). The influence of online product recommendations on consumers' online choices. *Journal of Retailing, 80*(2), 159–169.

Seno, D., & Lukas, B. (2007). Exploring the relationship between celebrity endorser effects and advertising effectiveness. *European Journal of Marketing, 41*(1/2), 121–134.

Sheth, J. (2011). Impact of emerging markets on marketing: Rethinking existing perspectives and practices. *Journal of Marketing, 74*(4), 166–182.

Sheth, J., & Parvatlyar, A. (1995). Relationship marketing in consumer markets: Antecedents and consequences. *Journal of the Academy of Marketing Science, 23*(4), 255–271.

Shibutani, T. (1955). Reference groups as perspectives. *American Journal of Sociology, 60*(6), 562–569.

Simmons, G. (2008). Marketing to postmodern consumers: Introducing the internet chameleon. *European Journal of Marketing, 42*(3/4), 299–310.

Simon, F., & Tossan, V. (2018). Does brand-consumer social sharing matter? A relational framework of customer engagement to brand-hosted social media. *Journal of Business Research, 85*, 175–184. doi:10.1016/j.jbusres.2017.12.050

Singh, S., & Sonnenburg, S. (2012). Brand performances in social media. *Journal of Interactive Marketing, 26*(4), 189–197.

Singh, T., Veron-Jackson, L., & Cullinane, J. (2008). Blogging: A new play in your marketing game plan. *Business Horizons, 51*(4), 281–292.

Smith, A., & Anderson, M. (2018). *Social Media Use in 2018* (pp. 1–7). America: PewResearch Center. Retrieved from http://assets.pewresearch. org/wp-content/uploads/sites/14/2018/03/01105133/PI_2018.03.01_ Social-Media_FINAL.pdf

Smith, P., & Zook, Z. (2011). *Marketing communications* (5th ed., pp. 3–26). London: Kogan Page.

Smith, T. (2009). The social media revolution. *International Journal of Market Research, 51*(4), 559–561.

Snap Inc.. (2018). *Snap.com.* Retrieved from https://www.snap.com/en-US/

Statista. (2016). *London Fashion Week: Social Buzz 2014.* Social Media & User-Generated Content. Statista - The Statistic Portal. Retrieved January 7, 2019, from http://www.statista.com/statistics/315224/social-media-mentions-london-fashion-week/

Statista. (2016). *Daily time spent on social networking by internet users worldwide as of 2nd quarter 2016, by age group (in minutes).* Retrieved January 5, 2019, from https://www.statista.com/statistics/613456/daily-social-media-usage-worldwide-age/

Statista. (2016). *Global apparel market size projections from 2012 to 2025, by region (in billion U.S. dollars).* Retrieved January 7, 2019, from https://www. statista.com/statistics/279757/apparel-market-size-projections-by-region/

Statista. (2017). *Daily time spent on social media by social video viewers worldwide as of 2nd quarter 2017, by age group.* Retrieved January 5, 2019, from https://www.statista.com/statistics/267138/social-media-usage-per-day-global-social-video-users-age/

Statista. (2017). *Sources used by Millennials to hear about the latest high-end fashion or luxury item trends worldwide in 2017.* Retrieved January 7, 2019, from https://www.statista.com/statistics/441758/sources-for-hearing-about-new-luxury-brands-worldwide/

Statista. (2018). *Instagram: active users 2018 | Statista.* Retrieved from https://www.statista.com/statistics/253577/number-of-monthly-active-instagram-users/

Statista. (2018). *Instagram luxury brands followers 2018 | Statistic.* Retrieved from https://www.statista.com/statistics/483753/leading-luxury-brands-instagram-followers/

Statista. (2017). *Instagram: most-followed fashion brands 2017.* Retrieved from https://www.statista.com/statistics/483738/leading-fashion-brands-instagram-followers/

Statista. (2018). *Most famous social network sites worldwide as of January 2018, ranked by number of active users (in millions).* Retrieved January 5, 2019, from https://www.statista.com/statistics/272014/global-social-networks-ranked-by-number-of-users/

Stephen, A., & Galak, J. (2010). The complementary roles of traditional and social media in driving marketing performance. *INSEAD Working Papers Collections, 2010*(97).

Stern, B. (1994). A revised communication model for advertising: Multiple dimensions of the source, the message, and the recipient. *Journal of Advertising, 23*(2), 5–15.

Stokinger, E., & Ozuem, W. (2015). Social media and customer retention in the luxury fashion sector. In G. Bowen & W. Ozuem (Eds.), *Computer-Mediated Marketing Strategies: Social Media and Online Brand Communities.* Hershey: IGI

Strauss, W., & Howe, N. (1991). *Generations: The history of America's future* (pp. 27–32). New York: Morrow.

Sung, Y., & Kim, J. (2010). Effects of brand personality on brand trust and brand affect. *Psychology and Marketing, 27*(7), 639–661.

Susarla, A., Oh, J., & Tan, Y. (2012). Social networks and the diffusion of user-generated content: Evidence from youtube. *Information Systems Research, 23*(1), 23–41.

Sweeney, J., Soutar, G., & Mazzarol, T. (2008). Factors influencing word of mouth effectiveness: Receiver perspectives. *European Journal of Marketing, 42*(3/4), 344–364.

Taken Smith, K. (2012). Longitudinal study of digital marketing strategies targeting Millennials. *Journal of Consumer Marketing, 29*(2), 86–92.

Tajfel, H., & Turner, J. (1985). The social identity theory of intergroup behaviour. In S. Worchel & W. Austen (Eds.), *Psychology of Intergroup Relations* (2nd ed., pp. 7–24). Chicago: Nelson-Hall.

Thompson, C., Rindfleisch, A., & Arsel, Z. (2006). Emotional branding and the strategic value of the doppelgänger brand image. *Journal of Marketing, 70*(1), 50–64.

Tiago, M., & Veríssimo, J. (2014). Digital marketing and social media: Why bother?. *Business Horizons, 57*(6), 703–708.

Tirunillai, S., & Tellis, G. (2017). Does offline TV advertising affect online chatter? Quasi-experimental analysis using synthetic control. *Marketing Science, 36*(6), 862–878. doi:10.1287/mksc.2017.1040

Trepte, S. (2008). Social identity theory. In J. Bryant & P. Vorderer (Eds.), *Psychology of Entertainment* (2nd ed., pp. 255–271). New York: Routledge.

Trusov, M., Bucklin, R., & Pauwels, K. (2009). Effects of word-of-mouth versus traditional marketing: Findings from an internet social networking site. *Journal of Marketing, 73*(5), 90–102.

Tsai, W., & Ghoshal, S. (1998). Social capital and value creation: The role of intrafirm networks. *Academy of Management Journal, 41*(4), 464–476.

Turner, J., Oakes, P., Haslam, S., & McGarty, C. (1994). Self and collective: Cognition and social context. *Personality and Social Psychology Bulletin, 20*(5), 454. doi:10.1177/0146167294205002

Tuten, T., & Solomon, M. (2014). *Social media marketing* (2nd ed.). Boston: Pearson.

Twenge, J. (2006). *Generation me: Why today's young americans are more confident, assertive, entitled—and more miserable than ever before*. New York: Free Press.

Twenge, J., Campbell, W., & Freeman, E. (2012). Generational differences in young adults' life goals, concern for others, and civic orientation, 1966–2009. *Journal of Personality and Social Psychology, 102*(5), 1045–1062.

v. Wangenheim, F., & Bayón, T. (2004). The effect of word of mouth on services switching. *European Journal of Marketing, 38*(9/10), 1173–1185.

Valentine, D., & Powers, T. (2013). Generation Y values and lifestyle segments. *Journal of Consumer Marketing, 30*(7), 597–606.

Valette-Florence, P., Guizani, H., & Merunka, D. (2011). The impact of brand personality and sales promotions on brand equity. *Journal of Business Research, 64*(1), 24–28.

Van Dijck, J. (2013). *The culture of connectivity*. Oxford: Oxford University Press.

Van Doorn, J., Lemon, K., Mittal, V., Nass, S., Pick, D., Pirner, P., & Verhoef, P. (2010). Customer engagement behavior: Theoretical foundations and research directions. *Journal of Service Research, 13*(3), 253–266. doi:10.1177/1094670510375599

Van Knippenberg, D., van Knippenberg, B., De Cremer, D., & Hogg, M. (2004). Leadership, self, and identity: A review and research agenda. *The Leadership Quarterly, 15*(6), 825–856.

Vargo, S., & Lusch, R. (2004). Evolving to a new dominant logic for marketing. *Journal of Marketing, 68*(1), 1–17.

Vázquez-Casielles, R., Suárez-Álvarez, L., & del Río-Lanza, A. (2013). The word of mouth dynamic: How positive (and negative) wom drives purchase probability. *Journal of Advertising Research, 53*(1), 43–60. doi:10.2501/jar-53-1-043-060

Valette-Florence, P., Guizani, H., & Merunka, D. (2011). The impact of brand personality and sales promotions on brand equity. *Journal of Business Research, 64*(1), 24–28.

Veletsianos, G. (2013). Open practices and identity: Evidence from researchers and educators' social media participation. *British Journal of Educational Technology, 44*(4), 639–651.

Veloutsou, C., & Moutinho, L. (2009). Brand relationships through brand reputation and brand tribalism. *Journal of Business Research, 62*(3), 314–322.

Vermeulen, I., & Seegers, D. (2009). Tried and tested: The impact of online hotel reviews on consumer consideration. *Tourism Management, 30*(1), 123–127.

Vernuccio, M., Pagani, M., Barbarossa, C., & Pastore, A. (2015). Antecedents of brand love in online network-based communities. A social identity perspective. *Journal of Product & Brand Management, 24*(7), 706–719. doi:10.1108/jpbm-12-2014-0772

Vogel, V., Evanschitzky, H., & Ramaseshan, B. (2008). Customer equity drivers and future sales. *Journal of Marketing, 72*(6), 98–108.

Wang, C., Lee, H., Wu, L., & Liu, C. (2017). Quality dimensions in online communities influence purchase intentions. *Management Decision, 55*(9), 1984–1998. doi:10.1108/md-11-2016-0822

Wee, T. (2004). Extending human personality to brands: The stability factor. *Journal of Brand Management, 11*(4), 317–330.

Weinberg, T. (2009). *The new community rules: Marketing on the social web* (pp. 2–17). Sebastopol, CA: O'Reilly Media, Inc.

Weinberg, B., & Pehlivan, E. (2011). Social spending: Managing the social media mix. *Business Horizons, 54*(3), 275–282.

Whan Park, C., MacInnis, D., Priester, J., Eisingerich, A., & Iacobucci, D. (2010). Brand attachment and brand attitude strength: Conceptual and empirical differentiation of two critical brand equity drivers. *Journal of Marketing, 74*(6), 1–17.

Wirtz, J., den Ambtman, A., Bloemer, J., Horváth, C., Ramaseshan, B., & van de Klundert, J. et al. (2013). Managing brands and customer engagement in online brand communities. *Journal of Service Management, 24*(3), 223–224.

Wolny, J., & Mueller, C. (2013). Analysis of fashion consumers' motives to engage in electronic word-of-mouth communication through social media platforms. *Journal of Marketing Management, 29*(5–6), 562–583.

You, Y., Vadakkepatt, G., & Joshi, A. (2015). A meta-analysis of electronic word-of-mouth elasticity. *Journal of Marketing, 79*(2), 1–39.

Yuan, C., Kim, J., & Kim, S. (2016). Parasocial relationship effects on customer equity in the social media context. *Journal of Business Research, 69*(9), 3795–3803. doi:10.1016/j.jbusres.2015.12.071

Zaglia, M. (2013). Brand communities embedded in social networks. *Journal of Business Research, 66*(2), 216–223. doi:10.1016/j.jbusres.2012.07.015

Zarrella, D. (2009). *The social media marketing book*. Sebastopol: O'Reilly Media, Inc.

Zhang, Y., & Leung, L. (2014). A review of social networking service (SNS) research in communication journals from 2006 to 2011. *New Media & Society, 17*(7), 1007–1024. doi:10.1177/1461444813520477

Zhu, Y., & Chen, H. (2015). Social media and human need satisfaction: Implications for social media marketing. *Business Horizons, 58*(3), 335–345.

Chapter 3

Social Media and Purchase Intentions: Strategic Marketing Implications

Ali Usman
University of the West of Scotland, UK

Sebastian Okafor
University of Cumbria, UK

ABSTRACT

Within the fashion industry, managing the consumer-brand relationship is always challenging. Web 2.0-based brand communities and groups on social networking sites henceforth provide the solution to this problem and enable the marketers to create maximum brand awareness and engagement of consumers with the interactive promotional and informational content. This chapter explains the ubiquitous role of social media in strengthening the consumer-brand relationship which subsequently develops the purchase intentions. It further explains the explicit role of social networking sites (SNS) based fashion brand communities and groups which provide the essential platform for heterogeneous social interactions (information, social, hedonic and economic). Such social interactions develop brand awareness, brand loyalty, brand identification, eWOM and ultimately consumers' purchase intentions. Furthermore, the chapter also discusses the conclusion and potential managerial implications of this knowledge in the fashion industry.

INTRODUCTION

Over the course of time, marketing trends have undergone changes from traditional and conventional methods of marketing to new, fast and improved modes of promoting products and services in the fashion industry using online media (Helal et al., 2018). The integration of mass media and individual social interactions as forms of interpersonal communication has long been considered the cornerstone of behavioural and attitudinal change amongst consumers (Li et al., 2018; Peng et al., 2017). Revolutionary development in inbound consumer-centric digital media, especially in terms of online social media, has created a dependence on alternative marketing practices. This has fundamentally changed the marketing landscape (Siikanen et al., 2018). Digital platforms that support communication and social interactions are the result of the extensive commercialisation of the Internet, which has created a shift in the network paradigm from traditional media to Web 2.0-based online social media. The invention of the Internet and subsequent development of Web 2.0-based technological applications such as social media have revolutionised social communications and online interactions (Siikanen et al., 2018). In today's world, the transition from conventional to social and digital media marketing plays an important role in creating fashion brand awareness (Kaplan & Haenlein, 2010; Kawaf & Istanbulluoglu, 2019), changing value perceptions, transforming thoughts and encouraging the adoption of new behaviours to create leads for brand recognition and to drive return on investment (ROI) (Fisher, 2009; Smith, 2012). The advantage of consumer dependence on digital and social media has been exploited by marketers to re-craft their marketing strategies using digital media to communicate and promote products and services to customers. Social media marketing strategies are unique since they make use of online SNSs as a medium for promoting goods and services to reach a wider audience and to receive quick customer responses (Stokinger & Ozuem, 2014). Social media marketing uses networking websites like Facebook, Twitter, MySpace, Instagram and YouTube through social media optimisation (Davis et al., 2012).

THEORETICAL CONTEXT

To grasp the concept of social media, three related concepts are fundamental: Web 2.0, Web 3.0 and User-Generated Content (UGC). Web 2.0 was coined in 2004 to describe a new method in which application programmers and end-users could utilise the World Wide Web (Klimis, 2010; Tong et al., 2018). Web 2.0 is a platform in which software and content are produced and published not by individual companies and people, but by different participants in a continuous and collaborative manner. UGC describes all the ways in which users create content and use social media (Ozuem et al., 2017). UGC-based social media enable individuals to represent their self-selected styles on social webs and have initiated the new mode of consumer-brand communication and engagement (Lin et al., 2012). The term 'content' has been the least defined and is not very familiar to online marketing research. This word is defined by Handley and Chapman (2011) as the formation of words, graphics and numerical figures that yield certain information and is available online to the users. Holliman and Rowley (2014) rightly defined the term content as the display of information to online users in the form of words, podcasts, videos and infographics. Halvorson and Rach (2012) defined content as messaging about products and services for attracting customers towards those products and services and convincing them to buy through promotional stories. The concept reached significant levels of popularity in 2005. Web 2.0 is an umbrella term that describes various forms of media content that are publicly available and created by end-users, from text to video and audio materials (Kaplan & Haenlein, 2010; Kawaf & Istanbulluoglu, 2019). Web 3.0 is a technologically advanced form of Web 2.0 which can be explained as semantically integrated digital technologies or intelligent agents that are capable of manipulating web services (creating, reading and writing the user-generated content) in order to support human cooperation across the online network and enable firms to react to and adopt the changes into data and to implement those changes efficiently (Cabada et al., 2018).

The explicit role of social media comes into play as a mode of value creation for business. It provides a credible platform for online users to communicate and to enhance their social interactions and strengthen relationships with brands or firms as part of a wider socialisation process in B2C environments (Felix et al., 2017). The Internet has long been considered the primary component for communication and interactions as companies have grown to realise the importance of the transition from traditional modes of communication to Web 2.0-based online media, which are cost-effective and more rigorous in facilitating an exchange between consumers and retail fashion companies (Hardey, 2009; Klimis, 2010). Within the retail fashion industry the shift in the marketing paradigm as a result of Internet-based promotional broadcasting on multiple social media platforms has been recognised as a critical factor influencing online users' behaviour (De Bruyn & Lilien, 2008; Kawaf & Istanbulluoglu, 2019; Ozuem, Howell, & Lancaster, 2016). The most notable aspects of consumer behaviour that are influenced include information acquisition, evaluation of post-purchase experiences, and communication and changes in perceptions of the utility of products and services (Felix et al., 2017). Changes in consumers' behaviour are the outcome of social media communications and such behaviours represent a clear opportunity for companies to drive profit (Chan & Guillet, 2011; Hajli, 2014). First, promotional messages are broadcast to consumers following careful analysis of their online behaviour. Second, companies facilitate consumer-to-consumer interactions on social media to give their advertisements greater exposure. Consequently, this transforms the behaviour and perceptions of users and creates an opportunity for users to become potential consumers in the process of making rational purchase decisions (Ozuem & Tan, 2014).

The significant benefit of social networking sites over traditional media is the capability of such user-generated sites to offer greater user interactivity. For example, when online members of SNS on Facebook 'like' or follow a fashion brand's page or group they receive the updates on the newsfeed about the happenings within the specific fashion group or community. Such SNS groups and communities further enhance the interactive experience of the users with features of UGC whereby they can create content in the form of comments and opinions and share and propagate such content with friends in their SNS social circle (Helal et al., 2018). Upon sharing the UGC in the social circle their friends' interaction with the shared content rebroadcasts into their own networks and propagates further on. In this scenario the UGC undergoes a speedy exchange across the SNS network and transmitted to a significantly larger and broader audience at significantly lower cost compared to the traditional media.

SOCIAL MEDIA AND THE FASHION INDUSTRY

Social media has previously been used to study changes in consumers' behaviour, brand awareness, brand commitment and loyalty, attitudes and decision-making in the luxury fashion brand industry (Kedzior et al., 2016; Langaro et al., 2018; Tong et al., 2018; Zhang et al., 2015; Helal et al., 2018). Fashion has been classified as having high involvement as it refers to products which are expensive, reveal personal identity, are occasionally bought and hold a high purchase risk. Such high involvement brand products and services attract significant consumers' interest and become the point of conversation and social interaction on social media (Gu et al., 2012).

Through heterogeneous (informational, social, hedonic and economic) interactions on social media the consumer-brand relationship in the fashion industry helps in evaluating the social value and importance of fashion brand products. On social media Facebook is the most popular users' interaction site with over 2 billion users across the world (Alexa, 2018). More than 60 million businesses have already launched their consumer-brand relationship strategies and communicate their brands' messages with potential customers by setting up their Facebook pages (Vladlena et al., 2015). According to research, more than 2.5 million businesses pay to use Facebook for promotion and advertisements and 75 per cent of the fashion brands pay multiple social media platforms to promote their posts to maximise users' interaction with the brands (Smith, 2016). Kawaf and Istanbulluoglu (2019) stated that the fashion industry has become the leading industry in online shopping and is enjoying the maximum users' interaction and brand promotion by using multiple online social media platforms. Social media has enabled the fashion industry to maximise consumer-brand relationships and consumer brand identity by promoting consumer-to-consumer communication and knowledge sharing through heterogenic social interactions (informational, social, hedonic and economic).

Many scholars have studied consumer-brand relationships in the luxury fashion industry on social media in multiple perspectives. For example, Kedzior et al. (2016) investigated the role of social media by measuring the consumers' feedback on luxury fashion brand content on social media platforms. Langaro et al. (2018) studied the influence of social media on consumers' brand awareness and attitudes towards fashion brands, Tong et al. (2018) examined consumers' brand commitment and loyalty to luxury fashion brands on social media. Zhange et al. (2015) studied heterogenic consumer-brand interaction in the perspective of the creation and consumption of fashion brand content on multiple social media platforms, as social media users share fashion and style-related information on social networks consisting of peers, friends and acquaintances and receive feedback on their style-related choices. Within the fashion industry, consumer engagement with fashion brand content in the form of informational content, brand-sponsored videos and reviews helps companies to attract the attention of potential customers. Such consumer-brand engagement on social media enables the companies to better understand how to influence the consumers through using social media rather than traditional advertising techniques. The social media social networking sites hold ubiquitous importance for maximising consumers' engagement with fashion brands to create brand identity and brand awareness. The SNS fashion groups and communities enable the companies to enhance the consumers' engagement with brands through social information sharing and knowledge exchange. This changes the consumers' mindset and develops rational purchase intentions (Hajli, 2014).

Social media has changed the landscape of online communications and social networking because it functions on the principles of UGC, which harnesses Web 2.0 Internet technologies to facilitate communication between users. This is achieved in the form of content containing media-based impressions. It can be archived or published online as part of a user profile to facilitate easy access to content and information (Boyd & Ellison, 2007). The most important forms of social media are SNSs because they enable greater engagement and UGC interactions between online members. The literature includes extensive research that has been carried out on digital content promotion and distribution and their impact on electronic business promotion and products and services recognition (Pulizzi, 2013; Oestreicher-Singer & Zalmanson, 2013; Feng et al., 2009). The interactive and promotional content published in SNS fashion brand groups has been considered an integral part of online fashion business and marketing as an object of trade because the information is exchanged and traded through development of online content at a cost of resources to the consumers. This digital interaction boosts the credibility of online sources and helps bring potential customers to the fashion companies by promoting their products. Pulizzi's (2013) research stated that companies nowadays try to make their content available free online, increasing both its exposure to customers and their online traffic on websites. Distribution of the content in SNS brand communities facilitates customers' engagement with the content through increasing online interaction and communication, helping the companies to attract potential customers.

SOCIAL MEDIA AND FASHION BRAND COMMUNITIES

The ubiquitous social interactions have made SNS ever increasingly popular across the world. The most popular social networking sites are

Facebook, Twitter, Instagram and YouTube and online users actively interact using one or two of these sites in everyday life. Lu (2018) argued that SNS bring a defined benefit to both brand and relationship marketing due to their dynamic features and capability to increase brand awareness, exposure, brand identity, loyalty, consumer-brand engagement and website traffic. These pervasive online spaces have also enabled marketers to gain leads on market intelligence in the context of consumers' value perceptions and buying behaviour (Xie & Lee, 2015). Further, the accessibility of such SNS on mobile phones has increased the experiential value of SNS users and made it easy for the marketers to reach out to this expanded target audience to communicate and promote brand products and services. Such B2C communication in fashion industry creates consumers' brand awareness and develops a base of brands through consumers' utilitarian and hedonic social interactions with brand content. Similarly, the marketer-developed SNS brand communities and groups enhance consumer engagement, which resultantly strengthens consumer-brand relationships and influences purchase decisions (Goh et al., 2013). As such, the trend of incorporating SNS in corporate brand strategies has become indispensable for increasing consumer-brand engagement and experiential value through interacting, consuming, creating and sharing brand content. Millions of companies have set up their SNS brand communities and groups for the purpose of brand communication and to gain a theoretical understanding of how the informational, hedonic, economic and utilitarian social interactions in brand communities influence brand-related outcomes (Jin & Phua, 2014).

Such bottom-up media formats enable integrated marketing communications and social networking by connecting millions of online users who trust each other's opinions and experiences, creating greater brand awareness about the fashion brands.. The prospect of digital marketing has advanced the field of marketing research and marketers can now influence the behaviour of customers via SNS fashion brand group interactions (Peng et al., 2017). Such SNS fashion brand group interactions develop multiple levels of social influence, leading to the adoption of new behaviours and agreement as to common attitudes and opinions in online settings (Carr et al., 2016). Consequently, individual group-based social interactions in SNS brand communities lead to intentional social actions that are embedded in new behaviours and attitudes (Tsai & Man, 2013). Keeping this logic in mind, the prominence of social media use in online selling and commerce has increased, reaching new viewers and customers that use social media. It has become the core medium for interactions between consumers and sellers.

The fashion brand communities developed on Web 2.0-based social media platforms such as Facebook are one of the best examples in this context. Burson-Marsteller (2012) argued for the importance of such brand communities and groups on SNS by mentioning that 74 out of 100 Fortune 500 companies have their active SNS brand groups and 94 per cent of those companies update their content pages every week. With rapid diffusion of SNS and widespread use of SNS brand communities for consumer-brand communication, more and more firms are relying on their SNS brand communities to facilitate and encourage the community members to exchange information, knowledge and personal experiences about the usefulness of brand products and services. Commonly acclaimed benefits associated with these SNS brand communities are social and connectivity benefits (social interaction and exchange), informational benefits (sharing and seeking information), hedonic benefits such as entertainment, enjoyment and fun, and economic benefits such as engagement with promotional content. Dholakia et al. (2009) in their research argued that underpinning the above-mentioned benefits of the SNS fashion brand communities their members hold values of reciprocity and intimacy, enabling others to share the consumer-generated information for problem solving and technological support. A unique feature of the nature of SNS brand communities is that the members should not explicitly hold brand loyalty or be known as 'brand enthusiasts'. Rather, most members of these communities visit the communities and join on the basis of economic and utilitarian benefits such as exclusive offers, deals, promotions, bonuses, etc. (Schau et al., 2009; Jin & Phua, 2014). Having a distinctive nature and unique features embedded in SNS fashion, the brand communities have been explicitly used for brand communication and development of consumer-brand engagement, underlying the fact that consumers' social interactions in these communities transform their loyalty to the brand, leading to rational purchase decisions (Hennig-Thurau et al., 2010). The example of Facebook communities fits best in this regard where the community is developed, promoted, operated and controlled by the companies to extract the essential drivers (indicators of community growth and success) of the users' engagement with the brand and brand content. Such Facebook-based communities and brand pages strengthen the fashion industry firms' customer relationship-building capabilities through supporting the community members' interactive experience and consumers' engagement with the UGC. Jin et al. (2010a) stated that SNS brand communities attract the attention of individuals on social media having a common interest in interaction with the brand. Having a shared social interest the community members share information, personal experiences and socio-emotional support as a testimony to their strong engagement and consumer-brand ties. Zaglia (2013) argued that the SNS brand communities provide an essentially holistic social structure in online spaces, facilitating consumer-to-consumer communication and consumer-brand interaction.

The SNS fashion brand groups and communities enable experiences of utilitarian and hedonic interaction through sharing social information as well as knowledge and support amongst online members, further providing a fundamental basis for the development of online social influence with implications for consumers' online behavioural modelling (Gutiérrez-Cillán et al., 2017; Zaglia, 2013; Kang & Schuett, 2013). Moreover, such digital platforms help consumers and online users on social media to interact, influence, consume, co-create and communicate about products and services and share content with millions of other members to promote fashion goods and services sold by luxury fashion brand companies (Ozuem & Tan, 2014).

Marketers continue to examine the online behaviour of users on the basis of social interactions and this has led to the design of specific online programmes and marketing campaigns to attract the attention of users (Vemuri, 2010). For this purpose they gauge the extent to which the interactive content and posts within the SNS fashion brand communities created by the firms help in improving socially collaborative learning and experiences by maximising the consumer-brand engagement. Secondly, they ascertain the type and orientation of UGC yielding experiential value to the community members on basis of their engagement and consumption of content. Such experiential value through social, informational, hedonic and economic community interactions influences their loyalty and association with a luxury fashion brand, which subsequently determines the purchase decision-making. Furthermore, the commercialisation of social media has enabled companies to achieve this outcome with the development of social media brand communities or groups in which online users enjoy intimacy, interactivity, socialisation and engagement with fashion brand content (Bonson & Flores, 2011; Proenca et al., 2010; Jin & Phua, 2014).

FASHION BRAND COMMUNITIES AND ELECTRONIC WORD-OF-MOUTH (EWOM)

Through social media brand communities the firms aim to strengthen their communication and relationship with the customers by gaining their trust and loyalty. Such trust and loyalty develop electronic word-of-mouth (eWOM) on social media, which affects between 20 and 50 per cent of the consumers' buying decisions (Erkan & Evans, 2016; Bughin et al., 2010). The eWOM communication confirms the ubiquity of the social media and can be defined as the way of exchanging practical information about the brand that influences consumers' value perception about the brand and services (Farzin & Fatahi, 2018). Since eWOM is the product of social media and is transmitted through social media platforms such as SNS rather than being propagated in traditional media, this impacts its credibility and wider acceptance. The credibility and ubiquity of social media enhances its dependability in the sense that before making a purchase decision about certain fashion brand products consumers look for information about them on the social media. The consumers' dependence on social media-based eWOM is even higher when the fashion products and services they want to buy are expensive or they are buying for the first time, as consumers then tend to engage more with the informational content, brand group discussions, opinions and comments about those fashion products (Chu & Kim, 2011).

Laroche et al. (2013) state that the SNS brand communities have a positive influence on consumers' decisions and product promotion. Such positive influence not only affects the rational development of consumer-brand relationships but also increases the consumers' loyalty, association and identity with a fashion brand. Yet the consumer-to-consumer communication and social exchange of information and knowledge is what most influences trust and loyalty to a brand and this creates the foundation of eWOM development. Such communication is the fundamental feature of the user-generated content in which consumers share their ideas and opinions about the fashion brand products and services as it unveils the benefits and utility of the products in a short span of time, making it a cost-effective way of achieving a relationship marketing strategy. By having such communal and social features for supporting individuals' social interactions social media is widely known as 'people's media' (Fournier & Avery, 2011). Further, using the SNS fashion brand communities as a platform the firms utilise eWOM in the form of consumers' trust and loyalty with the brand to sell their products and achieve financial targets. Chang et al. (2013) argued that eWOM could be either positive or negative, with a corresponding subsequent impact on the consumers' value perception and decision-making. Positive eWOM reflects favourable comments and recommendations made by existing customers on the basis of current or past buying experience and value perception about the brand's products and services; negative eWOM is the opposite. On social media it is easy to gain wide knowledge and information about a brand's products and disseminate such knowledge further into the social networks of friends, family, peers and acquaintances.

Compared to traditional WOM, eWOM has a much wider coverage and impacts on the decisions of a broader audience in the fashion industry. Unlike the traditional media where firms influence the development of WOM through transmission of persuasive messages to the public, eWOM involves less effort and companies have lesser control over it since it is a product of consumer-to-consumer interaction and communication (Laroche et al., 2013). It has more impact on consumers' decision-making as it is propagated to a geographically wider audience but it has the embedded risk of propagating negative information or unpleasant customer experiences in the social networks. Consequently the circulation of negative product messages can deprive a company of its market share and brand identity in public perception.

For companies to maximise the influence of eWOM in fashion brand communications the identity of the consumer group or the individual plays a significant role. The influence of the eWOM would be positive and more productive of purchase decisions when members of a social group consider its source to be trustworthy and knowledgeable about the brand's products and services. Moreover, the environment where consumers can interact and express their ideas and views independently also plays the essential role in the validity of eWOM. Erkan and Evans (2016) in their research argued that within the online spaces consumer-brand relationships are strengthened when the individuals interact in geographically wide social groups compared to the when they interact in small groups and communities. In larger groups consumers are exposed to extensive positive and negative eWOM messages stating the pros and cons of a brand's products and their utility, essentially making it easier for other customers to make a rational decision about them (Bughin et al., 2010).

In order to take the maximum advantage of eWOM as a relationship marketing tool the fashion brand companies should monitor the dimensions of the products it communicates about. For example, eWOM should be based on the information, evidence and post-purchase experience that consumers trust, developed from individuals' social interaction and knowledge sharing in SNS brand communities. Secondly, the eWOM should explicitly originate from consumer-to-consumer communication in SNS fashion brand communities, and finally, the eWOM messages should be propagated so as to gain wide exposure across the social network, winning the trust of consumers. Augusto and Torres (2018) argue that the incentive for the consumers in UGC-based SNS fashion brand communities is the ability to generate eWOM. The mechanism involved in this includes the customers' involvement in the development of the fashion product through to their participation in online brand communities. Since consumers tend to share their views and opinions about a product in the early phase of its development and life cycle, the generation of eWOM on the basis of such customers' experiences with the launch of new products is of explicit benefit to the companies.

Social Media and Consumers' Purchase Intentions

Truong and Simmons (2010) in their research state that social media marketing is the future of marketing for all kinds of businesses in the retail and B2C environment. This concept contends with the transactional view of marketing and confirms that consumers in SNS brand communities use their interactive and relational experiences as a guide to strengthen their association, loyalty and purchase intentions towards a brand.

Hajli (2014, p. 388) explained this phenomenon as follows:

'The networking of individuals through social media provides shared values, leading to a positive i+1.99 ptmpact on trust. Today, with the expansion of social media and SNSs, a study of consumer behaviour on these platforms is a research agenda because social media are likely to develop marketing strategies in firms through trust-building mechanisms and affecting customers' intention to buy online products.'

On SNSs, online consumers engage with digital content and exchange thoughts, ideas and valuable information through self-generated posts, tags, and blogs about fashion brands, their latest trends and products (de Vries et al., 2012; Cvijikj & Michahelles, 2013; Sabate et al., 2014;

Ozuem, Thomas & Lancaster, 2016). The orientation and type of the content within these brand communities not only enhances the experiential value of heterogenic social interaction between the community members but also significantly enhances the popularity of the community on the basis of likes, content sharing and the number of comments and posts. The creation of new content and alterations to existing content by online users on SNSs involve multiple existing and new sources of information which are widely discussed and shared by online users individually or in social groups. These are created and shared for multiple purposes, including for education, speedy learning and exchanging information about brand products and services which lead to rational purchase decisions (Holsapple et al., 2018). The heterogenic nature of SNSs encourages complex interactions between users (Hoffman, 2010) and has at the same time enabled users to harness information relating to consumer purchase behavioural patterns while interacting and engaging with online content. Such intelligence provides a wider picture of aggregate behaviour and user opinions in order to tailor information for particular audiences (Hearn et al., 2009; Kaplan & Haenlein, 2010; Berthon et al., 2008). Members' activity and its experiential value as a result of their utilitarian and hedonic interactions and engagement with the content in the SNS brand community's public forum play a crucial role in a brand community's survival and endurance. In addition, such marketer-developed brand communities and brand groups hold embedded benefits for the firms' relationship marketing strategies, making them a focal point of research for marketers to evaluate the efficacy of the SNS brand communities in the context of their B2C relationship and communication (Lu, 2018). Because the benefits of brand communities are not limited to bringing people together on one public platform for their stipulated interest in brand awareness through discussions and reviews, the individuals' engagement in such SNS brand communities also provides the edge towards the success of a firm's relationship marketing strategy.

The greater the usefulness and value perception of the content-based information, the higher the expected online traffic of the users, and vice versa (Kietzmann et al., 2011). For marketers in today's world selling products and services online has become difficult because buyers prefer to look for the content themselves, which gives them smarter insight and leaves them with greater choices for purchase decisions. The future of digital content marketing will be centred more on communication and engagement between the customers and the business. The credibility of content sharing in SNS brand groups and communities is considered more reliable (Jin & Phua, 2014). The credibility and vitality of content are what every digital content marketer should be aiming at and these are enhanced when the sharing of consumer-generated content increases. Apart from the promotion of products and services, SNSs facilitate group-based social interactions and informational exchange between users to help them understand what benefits certain products or services can provide (Carr et al., 2016). Such speedy one-on-one communication removes time constraints and reduces the barriers to communication imposed by traditional media. This in turn empowers consumers to interact directly with companies rather than receive information passively. In addition, social media encompasses a variety of emerging information sources, enabling consumers to understand more about products and services and to compare and evaluate these against alternatives. It allows them to share personal views and experiences with large audiences on social media platforms (Greenhow & Robelia, 2009).

CONCLUSION AND MANAGERIAL IMPLICATIONS

Both consumer-developed and marketer-developed SNS fashion brand communities help to accelerate customers' engagement (Lu, 2018). This is determined by the choices of the consumers because technology merely serves as an instrument. It differs from the traditional media segmentation and has created advantages for companies depending upon SNS communities to determine consumers' needs and situations (Tsai & Men, 2013). The companies tailor the online behaviour of the customers through adding epic content into automatic pop-up adverts and visual ads to simultaneously promote and communicate their brand messages and give the customers the choice to accept or reject them by simply clicking on the pop-ups to access or cancel them. Zaglia (2013) in their research stated that social media is a vital scientific tool for the applicability of digital marketing by strengthening the engagement leads on brand-consumer relationships in SNS brand groups. The majority of the empirical findings reveal that creating leads with SNS brand communities has a significant relationship with customers' purchase intentions and return on investment (Fisher, 2009; Smith, 2012). SNS brand group interactions promote the customers' purchase intentions by raising awareness about the products and services to solve consumers' needs and educating customers to decide about buying services they have never tried before (Jin & Phua, 2014). The consumer-generated content published in these brand groups has a wider impact in practical marketing strategies when potential customers who are outside the contact list of the company find value in it. This increases the return on investment if the online content marketing is executed correctly. For example, most of the time the content attracts potential customers by its quality and by carrying extensive details of the fashion products through blogs, reviews, ratings, discussions, consumers' opinions and the number of times each post is shared. These benefit a variety of digital marketing channels by providing the additional content on social media marketing, raising brand awareness and brand equity and contributing to search engine optimisation by creating the inbound links, ensuring that the content is available on all the credible search engines (Helal & Ozuem, 2017).

Such an aggregate of opinions, online search data and interaction patterns yields valuable information and insight for marketers about trends in consumer society. It provides intelligence on consumer preferences and choices in relation to certain products and services, and offers clues as to the motivations of those that interact on social media (Hollebeek et al., 2014). The development of brand-related social media marketing strategies is effective in terms of engaging consumers, particularly in the context of the online luxury fashion industry (Park & Kim, 2015). Marketing communications involving the communication of information-based content about fashion products and services creates a sense of affiliation between online users and fashion brands (Ozuem & Tan, 2014). Indeed, such promotions presenting them with content in relation to the latest fashion trends and luxury product ranges accelerate the lines of communication between online users. This not only adds value to marketing communications by educating consumers about existing products and services but also communicates knowledge about forthcoming products and services as brand extensions. Consequently, this two-way communication significantly influences the socio-cognitive behaviours of online consumers, helping them to form rational buying decisions (Alalwan, 2018).

REFERENCES

Alalwan, A. A. (2018). Investigating the impact of social media advertising features on customer purchase intention. *International Journal of Information Management, 42*, 65–77.

Alexa. (2018). Alexa Site Info: Facebook. Retrieved April 12, 2019, from http://www.alexa.com/siteinfo/facebook.com

Augusto, M., & Torres, P. (2018). Effects of brand attitude and eWOM on consumers' willingness to pay in the banking industry: Mediating role of consumer-brand identification and brand equity. *Journal of Retailing and Consumer Services, 42*, 1–10.

Bagozzi, R. P., Dholakia, U. P., & Mookerjee, A. (2006). Individual and group bases of social influence in online environments. *Media Psychology, 8*(2), 95–126.

Berthon, P. R., Pitt, L., & Campbell, C. (2008). Ad lib: When customers create the ad. *California Management Review, 50*(4), 6–31.

Bonson, E., & Flores, F. (2011). Social media and corporate dialogue: The response of global financial institutions. *Online Information Review, 35*(1), 34–49.

Boyd, D., & Ellison, N. B. (2007). Social network sites: Definition, history, and scholarship. *Journal of Computer-Mediated Communication, 13*(1), 210–230.

Bughin, J., Doogan, J., & Vetvik, O. J. (2010). A new way to measure word-of-mouth marketing. *The McKinsey Quarterly, 2*, 113–116.

Burson-Marsteller. (2012). Largest Global Companies Mentioned More than 10 Million Times Online in One Month, Study Finds. Retrieved April 12, 2019, from http://www.burson-marsteller.com/social/Press Release.aspx

Cabada, R., Estrada, M., Hernández, F., Bustillos, R., & Reyes-García, C. (2018). An affective and Web 3.0-based learning environment for a programming language. *Telematics and Informatics, 35*(3), 611–628.

Carr, C. T., Wohn, Y. D., & Hayes, R. A. (2016). As social support: Relational closeness, automaticity, and interpreting social support from paralinguistic digital affordances in social media. *Computers in Human Behavior, 62*, 385–393.

Chan, N. L., & Guillet, B. D. (2011). Investigation of social media marketing: How does the hotel industry in Hong Kong perform in marketing on social media websites? *Journal of Travel and Tourism Marketing, 28*(4), 345–368.

Chang, A., Hsieh, S. H., & Tseng, T. H. (2013). Online brand community response to negative brand events: The role of group eWOM. *Internet Research, 23*(4), 486–506.

Christodoulides, G. (2009). Branding in the post-internet era. *Marketing Theory, 9*(1), 141–144.

Chu, S. C., & Kim, Y. (2011). Determinants of consumer engagement in electronic word-of-mouth (eWOM) in social networking sites. *International Journal of Advertising, 30*, 47–75.

Cvijikj, I. P., & Michahelles, F. (2013). Online engagement factors on Facebook brand pages. *Social Network Analysis and Mining, 3*(4), 843–861.

Davis, C. H. F., Canche, M. S. G., Deil-Amen, R., & Rios-Aguilar, C. (2012). *Social media in higher education: A literature review and research directions*. Arizona: The Center for the Study of Higher Education at the University of Arizona and Claremont Graduate University.

De Bruyn, A., & Lilien, G. (2008). A multi-stage model of word-of-mouth influence through viral marketing. *International Journal of Research in Marketing, 25*(3), 151–163.

De Vries, L., Gensler, S., & Leeflang, P. S. (2012). Popularity of brand posts on brand fan pages: An investigation of the effects of social media marketing. *Journal of Interactive Marketing, 26*(2), 83–91.

Dholakia, U., Bagozzi, R., & Pearo, L. (2004). A social influence model of consumer participation in network- and small-group-based virtual communities. *International Journal of Research in Marketing, 21*(3), 241–263.

Dholakia, U. M., Blazevic, V., Wiertz, C., & Algesheimer, R. (2009). Communal service delivery: How customers benefit from participation in firm-hosted virtual P3 communities. *SSRN Electronic Journal, 12*, 208–226.

Erkan, I., & Evans, C. (2016). The influence of eWOM in social media on consumers' purchase intentions: An extended approach to information adoption. *Computers in Human Behavior, 61*, 47–55.

Farzin, M., & Fattahi, M. (2018). eWOM through social networking sites and impact on purchase intention and brand image in Iran. *Journal of Advances in Management Research, 15*(2), 161–183.

Felix, R., Rauschnabel, P., & Hinsch, C. (2017). Elements of strategic social media marketing: A holistic framework. *Journal of Business Research, 70,* 118–126.

Feng, Y., Guo, Z., & Chiang, W. K. (2009). Optimal digital content distribution strategy in the presence of the consumer-to-consumer channel. *Journal of Management Information Systems, 25*(4), 241–270.

Fisher, T. (2009). ROI in social media: A look at the arguments. *Database Marketing and Customer Strategy Management, 16*(3), 189–195.

Fournier, S., & Avery, J. (2011). The uninvited brand. *Business Horizons, 54*(3), 193–207.

Goh, K. Y., Heng, C. S., & Lin, Z. (2013). Social media brand community and consumer behavior: Quantifying the relative impact of user- and marketer-generated content. *Information Systems Research, 24,* 88–107.

Greenhow, C., & Robelia, B. (2009). Old communication, new literacies: Social network sites as social learning resources. *Journal of Computer-Mediated Communication, 14*(4), 1130–1161.

Gutiérrez-Cillán, J., Camarero-Izquierdo, C., & San José-Cabezudo, R. (2017). How brand post content contributes to user's Facebook brand-page engagement. The experiential route of active participation. *BRQ Business Research Quarterly, 20*(4), 258–274.

Hajli, M. (2014). A study of the impact of social media on consumers. *International Journal of Market Research, 55*(6), 387–404.

Halvorson, K., & Rach, M. (2012). *Content strategy for the web* (2nd ed.). New Rides publishers.

Handley, A., & Chapman, C. C. (2011). Content Rules. Wiley, Hoboken, N. J. Hardey, M. (2009). The social context of online market research: An introduction to sociability of social media. *International Journal of Market Research, 51*(4), 562–564.

Hearn, G., Foth, M., & Gray, H. (2009). Applications and implementations of new media in corporate communications: An action research approach. *Corporate Communications: An International Journal, 14*(1), 49–61.

Hennig-Thurau, T., Malthouse, E. C., Friege, C., Gensler, S., Lobschat, L., Rangaswamy, A., & Skiera, B. (2010). The impact of new media on customer relationship. *Journal of Service Research, 13*(3), 311–330.

Helal, G., & Ozuem, W. (2017). Social identity matters: Social media and brand perceptions in the fashion apparel and accessories industries. In W. Ozuem & Y. Azemi (Eds.), *Digital Marketing Strategies for Fashion and Luxury Brands* (pp. 326–361). IGI Global, Hershey.

Helal, G., Ozuem, W., & Lancaster, G. (2018). Social media brand perceptions of millennials. *International Journal of Retail and Distribution Management, 46*(10), 977–998.

Hoffman, D. L., & Fodor, M. (2010). Can you measure the ROI of your social media marketing? *MIT Sloan Management Review, 52*(1), 41–49.

Holliman, G., & Rowley, J. (2014). Business to business digital content marketing: Marketers' perceptions of best practice. *Journal of Research in Interactive Marketing, 8*(4), 269–293.

Hollebeek, L. D., Glynn, M. S., & Brodie, R. J. (2014). Consumer brand engagement in social media: Conceptualization, scale, development and validation. *Journal of Interactive Marketing, 28*(2), 149–165.

Holsapple, C., Hsiao, S., & Pakath, R. (2018). Business social media analytics: Characterization and conceptual framework. *Decision Support Systems, 110*, 32–45.

Iyengar, R., Han, S., & Gupta, S. (2009). Do friends influence purchases in a social network? *SSRN Electronic Journal.*

Jin, B., Park, J. Y., & Kim, H. S. (2010). What makes online community members commit? A social exchange perspective. *Behaviour and Information Technology, 29*(6), 587–599.

Jin, S. A. A., & Phua, J. (2014). Following celebrities' tweets about brands: The impact of twitter-based electronic word-of-mouth on consumers' source credibility perception, buying intention, and social identification with celebrities. *Journal of Advertising, 43*, 181–195.

Kang, M., & Schuett, M. (2013). Determinants of sharing travel experiences in social media. *Journal of Travel and Tourism Marketing, 30*(1–2), 93–107.

Kawaf, F., & Istanbulluoglu, D. (2019). Online fashion shopping paradox: The role of customer reviews and Facebook marketing. *Journal of Retailing and Consumer Services, 48*, 144–153.

Kaplan, A. M., & Haenlein, M. (2010). Users of the world, unite! The challenges and opportunities of social media. *Business Horizons, 53*(1), 59–68.

Kedzior, R., Allen, D. E., & Schroeder, J. (2016). The selfie phenomenon– consumer identities in the social media marketplace. *European Journal of Marketing, 50*(9/10), 1767–1772.

Kietzmann, J. H., Hermkens, K., McCarthy, I. P., & Silvestre, B. S. (2011). Social media? Get serious! understanding the functional building blocks of social media. *Business Horizons, 54*(1), 241–251.

Klimis, C. (2010). Digital marketing: The gradual integration in retail banking. *EFMA Journal, 4*(226), 16–19.

Langaro, D., Rita, P., & Salgueiro, M. F. (2018). Do social networking sites contribute for building brands? Evaluating the impact of users' participation on brand awareness and brand attitude. *Journal of Marketing Communications, 24*(2), 146–168.

Laroche, M., Habibi, M. R., & Richard, M. O. (2013). To be or not to be in social media: How brand loyalty is affected by social media? *International Journal of Information Management, 33*(1), 76–82.

Lin, T. M. Y., Lu, K., & Wu, J. (2012). The effects of visual information in eWOM communication. *Journal of Research in Interactive Marketing, 6*(1), 7–26.

Li, K., Zhang, L., & Huang, H. (2018). Social influence analysis: Models, methods, and evaluation. *Engineering, 4*, 40–46.

Lu, X. (2018). Cultural differences in consumer engagement in brand related SNS groups: A cross-cultural study of China and the United States. *Journal of Global Marketing, 31*(5), 295–307.

Oestreicher-Singer, G., & Zalmanson, L. (2013). Content or community? A digital business strategy for content providers in the social age. *MIS Quarterly, 37*(2), 591–616.

Ozuem, W., Howell, K., & Lancaster, G. (2008). Communicating in the new interactive marketspace. *European Journal of Marketing, 42*(9/10), 1059–1083.

Ozuem, W., & Tan, K. (2014). Reconciling social media with luxury fashion brands: An exploratory study. In L. Aiello (Ed.), *Handbook of Research on Management of Cultural Products: E-Relationship Marketing and Accessibility Perspectives* (pp. 257–285). IGI Global.

Ozuem, W., Pinho, C. A., & Azemi, Y. (2016). User-generated content and perceived customer value. In W. Ozuem & G. Bowen (Eds.), *Competitive Social Media Marketing Strategies* (pp. 50–63). Mission IGI Global.

Ozuem, W., Thomas, T., & Lancaster, G. (2016). The influence of customer loyalty on small island economies: An empirical and exploratory study. *Journal of Strategic Marketing, 24*(6), 447–469.

Ozuem, W., Patel, A., Howell, K., & Lancaster, G. (2017). An exploration of consumers' response to online service recovery initiatives. *International Journal of Market Research, 59*(1), 97–115.

Park, H., & Kim, Y. (2015). Can a fashion brand be social? The role of benefits of brand community within social network sites. *Journal of Global Fashion Marketing, 6*(2), 75–86.

Peng, S., Yang, A., Cao, L., Yu, S., & Xie, D. (2017). Social influence modeling using information theory in mobile social networks. *Information Sciences, 379*, 146–159.

Proenca, J., Martins Silva, M., & Fernanades, T. (2010). The impact of the internet upon bank marketing. *Journal of Financial Services Marketing, 15*(2), 160–175.

Pulizzi, J. (2013). How to know content marketing when you see it. *E-Content, 36*(10), 16–17.

Sabate, F., Berbegal-Mirabent, J., Ca-abate, A., & Lebherz, P. R. (2014). Factors influencing popularity of branded content in Facebook fan pages. *European Management Journal, 32*(6), 1001–1011.

Schau, H. J., Muñiz, Jr., A. M., & Arnould, E. J. (2009). How brand community practices create value. *Journal of Marketing, 73*(5), 30–51. doi:10.1509/jmkg.73.5.30

Siikanen, M., Baltakys, K., Kannianinen, J., Mukkamala, R., & Hussain, A. (2018). Facebook drives behavior of passive households in stock markets. *Finance Research Letters*. In press.

Smith, K. T. (2012). Longitudinal study of digital marketing strategies targeting Millennials. *Journal of Consumer Marketing, 29*(2), 86–92.

Smith, K. (2016). Marketing: 47 Facebook Statistics for 2016. Brand-Watch (2016). Retrieved April 12, 2019, from https://www.brandwatch.com/2016/05/47-facebook-statistics-2016/

Stokinger, E., & Ozuem, W. (2014). Social media and customer retention: Implication for luxury beauty industry. In G. Bowen & W. Ozuem (Eds.), *Computer-Mediated Marketing Strategies: Social Media and Online Brand Communities* (pp. 200–222). Publisher: IGI Publication.

Tong, X., Su, J., & Xu, Y. (2018). Brand personality and its impact on brand trust and brand commitment: An empirical study of luxury fashion brands. *International Journal of Fashion Design, Technology and Education, 11*(2), 196–209.

Truong, Y., & Simmons, G. (2010). Perceived intrusiveness in digital advertising: Strategic marketing implications. *Journal of Strategic Marketing, 18*(3), 239–256.

Tsai, W., & Men, L. (2013). Motivations and antecedents of consumer engagement with brand pages on social networking sites. *Journal of Interactive Advertising, 13*(2), 76–87.

Vemuri, A. (2010). Getting social: Bridging the gap between banking and social media. *Global Finance, 24*(5), 20–21.

Vladlena, B., Saridakis, G., Tennakoon, H., & Ezingeard, J. N. (2015). The role of security notices and online consumer behaviour: An empirical study of social networking users. *International Journal of Human and Computer Studies, 80*, 36–44.

Xie, K., & Lee, Y. J. (2015). Social media and brand purchase: Quantifying the effects of exposures to earned and owned social media activities in a two-stage decision making model. *Journal of Management Information Systems, 32*(2), 204–238.

Zaglia, M. E. (2013). Brand communities embedded in social networks. *Journal of Business Research, 66*(2), 216–223.

Zhang, Y., Tang, J., Yang, Z., Pei, J., & Yu, P. U. (2015). Cosnet: Connecting heterogeneous social networks with local and global consistency. In *Proceedings of the 21th ACM SIGKDD International Conference on Knowledge Discovery and Data Mining (2015)*, pp. 1485–1494.

SEVEN KEY TERMS AND DEFINITIONS

Social media: A Web 2.0-based application that runs on the principles of user-generated content, enabling the online users to create, share, modify and alter the digital content and facilitating two-way communication on the Internet.

User-generated content: UGC represents all the ways in which users create and exchange digital content and use social media on the technological basis of Web 2.0.

Web 2.0: Web 2.0 is a platform in which software and digital content are produced and published not only by individual companies and people but also by different participants in a continuous and collaborative manner.

SNS brand community: An online Web 2.0-based platform of social media on which consumers can communicate brand-related content with companies and other consumers in a community and share such consumer-generated content in order to strengthen consumer-brand relationships.

B2C: The business environment where firms directly communicate and promote their products and services to the consumers by adopting multiple media and using integrated marketing communication strategies.

Purchase intention: The willingness of a customer to buy a product or service in a certain situation.

Social interaction: The communication or contact of an individual with another individual or a group of individuals for the purposes of information exchange or entertainment or to maintain essential social connections.

Chapter 4

A Store–Driven Luxury Fashion Omni–Channel Retailer: Emerging Practices from Luisaviaroma

Silvia Ranfagni
University of Florence, Italy

Danio Berti
University of Florence, Italy

ABSTRACT

This chapter investigates the case of Luisaviaroma, an emblematic company that pioneered online business in luxury fashion. Founded in Florence (Italy) as a physical retailer, it exploited its stores as a springboard to animate an e-commerce platform transforming itself over time into a digital enterprise. Today nearly all its turnover comes from online business. Nevertheless, the physical stores maintain a strategic role: they integrate the online business, acting as base for omni-channel strategies. Our aim is to investigate LVR's business integration and the related practices of omni-channel management.

KEYWORDS

Luxury Fashion Retailer, Online Business, Omni-Channel Management

INTRODUCTION

Digital culture and its effects. Today the growth of companies lies increasingly in the development of a digital culture. This development usually corresponds with investments in the creation of company websites (Murphy, 1998). In luxury companies the website has proved to be a way to increase brand visibility and interactivity (Seo & Buchanan-Oliver, 2015). Dall'Olmo Riley and Lacroix (2003) stress that a company website works better as a channel of communication than as one of distribution. However, if appropriately used as a distribution channel, it serves to reach online luxury shoppers (Seringhaus, 2005) in both local and foreign markets. Thus, it may become a way to transcend national boundaries (Moini & Tesar, 2005; Morgan-Thomas, 2009; Premazzi et al., 2010). In this regard, Sinkovics, Sinkovics and Bryan (2013) demonstrate that, especially in SMEs, a website can enhance export performance. This is because it acts positively on the speed of internationalization (Luo, Zhao, & Du, 2005; Hassouneh & Brengman, 2011) and on the efficiency of market transactions (Koth, Rindova, & Rotharmel, 2001; Petersen, Welch, & Liesch, 2002). Despite its positive effects, in the luxury fashion industry the company website as a selling tool has taken time to get off the ground. The prevailing conviction was that luxury, since it involves uniqueness, could not be sold without a physical contact with customers (Okonkwo, 2009; Guercini & Runfola, 2015). Luxury goods are sensory goods: the senses of sight, smell, touch and feel that they evoke pervade the relations they have with the market (Dennis et al., 2004; Hennis, Wiedmann, & Klarmann, 2012). As Okonkwo (2007) points out, luxury is made up of ingredients that on the whole speak more to feelings than to reason. Certain feelings are aroused by shopping experiences customers have in stores (Kapferer & Bastien, 2009; Dion & Arnould, 2011). Stores have been preferred by companies over online business also because, as Hennis, Wiedmann and Klarmann (2012) explain, the use of the website can feed the market for fakes by making possible the proliferation of counterfeit items.

Combining online and offline business: an evolving need. Recently luxury fashion companies have changed their attitude toward online business (Ashworth et al., 2016; Ozuem et al., 2017). They implement actions to integrate the *online channel* (e.g. mono- and multi-brand e-commerce platforms) with the *offline channel* (e.g. mono- and multi-brand stores). In doing so, they aim to make the online business an integral part of their business model. The choice was favoured by technological progress and by new ways of relating with luxury brands. It emerges that today consumers increasingly experience luxury brands in virtual spaces. These may be online brand communities (forums, blogs) and social network sites. On entering these spaces, they can discover and share brand values and personality. They can also narrate their brand experiences, communicating with each other free from temporal or spatial restrictions (Brogi et al., 2013). Besides, interactive technologies (Ozuem, Howell, & Lancaster, 2008). and innovative techniques of online visual merchandising (Okonkwo, 2009) enable companies to turn their websites into virtual spaces in which the relations that consumers build with brands become closer and more intimate (Ha & Stoel, 2012). The interactive brand spaces that consumers virtually inhabit require a strategic management. This is for several reasons. First, they impact on the development of brand awareness (Çukul, 2015). Secondly, they animate communication flows, thereby generating information exchanges in real time. As a result, consumers can become active players co-creating brand values if companies are able to "tap into [their] knowledge or discuss new ideas and developments" (Tynan, McKechniem, & Chhuon, 2010, p. 1160). Finally, the virtual spaces of brand interaction that consumers experience also influence brand performance. In this regard, Brogi et al. (2013) demonstrate that online brand communities can serve as powerful instruments to influence customers' purchasing behaviour, as can, according Chu, Kamal, and Kim (2013), social network sites. Twitter and Facebook in particular can be considered as business take-off tools that affect customer relationships and purchase intentions.

From a multi-channel to omni-channel retailing strategy. Social media sites, along with companies' apps, constitute some of the ways to provide access to luxury brands. Their management, combined with the company website as e-commerce platform (online business) and with the stores (offline business), is strategically challenging. It induces companies to abandon a multi-channel in favour of an omni-channel strategy. In the former, the company's aim is to increase sales in different markets through cross-channel interactions and to gain valuable insight into consumer behaviour (Kent et al., 2016). In the latter, the focus is on the interplay between offline and online channels, touchpoints and brands. Omni-channel retailing is understood as "the synergetic management of the numerous available channels and customer touch points, in such a way that the customer experience across channels and the performance over channels is optimized" (Verhoef, Kannan, & Inman, 2015, p. 3). The levels to manage in this approach are more numerous than those of multi-channel customer management, which Neslin et al. (2006) formally define as "the design, deployment, coordination, and evaluation of channels to enhance customer value through effective customer acquisition, retention, and development" (p. 96). In luxury fashion companies omni-channel retailing leads companies to define, design, implement and manage the brand experience, providing customers with a harmonious and coherent way to move around as they wish in the online and offline channels made available by the company during the buying process. As Gao and Yang (2016) observe it makes it possible to shop across channels anywhere and at any time, thereby providing customers with a unique, complete, and seamless shopping experience that breaks down barriers between channels. Like the touchpoints it encompasses, the omni-channel approach triggers an online purchasing perspective. It may also impact on purchasing intentions. According to Juaneda-Ayensa, Mosquera, and Sierra Murillo (2016) there are three key factors in influencing intentions. The first is *personal innovativeness*, that is the degree to which a person prefers to try new and different products or channels and, thus, to seek new shopping experiences. The second is *effort expectancy*, understood as the degree of ease associated with consumers' use of different touchpoints during the shopping process. Finally, there is *performance expectancy*, which can be defined as the degree to which using different channels and technologies during the shopping journey will provide consumers with benefits when they are buying fashion.

Our research. Although the omni-channel approach is a strategy which is spreading among luxury fashion companies, there is very little scientific literature on its practices of implementation. It is interesting to investigate how luxury fashion companies effectively approach the integration between the offline channel, online channel and consumer interactive touchpoints. In this chapter we examine the *case of Luisaviaroma* (henceforth LVR). Its history is emblematic of the evolution of a company which began as a physical retailer and was a pioneer in providing itself with an e-commerce platform. It was able to integrate its offline business with the online one and turn the two into communicating vessels for the customer by elaborating a full-fledged omni-channel strategy. The case we propose is based on the analysis of secondary data and qualitative face-to-face interviews, one of the most widely employed methods for gathering data in social and business research (Stewart & Kamins, 1993; Eisenhardt & Graebner, 2007). The interviews involved the Project Manager and the Chief Financial Officer (CFO) of LVR. All the interviews were carried out according to a protocol of analysis to investigate the origin of the company, its evolution and the factors that have driven its digitalization in a logic of coevolution between the online and the offline business.

WHY LUISAVIAROMA? A COMPARISON
WITH ITS COMPETITORS

LVR is a fashion luxury retailer which was a pioneer in launching an e-commerce platform to intermediate luxury products, thereby laying the basis for the development of online business. Today over 90% of its sales volume comes from the online business. It is, then, a digital company. Nevertheless, LVR is to this day a family company. This feature distinguishes it from its direct competitors. The more outstanding of these are Matches Fashion and Mytheresa. Like LVR, both are "off- and online retailers". About 95% of their business is carried out online, but the former is owned by the Apax Investment Fund, while the latter was recently acquired by the Newman Marcus Group. Moreover, in contrast to these companies, LVR cannot be defined as "an online supermarket of luxury fashion": it does not sell a bit of everything relative to luxury brands in its portfolio but rather iconic products, that is products selected as an ultimate expression of the values of the brand they represent. For this reason, LVR sets itself apart from other fashion luxury retailers like Yoox and Net-a-Porter. Acquired by Compagnie Financière Richemont in 2008, both offer a brand portfolio which is vast and wide-ranging but quite generalist. In contrast to LVR, they are also "pure digital retailers": their online business is not integrated with offline in-store activities. What is more, Yoox is even an "off-price retailer": it buys in-stock luxury brand products and resells them employing aggressive discount policies. Finally, LVR does not rent online commercial spaces to luxury brands which then manage them autonomously as sales platforms. This trait distinguishes LVR also from Farfetch, which is a "drop shipping retailer", a hub which rather than intermediating luxury goods hosts a wide assortment of luxury brands (more than 850). These brands exploit the hub to act as online retailers. Keeping these peculiarities in mind, we can now examine the identity of LVR.

WHO IS LUISAVIAROMA? AN OVERVIEW
OF THE COMPANY

LVR began as a physical retailer in fashion luxury. The first store was opened in 1930 in the centre of Florence (in via Roma). It offers products from first line collections of the world's most renowned fashion designers. In 2008, a second store was inaugurated. Unlike the first, this one is located in a more peripheral area of the city and it has collections by contemporary designers as well as items from previous seasons or from second line collections by well-known fashion luxury designers. The first store (the Florentine boutique) has played a strategic role in LVR as it has fostered over time the growth of its online business. Set up through an e-commerce platform made accessible from the company website, the online business has undergone an acceleration since 2008 and has become LVR's main source of turnover. In 2008 total sales volume was 8 million Euros (Figure 1), of which 3 million came from online sales. Nine years later, in 2017, sales were 125 million Euros, 112 million of which from online sales. The main European countries in terms of online sales (Figure 2) are the UK (9%) and Germany (11%), while among the non-EU markets Asia stands out (15%) together with the US (13%). The progress of LVR as online luxury retailer has been facilitated by the many and diversified brands composing its portfolio. It includes as many as 600 brands. The more productive in terms of sales are Gucci, Balenciaga, Off White, Moncler, Dsquared, Dolce & Gabbana, Fendi, Saint Laurent, Givenchy and Valentino. These brands embrace total look collections for men, women and children. LVR's brand portfolio has progressively expanded. In 2014 the company launched the line "home", introducing new brands such as Kartell, Alessi, Fornasetti, Vitra, Foscarini and Seletti. In all, there are 174 home line brands. Later, in 2018, LVR launched the line "beauty", composed of 40 of the most prestigious brands in the sector, such as Mac, R+Co, Oribe and Foreo. Thanks to its brand assortment, today LVR satisfies over 165,000 loyal and highly selected customers. The brands LVR offers may vary considerably in their performance. In fact, as the LVR Project Manager explains, "there are brands that sell well in certain markets and others that sell well everywhere. Gucci is a good example: it is our top designer in terms of sales". The manager also points out that "expanding to many markets does not guarantee positive results…. in fact, if we look at our second designer, Balenciaga, we see that even though their products reach many international markets, their sales amount to about half those of Gucci".

Shifting to the organizational side, LVR currently employs about 200 people hailing from 15 different countries. Of the 200 employees, 150 are involved in the online business, the other 50 in the stores management. The stores absorb a significant number of employees because of their size and the long opening hours. As the CFO explains, "each of the stores is nearly 500 square meters in size and is open 7 days a week, 9 hours a

Figure 1. Sales trend in LVR (Million Euro)

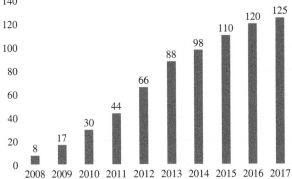

Source: LVR.

Figure 2. E-commerce sales per country (2017)

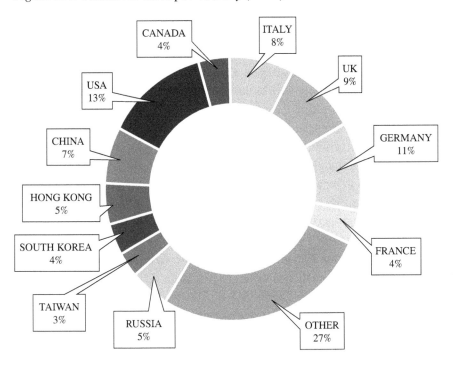

Source: LVR.

day on average". Overall, LVR is an integrated retailer. The different company functions are carried out internally, with the exception of the logistic function. Its outsourcing was made necessary by the need to efficiently deal with the shipping of 30,000 articles every month from the company's logistics centre. The other functions are those of administration (invoicing, cashing, refunds), marketing, customer care service, buying and ITC (information, technology and communication). In addition to these, the periodic updating of the company's annual catalogue is also internalised. LVR's catalogue is entrusted to an international team that renews the product descriptions every season inserting between 20,000 and 30,000 articles and translating the relevant information about each into at least nine different languages.

COMPANY HISTORY: THE PATH TO BECOMING A DIGITAL BUSINESS

The origins of LVR as luxury offline retailer. The origins of LVR as physical retailer date back to the 1920s when Luisa Jaquin and her husband Lido Panconesi opened a straw hat boutique in Paris. Subsequently they transferred their activity to Florence, Lido's hometown, and inaugurated the first boutique seeking to expand the hat business. The real changes for LVR took place when, in the late 60s, Andrea Panconesi, Lido's grandson, extended and diversified the store's assortment by signing exclusive contracts with important luxury fashion brands. As a result, LVR began to take the shape of a luxury fashion retailer. From the beginning, LVR sought to distinguish itself by offering a wide variety of products including selected iconic brand products. It is precisely for this reason that in 1968 Kenzo chose LVR to present a European preview of his autumn/winter collection.

    The mail order service as basis for the development of an online business. LVR's growth was gradual. It was facilitated by a business formula the company adopted in the 90s and centred on the mail order service of in-store products. The project manager of LVR details this service as follows: "When I was engaged in the training of some employees... I saw customers, foreigners as well, who had visited the store, sending faxes... with copies of their credit cards... in this way, they booked the latest products of the season that LVR had in its brand portfolio". In response to the requests received, the manager adds, "the company did everything possible to arrange the mail orders". Despite all the sustained efforts, the positive impact of the new formula was not on the company's turnover, which remained solidly driven by the Florentine boutique performance, but on laying the foundations for the development of LVR's online business (Figure 3). In fact, to stimulate this development, the company had only to automate a selling process which, internally, was already in place. This was made possible by creating an e-commerce platform; its effective launch took place on December 15, 1999. With this decision, the company emerged as a pioneer retailer in the luxury fashion sector. At that time, in the sector the idea of doing business online was considered pure folly. Indeed, the prevailing conviction was that the luxury fashion market contrasted with digitalization, given the importance of personal relationships in the customer purchase experience.

Figure 3. LVR: the path to become a digital company

Period: 1990s
• Offline business: Florentine boutique (mail order services of in-store products)
• Online business: E-commerce platform development—15 December 1999

Period: 2000–2004
• Offline business: Florentine boutique
• Online business: E-commerce platform managed on the basis of the "vente privée" model (online shopping granted to selected customers)
The online business is complementary to the offline business

Period: 2004–2008
• Offline business: Florentine boutique
• Online business: E-commerce platform accessible to all potential customers
The online business grows, but remains complementary to the offline business

Period: From 2008 to today
• Online business: An open e-commerce platform and development of interactive touchpoints (social media sites, app)
• Offline business: Florentine boutique and the opening of a new "pheripheral" store
LVR is coverted into a digital company: the online business becomes the motor of the company growth

"Vente Privée" as the first online business model. The online business model that LVR developed initially followed the logic of "vente privée": access to the e-commerce platform was granted only to certain customers. In order to be selected, customers were required to register on the company website providing their personal information (name, email, nationality, age and occupation). The uploaded data were analysed together with other available information on customers. In determining who could benefit from access to the e-commerce platform, LVR gave priority to loyal customers from the USA, the UK, France, Germany, Italy and Japan. The model of "vente privée" remained active from 2000 to 2004 (Figure 3). It contributed to reinforcing the reputation of the LVR brand on international markets. Moreover, its implementation reduced the company's risk of not being able to fulfil online orders because of inadequate logistic resources. The impact it had on company performance was significant. When it began in 2000, the sales volume of LVR amounted to 30,000 Euros. Only four years later, in 2004, it was up to 500,000 Euros. The investments required were limited mainly to the management of the e-commerce platform and to the production of promotional material distributed in store explaining how to access the online offer. A decisive role in the development of LVR's online business was played by word-of-mouth.

The march of digitalization: toward the domination of the online business. In 2004, LVR opened its e-commerce platform to all potential customers. In doing so, it cleared the path toward a specific objective: the conversion of the e-commerce platform from online business complementary to offline stores into a full-fledged autonomous business. Its achievement presupposed strategic interventions fostering traffic within the e-commerce platform (Figure 3). One of these entails the store management. The store, in addition to being a selling place, becomes also a site of digital skill acquisition. More specifically, it is transformed into a space where customers are instructed how to make online purchases by using a touch screen. Another intervention concerned changes in communication. In particular, LVR decided to intensify the participation in events held in strategic contexts, such as the fair at Pitti Palace in Florence, and began to develop co-marketing projects in collaboration with companies like Fiat, Puma, Adidas, Missoni, Lacoste, Levi's and Tim. Among all the events LVR attended, "Firenze4ever" was particularly important as it helped create brand awareness among important international bloggers. Overall, what followed was an increase in sales up to 8 million Euros along with an enhanced reputation of the LVR brand.

The achievement of a "pure digital" business model. In 2008, the objective that LVR had pursued—making the online business the motor of company growth—became concrete (Figure 3). The CFO captures this transformation succinctly: "LVR became a truly digital business, and as such it is comparable to companies like Google and Facebook; not so much in terms of dimensions as in terms of the centrality of the online business". On this point he remarks: "From 2000 to 2008 LVR was an offline business, a physical retailer that also had e-commerce; it was not a pure digital business. As of 2008 our core business has become digital … as if we were born again with a new skin. In the process, the physical store has supported the growth of online business". Finally, the manager adds, "now we are a sort of start-up … even though in reality we've been around for three generations… the sales volume was 8 million Euros in 2008. Now, thanks to the new business model, we are up to 125 million Euros. By adopting a "pure digital business model", LVR increased its presence on social networks (especially Facebook, Instagram, Weibo, Twitter, Pinterest and Wecha) and also created an app. All the different digital tools are used by the digital marketing team to create, develop and reinforce relations with the market. In time the company also expanded physically, and in 2008 it opened its second peripheral store.

HOW TO INTEGRATE ONLINE AND OFFLINE BUSINESS: TEACHING AN OMNI-CHANNEL PURCHASING APPROACH

LVR is now a digital company. Today the online business drives its turnover. However, it did not evolve on its own, but by combining with the offline business. In LVR's history, the first store (the boutique in Florence) has played a key role in the development of the online business. Together with specific communication actions, it has propelled the growth of online sales contributing to LVR's transformation into a digital company.

Iconic products. The Florentine boutique and the online business share a common base: the offer of iconic products. These products define LVR's competitive positioning as fashion luxury retailer. The search for them is far from simple. It is a task that is assigned to buyers. The buyers are LVR employees hired for their ability to pick out in brand collections product uniqueness as expression of the correlated brand values. It is interesting to note that, in their scouting activity, buyers are shifting their attention toward products which, although branded, embody a synthesis not so much of an ostentatious luxury as of a luxury-awareness, where the search for self prevails over the need to show one's status. It is a type of luxury, then, that responds not to the consumer's craving to "own" but rather to his desire to "be". The interface that iconicity generates between in-store and online business enables their integration. In LVR the in-store activities integrate with the online business. And thanks to them, the online business grows. The boutique in fact, has served as basis for the activation of an online purchasing perspective by educating customers on developing an omni-channel behaviour, that is on using all the available touchpoints to access the company's offer. In addition to the stores, in LVR they include the website and social networks sites. e Thus, an omni-channel approach opens to holistic brand experiences. In LVR this approach is store-driven: it finds its source in the store.

A new conception of the store. The Florentine boutique has always played a central role in LVR's strategy, while undergoing significant changes over time (Figure 4). The store has gone from being simply a place of sale to also becoming a place where customers *learn ways to engage in omni-channel interactions* with the company. The environment is essential: the merchandising is minimalist and leaves room for interactive technologies that instruct customers on an omni-channel shopping approach by showing LVR's vast online offer. This offer includes all the 600 brands in LVR's portfolio, far more than the 70 customers find in the store. The Project Manager describes the connective role of the store in these terms: "The shop assistants welcome the customers and listen to their desires. Then they take them to the touch screens. The screens are crucial ... the store revolves around them. They are used to show the customers the assortment of the e-commerce platform and to explain how to access it using the website and social networks". The store helps customers gain awareness of the various ways to connect with LVR. They discover, in other words, the different possible routes of their brand journey. They can, in fact, begin

Figure 4. A store-driven omni-channel retailing: the leading role of the Florentine boutique

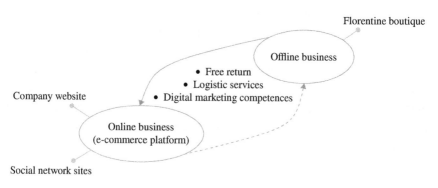

their journey in-store and continue in virtual environments or do exactly the opposite. They can also experience more than one environment at the same time. Using the in-store touch screen, customers can access the company website and decide whether to buy an article which is sold online in-store. The in-store items are not numerous but also not few. They create atmosphere, but at the same time they are functional: they serve to meet the customer's need to try out products where he buys them. If he is satisfied with the item, he may decide to buy it directly in the store. Otherwise, if he opts for different size, model or colour, he may decide to buy it online, either from the store or from home.

SERVICES AND COMPETENCES: THE FOUNDATIONS OF LVR'S BUSINESS INTEGRATION

The LVR store animates the online business, transmitting to its customers an omni-channel culture enabling holistic brand experiences and contributing to the development of a perspective on online purchasing. The integrating role of the LVR store requires the activation of certain services that can facilitate online buying. The most important of these are free return and logistics services (Figure 4).

Free return: alignment between online and offline shopping. Free return fosters online buying as it reduces in consumer perception the distance between online and offline shopping. Just as in physical stores, products purchased online can be returned or exchanged for other articles free of charge. LVR was a pioneer in introducing this service. The result is a more enduring relationship with customers. The CFO says, in this connection: "We deliver our products and if customers are not satisfied they can send them back free of charge... so we create an aura of seriousness and reliability, which connects us more closely to our customers". He adds that "the more customers use the service, the more they become accustomed to it". For some customers a certain attitude toward recourse to free return is not acquired but, as it were, innate in their consumption culture. Germans constitute an emblematic case. Free return was a component of buying by catalogue, widespread in Germany thanks to companies like Burda and Postalmarket. Other consumers who regularly use free return are the Austrians and the Dutch. Less accustomed, on the other hand, are the Japanese. In Europe, the Italians are among those who do not yet consider return, even if free, a real incentive to purchase.

The logistics services: the activation of a controlled outsourcing. Another service that can enhance online sales if managed efficiently is the logistics service. LVR outsourced logistics in 2015. The decision became inevitable when the e-commerce began to take off and the path toward the transformation of the company into a digital business was cleared. The step was taken in response to an extraordinary event which revealed all the weaknesses in LVR's management of logistics services. This was the Black Friday in November 2014. Although the company had activated only promotions targeting the US market, it received such a quantity of orders that it quickly encountered serious logistics problems. The main consequence was that delivery times stretched from two days on average to four. The Project Manager describes the situation in these terms: "We were immersed in Black Friday from November to April ... the bottleneck that had been created extended for months, literally hurling us into crisis. So finding external suppliers became absolutely urgent". The model of outsourcing that LVR adopted is somewhat unusual as it is "controlled". The company's employees work in the warehouse together with those of the logistics company in order to monitor operations. The CFO points out that "some products may come back ... and in this case it's necessary to check the security seal." "The security seal", he explains, "shows that the product is ours. If it has been broken or removed, our people have to step in and examine the article. The verification is important. We've had cases where a customer has removed the security seal and 'returned' a garment which turned out to be an imitation of the one we sent".

Beyond the services: the need for digital marketing competences. Free return services and logistics services are important for the development of online business, but they are not sufficient. The company must also have digital marketing competences. Initially, in LVR, these were regarded as a hindrance to the growth of the company. The owner was quite explicit: "I don't see the point in investing resources in the management of social media ... in my opinion, these are wasted resources that don't impact on our performance". In reality, these competences revealed themselves to be very useful. Thanks to them LVR is able to manage new instruments of interaction with the market (social networks, website, etc.) as paths to an omni-channel offer. And thanks to them, LVR has designed and developed the online business coherently with the offline business and merging with it (a sort of spontaneous budding). Therefore, the company has read and interpreted strategically the online business according to a unitary business vision.

OMNI-CHANNEL MANAGEMENT: ITS EVOLUTION THROUGH NEW INTERACTIVE SPACES

In LVR's business model the store drives online sales. This model has dealt over time with a structural limitation given by the availability of the single Florentine store. Although territorially well situated (Florence, city of made in Italy luxury), it could not influence the online business growth beyond a certain point. For this reason, LVR has recently started investing in new stores. They have been opened not on the home market but abroad. For their location the company has chosen prestigious international cities such as Los Angeles and Shanghai (Figure 5). These stores are not traditional luxury shops but pop-up stores, that is temporary retail spaces. Internally, they reproduce the concept of LVR's Florentine boutique: interactive technologies acting as promoting platforms stand out against an essential merchandising. The role they play in LVR is strategic. They are used to expand on international markets the basis to create knowledge about the omni-channel accesses offered. Moreover, they are a means to enhance LVR customers' opportunities to have omni-channel experiences (until then limited to the Florentine store only). Thus, LVR's omni-channel approach has developed progressively. Omni-channel fact-finding actions have intensified and combined with implementative actions. Both, once undertaken, have positively impacted on LVR's brand reputation. Along with pop-up stores as ways to access omni-channel experiences, LVR has also introduced a new interactive touchpoint. In addition to the website and the social network sites, the company has created an app to facilitate interactions with customers.

Figure 5. A store-driven omni-channel retailing: its evolution through new interactive spaces

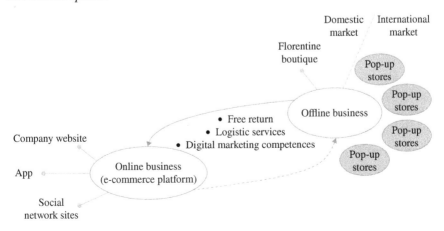

This resulted in a significant increase in monthly virtual contacts. Data on website contacts show that the current total amounts to about 7 million. The number of visitors rose to 60 million in 2016 (+17 million compared to 2015). In 2017 the upward trend continued, reaching 72 million. More specifically, there were 250 million page views, of which 30% single page visits (bounce rate), and on average six pages per visit and five minutes on site. In 2017 as well LVR had 2.2 billion monthly contacts on Facebook, 800 million on Instagram, 1 billion on Whatsapp Daily and 1 billion on Audience Network. The multiple ways of accessing LVR allow customers to differentiate their brand journeys and intensify their shifts from stores to virtual environments and vice versa. The consequence is an increase in online rather than in-store sales. The stores serve more to orient customer choices rather than to sell; as such they absorb more economic resources than they generate. Stores are an on-going investment made to further the online business development. This involves an increase in the number and variety of customers. What is more, since customers can journey in both online (website, app) and offline (stores) environments, the relations the company maintains with them are enhanced and more intense. Omni-channel interactions, then, result in increasing relational complexity. To manage this complexity LVR has developed a system of artificial intelligence which automatizes communication processes addressed to consumers embracing the various virtual environments (website, app, social network sites). Customers receive periodic messages concerning LVR's offer that can also be personalized. The artificial intelligence system profiles customers combining sociodemographic traits (age, gender, location, etc.), omni-channel behaviours, and purchase choices. This facilitates the development of one-to-one relations with customers.

DISCUSSION: EMERGING OMNI-CHANNEL PRACTICES

LVR is a case of a fashion luxury retailer in which the stores propel the online business inducing omni-channel consumption behaviours. The omni-channel retailing approach answers the need to encourage a perspective on online purchasing (Gao & Yang, 2016; Juaneda-Ayensa, Mosquera, & Sierra Murillo, 2016) by integrating in-store activities with online business. Thus, this chapter has investigated a particular omni-channel formula. Its development o translates into omni-channel practices which we will now detail.

(a) *Educate* the *customer* in-store in the use of different touchpoints as ways of accessing the brand

(b) Reconsider the *concept of store*, to be viewed no longer as simply a place where the customer has purchasing experiences but as a venue to learn about omni-channel shopping.

(c) Build a *network* of *temporary stores* in foreign markets as a new basis to generate knowledge about omni-channel accesses and to enable holistic brand experiences.

(d) *Integrate digital marketing* with *artificial intelligence activities*: marketing managers focus on strategic decisions (selection and analysis of target, brand positioning, creation of communication contents, etc.) and employ interactive artificial intelligence instruments to manage relations with customers.

The practice of "educating" acts on *personal innovativeness* (Juaneda-Ayensa, Mosquera, & Sierra Murillo, 2016), encouraging customers to try out new paths of access to the brand; the practice of "redefining the concept of the store" impacts on *effort expectancy* (Juaneda-Ayensa, Mosquera, & Sierra Murillo, 2016) and thus induces them to seek new shopping experiences. Both of these practices are activated in store and determine the other two. All four together impact positively on LVR's online performance.

What are the implications of such practices? If we were to suggest to important luxury brands how to develop an omni-channel approach in which the stores drive the online business, in the light of the LVR experience, we could make the following recommendations. They could use their points of sale (which are usually numerous) as venues to guide the customer toward the integration of online and offline purchasing experiences. They could also reconceptualise the notion of the store, no longer considered as a point of sale but as a place where the customer learns how to have holistic brand experiences. The store remains a focal point of these experiences. Its centrality could lead the luxury brand to reconsider the geographic configuration of its stores, combining a stable network with a mobile network of experiential spaces corresponding to temporary stores. The ensuing relational complexity could be then controlled with the aid of artificial intelligence-based interactive devices. The employment of such devices is essential for the management of omni-channel interactions. Once initiated, it can lead to redesigning the role that digital marketing plays in the company; this role will tend to be less operative and more strategic. The analysis of customers, the study of their profiles, and the personalization of communication contents become priorities in digital marketing. These activities will be supported by a system that automatically manages processes of interaction with the market. The omni-channel culture generates the effect of "everything always and everywhere" enabling consumers to immerse themselves in the brand and to experience it without temporal or spatial constraints. As a result, competitive edge lies in enabling consumers to steep themselves in holistic brand experiences; these experiences are interactive spaces to share brand values but not only. They are also spaces where the relation between consumers and brand may be so deeply experienced as to become a field in which consumers recognize themselves, evolve and grow. Thus, the competitive game that companies poses increasing challenges: its outcomes depends on how they are able to harmonize personal insights with brand values and innovative technologies generating interactions with consumers.

REFERENCES

Ashworth, C. J., Schmidt, R. Ä., Pioch, E. A., & Hallsworth, A. (2006). An approach to sustainable 'fashion' e-retail: A five-stage evolutionary strategy for 'Clicks-and-Mortar' and 'Pure-Play' enterprises. *Journal of Retailing and Consumer Services, 13*(4), 289–299.

Brogi, S., Calabrese, A., Campisi, D., Capece, G., Costa, R., & Di Pillo, F. (2013). The effects of online brand communities on brand equity in the luxury fashion industry. *International Journal of Engineering Business Management, 5*(Godište 2013), 5–32.

Chu, S. C., Kamal, S., & Kim, Y. (2013). Understanding consumers' responses toward social media advertising and purchase intention toward luxury products. *Journal of Global Fashion Marketing, 4*(3), 158–174.

Çukul, D. (2015). Fashion marketing in social media: Using instagram for fashion branding (No. 2304324). *International Institute of Social and Economic Sciences.*

Dall'Olmo Riley, F., & Lacroix, C. (2003). Luxury branding on the Internet: Lost opportunity or impossibility? *Marketing Intelligence & Planning, 21*(2), 96–104.

Dennis, C., Fenech, T., Pantano, E., Gerlach, S., & Merrilees, B. (2004). *E-retailing.* Routledge.

Dion, D., & Arnould, E. (2011). Retail luxury strategy: Assembling charisma through art and magic. *Journal of Retailing, 87*(4), 502–520.

Eisenhardt, K. M., & Graebner, M. E. (2007). Theory building from cases: Opportunities and challenges. *Academy of Management Journal, 50*(1), 25–32.

Gao, R., & Yang, Y. X. (2016). Consumers' decision: Fashion omni-channel retailing. *Journal of Information Hiding and Multimedia Signal Processing, 7*(2), 325–342.

Guercini, S., & Runfola, A. (2015). Internationalization Through E-Commerce. The Case of Multibrand Luxury Retailers in the Fashion Industry. In *International Marketing in the Fast Changing World* (pp. 15–31). Emerald Group Publishing Limited.

Ha, S., & Stoel, L. (2012). Online apparel retailing: Roles of e-shopping quality and experiential e-shopping motives. *Journal of Service Management, 23*(2), 197–215.

Hassouneh, D., & Brengman, M. (2011). Virtual worlds: A gateway for SMEs toward internationalization. *Journal of Brand Management, 19*(1), 72–90.

Hennigs, N., Wiedmann, K. P., & Klarmann, D. O. C. (2012). Luxury brands in the digital age–exclusivity versus ubiquity. *Marketing Review St. Gallen, 29*(1), 30–35.

Juaneda-Ayensa, E., Mosquera, A., & Sierra Murillo, Y. (2016). Omnichannel customer behavior: Key drivers of technology acceptance and use and their effects on purchase intention. *Frontiers in Psychology, 7*, 1117.

Kapferer, J. N., & Bastien, V. (2009). The specificity of luxury management: Turning marketing upside down. *Journal of Brand Management, 16*(5–6), 311–322.

Kent, A., Vianello, M., Cano, M. B., & Helberger, E. (2016). Omnichannel Fashion Retail and Channel Integration: The Case of Department Stores. In *Handbook of Research on Global Fashion Management and Merchandising* (pp. 398–419). IGI Global.

Koth, S., Rindova, V. R., & Rotharmel, F. T. (2001). Asset and actions: Firm-specific factors in Internationalization of U.S. Internet firms. *Journal of International Business Studies, 32*(4), 769–791.

Luo, Y., Hongxin Zhao, J., & Du, J. (2005). The internationalization speed of e-commerce companies: An empirical analysis. *International Marketing Review, 22*(6), 693–709.

Moini, H., & Tesar, G. (2005). The internet and internationalization of smaller manufacturing enterprises. *Journal of Global Marketing, 18*(3–4), 79–94.

Morgan-Thomas, A. (2009). Online activities and export performance of the smaller firm: A capability perspective. *European Journal of International Management, 3*(3), 266–285.

Murphy, R. (1998). The Internet: A viable strategy for fashion retail marketing? *Journal of Fashion Marketing and Management: An International Journal, 2*(3), 209–216.

Neslin, S. A., Grewal, D., Leghorn, R., Shankar, V., Teerling, M. L., Thomas, J. S., & Verhoef, P. C. (2006). Challenges and opportunities in multichannel customer management. *Journal of Service Research, 9*(2), 95–112.

Okonkwo, U. (2007). Luxury fashion branding: Trends. *Tactics, Techniques, New York.*

Okonkwo, U. (2009). Sustaining the luxury brand on the Internet. *Journal of Brand Management, 16*(5–6), 302–310.

Ozuem, W., Howell, K., & Lancaster, G. (2017). An exploration of consumers' response to online service recovery initiatives. *International Journal of Market Research, 59*(1), 97–115.

Ozuem, W., Howell, K. E., & Lancaster, G. (2008). Communicating in the new interactive marketspace. *European Journal of Marketing, 42*(9/10), 1059–1083.

Petersen, B., Welch, L. S., & Liesch, P. W. (2002). The Internet and foreign market expansion by firms. *Management International Review, 42*(2), 207–222.

Pezderka, N., & Sinkovics, R. R. (2011). A conceptualization of e-risk perceptions and implications for small firm active online internationalization. *International Business Review, 20*(4), 409–422.

Premazzi, K., Castaldo, S., Grosso, M., Raman, P., Brudvig, S., & Hofacker, C. F. (2010). Customer information sharing with e-vendors: The roles of incentives and trust. *International Journal of Electronic Commerce, 14*(3), 63–91.

Seo, Y., & Buchanan-Oliver, M. (2015). Luxury branding: The industry, trends, and future conceptualisations. *Asia Pacific Journal of Marketing and Logistics, 27*(1), 82–98.

Seringhaus, F. R. (2005). Selling luxury brands online. *Journal of Internet Commerce, 4*(1), 1–25.

Sinkovics, N., Sinkovics, R. R., & "Bryan" Jean, R. J. (2013). The internet as an alternative path to internationalization? *International Marketing Review, 30*(2), 130–155.

Stewart, D. W., & Kamins, M. A. (1993). *Secondary Research: Information Sources and Methods* (Vol. 4). Sage.

Tynan, C., McKechnie, S., & Chhuon, C. (2010). Co-creating value for luxury brands. *Journal of Business Research, 63*(11), 1156–1163.

Verhoef, P. C., Kannan, P. K., & Inman, J. J. (2015). From multi-channel retailing to omni-channel retailing: Introduction to the special issue on multi-channel retailing. *Journal of Retailing, 91*(2), 174–181.

KEY TERMS AND DEFINITION

Omni-channel retailing is the synergetic management of the numerous available channels and customer touch points, in such a way that the customer experience across channels and the performance over channels is optimized.

Multi-channel customer management is the design, deployment, coordination, and evaluation of channels to enhance customer value through effective customer acquisition, retention, and development.

"Vente Privée" business model is based on the access to the e-commerce platform granted only to a selection of customers.

Digital company is a company whose turnover mainly comes from online business.

A store driven omni-channel retailer is a retailer in which the stores propel the online business inducing omni-channel consumption behaviours.

Artificial intelligence is a machine intelligence that authomatise communication processes addressed to consumers embracing virtual environments (website, app, social network sites).

Chapter 5

Enhancing Online Brand Relationship Performance: Insights and Reflections

Michelle Willis, Wilson Ozuem, and Raye Ng
University of Cumbria, UK

ABSTRACT

It is widely recognised that an in-depth understanding of online brand communities and their implications is vitally important for enhancing online relationships. However, although various studies examine how online brand communities impact consumer behaviour, very few have examined how fashion brands can enhance online relationships with their consumers through online communities. The concept of online brand communities has been applied to a range of marketing studies on purchase experience, brand equity, customer participation and brand loyalty. Additionally, it has been applied to understand social behaviours of consumers including their individual motives, group intentions, social identity, and interactions between consumers. The various studies focus on different marketing characteristics concerning online brand communities; researchers provide mixed conclusions on how brands' online relationships with consumers are maintained; specifically, limited studies have focused on online brand communities in the fashion industry. The chapter offers insight into underpinning debates but also practical guidance and advice on the development and nurturing of sustainable online brand communities.

INTRODUCTION

The understanding of online communities can be dated back to the early concept of 'Imagined Community' developed by Anderson (1983). Several studies have taken this concept to apply the understanding of communities to the online digital environment (Gruzd, Wellman, & Takhteyev, 2011; Cayla & Eckhardt, 2008; Coles & West, 2016; Ozuem et al., 2018). Although communities have advanced to the digital 21st century the concept of individuals being part of a community has remained similar to how it was a decade ago. With the advancement of technology, there is a greater need for brands to develop relationships with consumers which has encouraged the use of online brand communities. Brands are compelled to look beyond the consumers' need for the products and promotional offers they offer and extend their activities to include facilitating communities that enable them to have interactive communication with their consumers and enable consumers to interact with each other.

Brands' increased activity of enabling shared communications between consumers has a great influence on the consumers' relationship with brands. Increased customer participation in online brand communities has transformed their consumption experience, as it has increased their control over their experience including obtaining brand-related information and promotion deals in the online communities. Furthermore, studies indicate that entertainment and enjoyment arises from interacting with the brand in an online community (De Vries & Carlson, 2014; Carlson, Rahman, Taylor, & Voola, 2019). Participation of consumers is not directly limited towards the brand; consumers' interaction with other consumers has been a key subject in several studies (Cheng, Wu, & Chen, 2018; Huang, Chen, Ou, Davison, & Hua, 2017; Wu, Vassileva, & Zhao, 2017) identifying social capital as a key factor that influences loyalty in online brand communities.

Some consumers perceive the value of an online community through its members' community and its 'we' culture which they may identify with as an individual, thus motivating them to become part of that community (Fournier, 1998; Bergami & Bagozzi, 2000; Bagozzi & Dholakia, 2006). This concept has also been applied to the consumers' brand love, of which they participate in online communities that are specifically linked to their brand preferences (Coelho, Bairrada, & Peres, 2019). From the individuals' perspective, belonging to a brand provides a uniqueness to their identity as it implies an emotional involvement with a group that shares values and preferences (Dholakia, Bagozzi, & Pearo, 2004). It is clear that financial motives are not the only concerns for consumers in online brand communities. The studies on the diverse online habits have helped to identify and extend the different values consumers develop from participating within online communities, including emotional value, relational value and entitativity values, as well as functional values (Carlson, Wyllie, Rahman, & Voola, 2018; Ozuem & Lancaster, 2014). These can be linked to consumers with various community motivations whether it be for their individual benefits or group-orientated goals.

The diverse habits and behaviours of consumers in online communities can be linked to the complex nature of fashion. Fashion is considered to be a powerful social symbol that creates and groups several identities (Ahuvia, 2005) and is adapted according to the norms, values and preferences adapted by the consumers (Ranfagni, Crawford-Camiciottoli, & Faraoni, 2016; Helal, Ozuem, & Lancaster, 2018). The degree of similarity between the company and consumers' personality, as well as the community environment, are likely to be key factors that influence the response within brand communities linked to fashion brands. This chapter considers the various concepts of brand communities and how consumers' behaviour will vary depending on their motivations and how relationships are developed in the online environment.

THEORETICAL FOUNDATION AND CONTEXT

Historically, the definition of what a 'community' is was thought to be based on geographically bounded populations, a diverse group of people with multiple differences including age, gender, religion, ethnicity, religion, wealth and even power (Cornwall, 1995; Navarro, 1984). 'Imagined Community' is a concept developed by Anderson (1983) to understand and analyse nationalism. According to Anderson's theory of imagined communities in his early studies, the main causes of nationalism are: (1) the increased acceptance of a universal language accepted by large populations over a perceived language that is accessible based on privilege, (2) the movement to eliminate the idea of 'rule by divine right' and (3) the emergence of printing press capitalism. Anderson depicts a nation as a socially constructed community, and as something that is not materially orientated but that exists in between culture and psychology. Although Anderson focuses on the historical concern for state-building within communist societies, his concept is useful to understand behaviour in online communities.

Online community platforms like social media may create an 'imagined community' among their targeted groups, exceeding the boundaries that physical communities were limited to (Danias & Kavoura, 2013; Kavoura, Pelet, Rundle-Thiele, & Lecat, 2014). The concept has been applied in other studies (Beck, 2011; Cayla & Eckhardt, 2008) but its application in online community studies has been limited (Gruzd, Wellman, & Takhteyev, 2011; Cayla & Eckhardt, 2008; Coles & West, 2016). Gruzd et al. (2011) used the 'imagined community' concept as a starting point to understand the environment and behavioural patterns within Twitter. Anderson stated: 'the members of even the smallest nation will never know most of their fellow-members, meet them, or even hear of them, yet in the minds of each lives the image of their communion' (p. 6). Users on online communities will most likely not know everyone within the community, but they would be aware of their presence. An important foundation of Anderson's 'imagined community' concept is an individual's conscious recognition that they are following similar events with others and that they share common affects with each other (Beck, 2011). Thus, when individuals have interests and values and they find a community with a large population that shows similar interests, value or hobbies, they are likely to feel part of such a community even though they may not know the people within that community. Whether the goal is to follow others, promote ideas or broadcast their daily activities through online communities, it is not possible for members to be unaware of the perceived group they feel part of in the virtual community, similarly to Anderson's summarised concept of an 'imagined community' in the physical world.

The development of the mass media and telecommunications technologies transformed people's ability to share an identity surpassing the geographical boundaries. Researchers have argued that virtual media can create an 'imagined community' among groups, exceeding the physical boundaries (Grudz et al., 2011; Danias & Kavoura, 2013; Kavoura, 2014). Technology development contributed to the emergence of consumer brands becoming part of consumer identity culture as firms' accessibility to consumers became less restricted and cheaper (Muniz & O'Guinn, 2001). The increased involvement of brands within communities attracted a variety of scholars to examine online communities and their connection to consumers (Algesheimer, Dholakia, & Herrmann, 2005; Muniz

& O'Guinn, 2001; Albert, Merunka, & Valette-Florence, 2008; Baldus, Voorhees, & Calantone, 2015). Brand communities are different from traditional communities; their core focus is on branded goods or services, and their community members are typically interested in and admirers of a brand (Albert et al., 2008). Although each brand community has unique purposes, they are universally considered a marketing investment for firms to develop and maintain long-term relations with their current and potential consumers (Zaglia, 2013) and achieve favourable brand outcomes (Relling, Schnittka, Sattler, & Johnen, 2016, p. 107). According to Baldus et al. (2015), brand communities began as simple text forums where consumers shared thoughts and questions regarding the brand; but have evolved to offer unique interactive brand experiences.

Li, Wang, and Lin (2018) identify two types of online intermediaries: online communities and product channels. The distinct difference between the two is that product channels are mostly information sites and are not used for interaction purposes, whereas online communities facilitate mutual communications between multiple parties. Li et al. (2018) justified firms seeking to generate online platforms that provide both product channel information and interactive communication to reduce consumers' uncertainties in their purchase decisions. The study provides a quantitative result that firms' sales benefited from using both these intermediaries, but there is a lack of understanding of how online communities benefit the firms' brand image. The study does not explore how firms create customer loyalty or how they can effectively maintain long-term relations with customers with the use of an online community, and does not consider the different values of online communities that individual consumers may look for.

DEVELOPING BRAND RELATIONSHIPS

Customer participation in online brand communities is important for improving brand relationship performance and creating value within such a community. Carlson et al. (2018) proposed a model that depicts how customer participation in virtual brand communities in the retail sector enables to customers to co-create functional value, emotional value, relational value and entitativity values, which affect their brand relationship performance. Through social media, customers' motivations to partake in online brand communities to drive functional benefits include: (1) solving problems,

(2) sending specific inquires, (3) searching for brand-related information to enhance learning, (4) benefiting from pre-purchasing outcomes, and (5) gaining access to promotion deals (Davis, Piven, & Breazeale, 2014). Such active participation allows consumers a degree of control over the brand consumption experience they seek, resulting in greater opportunities to obtain higher functional value. From studies in social media, entertainment and enjoyment from interacting with a brand's social media presence involving brand and social interactions are identified as the source motivators for customer participation (De Vries & Carlson, 2014; Carlson et al., 2019). As a result, they generate greater emotional value from the retail consumption experience.

Relational consumption occurs between the consumer and the brand based on interactions (Ramaswamy & Ozcan, 2016). According to Davis et al. (2014), personalised brand communications and engagement in the brands' daily activities are key elements of the relational aspect in online brand communities. This supports that consumption experience is enhanced when consumers feel that their interaction with the brand has been personalised to their individual preference (Merz, Zarantonello, & Grappi, 2018; Ramaswamy & Ozcan, 2016). Entitativity refers to situations where people can be described as a single meaningful unit (Vock, Dolen, & Ruyter, 2013). The level of perceived entitativity is built upon the interactions among members and the nature of interactions may include: (1) experience exchange, (2) community attachment, (3) building links, and (4) social interaction (Davies et al., 2014). With such interactions being facilitated, virtual community users share their personal brand experience with others with the willingness to generate benefits for others as well as for themselves. Carlson et al.'s (2018) study demonstrates the different features of an online community and how its online activities, particularly purchase experience, influence consumers' perspectives of the value it brings to them individually. However, the mechanisms of what encourages consumers to become part of a community founded on group intentions and influence is equally vital to understand, initially based on non-purchasing activities.

The study by Cheng et al. (2018) proposed a framework to identify how firms can create customer loyalty in online brand communities. The model showed that information quality, need for social capital, emotion and perceived critical mass are expected to influence customer satisfaction and relationship commitment, which eventually will lead to loyalty intentions in online communities. Like Li's et al.'s (2018) study, Cheng et al. (2018) argue that firms must ensure they provide cohesive product information online for consumers to access on online communities, as it is one of the major activities for online customers in the purchase-making process (Ho, Lin, & Chen, 2012; Klein & Ford, 2003; Ozuem & Azemi, 2018). However, Cheng et al. (2018) explored in greater detail how the quality of information could influence loyalty intentions; their model shows that completeness, believability, timeliness and the amount of information would influence customer satisfaction and relationship commitment. This is supported by Kim and Niehm (2009), who found that perceived information quality affects perceived value and loyalty intentions on retail websites.

Compared to Li's et al.'s (2018) and Carlson et al.'s (2018) studies, Cheng et al.'s (2018) study greatly emphasised the importance of the consumers' need to build and maintain networks within the online brand community as it generates capital for the firm. Huang et al. (2017) found that online social capital can enhance customers' satisfaction with the sellers, which can eventually affect consumers' loyalty to the company. Furthermore, with a perceived critical mass, consumers may be influenced to shift to other brands if there is proof of an increasing number of individuals involved in the online brand community (Wu et al., 2017). This confirms that firms can increase their perceived community value by enabling consumers' access to other consumers who could benefit them in a variety of ways, including information sharing and grouping with individuals for relational reasons, as implied by Carlson et al. (2018).

Cheng et al. (2018) indicate that firms must consider the non-financial motivations consumers have for participating in online communities, providing a balanced argument that quality of information and networking activities are equally important to influence consumer loyalty within the online brand. However, that study focuses on actions firms should take to generate and maintain consumer loyalty through online brand communities. Although it mentions the important influence consumer network building can have for influencing other consumers' perception of the brand and their purchasing decisions, its explanation for why consumers feel motivated to participate in the community itself is unclear. The benefits and values that consumers obtain from partaking in online communities have been addressed by Carlson et al. (2018) and the return in positive loyalty that firms gain from consumers when they facilitate and enable effective online activities has been covered by Cheng et al. (2018). However, consumers' motivation to remain loyal to a brand community and their motivation to participate within it still has to be understood.

ONLINE COMMUNITY IDENTIFICATION AND ACTIVE PARTICIPATION

The advancement of Internet technology and its commercialisation have redefined brand communities and how consumers interact and build engaging experiences (Brown, Dacin, Pratt, & Whetten, 2006), making the sharing of information and mutual communication more accessible (Kietzmann, Hermkens, McCarthy, & Silvestre, 2011). In contrast to focusing studies on the online community and the features and elements it facilitates (Cheng et al., 2018; Li et al., 2018; Carlson et al., 2018), other researchers have directed their attention to the consumers' part in these communities, and particularly the individual's sense of belonging to a community and community identification (Algesheimer et al., 2005; McAlexander, Schouten, & Koenig, 2002). The study of virtual communities by Dholakia et al. (2004) showed that higher levels of perceived value lead to stronger community identification. From an individual's point of view, belonging to a brand is of unique significance as it implies an emotional group involvement resulting in attachment or commitment to the community and brand. Other researchers' studies have focused on the connection between consumer members, identifying a 'we' culture in which there is a shared feeling of belonging with other users that separates them from users of other brands (Fournier, 1998; Bergami & Bagozzi, 2000; Bagozzi & Dholakia, 2006). According to the studies this was stronger than the relationship between the firms and the consumers. These authors address the mechanisms that enable consumers to feel a sense of belonging within a community, yet the instruments that lead to identification and active participation are unclear.

Gong's (2018) study on online brand communities focused on countries' cultural value orientations from the USA and South Korea and tested Merz, He and Vargo's (2009) 'Brand Value Co-creation' (BVCC) model. According to the BVCC model, a significantly high number of interactions between brands and customers create co-created brand value. Gong's findings indicate that brand value co-creation, a form of customer brand engagement, is driven by customer brand ownership and bounded by customers' cultural value orientation. The findings indicate that individualism-collectivism and power distance indirectly affect brand responsibility and self-enhancement in the relationship between brand ownership and customer brand engagement behaviour. While this study provides insight and illustration of the cultural environment and the different levels of online brand community engagement, it is limited to cultural value orientation and is unclear about the consumers' association with the brand's community culture and what leads them to be involved in such a community. Furthermore, although the study emphasises brand familiarity, it does not specifically explore the significant importance of the firms' and other consumer members' involvement in the community and how they affect the interaction of the community and how these can affect consumers' choice to actively partake in brand communities.

Coelho et al.'s (2019) study focused on identifying how brand communities may contribute to establishing long-lasting relationships with customers based on the mediating effects of brand love. The study focused on the relational reasoning and outcomes for members to be part of a brand's community, indicating that commitment to a brand is more important than commitment to the group. This study places the brand itself as of central importance in the online brand community in contrast to the members. It could be argued that the brand's appeal to the consumers is the supporting source of online community identification, which can motivate individuals to actively participate as a member of the brand community and maintain relations with other members (Bhattacharya & Sen, 2003; Bergami & Bagozzi, 2000).

However, even with a self-created identity, a brand's appeal to does not mean that consumers will have the self-motivation to demonstrate active participation with the brand's online community. The existence of a virtual brand community will not guarantee a company will establish an ongoing relationship with consumers of a brand and build a long-term brand community (Culnan, McHugh, & Zubillaga, 2010). Some consumers may be impacted more by the wide network of members involved in the community, especially if there is a lack of firm-generated interactions. Consumers may feel more motivated to engage in an online brand community and build a brand through expanding their network of connections, which can redefine value creation as co-creation between brand and consumers (He, Chen, Lee, & Pohlman, 2017; VanMeter, Syrdal, Powell-Mantel, Grisaffe, & Nesson, 2018). Essamri, McKechnie and Winklhofer's (2019) study emphasised the importance of maintaining socially negotiated processes in brand identity and co-creation with brand community; they introduced a model that visualises the context in which firm's management participates in brand identity but also maintains 'bridges' and 'bonding' with the online community members. The model illustrates brand identity connection with a long socio-cultural process with various stakeholders such as a brand community, recognising that the brand's 'fans' and consumers continuously reflect and validate their perception of the brand's identity. This demonstrates that a brand's appeal to consumers alone is not enough to maintain online brand community engagement, and the number of memberships it has is only effective if it maintains a significant level of interactions.

Bang, Youn, Rowean, Jennings, and Austin's (2018) study supports that community members' involvement is important to brands. Bang et al. (2018) identified six motivations for consumers' participation in company-sponsored market research online communities (MROCs): knowledge, utilitarian, value-expressive, ego-defensive, social, and helping the company. The authors found that online members involved in such communities enhanced the members' sense of identification, initially making them feel they had a voice within a sponsored company and increasing the likelihood of continuous participation in MROCs. As firms attempt to improve their services, their understanding of how to attract consumers to provide their perspectives and feedback of the firm is critical to comprehend (Baldus et al., 2015). Although this study focuses on private membership online communities, it does support the perspective that firms must ensure engagement is maintained within communities and generate the favourable outcomes for the firm. Therefore, while the brand is essential to the online community, the community's members can generate the perceived value to firms-generated interaction and influence active engagement both between the consumers as well as interactions between the brand and its consumers. As mentioned before, the existence of a virtual community page will not guarantee a firm will encourage consumers to build a connection with the brand online (Culnan et al., 2010). While some authors have focused on community membership bonding and interaction between consumers as key to attract and maintain interaction (Bang et al., 2018; Essamri et al., 2019; Bagozzi & Dholakia, 2006), others have investigated the elements of trust and loyalty in their studies on online brand communities (Coelho, Rita, & Santos, 2018; Akrout & Nagy, 2018; Vohra & Bhardwaj, 2019).

ONLINE BRAND COMMUNITY AND CONSUMER ENGAGEMENT

Akrout and Nagy's (2018) study investigated the determinants of trust and commitment to the virtual brand community in the firm-initiated virtual brand community (FiVBC) setting. They adapted their study from prior research that tackled the central enjoyment consumers may obtain from being actively part of activities that stem from their interests (Nambisan & Watt, 2011; Jahn & Kunz, 2012) and the effect of relationship benefits on participation (Dholakia, Blazevic, Wiertz, & Algesheimer, 2009; Ozuem et al., 2016). Akrout and Nagy (2018) go further by including the direct role of economic and hedonic benefits provided by the firm that initiates trust and commitment. This indicates that if a brand demonstrates it can offer consumers appropriate economic benefits, the FiVBC reinforces the brand's perceived competence and trustworthiness. However, Akrout and Nagy (2018) also point out that the brands can use their current 'fan followers' to refer their fan pages to their own personal networks. A brand's strong fan networks are likely in a better position to be motivated to generate positive word-of-mouth, making them essential networks to the FiVBC. This study focuses on the perspective of the ability of a brand community page to obtain trust from consumers within the community through the firm's competency actions but also with the use of current networks that can be useful mediators to other networks. The limitation to this study is quite generic in how a firm's loyal followers can generate positive WOM to other consumers, and what the information should be about. Not all consumers will have financial or promotion motivations; therefore it is important to understand what types of conversations would mutually benefit the brand's community image and sales. Additionally, it needs to be established whether trust is developed with positive WOM before or after active participation. Therefore, it is important to understand how interactions within a brand community can encourage consumers to form relationships within the online brand community.

Vohra and Bhardwaj (2019) identified three competing models of customer engagement in the context of social media for emerging markets. Their study recognised the role and importance of active participation in a brand community and identified community trust and commitment to be based on the consumers' experience of the online engagement activities. Kang, Tang, and Fiore (2014) and Tonteri, Kosonen, Ellonen, and Tarkiainen (2011) found two types of online participating users: active and passive. Most studies on online customer participation do not differentiate between active and passive participation, whereas Vohra and Bhardwaj offer a distinct difference between the two, and position active participation as the main feature of their conceptual models. The first nomological network (NN1) model proposed that active participation is a consequence of customer engagement with the community, thus leading to community trust and commitment.

Participation is a starting point for both NN2 and NN3. NN2 presented community trust and commitment as influenced by active participation, resulting in customer engagement with the community, whereas NN3 presented community trust and commitment to be a result from customer engagement with the community. Vohra and Bhardwaj concluded that NN2 was the most suitable model to describe the conceptual dimensions of customer engagement in the online community. The study yields the understanding that online community managers must create an environment that maintains trust and commitment, which may result in increased loyalty and positive perceptions from the consumers. The study does not determine what online users perceive as trustworthy in an online community, and whether that trust stems from the brand itself or the community members that the brand has already acquired. It is unclear on the motivations that consumers have for choosing to actively partake in online communities and how they are influenced to become engaged with the community as a result. Vohra and Bhardwaj (2019) provide a thorough conceptual model on what leads consumers to become engaged in online communities, but it is important to understand where the influence to do so comes from.

Coelho et al. (2018) proposed a conceptual model in which placed consumer engagement as the essential motivation for consumers to continue interacting with an online brand community. This is supported by Baldus et al. (2015) who provided a summary of eleven dimensions: brand influence, brand passion, connecting, helping, like-minded discussion, hedonic rewards, utilitarian rewards, seeking assistance, self-expression, up-to-date information, and validation; according to the study, these affect consumers' motivation to continue partaking in online brand communities. The model indicates that the firm obtains trust and loyalty from the consumers, which ultimately leads to consumer-brand identification and brand identity.

Coelho et al.'s (2018) model is directed to online communities of mass-market products, focusing on products that are part of highly competitive market and do not target a specific segment of consumers. It can be argued that with mass product categories, a direct relationship is not expected as the fundamental element affecting brand choice would be the price. Conversely, brands which are mostly based on experience or products that are part of the luxury or fashion industry will more likely need to consider how online communities can generate relationships between the firm and its consumers. Luxury and experience brands are often associated with consumers' image and appeal to the emotional values of the consumer, which can be linked to online social identity (Helal, Ozuem, & Lancaster, 2018).

A wide network linked to such a brand may often motivate consumers to join the community to improve their online image and for relational reasons. Although some online brands may not have a large market to target compared to mass-market products, the size of the market segment is not equal to the number of followers the brand will receive within a community. Therefore, it is important to understand what attracts consumers to an online brand when emotional appeal and engagement are the core factors of the online community.

Shukla and Drennan (2018) studied the interactive effects of individual and group level variables on virtual purchase behaviour in online communities. Community influence was a major key variable mentioned in the study, supporting that strong relations between community members encourage active participation within the community. Social identification was also a major variable in the group-influence variable. According to Wasko and Faraj (2005), increased identification improves the human capital encouraging users to interact more within the online community. This study argues that developing community members' sense of belonging and identity within a community is important to encouraging consumer engagement (Algesheimer et al., 2005; McAlexander et al., 2002) and having a 'we' community culture can increase its perceived value (Fournier, 1998; Bergami & Bagozzi, 2000; Bagozzi & Dholakia, 2006). The study equally notes the importance of the consumers' intrinsic motivations for engaging online including the enjoyment they obtain from online activity and individualism within the community (Verhagen, Feldberg, van den Hooff, Meents, & Merikivi, 2012). It can be argued that even within a community where product and service purchasing activities occur, community interaction is vital to maintaining long-term relationships with customers. While some brands may benefit from direct involvement in the online brand community, others obtain higher online engagement from encouraging consumers to interact with each other. Therefore, the study identifies the importance for brands to consider both customisation of interaction media within the community for individuals and maintaining the 'we' culture to ensure that interactions between the online community members continue.

ONLINE BRAND VALUES AND PREFERENCES

Fashion is a powerful social symbol used to create individual and group identities (Ahuvia, 2005); it is also adapted according to the users' norms, values and preferences, and arguably trends are co-created by consumers who both preserve and adapt them along the way (Wolny & Muller, 2013). Therefore, if a trend is adopted by a significant number of people, the products' perceived value will be affected, either positively or negatively, depending on the references. Fashion is categorised as a high involvement product, which implies that products are either expensive, rarely bought, linked to individual identities, or come with high risks socially as well as functionally. According to Gu, Park, and Konana (2012) high involvement products attract high numbers of online conversations. This may be due to the complex process of evaluating the value of individual fashion brands and their products, particularly its social value (Wolny & Muller, 2013). Fashion brands are often described in terms of human personality traits (Thompson & Haytko, 1997) that may possess an emotional component that evokes strong attitudes. Online users share information related to their stylistic choices to their peers with intentions of obtaining feedback responses on their choices (Lin, Lu, & Wu, 2012). This supports that consumers are highly conscious of their fashion brand choices, placing their image on online communities as the major priority for their decision-making. The complexity of the fashion industry has attracted many authors to explore aspects of its presence in the online community including brand personality (Wolny & Muller, 2013; Ranfagni et al., 2016) and social identity (Helal et al., 2018; Carlson, Suter, & Brown, 2008; Nowak, Szamrej, & Latané, 1990).

Heine and Berghaus (2014) have classified eight digital platforms that provide an understanding of the online tools and social media sites which managers of luxury brands can use to manage their information and marketing activities effectively. These are:

- Luxury brand website (representing the first source in searching for information)
- Search engine optimization (to increase the luxury brand's website traffic)
- Direct mailing (for customer relationship management purposes)
- Online advertising (for customer purchase)
- Brand communities (to share content with customers)
- Social campaigns (for storing and sharing content)
- Phone and tablet apps
- E-commerce

The identification of these platforms is important for companies to understand, as each has its own level of interactions it allows for consumers to have with the firm or with other consumers as well as different activities that consumers can participate in. Therefore, it is important to know which platforms enable consumers access to relevant information and facilitates their voice within the community to impact the engagement levels within the community. However, the major factor to understand is what are the key elements that drive consumers to interact in fashion brands' online communities and how firms can get consumers' perception of the brand to correlate with the firms' intended message.

Ranfagni et al.'s (2016) study on measuring brand personality identified the complex action of communication between fashion firms and consumers in online communities. Using Aakar's (1997) summary on brand personality dimensions, Ranfagni et al. (2016) analysed adjectives that presented the verbal expression of brand personality in consumer-generated texts in online fashion communities and by fashion companies in their firm-generated communications. These adjectives were used to calculate three key quantitative indicators that measure (1) the degree of alignment between company-defined and consumer-perceived brand personality, (2) the degree of similarity in personality between different brands, and (3) the degree to which consumers perceive brands as similar. One of the major concerns the study expresses is that managers of fashion brands face loss of control over what consumers say about the brands. From this the authors advise using analytical instruments that verify gaps between what a brand aims to be and how it is perceived online. They also express the need to not only preserve but also refresh existing brand personality traits or identify new ones, thereby generating changes in competitive positioning, while also performing a comparative analysis of brand personality perceptions of other brands. This study proposes that companies need to critically consider what they communicate and what intended responses they want from consumers, especially through online brand communities, as consumers are more conscious of their online presence, and that they should therefore critically consider their online network associations. Furthermore, with brands' increasing presence through online communities it is majorly important for them to identify their differences among other brands to obtain that competitive advantage, making sure consumers understand the brands' identity categories whilst also aligning with consumers' own social identities.

Consumers of fashion interact far more through digital platforms (Thomas, Peters, & Tolson, 2007) providing textual resources that can yield indications of the brand-related perceptions consumers have. Fashion blogs contain texts written by opinion leaders or experts as well as consumers who feel positively associated with the brand; therefore the information may be perceived as richer compared to regular fashion consumer forums. Additionally, fashion blogs can be perceived as a community in which all members are 'real' consumers (Pettit, 2010, p. 241) and thus are representatives of the brand's consumer population. The study by Crawford-Camiciottoli et al. (2014) aimed to show how brand associations can be identified and analysed in an online community. The authors focused on three leading fashion companies: Valentino, Dolce & Gabbana, and Giorgio Armani, all of which can be linked with iconic personalities and the luxury sector and have obtained rich expressed comments from consumers of fashion. The authors presented three major categories of brand associations: product-related attributes, non-product-related attributes, and designer identity. The first two aligned with Keller's (1993) framework, while Crawford-Camiciottoli et al. (2014) discovered that the strong presence of the designer's name implied the need for a specific category. This verified Thomas et al.'s (2007) study which similarly found individual designers in their analysis of online fashion forums.

According to the results Valentino has a stronger level of brand associations linked to the designer identity, with Valentino himself contributing. Seemingly, fashion bloggers still associate the brand with its original designer. In contrast, Dolce & Gabbana has relatively high levels of product-related attributes. Armani had the highest level of non-product-related attributes, though product-related attributes similarly characterised Armani's brand associations and it has a strong designer identity. Compared to the other two, consumers of Armani perceive its network of brand associations in a more balanced way (Broniarczyk & Gershoff, 2003). Crawford-Camiciottoli et al. (2014) mentioned that in some cases, fashion bloggers introduce creative alternatives such as Bejewelled that reinforce the company-defined brand associations. This can allow companies to determine which shared brand associations are strong in the consumer's mind, which can improve the brands' competitive positioning. Like Ranfagni et al.'s (2016) study, that of Crawford-Camiciottoli et al. (2014) provides analytical tools to determine whether the brand aligns in the mind of the consumer with the attributes that define its competitive positioning, but it focuses on the brand associations rather than just the brand itself. The study's analytical tools also help reveal possible new themes of brand associations which can be identified within online communities and analyse the impact of previous posts on new brand associations. This study shows that internal cohesiveness is a major factor that determines the successful outcome of fashion online communities, emphasising the need for brands to have an established strong identity that consumers can relate to but also the need to keep the community's conversations fresh and have continuing and adapting changes that reinforce the brand's and the consumers' identity.

In contrast to the two previous studies by Ranfagni et al. (2016) and Crawford-Camiciottoli et al. (2014), Kim and Ko (2012) addressed the success of social media marketing activities in enhancing equity for luxury fashion brands. This study comprised five concepts: entertainment, interaction, trendiness, customisation, and word-of-mouth. It indicated that customisation and word-of-mouth were important for fashion brands in the online community. The findings presented a positive connection between the application of social media marketing, purchase intentions and customer equity within the luxury fashion industry. Kim and Ko's perception of relationship equity is that special treatment or recognition of consumers is necessary to build strong customer relationships and enhance relationship equity. This indicates that marketing promotion techniques like loyalty programmes are the least effective for maintaining long-term customer relationships as many alternatives are available from other brands. However, the study also points out the 'shallow loyalty nature' of consumers in the fashion luxury industry. As mentioned before, individuals may associate with a brand that correlates with their own individual identity and are more conscious about their image online, which significantly influences their brand choices. While Kim and Ko reveal the fundamental role that social media marketing activities play in presenting the visual activity of the luxury fashion brand, it is important to consider how the consumer relates to the brand itself and how the firm can channel that enthusiasm in the online community and encourage the consumer to become interactive in the online community. Therefore, the internal attributes, identity and values that the firm promotes can increase consumers' perceived value of the firm's online activity and thus impact relationship equity.

Helal et al.'s (2018) study draws from the social identity theory to examine how evolving social media platforms have impacted brand perceptions in the fashion and accessories industries. The dynamic nature of online marketing has caused companies to be constantly seeking development in their activity (Jayachandran, Gimeno, & Varadarajan, 1999; Lusch, 2007; Vargo & Lusch, 2004; Webster, 1992) and has since resulted in their using online platforms that enable them to contribute content to followers (Hoffman & Novak, 1996). The fashion industry is known for establishing the concept of embracing individuality amongst the consumer population. Thus, consumers seek to individually establish their unique manner of behaviour, speech and appearance that is noticeable and significant but also found with presumed group norms. According to Carlson et al. (2008) and Nowak et al. (1990) a consumer is placed amid two forces, the individual or psychological influence of personal opinions and preferences, and the social weight of beliefs and attitudes. This strengthens the argument that consumers consider how their personal brand choices impact their image in an online community and how they choose and act accordingly. Researchers have thus recognised a need for a more relational social identity perspective in conceptualising the computer-mediated marketing environments (Ozuem, Howell, & Lancaster, 2008; Moon & Sprott, 2016). Consumer brand judgement is influenced according to the value a brand is perceived to deliver, as customers are encouraged to voice their association with a brand that enhances self-presentation and builds social identity (Algesheimer et al., 2005; Dholakia et al., 2004; Ozuem, Thomas, & Lancaster, 2016).

CONCLUSION

The literature examined indicates that brands need to distinguish online communities from product information channels. While online brand communities impact the consumers' consumption experience it is important to consider how to enhance long-term online relationships which, for different consumers, do not necessarily continue even after purchasing products from specific fashion brands. Though followers may be typical admirers of a fashion brand (Albert et al., 2008) the dynamic nature of online marketing compels brands to seek new activity development (Jayachandran et al., 1999; Lusch, 2007; Vargo & Lusch, 2004; Webster, 1992) which is vitally important to ensure consumers maintain interest in the online brand community and develop loyalty. This issue identifies the need to maintain consumers' perceptions that fashion brands are relevant to their online motivations, identities and personalities. This is a major challenge in view of the diverse values and needs consumers have despite sharing a common preference towards specific fashion brands with other consumers.

A significant determinant that affects relationships in online brand communities is customer participation. Vohra and Bhardwaj's (2019) framework on customer engagement concluded that active participation is the key starting point, which then generates trust and commitment resulting in further commitment from the consumer. However, what consumers perceive as trustworthy and motivates them to participate is complex as well as distinctive across different consumers. This is significant to individual and group-orientated motivated consumers. Essamri et al. (2019) note the social bonding and bridging motivations consumers have, whereas Bang et al. (2018) and Kim and Ko (2012) identify the 'ego-shallow' nature of consumers in online communities. Cheng et al. (2018) consider consumers with various mentally processed values including their perception of information quality, need for social capital, emotion and perceived critical mass. Fashion is linked to individual identities, and consumers often consider the potential social risks as well as the functional risks of being part of a community. Thus, brands must ensure that they understand their consumers' personality, which is often reflected in their habits in online communities, and ensure they maintain consumers' perception that they are relevant to their identity in order to maintain long-term relationships.

Academics clearly identify that functional values are not the only factors that determine a consumer's perceptions of the perceived value of an online brand community. Brands must ensure they approach consumers online in ways that appeal to their emotional and relational values. Carlson et al. (2018) and Ramaswamy and Ozcan (2016) identify the diverse mental processes that consumers have, presenting the challenges brands will face when meeting the different values consumers maintain in their online activity. For example, several papers have identified online behaviours of consumers in virtual communities, focusing on consumers' individual motivations to maintain their social identity (Helal et al., 2018; Carlson et al., 2008; Nowak et al., 1990). Often individuals' fashion brand preferences reflect their individual identity, and though they may not have originally intended to join an online community for group motivations, it can be argued that the increased sense of belonging to a specific community because of universally agreed norms and values can motivate consumers to partake in the community. This applies to any consumer regardless of whether they are participating for the 'we' culture of the community (Fournier, 1998; Bergami & Bagozzi, 2000; Bagozzi & Dholakia, 2006) or to build a network to promote their own online image in that community. Therefore, brands need to ensure they are transparent in their activity in online brand communities, ensuring that the majority of consumers feel their values are being represented there.

REFERENCES

Aaker, J. L. (1997). Dimensions of brand personality. *Journal of Marketing Research, 34*(3), 347–356.

Ahuvia, A. C. (2005). Beyond the extended self: Loved objects and consumers' identity narratives. *Journal of Consumer Research, 32*(6), 171–184.

Akrout, H., & Nagy, G. (2018). Trust and commitment within a virtual brand community: The mediating role of brand relationship quality. *Information and Management, 55*(8), 939–955.

Albert, N., Merunka, D., & Valette-Florence, P. (2008). When consumers love their brands: Exploring the concept and its dimensions. *Journal of Business Research, 61*(10), 1062–1075.

Algesheimer, R., Dholakia, U. M., & Herrmann, A. (2005). The social influence of brand community: Evidence from European car clubs. *Journal of Marketing, 69*(3), 19–34.

Anderson, B. (1983). *Imagined communities: Reflections on the origin and spread of nationalism.* London: Verso.

Bagozzi, R. P., & Dholakia, U. M. (2006). Antecedents and purchase consequences of customer participation in small group brand communities. *International Journal of Research in Marketing, 23*(1), 45–61.

Baldus, B. J., Voorhees, C., & Calantone, R. (2015). Online brand community engagement: Scale development and validation. *Journal of Business Research, 68*(5), 978–985.

Bang, J., Youn, S., Rowean, J., Jennings, M., & Austin, M. (2018). Motivations for and outcomes of participating in research online communities. *International Journal of Market Research, 60*(3), 238–256.

Beck, U. (2011). Cosmopolitanism as imagined communities of global risk. *American Behavioral Scientist, 55*(10), 1346–1361.

Bergami, M., & Bagozzi, R. P. (2000). Self-categorization, affective commitment and group self-esteem as distinct aspects of social identity in the organization. *British Journal of Social Psychology, 39*(4), 555–577.

Bhattacharya, C. B., & Sen, S. (2003). Consumer–company identification: A framework for understanding consumers' relationships with companies. *Journal of Marketing, 67*(2), 76–88.

Broniarczyk, S. M., & Gershoff, A. D. (2003). The reciprocal effect on brand equity and trivial attributes. *Journal of Marketing Research, 40*(2), 161–175.

Brown, T. J., Dacin, P. A., Pratt, M. G., & Whetten, D. A. (2006). Identity, intended image, construed image, and reputation: An interdisciplinary framework and suggested terminology. *Journal of the Academy of Marketing Science, 34*(2), 99–106.

Carlson, B., Suter, T., & Brown, T. (2008). Social versus psychological brand community: The role of psychological sense of brand community. *Journal of Business Research, 61*(4), 284–291.

Carlson, J., Rahman, M. M., Taylor, A., & Voola, R. (2019). Feel the VIBE: Examining value-in-the-brand-page-experience and its impact on satisfaction and customer engagement behaviours in mobile social media. *Journal of Retailing and Consumer Services, 46*, 149–162.

Carlson, J., Wyllie, J., Rahman, M. M., & Voola, R. (2018). Enhancing brand relationship performance through customer participation and value creation in social media brand communities. *Journal of Retailing and Consumer Services*. doi:10.1016/j.jretconser.2018.07.008

Cayla, J., & Eckhardt, G. M. (2008). Asian brands and the shaping of a transnational imagined community. *Journal of Consumer Research, 35*(2), 216–230.

Cheng, F., Wu, C., & Chen, Y. (2018). Creating customer loyalty in online brand communities. *Computers in Human Behavior*.

Coelho, A., Bairrada, C., & Peres, F. (2019). Brand communities' relational outcomes, through brand love. *Journal of Product and Brand Management, 28*(2), 154–165.

Coelho, P. S., Rita, P., & Santos, Z. R. (2018). On the relationship between consumer-brand identification, brand community, and brand loyalty. *Journal of Retailing and Consumer Services, 43*, 101–110.

Coles, B. A., & West, M. (2016). Weaving the internet together: Imagined communities in newspaper comment threads. *Computers in Human Behavior, 60*, 44–53.

Cornwall, A., & Jewkes, R. (1995). What is participatory research? *Social Science and Medicine, 41*(12), 1667–1676.

Crawford-Camiciottoli, B., Ranfagni, S., & Guercini, S. (2014). Exploring brand associations: An innovative methodological approach. *European Journal of Marketing, 48*(5/6), 1092–1112.

Culnan, M. J., McHugh, P. J., & Zubillaga, J. I. (2010). How large U.S. companies can use Twitter and other social media to gain business value. *MIS Quarterly Executive, 9*(4), 243–259.

Danias, K., & Kavoura, A. (2013). The role of social media as a tool of a company's innovative communication activities. *The Małopolska School of Economics in Tarnów Research Papers Collection, 23*(2), 75–83.

Davis, R., Piven, I., & Breazeale, M. (2014). Conceptualizing the brand in social media community: The five sources model. *Journal of Retailing and Consumer Services, 21*(4), 468–481.

De Vries, N. J., & Carlson, J. (2014). Examining the drivers and brand performance implications of customer engagement with brands in the social media environment. *Journal of Brand Management, 21*(6), 495–515.

Dholakia, U. M., Bagozzi, R. P., & Pearo, L. K. (2004). A social influence model of consumer participation in network- and small-group-based virtual communities. *International Journal of Research in Marketing, 21*(3), 241–263.

Dholakia, U. M., Blazevic, V., Wiertz, C., & Algesheimer, R. (2009). Communal service delivery: How customers benefit from participation in firm-hosted virtual P3 communities. *Journal of Service Research, 12*(2), 208–226.

Essamri, A., McKechnie, S., & Winklhofer, H. (2019). Co-creating corporate brand identity with online brand communities: A managerial perspective. *Journal of Business Research, 96*, 366–375.

Fournier, S. (1998). Consumers and their brands: Developing relationship theory in consumer research. *Journal of Consumer Research, 24*(4), 343–373.

Gong, T. (2018). Customer brand engagement behavior in online brand communities. *Journal of Services Marketing, 32*(3), 286–299.

Gruzd, A., Wellman, B., & Takhteyev, Y. (2011). Imagining Twitter as an imagined community. *American Behavioral Scientist, 55*(10), 1294–1318.

Gu, B., Park, J., & Konana, P. (2012). The impact of external word-of-mouth sources on retailer sales of high-involvement products. *Information Systems Research, 23*(1), 182–196.

He, Y., Chen, Q., Lee, R., & Pohlman, A. (2017). Consumers' role performance and brand identification: Evidence from a survey and a longitudinal field experiment. *Journal of Interactive Marketing, 38*(2), 1–11.

Heine, K., & Berghaus, B. (2014). Luxury goes digital: How to tackle the digital luxury brand-consumer touchpoints. *Journal of Global Fashion Marketing, 5*(3), 223–234.

Helal, G., Ozuem, W., & Lancaster, G. (2018). Social media brand perceptions of millennials. *International Journal of Retail and Distribution Management, 46*(10), 977–998.

Ho, C. I., Lin, M. H., & Chen, H. M. (2012). Web users' behavioural patterns of tourism information search: From online to offline. *Tourism Management, 33*(6), 1468–1482.

Hoffman, D., & Novak, T. (1996). Marketing in hypermedia computer-mediated environments: Conceptual foundations. *Journal of Marketing, 60*(3), 50–68.

Huang, Q., Chen, X. Y., Ou, C., Davison, R. M., & Hua, Z. S. (2017). Understanding buyers' loyalty to a C2C platform: The roles of social capital, satisfaction and perceived effectiveness of E-commerce institutional mechanisms. *Information Systems Journal, 27*(1), 91–119.

Jahn, B., & Kunz, W. (2012). How to transform consumers into fans of your brand. *Journal of Service Management, 23*(3), 344–361.

Jayachandran, S., Gimeno, J., & Varadarajan, R. (1999). The theory of multimarket competition: A synthesis and implications for marketing strategy. *Journal of Marketing, 63*(3), 49–66.

Kang, J., Tang, L., & Fiore, A. M. (2014). Enhancing consumer–brand relationships on restaurant Facebook fan pages: Maximizing consumer benefits and increasing active participation. *International Journal of Hospitality Management, 36*, 145–155.

Kavoura, A. (2014). Social media, online imagined communities and communication research. *Library Review, 63*(6/7), 490–504.

Kavoura, A., Pelet, J. E., Rundle-Thiele, S., & Lecat, B. (2014). Experience matters: Exploring the experience behavioral loyalty relationship in wine. In *2014 Global Marketing Conference at Singapore*, 1757–1762.

Keller, K. L. (1993). Conceptualizing, measuring and managing customer-based brand equity. *Journal of Marketing, 57*, 1–22.

Kietzmann, J., Hermkens, K., McCarthy, I., & Silvestre, B. (2011). Social media? Get serious! Understanding the functional building blocks of social media. *Business Horizons, 54*(3), 241–251.

Kim, A. J., & Ko, E. (2012). Do social media marketing activities enhance customer equity? An empirical study of luxury fashion brand. *Journal of Business Research, 65*(10), 1480–1486.

Kim, H., & Niehm, L. S. (2009). The impact of website quality on information quality, value, and loyalty intentions in apparel retailing. *Journal of Interactive Marketing, 23*(3), 221–233.

Klein, L. R., & Ford, G. T. (2003). Consumer search for information in the digital age: An empirical study of prepurchase search for automobiles. *Journal of Interactive Marketing, 17*(3), 29–49.

Li, Q., Wang, Q., & Lin, Z. (2018). Effects of consumer visit to online community and product channel on local sales of large consumer goods: Evidence from real estate industry. *Journal of Strategic Information Systems, 27*(2), 191–204.

Lin, T. M. Y., Lu, K., & Wu, J. (2012). The effects of visual information in eWOM communication. *Journal of Research in Interactive Marketing, 6*(1), 7–26.

Lusch, R. (2007). Marketing's evolving identity: Defining our future'. *Journal of Public Policy and Marketing, 26*(2), 261–268.

Merz, M. A., He, Y., & Vargo, S. L. (2009). The evolving brand logic: A service-dominant logic perspective. *Journal of the Academy of Marketing Science, 37*(3), 328–344.

Merz, M. A., Zarantonello, L., & Grappi, S. (2018). How valuable are your customers in the brand value co-creation process? The development of a customer co-creation value (CCCV) scale. *Journal of Business Research, 82*, 79–89.

Moon, H., & Sprott, D. E. (2016). Ingredient branding for a luxury brand: The role of brand and product fit. *Journal of Business Research, 69*(12), 5768–5774.

Muniz, A. M., & O'Guinn, T. C. (2001). Brand community. *Journal of Consumer Research, 27*(4), 412–432.

Nambisan, P., & Watt, J. H. (2011). Managing customer experiences in online product communities. *Journal of Business Research, 64*(8), 889–895.

Navarro, V. (1984). A critique of the ideological and political positions of the Willy Brandt Report and the WHO Alma Ata Declaration. *Social Science and Medicine, 18*(6), 467–474.

Nowak, A., Szamrej, J., & Latané, B. (1990). From private attitude to public opinion: A dynamic theory of social impact. *Psychological Review, 97*(3), 362–376.

Ozuem, W., & Azemi, Y. (2018). Online service failure and recovery strategies in luxury brands: a view from justice theory. In W. Ozuem & Y. Azemi (Eds.), *Digital Marketing Strategies for Fashion and Luxury Brands* (pp. 108–125). Hershey: IGI Global.

Ozuem, W., Howell, K., & Lancaster, G. (2008). Communicating in the new interactive marketspace. *European Journal of Marketing, 42*(9/10), 1059–1083.

Ozuem, W., Howell, K. E., & Lancaster, G. (2016). Understanding technologically-induced customer services in the Nigerian banking sector: the internet as a post-modern phenomenon. *International Journal of Information Technology and Management, 15*(3), 272–290.

Ozuem, W., Howell, K. E., & Lancaster, G. (2018). Developing technologically induced environments: the case of the Nigerian banking sector. *Journal of Financial Services Marketing, 23*(1), 50–61.

Ozuem, W., & Lancaster, G. (2014). Recovery strategies in on-line service failure. In A. Ghorbani (Ed.), *Marketing in the Cyber Era: Strategies and Emerging Trends* (pp. 143–159). Hershey: IGI Global.

Ozuem, W., Patel, A., Howell, K., & Lancaster, G. (2017). An exploration of consumers' response to online service recovery initiatives. *International Journal of Market Research, 59*(1), 97–115.

Ozuem, W., Thomas, T., & Lancaster, G. (2016). The influence of customer loyalty on small island economies: An empirical and exploratory study. *Journal of Strategic Marketing, 24*(6), 447–469.

Pettit, R. (2010). Digital anthropology: How ethnography can improve online research. *Journal of Advertising Research, 50*(3), 240–242.

Ramaswamy, V., & Ozcan, K. (2016). Brand value co-creation in a digitalized world: An integrative framework and research implications. *International Journal of Research in Marketing, 33*(1), 93–106.

Ranfagni, S., Crawford-Camiciottoli, B., & Faraoni, M. (2016). How to measure alignment in perceptions of brand personality within online communities: Interdisciplinary insights. *Journal of Interactive Marketing, 35*, 70–85.

Relling, M., Schnittka, O., Sattler, H., & Johnen, M. (2016). Each can help or hurt: Negative and positive word of mouth in social network brand communities. *International Journal of Research in Marketing, 33*(1), 42–58.

Shukla, P., & Drennan, J. (2018). Interactive effects of individual- and group-level variables on virtual purchase behavior in online communities. *Information and Management, 55*(5), 598–607.

Thomas, J. B., Peters, C. O., & Tolson, H. (2007). An exploratory investigation of the virtual community MySpace.Com. What are consumers saying about fashion? *Journal of Fashion Marketing and Management, 11*(4), 587–603.

Thompson, C. J., & Haytko, D. L. (1997). Speaking of fashion: Consumers' uses of fashion discourses and the appropriation of countervailing cultural meanings. *Journal of Consumer Research, 24*(1), 15–42.

Tonteri, L., Kosonen, M., Ellonen, H. K., & Tarkiainen, A. (2011). Antecedents of an experienced sense of virtual community. *Computers in Human Behavior, 27*(6), 2215–2223.

VanMeter, R., Syrdal, H. A., Powell-Mantel, S., Grisaffe, D. B., & Nesson, E. T. (2018). Don't just "Like" me, promote me: How attachment and attitude influence brand related behaviors on social media. *Journal of Interactive Marketing, 43*, 83–97.

Vargo, S., & Lusch, R. (2004). Evolving to a new dominant logic for marketing. *Journal of Marketing, 68*(1), 1–17.

Verhagen, T., Feldberg, F., van den Hooff, B., Meents, S., & Merikivi, J. (2012). Understanding users' motivations to engage in virtual worlds: A multipurpose model and empirical testing. *Computers in Human Behavior, 28*(2), 484–495.

Vock, M., Dolen, W., & Ruyter, K. (2013). Understanding willingness to pay for social network sites. *Journal of Service Research, 16*(3), 311–325.

Vohra, A., & Bhardwaj, N. (2019). Customer engagement in an e-commerce brand community: An empirical comparison of alternate models. *Journal of Research in Interactive Marketing, 13*(1), 2–25.

Wasko, M. M., & Faraj, S. (2005). Why should I share? Examining social capital and knowledge contribution in electronic networks of practice. *MIS Quarterly, 29*(1), 35–57.

Webster, F. (1992). The changing role of marketing in the corporation. *Journal of Marketing, 56*(4), 1–17.

Wolny, J., & Mueller, C. (2013). Analysis of fashion consumers' motives to engage in electronic word-of-mouth communication through social media platforms. *Journal of Marketing Management, 29*(5–6), 562–583.

Wu, K., Vassileva, J., & Zhao, Y. (2017). Understanding users' intention to switch personal cloud storage services: Evidence from the Chinese market. *Computers in Human Behavior, 68*, 300–314.

Zaglia, M. E. (2013). Brand communities embedded in social networks. *Journal of Business Research, 66*(2), 216–223.

Chapter 6

Social Media Managed Brand Communities

Guida Helal
American University of Beirut, Lebanon

ABSTRACT

Organisations have veered communication to social media platforms in pursuit of the new-age vocal consumer. Social media means have allowed brands and customer to engage in real-time interchange, facilitating for the transposition of traditional brand communities to virtual communities. Social media brand communities produce interactive spaces of variable extents across global consumers. Through social media platforms, brands are able to produce content that resonates with customers, expanding brand awareness, inducing brand impressions, and fostering brand-customer relationships that constitute the foundation for brand communities. Such social media brand communities have instigated a sense of belonging across worldwide consumers, allowing individuals to utilise overt brand associations through online brand communities as a means to further social identities. The following chapter examines the influence of social media brand communities on the Millennial generation in the fashion industry, from a social identity theory perspective. This chapter focuses on theoretical and managerial implications.

INTRODUCTION

Over the years, marketing methods have contextually evolved parallel to external realities consisting of the economy, society, technology, or

157

globalisation, among other factors (Sheth, 2011; Sheth & Sisodia, 1999; Zinkhan & Hirschheim, 1992). This elucidates industries' imperative adoption of fluid marketing disciplines that are susceptible to variable externalities (Jayachandran, Gimeno, & Varadarajan, 1999; Vargo & Lusch, 2004). One revolutionary episode that has induced societal influence is the modern-day integration of the Internet. Communication bears a reconditioned focus amid the tech-savvy Millennial generation, who have embodied the Internet as a prominent avenue for dialogue. In keeping with contemporary advancements, marketers have assumed Internet means in approaching consumers (Hudson et al., 2016; Chappuis, Gaffey, & Parvizi, 2011), as the dynamic two-way interchange of social media supersedes traditional manners of marketing (Houman Andersen, 2001; Ozuem, Howell, & Lancaster, 2008). Brands are impelled to undertake a virtual presence in the quest to establish real-time eminence amid engaging consumer-centric environments (Evans, 2012; Hoffman & Novak, 1996). Fashion labels have especially embraced social media platforms as direct outlets to first-hand brand-customer interactions that cannot be mirrored through offline channels (Kim & Ko, 2012; Phan, Thomas & Heine, 2011; Helal & Ozuem, 2018). There exists extensive literature on the integration of social media as a prominent influence on consumer intentions (Fischer & Reuber, 2011; Hoffman & Fodor, 2016; Huy & Shipilov, 2012; Kaplan & Haenlein, 2010; Kietzmann et al., 2011; Qualman, 2013). Further research has investigated the conclusive application of social media within brand marketing methods (Habibi, Laroche, & Richard, 2014; Naylor, Lamberton, & West, 2012; Simmons, 2008).

Habibi, Laroche, and Richard (2014) consider the transposition of brand communities to online mediums in a study addressing the outcome of social media brand communities on brand trust. The findings of the research unfolded a positive relationship between interaction in social media brand communities and ensuing brand trust. As this study was performed on a wider age group, it appointed little attention to an age bracket that is most adept to social media use in routine life. Another limitation is the general use of brand communities and industries in the study, prompting leniency in the definition and attribution of what a brand community is, thus contributing to a general outlook of results. In a demographic evaluation of social media use, Pew Research Center revealed that maximum usage rates from 2006 to 2018 lay among ages 18 to 29 years (Smith & Anderson, 2018). Despite the extensive literature on the vast development of social media, few studies have explored the implementation of social media brand communities among Millennials in the fashion realm.

The marketing discipline has retained a progressive disposition projected in its continual evolution over the years, a steady deviation from a tangible approach of commodities to an intangible focus of service marketing (Vargo & Lusch, 2004; Lusch, 2007; Vargo, Lusch, & Morgan, 2015; Hunt & Madhavaram, 2015). The mere promotion of material goods no longer suffices as marketing practices have veered to value-driven logics of establishing relationships between brands and customers (Grönroos & Voima, 2013; Prahalad & Ramaswamy, 2000; Ozuem et al., 2017). Lusch (2007) interprets the progression of marketing practices over the past 100-year period into three developmental stages. The initial stage embodies the 'to market' approach, whereby the marketer serves as the bridge between two separate beings, the seller and the buyer. During the industrial revolution, marketing practices entered a second stage of 'market to', which consisted of stimulating demand from customers. The final stage, 'market with', embodies the vital shift from a receiving customer to an active value-contributing customer (Lusch, 2007). Brands have acknowledged the magnitude of generating reciprocity with customers (Ramaswamy, 2008). Brand-customer interaction represents the underlying basis of co-creating value, inducing brands to embolden consumer interchange as a means of furthering value creation (Prahalad & Ramaswamy, 2004).

Prahalad and Ramaswamy (2004) adopt the DART model as the building blocks to value co-creation. The first block consists of *dialogue*, which involves the circulation of information and conversations between brands and customers. The second block, *access*, considers the ease of information accessibility for both brand and customer. *Risk assessment*, the third block, involves the probable risk for a consumer associated with consumption of a product. Lastly, *transparency* regards brands' lucid communication of product details with consumers. The combination of the building blocks produces an approachable setting that invites interplay among brands and customers. The distribution of information, awareness and accountability incites participation amid brand-customer and customer-customer, thus conceiving a community (Hatch & Schultz, 2010; Muniz & O'Guinn, 2001; Pongsakornrungslip & Schroeder, 2011). By way of brand communities, invested members are granted the context to initiate and pursue social relations (Muniz & O'Guinn, 2001). The transposition of offline to online brand communities invites affiliates to venture into novel, prevalent channels (Romero & Molina, 2011), whereby recurring social interchange nourishes brand-customer bonds (Manville, 2004). Virtual brand presence introduces an inflow of multinational followers bound together under a devotion to the social media brand community at hand (Habibi, Laroche, & Richard, 2014; Pitta & Fowler, 2005). The accessibility of social media posits a greater reliance on such platforms for attainment of global information rather than traditional media outlets (Mangold & Faulds, 2009; Schivinski & Dabrowski, 2016).

Social media have increasingly penetrated global societies over the past years. One study, concerning the degree of worldwide social network users, demonstrated an annual surge of active users from 1 billion users in 2010 to a projected 3 billion by 2021 (Statista, 2017). Social media platforms are regarded as the favoured information outlets among Millennials and are notably the sought and preferred channels for obtaining updates on the fashion industry (Statista, 2017). The fashion world has also demonstrated dedication to social media mediums, as the 2016 Milan Fashion Week revealed heavy Instagram traffic of over 60 per cent of users relying on online influential personalities for the latest happenings (Statista, 2016). This exhibits the degree of clout social media communication has acquired within the fashion industry in relaying real-time material. Fashion labels build on the potential of virtual mediums in disseminating content across a wide scope. The Millennial group has inherently assumed social media channels as information portals powered by user interactions (Kilian, Hennigs, & Langner, 2012; Williams et al., 2012; Whiting & Williams, 2013). Recurring social interactions evolve into relationships among participants, enabling brands to pursue ties with customers into those of devotion, trust and loyalty, constituting a foundation for promised relationship equity that consumer and brand can profit from (Lemon, Rust, & Zeithaml, 2001; Kim & Ko, 2012; Vogel, Evanschitzky, & Ramaseshan, 2008).

In considering the social identity theory, this chapter investigates how the application of social media brand communities, and its manifestations, may engage customers by influencing social identity. The social identity theory embroils an individual's chase to allocate him/herself or others to social groups that embody a symbolic value (Tajfel, 1972). Individuals are drawn to social collectives that offer grounds to build the self through associations (Ashforth & Mael, 1989; Hogg & Terry, 2000). Much research has been dedicated to the underlying consumer motive of exercising brand affiliations in developing a desired social identity (Arnett, German, & Hunt, 2003; Bhattacharya & Sen, 2003; Lam et al., 2010). An individual seeks to employ the consumption of recognised brands in constructing his/her own identity while decoding others' identities (Elliot & Wattanasuwan, 1998; Helal, Ozuem, & Lancaster, 2018; Kleine, Kleine, & Kernan, 1993). Social eminence can be furthered via conspicuous consumption of what constitutes popular culture at a given time. The fashion world is an essential contributor to popular culture that can be utilised in acquiring social placement (Barron, 2012). Social placement is secured by affiliating to fashion labels that personify a lifestyle or personality akin to the lifestyle exalted by the desired social group. Consumers exploit discernible fashion brands that may offer a 'distinctive' identity but conform to a social circle of identical social identities. Social inclusion is achieved by an individual's ability to inhabit an identity enacted by a social group and its members, demonstrating the degree of influence a sought after community is capable of imparting to the development of self-identity (Ashmore et al., 2004; Heere et al., 2011).

A brand's online presence serves a functional intent of extending visibility while retaining a symbolic ambition that consumers may deploy in advancing social identities through brand affiliation. By employing social media brand communities, brands present consumers with fundamental grounds from which to derive tangible and intangible benefits. The virtual world represents the anomalous evolution of brand-customer interactivity from the physical bounds of brick-and-mortar sites to immeasurable, informal engagement through social media (Edelman, 2010; Fromm & Garton, 2013); a dynamic of communication that the Millennial age has normalised. Extensive literature is available on the administration of social media marketing advances, yet present studies do not address social media brand communities among Millennials in the fashion industry. This research seeks to expand on the influence of social media brand communities as marketing practices on the Millennial age, and this generation's pursuit of social identity through brand interactions. This study provides a foundation for fashion labels to progress the application of online brand communities in reaching consumers.

BACKGROUND

The fashion industry comprises an approximate 2 per cent of the world's Gross Domestic Product and is valued at over 2.4 trillion US dollars (McKinsey, 2016). The McKinsey Global Fashion Index projects industry sales growth of 3.5 to 4.5 per cent in 2019, highlighting growth in the premium and luxury sectors (BOF & McKinsey & Co., 2019). An in-depth analysis, The State of Fashion 2019, by UK-based Business of Fashion and renowned McKinsey & Company, considers the anticipated internal and external shifts in the retail and fashion industry for 2019. The active consumer is only projected to gain importance, as consumers uphold as primary contributors to product recognition through online channels. This consumer values omni-channel experiences incorporating social media platforms as information search points that lead to brand websites, in-store click-and-collect and comparable services, facilitating the movement between offline and online channels (BOF & McKinsey & Co., 2018). Brands are encouraged to adopt a disruptive approach in exceling within a highly competitive market. Social media provides the chief channel for fashion labels to veer from traditional methods in establishing inventive advances as digitised, impulsive innovators (BOF & McKinsey & Co., 2019). Brands are consequently emboldened to re-invent user-experiences through disruptive digitisation.

Social networking sites have achieved global penetration of approximately 71 per cent as of 2018, followed by an anticipated growth to over 73 per cent by 2021 (Statista, 2017). Such figures accentuate the extent of widespread online saturation within day-to-day interactions. The degree of social media adoption varies between regions as North America leads with 70 per cent penetration, followed by Europe and Asia-Pacific respectively (Statista, 2018). Universal exposure is guaranteed through the stretch social media outlets provide. Fashion labels from fast fashion to high-end sectors such as H&M, Zara, Louis Vuitton and Chanel, among others, have comparably achieved impressive visibility percentages through social networking avenues (Statista, 2016). Influential online presence can be attained through platforms like Instagram, a multibillion-dollar networking service enabling fashion brands to effectuate a 98 per cent penetration rate (Statista, 2016). Snap's ephemeral images and live video posts have similarly provided retail brands with leading penetration rates among consumers (Statista, 2017). Fashion industry frontrunners demonstrate reliance on prominent social media sites to ensure awareness as studies demonstrate the importance Millennials place on social media in remaining up-to-date on fashion trends (Statista, 2017).

The fashion industry has adapted to a contemporary virtual realm of unreserved reciprocity of content among brands and consumers. This communal platform enriches brand-customer relationships, reinforcing brand communities and emboldening customers to exert affiliation to esteemed brands. The nature of consumer-centric, user-generated content conduces to the development of brand perceptions (Berthon, Pitt, & Campbell, 2008; Christodoulides, Jevons, & Bonhomme, 2012). As customers are encouraged to readily participate with opinions, reviews, admiration, and brand association, brand impressions are elicited among a community of consumers, indicating optimistic correlations between a brand's social media activity and ensuing brand recognition (Hutter et al., 2013). Consumers comparably benefit from association with a brand community that retains the potential to further social identity based on a brand's perceived impression (Bhattacharya & Sen, 2003; Escalas & Bettman, 2005; Helal, 2019). Lemon, Rust, and Zeithaml (2001) explore the drivers of customer equity as an imperative foundation for marketing practices. *Value* and *brand equity* consider a purchaser's brand evaluation derived from the monetary or non-monetary cost of possessing the brand and the inclusive perception of the brand, respectively. *Relationship equity* refers to the non-functional exchange between a brand and customer, alluding to a deeper relation that bonds customers to brands. The potential of added value from consuming or being affiliated with a brand name enhance the bond shared between brand and customer (Lemon, Rust, & Zeithaml, 2001). Sentimental interactions are cultivated through social media brand communities that encourage members to chase brand affiliation for the perceived outcome of social enhancement.

The notion of social media stems from a basis of free-flowing user-generated content that inherently prompts the universal contribution of global societies (Van Dijck, 2013). According to Evans (2012), 'Social media is the democratisation of information, transforming people from content readers to content publishers. It is the shift from a broadcast mechanism to a many-to-many model, rooted in conversations between authors, people, and peers' (Evans, 2012, p. 32). This democratic setting allows for an equality-driven awareness of content reciprocity among all participating members. By route of social media, conversations have reformed to embody a casual, back-and-forth standard for interacting.

Millennials represent the prominent technologically integrated age, engaging diverse platforms for daily communication. Platforms such as Facebook, Instagram, Twitter and Snap each distinctively exemplify a disposition that users appropriately access to communicate on matters of politics, economy, society and environment. The Millennial cohort, particularly between 18 to 29 years of age, holds the highest degree of social media usage (Deloitte, 2017; Smith & Anderson, 2018; Statista, 2016). This age group does not have precise beginning and end dates but some researchers believe Millennials' birth years fall between the early 1980s and the early 2000s (Ng, Schweitxer & Lyons, 2010; Rainer & Rainer, 2011). Howe and Strauss (2000) define the generation as individuals born between 1982 and 2004. This generation values the reach of social media that allows users to be integrated into different community environments across varied networking sites (Bolton et al., 2013; Rainer & Rainer, 2011). Internet-instituted networks disregard the physicality of geographic boundaries, impelling widespread Millennials to emulate a prevalent culture of worldwide homogeneous behaviour (Moore, 2012). Marketers excel from targeting Millennial ages based on the collectively harmonised approval of definite values and attitudes (Schewe & Meredith, 2004).

CONTEXT AND FOUNDATION

Social media has progressively immersed into routine, day-to-day interactions over the past decade. While this phenomenon was primarily centred on an unregulated free-flow of content by individual users, it later evolved to outlets embraced by individuals, organisations and industries alike (Hennig-Thurau et al., 2010; Kaplan & Haenlein, 2012). Extensive literature has explored the development of social media (Hanna, Rohm, & Crittenden, 2011; Kaplan & Haenlein, 2012; Kietzmann et al., 2011; Mangold & Faulds, 2009; Murugesan, 2007; Whiting & Williams, 2013; Williams, Crittenden, Keo, & McCarty, 2012). Kaplan and Haenlein (2010) famously defined social media as a 'group of Internet-based applications that build on the ideological and technological foundations of Web 2.0, and allow the creation and exchange of user generated content' (Kaplan & Haenlein, 2010, p. 61). Social media is built on a body of networks that is powered by the notion of an accessible flow of user-generated information (Van Dijck & Poell, 2013). Online participants produce an informative environment by circulating news on various topics, including product and service feedback (Blackshaw & Nazzaro, 2006). An era of technologically apt Millennial consumers is actuated, empowered by the unreserved dynamic of the virtual realm (Kozinets, 1999; Williams et al., 2012). Social media participants are motivated to interconnect in social interchange (Fischer &

Reuber, 2011; Susarla, Oh, & Tan, 2012), effectuating a social setting that converges individual inputs into consolidated reflections that weigh on the other participating users (Parameswaran & Whinston, 2007).

Whiting and Williams (2013) derive seven themes of using social media in a study considering the reasoning of social media usage based on extensive literature of current uses and gratifications. The themes, including social interaction, information seeking, entertainment, relaxation, passing time, convenience utility and communicatory utility, uphold a composition of social media use that is founded on social interchange for functional and symbolic self-enhancement. User relations and communities are formed and strengthened from frequent back-and-forth exchange (Hansen, Schneirderman, & Smith, 2011; Ozuem, Thomas & Lancaster, 2016). The nature of virtual outlets motivates consumers to freely voice personal viewpoints, tipping the balance of power to consumers within a transition of 'bottom-up marketing' (Karpinski, 2005). As brand marketers seek to engage consumers in co-creative settings, social media is recognised as a manifestation of societies that marketers can administer in stimulating audiences (Hanna, Rohm, & Crittenden, 2011). Social media presents brands and customers with a limitless outlet to build relations and affiliations through online societies. In the process of identifying online communities, it is imperative to outline what brand communities entail.

Brand communities have been extensively acknowledged in academia and corporate markets among researchers and marketers (Muniz & O'Guinn, 2001; Cova & Pace, 2006; Stokburger-Sauer, 2010; McAlexander, Koenig, & Schouten, 2006; Schau, Muniz, & Arnould, 2009). Industry professionals have advanced marketing methods past the limits of an individualist understanding to a collective approach to consumption (Cova, 1997). Social influences are heightened among individuals in groups they identify with, creating a 'tribal' effect that bonds group members (Cova & Cova, 2002; Gainer & Fischer, 1994). Individualised brand-customer relationships recede in solely sustaining solid affinity (Berry, 1995; Iacobucci, 1994) as marketers recognise the gravity of social influence in brand communities (Cova & Cova, 2002; Dholakia, Bagozzi, & Pearo, 2004; McAlexander, Koenig, & Schouten, 2006; Schouten & McAlexander, 1995). Muniz and O'Guinn (2001) define brand community as a physically boundless society of consumer relations based on the shared admiration of a brand. Communities can be identified through three fundamental markers. The first, concerning consciousness of kind, involves the sentiments that consolidate community affiliates to one another while inflating the gap between non-members of the community (Bagozzi & Dholakia, 2006; Gusfield, 1978; Muniz & O'Guinn, 2001). Weber (1978) establishes joint consciousness as an indicator of belonging. The next marker comprises shared rituals and traditions ingrained in a brand's history and emblematically practised as the culture of a community (Muniz & O'Guinn, 2001). The third marker involves the personal dedication invested as members harbour an obligation to other members, the group and a brand (Muniz & O'Guinn, 2001). The following indicators serve as the bases of communities in nurturing connections and relationships among members.

In asserting the dominance of customer experience in perpetuating brand communities, McAlexander, Schouten, and Koenig (2002) proposed a customer-centric model of brand community. The paradigm accentuates a customer's positioning as the focal explication in instituting the necessary member integration to ensue positive aftermaths. McAlexander, Schouten, and Koenig (2006) explore four component relationships of the conceptualised model. *Customer-product relationship* refers to the quality of the products or services exchanged by brand and customer, whereby optimistic experiences facilitate encouraging consumer perceptions of brand affiliation. *Consumer-brand relationship* reveals the symbolic attachment consumers may form with brands. *Customer-institution relationship* refers to the ensuing connection a customer develops with the housing company of the brand. Lastly, the *customer-customer relationship* explores the weight of community word-of-mouth on receiving consumers. Brand community members' opinions and purchase intentions are inclined to divert based on the unified disposition of majority community members (McAlexander, Schouten, & Koenig, 2006). This extensive examination of brand community relationships displays the complex underlying forces that comprise a community and drive its success.

Customers branch across widespread scopes in building networks through the reach of social media outlets (Mangold & Faulds, 2009). Kozinets (1999) identifies 'e-tribalizing' as an emergence of virtual tribal societies arising from networked interactions. Consumer behaviour is observed by marketers from a novel standpoint (Kozinets, 1999, 2002) in the way that social media lends a comprehensive insight absent from traditional interaction. The Internet has occupied platforms for user-generated dialogue in different forms since its inception, yet social media outlets have triggered personalised interactions by offering users accounts to project their own identity comparable to realistic offline contact (Ross et al., 2009). The open display of interpersonal relationships publicised through networked platforms like Facebook or Instagram enables organisations to reap greater knowledge of consumers.

In an extensive exploration of social media based brand communities, Habibi, Laroche, and Richard (2014) address five underlying factors that distinguish brand communities on social media from other brand communities. The first element is *social context* including the intricate consumer/member information gained from social media services. The second aspect refers to the adaptable and casual *structure* held by communities. The third factor of social media based brand communities is the vast *scale* embodied by communities operating on such avenues. Fourth is the unique nature of social media in offering platforms for creative posts that instigate engagement and represent a notion of *storytelling*. Finally, an imperative dimension to collective societies effectuated on social media is *affiliated brand communities* arising from participating members cultivating deeper connections to form in-groups of smaller circles within a brand community (Habibi, Laroche, & Richard, 2014). Social media dynamics facilitate brand communities with engaging settings consumers utilise in self-expression and brand identification for individualised motives. Online social networks are an essential contributor to valuable brand communities, offering human connections and memorable experiences (Fournier & Lee, 2009). Virtual brand communities conduce to consumer experiences on a scope that exceeds definitive limitations through vast networks on social media.

ADDED VALUE THROUGH SOCIAL MEDIA BRAND COMMUNITIES

Brands recognise the advantages of engaging in the two-way communication social media entails as a potential for leveraging brand-customer interactions (Helal & Ozuem, 2019; Hudson et al., 2016; Laroche, Habibi, Richard, & Sankaranarayanan, 2012; Pentina, Gammoh, Zhang, & Mallin, 2013; Schivinski & Dabrowski, 2016; Zhang, Benyoucef, & Zhao, 2016). Social interplay within brand communities flourishes across the web of networks social media extends (Habibi, Laroche, & Richard, 2014; Zaglia, 2013), fostering brand and consumer engagement. Marketers have drawn primary attention to brand-customer relationships elicited via social media

(Fournier & Avery, 2011). This chapter addresses the leverage of social media brand communities in impacting Millennial consumers.

Knowledge Seeking/Sharing and EWOM

The clout one social media brand mention carries the potential of yielding is demonstrated by the global permeation of over 2.4 billion social network users in 2017, a number only estimated to reach 3 billion users in 2021 (Statista, 2017). As Millennial consumers rally to universal social networking sites in remaining relevant, brands emulate this transition to access new-age consumers (Tiago & Veríssimo, 2014). Internet technologies intensify brand-customer interchange in the way that joining parties are devoted social media platforms fitted for production and circulation of content (Brown, Kozinets, & Sherry, Jr., 2003; Gallaugher & Ransbotham, 2010). The ample presence of contributing consumers, brands and content dissemination produces affluent and sustainable brand community environments. The freedom to produce and distribute material invokes a source of information known as electronic word-of-mouth (eWOM) (Hennig-Thurau et al., 2004; Trusov, Buckin, & Pauwels, 2009). Brands acknowledge the implications of upholding eWOM as a marketing instrument to consumers chasing authentic feedback for brand knowledge (Cheung & Thadani, 2012; Chevalier & Mayzlin, 2006; Dellarocas, 2003; Duan, Gu, & Whinston, 2008). Social media's elaborate networked society draws consumer attention to trending brands (Daugherty & Hoffman, 2014), extending simple attention into awareness and stimulating purchasing decisions among customers (Godes & Mayzlin, 2004; Park, Lee, & Han, 2007).

Virtual means have propagated the use and acceptance of eWOM among individual and communes of consumers to a measure far superior to offline mediums (Gruen, Osmonbekov, & Czaplewski, 2006; Taken Smith, 2012; Veloutsou & McAlonan, 2012). Both brands and customers profit from the generous movement of information propelled by online social interplay (Tikkanen, Hietanen, Henttonen, & Rokka, 2009). Various motives may drive customers to seek out and partake in eWOM (Balasubramanian & Mahajan, 2001; Hennig-Thurau et al., 2004). Balasubramanian and Mahajan (2001) examine the underlying utility factors of intrinsic adoption of eWOM in communities, citing *focus-related utility* as the gratification a customer derives from sharing information and evidently value to the community. *Consumption utility* deliberates the value gained from receiving other community members' inputs. *Approval utility* considers the value of validation acquired from community members accepting an associate's contribution (Balasubramanian & Mahajan, 2001). Such utility types unfold the incentives that drive customers to engage in eWOM in online brand communities. Hennig-Thurau et al. (2004) consider a further two utility types in the dynamic of brand communities: *moderator-related utility* considers a moderator responsible for managing the influx of material from consumers, and *homeostase utility* is formulated on the notion of balance theory (Heider, 1946; Newcomb, 1953) concerning the demand for balance in individuals' lives by maintaining neutrality through positive and negative expressions (Hennig-Thurau et al., 2004). While organisations may be hesitant of the loss of power within settings of user-generated and led information, negative eWOM can be monitored and amended accordingly (Brown, Broderick, & Lee, 2007; Kozinets, de Valck, Wojnicki, & Wilner, 2010). Existing literature debates that positive or negative eWOM bears encouraging outcomes as any exposure advances brand awareness in one form or another (Berger, Sorensen, & Rasmussen, 2010; Duan, Gu, & Whinston, 2008; Liu, 2006). The fashion industry can expect to prosper from optimistic outcomes of eWOM circulation as such interaction is regarded as authentic (Kulmala, Mesiranta, & Tuominen, 2013; Wolny & Mueller, 2013), which becomes all the more feasible through virtual brand communities of extensive user-generated communication.

Community Participation and Consumer Engagement

Online brand communities encourage and facilitate the direct participation of community members (Woisetschlager, Hartleb, & Blut, 2008). The core interest that consolidates a community (Muniz & O'Guinn, 2001) invites members to partake in that community (Royo-Vela & Casamassima, 2011). Active participation is necessary to uphold communities and ensure continuity (Casalo, Flavián, & Guinalíu, 2007). Frequent engagement guarantees appealing, interactive environments that fuel long-run community endurance (Koh & Kim, 2004). Koh and Kim (2004) indicate the direct correlation between the degree of knowledge shared and community engagement in a research that examines the knowledge dispensed within online communities. Higher outputs of participation within virtual communities accounted for comparably larger levels of distributed knowledge (Koh & Kim, 2004). Emotive development in the form of trust and loyalty can be expected among consumers in brand communities evoking continual participation (Casalo, Flavián, & Guinalíu, 2007; Holland & Baker, 2001; Koh & Kim, 2004).

The digital empowerment of consumers has propelled the progression of customer-centric methods in marketing brands (Sashi, 2012). In the advent of virtual communicative platforms that promote interaction, industry professionals have realised the relevance of consumer engagement in modern-day dynamics (Baldus, Voorhees, & Calantone, 2014; Dessart, Veloutsou, & Morgan-Thomas, 2015; Sashi, 2012; Wirtz et al., 2013). Hollebeek, Glynn and Brodie (2014) define consumer-brand engagement as 'a consumer's positively valenced cognitive, emotional and behavioural brand-related activity during, or related to, specific consumer/brand interactions' (Hollebeek, Glynn, & Brodie, 2014). Social media offers outlets of give-and-take activities including posts of photos, live feeds, shares, comments and 'likes' of other members' posts. Social media brand communities accommodate real-time interactions that augment community engagement, consequently generating positive settings of copious community member relationships (Habibi, Laroche, & Richard, 2014). Social media's interactivity paves the route for continual instant contact that bears the potential to elicit deeper ties among community members.

Sashi (2012) identifies seven stages of a customer engagement cycle, commencing with an introductory stage of *connection* that a customer instigates with a brand or comparable customers in the quest for a desired product. The next step is the *interaction* assumed from recurring contact, which intrinsically assists in the co-creation of value between brands and consumers (Prahalad & Ramaswamy, 2004; Sashi, 2012). Sashi (2012) explores the third stage, *satisfaction* as the deciding factor of a member's continuity extracted from contentment with community interactions. With time, satisfaction engenders the fourth stage, *customer retention*. The fifth stage, *commitment*, subsumes calculative commitment, an approach of practicality based on the lack of substitute possibilities, and affective commitment, an emotional approach that arises from mutuality in a relationship (Gounaris, 2005; Kumar, Hibbard, & Stern, 1994; de Ruyter, Moorman, & Lemmink, 2001). Emotional bonds compel customers to partake in social media brand communities and share brand experiences as part of the sixth stage, *advocacy* (Sashi, 2012). The preceding stages of brand familiarisation lead to the final stage of *engagement*, whereby community relationships evolve to an arrangement of co-creating value (Sashi, 2012). Fashion brands have joined consumers in establishing a collaborative environment of value creation via social networking sites.

Customer Equity

Companies hold the obligation of preserving customer equity by managing and augmenting customer value as an asset comparable to other company assets (Blattberg, Getz, & Thomas, 2001; Kumar & George, 2007; Rust, Lemon, & Zeithaml, 2004). Lemon, Rust, and Zeithaml (2001) and Rust, Lemon, and Zeithaml (2004) classify customer equity into value, brand and relationship equity. Value equity refers to a customer's assessment of brand utility by appraising what is given up in acquisition of the brand. Brand equity considers a customer's subjective view of what the brand entails. Relationship equity focuses on the ties developed between a brand and customer inclusive of objective and subjective brand impressions (Rust, Lemon, & Zeithaml, 2000).

Brand Equity

Lemon, Rust, and Zeithaml (2001) construe brand equity to embody a consumer's symbolic evaluation of what is gained from brand consumption. According to Keller (1993), *customer-based brand equity* alludes to the impact brand recognition has on consumer response to brand advertising. Keller (1993) delves into brand knowledge as a brand node in customers' minds connected to brand associations, made up of brand awareness and brand image. Brand awareness alludes to a brand's potent positioning in the market demonstrated in a consumer's ability to identify a brand (Rossiter & Percy, 1987). Awareness includes brand *recognition*, determined by consumers distinguishing a brand from others, and brand *recall*, concerning consumers extracting a brand from memory (Keller, 1993). Within a continuum of brand knowledge, brand awareness indicates the preliminary point of brand recognition (Hoyer & Brown, 1990). A brand's saturation of its industry offers recognition that familiarises brand presence and reduces uncertainty and presumed risk among customers (Huang, Schrank, & Dubinsky, 2004). The image of a brand is derived from brand perceptions influenced by brand associations stored in consumers' minds (Keller, 1993). Customer brand impressions take the form of brand nodes assumed within clientele recollections. Unique, optimistic brand associations discern one brand from an assembly of brands, shaping brand equity (Keller, 1993).

Keller's (2009) research on brand equity management in multimedia retail environments applies the brand resonance model (Keller, 2001) to delineate effective scenarios of accessing customers and fortifying brand-consumer ties. The extension of marketing communicative methods into the domain of new-age virtual platforms has expedited brand resonance and ultimately strengthened brand equity. Initially, *brand awareness* is magnified through online interactive forums that present consumers with ample information for purchase decisions. Second, *brand associations* are escalated as imagery overtones contribute to the creative content that constitutes brand personality. *Brand attitudes* arise from interactions in collaborative settings in the manner of brand communities. *Brand activity* is particularly apparent in online interactive environments as it suggests effective consumer engagement that fulfils functional requests of information while imbuing symbolic attachments of brand loyalty (Keller, 2009). Social media brand communities comprise separate factors that collaboratively evince brand equity among an engrossed community; demonstrating the progression in brand-customer dynamics to jointly conduce value. Brand experiences in social media brand communities guide Millennials' input on the perception and equity formed of a brand.

Relationship Equity

Relationship equity examines the connection between a brand and customer past the brand and value equity. Relationship equity considers the aspects that bind a brand and customer beyond brand and value equity (Richards & Jones, 2008; Rust, Lemon, & Zeithaml, 2000). Emotional ties in the form of interactional activities, such as loyalty schemes or brand communities, allow brands to conserve relationship equity (Rust, Zeithaml, & Lemon, 2000). The instigation of attachment and trust drive the contact between a brand and customer from one of mere transactional communication to revered relationship (Morgan & Hunt, 1994). Higher degrees of participation in brand communities produce surroundings of trust and commitment among members. Trust is argued to be an antecedent of loyalty (Chaudhuri & Holbrook, 2001; Chiu, Huang, & Yen, 2010; Kim, Chung, & Lee, 2011). Brand communities via social media elicit interplay that empowers social structures and builds brand trust, ultimately inspiring loyalty (Ba, 2001; Walden, 2000; Zheng,

Cheung, Lee, & Liang, 2015). Habibi, Laroche, and Richard (2014) surmise two methods whereby enhancement of brand-customer ties could fortify brand trust. The first sees that frequent interactions across an extended time period through settings of brand communities intensify relationships and reinforce trust. The second identifies the parallel correlation of relationships and information sharing as ample information in brand communities allows trust to supersede any feelings of doubt consumers may experience (Habibi, Laroche, & Richard, 2014; Ba, 2001). The outcome of positive consumer engagement on social media invites encouraging functional and symbolic interactions that advance brand loyalty (Bruhn, Schnebelen, & Schafer, 2014; Schivinski & Dabrowski, 2016). Passive consumer actions such as 'lurking' or observing interactions have also demonstrated impressive aftermaths in garnering loyalty (Shang et al., 2006).

MOTIVATOR FOR SOCIAL MEDIA BRAND COMMUNITIES

Social media brand communities present Millennial users with a medium to gather information, engage, and build brand perceptions and relationships from. Such mediums have also been adopted by Millennials as platforms for self-expression. Consumers identify with brand communities that ensure integration into a desired social collective (Algesheimer, Dholakia, & Herrmann, 2005).

Social Media and Social Identity

Users are extended the platform to openly relay identities via the broad reach social media networks afford (Bagozzi & Dholakia, 2002; Bargh & McKenna, 2004; Dholakia, Bagozzi, & Pearo, 2004; Helal & Ozuem, 2016, 2018; Hogg & Reid, 2006; Pentina, Prybutok, & Zhang, 2008; Hennig-Thurau, Gwinner, Walsh, & Gremler, 2004; Kane, Alavi, Labianca, & Borgatti, 2014; Schivinski & Dabrowski, 2016; Veletsianos, 2013). The networks of contacts interlinked into circles based on brands and shared social interests across social media outlets embolden brand devotees to affiliate with that brand for self-enrichment. Customers flaunt their involvement to conspicuous social media brand communities in their quest to frame and affirm identity. Apart from attending to functional varieties of information distribution and customer engagement (Ma & Agarwal, 2007), brand communities avail in inflating customers' self-worth by producing formulas of social interactions that embody the individual he/she wishes to be perceived as (Donath, 1999). Such valued member interactions are fostered into bonds that feed consumers' demand for social placement (Ma & Agarwal, 2007; Ren et al., 2012; Zhu & Chen, 2015). Brand association carries the promise of retaining an identity that incites social placement.

Social identity theory maintains that an individual wishes to assign him/ herself or others into social groupings (Ashforth & Mael, 1989; Tajfel & Turner, 1985). Turner (1985) identifies groupings or categories to be archetypal qualities held by group members. Social classification effectuates inclusion in an aggregate, as individuals cognitively allot one another into decisive settings as a way of defining each other (Ashforth & Mael, 1989). An individual identifies him/herself to groups that epitomise social categories with which that individual seeks to align (Hogg & Abrams, 1988; Hogg, Terry, & White, 1995). Individuals chase after social categories on the premise that social consensus is attained from exercising such categories and being associated with a corresponding group (Jenkins, 2008; Trepte, 2008). Social consent secured within a group enriches an individual's sense of 'belonging', thus elevating self-identity. The terms social identification and group identification are used interchangeably for the reason that social identity stems from identification with a group (Tolman, 1943; Tajfel, 1982). Tajfel (1978) outlines social identity as 'that part of an individual's self-concept which derives from his knowledge of his membership of a social group (or groups) together with the value and emotional significance attached to that membership' (Tajfel, 1978, p. 62). Social identity is inferred to contain three factors: a *cognitive* factor considering the recognition of inclusion in a group, an *evaluative* component of positive or negative value implications of group inclusion, and an *emotional* factor of emotional absorption in a group (Tajfel, 1978, 1982). The three components collectively evoke group identification. Individuals chase social categories and associate with groups that reward them with the cognitive and emotional convenience they covet (Fisher & Wakefield, 1998). In overtly expressing affiliation to a society, a follower may pursue the compass to invest in a sought social perspective that incites self-worth and advances identity.

Social categorisation creates mutuality in groups based on similarities shared between members (in-group), whereas the categories that accentuate the bond within a group comparably isolate members of different groups from one another (out-group) (Tajfel, 1959, 1969). This is termed *depersonalisation*, the resolve that members are viewed as group affiliates as opposed to separate entities. The notion of depersonalisation alters an individual's self-perception as his/her beliefs and behaviours veer to mirror the all-embracing perspective held by the pursued group (Hogg, 2001; Hogg & Terry, 2000). Social identity theory comprises two outlooks, a personal disposition and a social view of the aggregate an individual attaches to (Luhtanen & Crocker, 1992; Nowak, Szamrej, & Latané, 1990). Personal and social identities are both sought through behaviour that centres on individuality, yet an individualism that appertains to the quintessential values of the group socially followed by an individual. Brand consumption exposes a manner of expression individuals manipulate to convey personal qualities that overall appeal their position within their social group. Personal identity is moderated to shadow the social identity an individual aspires to personify, a response that is heightened in salient environments (Onorato & Turner, 2004; Turner, 1982). Individuals are more inclined to exercise behaviour, in public settings of product and brand consumption, which accommodates a salient identity they socially communicate. In doubtful times, individuals deliberate in-group identification in adapting attitudes and behaviours to align with group perceptions that sequentially affirm an individual's sense of self (Hogg et al., 2006). While individuals tend to resort to a range of daily activities to foment self-expression, particular brand consumption has been a major approach to detailing the self (Belk, 1988; Schembri, Merrilees, & Kristiansen, 2010; Stokburger-Sauer & Teichmann, 2013). Consumption is representative as it allots individuals an instrument to inflate identity that symbolically relates to the social collective to which they aspire to mimic a similar lifestyle (Gabriel & Lang, 1995; Wattanasuwan, 2005). Consumers pursue brands that promise societal inclusion and reassert social presence. Customers are attracted to brands that entail symbolic outcomes of self-enhancement through brand identification (Bhattacharya & Sen, 2003).

Social media offers visibility that exudes a social influence over users' interactions. Users are presented the global platforms to vocalise personal viewpoints across various topics. However, in keeping with a personal identity that coheres with the coveted social identity (Clement & Krueger, 2002; Haslam, Oakes, Reynolds, & Turner, 1999; Hogg & Turner, 1987; Kietzmann et al., 2011), social media users are cautious to align verbalisations and behaviours with those of the desired social circle. Kleine, Kleine & Kernan (1993) deliberated the influence of social acceptance on the self-fulfilment an individual receives from imparting a social identity. The findings indicated higher importance placed on an identity that is socially commended, thus demonstrating a parallel correspondence between communal affirmation and significance of social identity. Social media brand communities have made salience progressively predominant as widespread circles converge into brand followers over a common platform. These online communities offer users the channel to attain both individual and collective objectives (Rheingold, 2002; Bagozzi & Dholakia, 2002). The three components previously mentioned by Tajfel (1978) are read-dressed in examining an individual's *cognition* of his/her own involvement in a brand community, which fosters the *emotional* belonging and commitment that matures into relationships (Ashforth & Mael, 1989; Bagozzi & Dholakia, 2002; Bergami & Bagozzi, 2000; Bhattacharya & Sen, 2003). The *evaluative* component is observed in community members' value of social identity dependent on the overall self-worth acquired from group engagements (Dholakia, Bagozzi, & Pearo, 2004).

Social media brand communities appeal to consumers' urge to employ brand association in their aspiration to establish social accord among a desired collective. Social media users access fashion brand communities to publicly proclaim brand affiliation through social networking sites and instil presence in a particular society.

MANAGERIAL IMPLICATIONS AND RECOMMENDATIONS

This chapter seeks to offer an insight into how social media brand communities have impacted Millennials in the fashion industry (Godey et al., 2016; Gummerus, Liljander, Weman, & Pihlstrom, 2012; Habibi, Laroche, & Richard, 2014; Kim & Ko, 2012; Laroche, Habibi, Richard, & Sankaranarayanan, 2012; Zheng, Cheung, Lee, & Liang, 2015). Social media's immense induction as the contemporary means of communication has induced Millennials' adoption of virtual avenues in self-expression, including showcasing brand affiliations. This chapter reveals the possibilities of brand communities in global social media platforms as means to advance concerted symbolic engagements that progress consumers' social identities. In the quest to access the aspired public prestige, consumers are fascinated by the overt interactions with a brand and its community.

Brands profit from engaging social media communities that bring together global users, allowing brands to deliver information in real-time. The distribution of information is expedited with every exchange, comment or share that additionally broadcasts brand messages to multitudes of networks. Consumers develop affection for brands as they attribute greater attention to relaying brand information in communities (Algesheimer, Dholakia, & Herrmann, 2005; Fournier & Lee, 2009; Hatch & Schultz, 2010; Muniz & O'Guinn, 2001). Customer accessibility is heightened and brand awareness is enriched through social media marketing techniques (Godey et al., 2016). Social media's progressive environment allows fashion companies to share live feeds featuring collection and product campaigns, fashion runs, and 'influential' endorsers that shape brand perceptions and progress brand equity. Brand devotees are consequently exposed to a symbolic representation of what the brand personifies and potentially depicts as a lifestyle. Social media brand communities are utilised by consumers to express affiliation and identification with what a brand epitomises. This research can be applied as a foundation for future studies to build on.

While marketing disciplines continue to unfold in adapting to the new balance of consumer power shifts and significance of value co-creation (Grönroos & Voima, 2012; Prahalad & Ramaswamy, 2000), social media has contributed to consumer entitlement by offering global platforms for unrestricted vocalisation (Hanna, Rohm, & Crittenden, 2011; Kaplan & Haenlein, 2010). Brands can take advantage of such channels in reaching consumers and co-creating value. This study examines the use of social media brand communities in the fashion industry among Millennials. Since inception, the fashion realm has embodied rigid approaches of top-to-bottom deliveries and brand-customer interactions within physical outlets. However, brand-customer relationships have been evolved and transposed to virtual channels through the likes of social media, as brands gain real-time access to consumers and consumers revel in broader understanding of brands. Consumers, today, seek greater insight than functional product information; rather they demand and value insight that uncovers a brand's societal and environmental stance in the market (State of Fashion, 2019). Engaging brand communities via social media lends flexibility for brands and consumers to create value through loyal relationships between parties. This study seeks to underline the importance of employing modern channels that appeal to Millennials, particularly within a dynamic industry widely populated with competing brands. Brands recognise that the boundless adoption of social media curtails the control brands are accustomed to imposing through traditional methods. However, customer relationship management through overt channels multiplies positive eWOM from optimistic experiences. The accessibility and ease of communication with consumers extends a promotional instrument brands can utilise in conveying an inclusive brand image worldwide through a consistent brand tone.

This study considers the presence of social identity theory in social media and brand communities (Bagozzi & Dholakia, 2002; Dholakia, Bagozzi, & Pearo, 2004; Hogg & Reid, 2006; Pentina, Prybutok, & Zhang, 2008). This research acknowledges the underlying motivations of Millennials in participating with social media brand communities to further their own urgency for social identity. Consumers pursue brands for personal aspirational motivations while brands are responsive to encouraging brand images that flatter a particular lifestyle. Brand community members are motivated to support brand perceptions through group identification that unites community members and distances other individuals or collectives, who are not members. Social media brand communities allow self-expression through brand association to be witnessed by a wider network of connections that may or may not belong to the community, allowing social identity to be expressed on a larger scale.

REFERENCES

Algesheimer, R., Dholakia, U., & Herrmann, A. (2005). The social influence of brand community: Evidence from European car clubs. *Journal of Marketing, 69*(3), 19–34.

Arnett, D., German, S., & Hunt, S. (2003). The identity salience model of relationship marketing success: The case of nonprofit marketing. *Journal of Marketing, 67*(2), 89–105.

Arora, P. (2014). *The leisure commons.* New York: Routledge.

Ashforth, B., & Mael, F. (1989). Social identity theory and the organization. *The Academy of Management Review, 14*(1), 20–39.

Ashmore, R., Deaux, K., & McLaughlin-Volpe, T. (2004). An organizing framework for collective identity: Articulation and significance of multidimensionality. *Psychological Bulletin, 130*(1), 80–114.

Ba, S. (2001). Establishing online trust through a community responsibility system. *Decision Support Systems, 31*(3), 323–336.

Bagozzi, R., & Dholakia, U. (2002). Intentional social action in virtual communities. *Journal of Interactive Marketing, 16*(2), 2–21.

Bagozzi, R., & Dholakia, U. (2006). Open source software user communities: A study of participation in linux user groups. *Management Science, 52*(7), 1099–1115.

Balasubramanian, S., & Mahajan, V. (2001). The economic leverage of the virtual community. *International Journal of Electronic Commerce, 5*(3), 103–138.

Baldus, B., Voorhees, C., & Calantone, R. (2015). Online brand community engagement: Scale development and validation. *Journal of Business Research, 68*(5), 2.

Bargh, J., & McKenna, K. (2004). The internet and social life. *Annual Review of Psychology, 55*(1), 573–590.

Barron, L. (2012). *Social theory in popular culture.* Basingstoke: Palgrave Macmillan.

Belk, R. (1988). Possessions and the extended self. *Journal of Consumer Research, 15*(2), 139.

Bergami, M., & Bagozzi, R. (2000). Self-categorization, affective commitment and group self-esteem as distinct aspects of social identity in the organization. *British Journal of Social Psychology, 39*(4), 555–577.

Berger, J., Sorensen, A., & Rasmussen, S. (2010). Positive effects of negative publicity: When negative reviews increase sales. *Marketing Science, 29*(5), 815–827.

Berry, L. (1995). Relationship marketing of services—growing interest, emerging perspectives. *Journal of The Academy of Marketing Science, 23*(4), 236–245.

Berthon, P., Pitt, L., & Campbell, C. (2008). Ad lib: When customers create the ad. *California Management Review, 50*(4), 6–30.

Bhattacharya, C., & Sen, S. (2003). Consumer-company identification: A framework for understanding consumers' relationships with companies. *Journal of Marketing, 67*(2), 76–88.

Blackshaw, P., & Nazzaro, M. (2006) Consumer-Generated Media (CGM) 101: Word-of-Mouth in the Age of the Web-Fortified Consumer. New York: Nielsen.

Blattberg, R., Getz, G., & Thomas, J. (2001). *Customer equity: Building and managing relationships as valuable assets.* Boston, Mass: Harvard Business School Press.

BOF & McKinsey & Co. (2018). *The state of fashion* (pp. 1–83). McKinsey & Co. Retrieved from https://cdn.businessoffashion.com/reports/ The_State_of_Fashion_2018_v2.pdf

BOF & McKinsey & Co. *The state of fashion* (pp. 1–102). McKinsey & Co. Retrieved from https://www.mckinsey.com/~/media/mckinsey/industries/ retail/our%20insights/the%20state%20of%20fashion%202019%20a%20 year%20of%20awakening/the-state-of-fashion-2019-final.ashx

Bolton, R., Parasuraman, A., Hoefnagels, A., Migchels, N., Kabadayi, S., & Gruber, T. et al. (2013). Understanding generation Y and their use of social media: A review and research agenda. *Journal of Service Management, 24*(3), 245–267.

Brown, J., Broderick, A., & Lee, N. (2007). Word of mouth communication within online communities: Conceptualizing the online social network. *Journal of Interactive Marketing, 21*(3), 2–20.

Brown, S., Kozinets, R., & Sherry, J. (2003). Teaching old brands new tricks: Retro branding and the revival of brand meaning. *Journal of Marketing, 67*(3), 19–33.

Bruhn, M., Schnebelen, S., & Schäfer, D. (2014). Antecedents and consequences of the quality of e-customer-to-customer interactions in B2B brand communities. *Industrial Marketing Management, 43*(1), 164–176.

Butler, B. (2001). Membership size, communication activity, and sustainability: A resource-based model of online social structures. *Information Systems Research, 12*(4), 346–362.

Casalo, L., Flavián, C., & Guinalíu, M. (2007). The influence of satisfaction, perceived reputation and trust on a consumer's commitment to a website. *Journal of Marketing Communications, 13*(1), 1–17.

Chappuis, B., Gaffey, B., & Parvizi, P. (2011). Are your customers becoming digital junkies? Retrieved from https://www.mckinsey.com/business-functions/marketing-and-sales/our-insights/are-your-customers-becoming-digital-junkies

Chaudhuri, A., & Holbrook, M. (2001). The chain of effects from brand trust and brand affect to brand performance: The role of brand loyalty. *Journal of Marketing, 65*(2), 81–93.

Cheung, C., & Thadani, D. (2012). The impact of electronic word-of-mouth communication: A literature analysis and integrative model. *Decision Support Systems, 54*(1), 461–470.

Chevalier, J., & Mayzlin, D. (2006). The effect of word of mouth on sales: Online book reviews. *Journal of Marketing Research, 43*(3), 345–354.

Chiu, C., Huang, H., & Yen, C. (2010). Antecedents of trust in online auctions. *Electronic Commerce Research and Applications, 9*(2), 148–159.

Christodoulides, G., Jevons, C., & Bonhomme, J. (2012). Memo to marketers: Quantitative evidence for change. *Journal of Advertising Research, 52*(1), 53–64.

Clement, R., & Krueger, J. (2002). Social categorization moderates social projection. *Journal of Experimental Social Psychology, 38*(3), 219–231.

Cova, B. (1997). Community and consumption. *European Journal of Marketing, 31*(3/4), 297–316.

Cova, B., & Cova, V. (2002). Tribal marketing: The tribalisation of society and its impact on the conduct of marketing. *European Journal of Marketing, 36*(5/6), 595–620.

Cova, B., & Pace, S. (2006). Brand community of convenience products: New forms of customer empowerment—the case "my Nutella The Community". *European Journal of Marketing, 40*(9/10), 1087–1105.

Daugherty, T., & Hoffman, E. (2014). eWOM and the importance of capturing consumer attention within social media. *Journal of Marketing Communications, 20*(1–2), 82–102.

de Ruyter, K., Moorman, L., & Lemmink, J. (2001). Antecedents of commitment and trust in customer–supplier relationships in high technology markets. *Industrial Marketing Management, 30*(3), 271–286.

Dellarocas, C. (2006). Strategic manipulation of internet opinion forums: Implications for consumers and firms. *Management Science, 52*(10), 1577–1593.

Deloitte. (2017). *The 2017 deloitte millennial survey* (pp. 1–31). United Kingdom: Deloitte. Retrieved from https://www2.deloitte.com/content/dam/Deloitte/global/Documents/About-Deloitte/gx-deloitte-millennial-survey-2017-executive-summary.pdf

Dessart, L., Veloutsou, C., & Thomas, A. (2015). Consumer engagement in online brand communities: A social media perspective. *Journal of Product & Brand Management, 24*(1), 28–42.

Dewing, M. (2010). *Social media: An introduction.* Ottawa: Library of Parliament.

Dholakia, U., Bagozzi, R., & Pearo, L. (2004). A social influence model of consumer participation in network- and small-group-based virtual communities. *International Journal of Research in Marketing, 21*(3), 241–263.

Donath, J. (1999). Identity and deception in the virtual community. In P. Kollack & M. Smith (Eds.), *Communities in Cyberspace* (1st ed., pp. 27–58). New York: Routledge.

Duan, W., Gu, B., & Whinston, A. (2008). The dynamics of online word-of-mouth and product sales—An empirical investigation of the movie industry. *Journal of Retailing, 84*(2), 233–242.

Edelman, D. (2010). Branding in the digital age: You're spending your money in all the wrong places. *Harvard Business Review, 88,* 62–69.

Elliott, R., & Wattanasuwan, K. (1998). Brands as symbolic resources for the construction of identity. *International Journal of Advertising, 17*(2), 131–144.

Escalas, J., & Bettman, J. (2003). You are what they eat: The influence of reference groups on consumers' connections to brands. *Journal of Consumer Psychology, 13*(3), 339–348.

Evans, D. (2012). *Social media marketing* (2nd ed.). Indianapolis, Ind.: John Wiley & Sons Publishing, Inc.

Evans, D. (2012). *Social media marketing* (2nd ed.). Indianapolis, Ind.: John Wiley & Sons Publishing, Inc. 32.

Fromm, J., & Garton, C. (2013). *Marketing to millennials* (pp. 60–87). United States of America: Barkley, Inc.

Fischer, E., & Reuber, A. (2011). Social interaction via new social media: (How) can interactions on Twitter affect effectual thinking and behavior? *Journal of Business Venturing, 26*(1), 1–18.

Fisher, R., & Wakefield, K. (1998). Factors leading to group identification: A field study of winners and losers. *Psychology and Marketing, 15*(1), 23–40.

Fournier, S., & Avery, J. (2011). The uninvited brand. *Business Horizons, 54*(3), 193–207.

Fournier, S., & Lee, L. (2009). Getting brand communities right. *Harvard Business Review*, 2–8.

Fuchs, C. (2014). *Social media: A critical introduction*. London: Sage Publications, Ltd.

Gabriel, Y., & Lang, T. (1995). *The unmanageable consumer*. London: Sage Publications.

Gainer, B., & Fischer, E. (1994). Community and consumption. *Advances in Consumer Research, 21*, p. 137.

Gallaugher, J., & Ransbotham, S. (2010). Social media and customer dialog management at starbucks. *MIS Quarterly Executive, 9*(4), 197–212.

Gillies, J., & Cailliau, R. (2000). *How the Web was born*. Oxford: Oxford University Press.

Godes, D., & Mayzlin, D. (2009). Firm-created word-of-mouth communication: Evidence from a field test. *Marketing Science, 28*(4), 721–739.

Godey, B., Manthiou, A., Pederzoli, D., Rokka, J., Aiello, G., Donvito, R., & Singh, R. (2016). Social media marketing efforts of luxury brands: Influence on brand equity and consumer behavior. *Journal of Business Research, 69*(12), 5833–5841.

Gounaris, S. (2005). Trust and commitment influences on customer retention: Insights from business-to-business services. *Journal of Business Research, 58*(2), 126–140.

Grönroos, C., & Voima, P. (2013). Critical service logic: Making sense of value creation and co-creation. *Journal of The Academy of Marketing Science, 41*(2), 133–150.

Gruen, T., Osmonbekov, T., & Czaplewski, A. (2006). eWOM: The impact of customer-to-customer online know-how exchange on customer value and loyalty. *Journal of Business Research, 59*(4), 449–456.

Gummerus, J., Liljander, V., Weman, E., & Pihlström, M. (2012). Customer engagement in a Facebook brand community. *Management Research Review, 35*(9), 857–877.

Gusfield, J. (1978). *Community: A critical response* (2nd ed.). New York: Harper Collophon Books.

Habibi, M., Laroche, M., & Richard, M. (2014). Brand communities based in social media: How unique are they? Evidence from two exemplary brand communities. *International Journal of Information Management, 34*(2), 123–132.

Hanna, R., Rohm, A., & Crittenden, V. (2011). We're all connected: The power of the social media ecosystem. *Business Horizons, 54*(3), 265–273.

Hansen, D., Schneiderman, B., & Smith, M. (2011). *Analyzing social media networks with NodeXL*. Amsterdam: Elsevier.

Haslam, S., Oakes, P., Reynolds, K., & Turner, J. (1999). Social identity salience and the emergence of stereotype consensus. *Personality and Social Psychology Bulletin, 25*(7), 809–818.

Hatch, M., & Schultz, M. (2010). Toward a theory of brand co-creation with implications for brand governance. *Journal of Brand Management, 17*(8), 590–604.

Heere, B., Walker, M., Yoshida, M., Ko, Y., Jordan, J., & James, J. (2011). Brand community development through associated communities: Grounding community measurement within social identity theory. *The Journal of Marketing Theory and Practice, 19*(4), 407–422.

Heider, F. (1946). Attitudes and cognitive organization. *The Journal of Psychology, 21*(1), 107–112.

Helal, G. (2019). The influence of social media brand communities on millennial brand perceptions in the fashion industry: A social identity outlook. In G. Bowen & W. Ozuem (Eds.), *Leveraging Computer-Mediated Marketing Environments* (pp. 143–172).

Helal, G., & Ozuem, W. (2016). The dynamics of social media in the fashion industry: The case of the millennial generation. In *Exceeding the Vision: Innovate, Integrate and Motivate* (pp. 194–202). United States of America: The Global Business and Technology Association.

Helal, G., & Ozuem, W. (2018). Social identity matters: Social media and brand perceptions in the fashion apparel and accessories industries. In W. Ozuem & Y. Azemi (Eds.), *Digital Marketing Strategies for Fashion and Luxury Brands* (pp. 326–361). Hershey, U.S.A: IGI Global.

Helal, G., & Ozuem, W. (2018). The emerging, evolving social media platforms and social identity: Implications for the fashion industry. In *Shaping the Next Wave of Globalization: Using Current Trends to Reconnect with Markets and Create Value* (pp. 204–211). United States of America: The Global Business and Technology Association.

Helal, G., & Ozuem, W. (2019). Social media and social identity in the fashion industry: Among the millennial generation. In G. Bowen & W. Ozuem (Eds.), *Leveraging Computer-Mediated Marketing Environments* (1st ed., pp. 43–82). Hershey, U.S.A: IGI Global.

Helal, G., Ozuem, W., & Lancaster, G. (2018). Social media brand perceptions of millennials. *International Journal of Retail & Distribution Management, 46*(10), 977–998.

Hennig-Thurau, T., Gwinner, K., Walsh, G., & Gremler, D. (2004). Electronic word-of-mouth via consumer-opinion platforms: What motivates consumers to articulate themselves on the Internet? *Journal of Interactive Marketing, 18*(1), 38–52.

Hennig-Thurau, T., Malthouse, E., Friege, C., Gensler, S., Lobschat, L., Rangaswamy, A., & Skiera, B. (2010). The impact of new media on customer relationships. *Journal of Service Research, 13*(3), 311–330.

Hoffman, D., & Fodor, M. (2016). Can you measure the ROI of your social media marketing? *Sloan Management Review, 52*(1), 41–49.

Hoffman, D., & Novak, T. (1996). Marketing in hypermedia computer-mediated environments: Conceptual foundations. *Journal of Marketing, 60*(3), 50–68.

Hogg, M. (2001). A social identity theory of leadership. *Personality and Social Psychology Review, 5*(3), 184–200.

Hogg, M., & Abrams, D. (1988). *Social identifications*. London: Routledge.

Hogg, M., & Reid, S. (2006). Social identity, self-categorization, and the communication of group norms. *Communication Theory, 16*(1), 7–30.

Hogg, M., & Terry, D. (2000). Social identity and self-categorization processes in organizational contexts. *The Academy of Management Review, 25*(1), 121–140.

Hogg, M., & Turner, J. (1987). Intergroup behaviour, self-stereotyping and the salience of social categories. *British Journal of Social Psychology, 26*(4), 325–340.

Hogg, M., Sherman, D., Dierselhuis, J., Maitner, A., & Moffitt, G. (2006). Uncertainty, entitativity, and group identification. *Journal of Experimental Social Psychology, 43*(1), 135–142.

Hogg, M., Terry, D., & White, K. (1995). A tale of two theories: A critical comparison of identity theory with social identity theory. *Social Psychology Quarterly, 58*(4), 255–269.

Holland, J., & Baker, S. (2001). Customer participation in creating site brand loyalty. *Journal of Interactive Marketing, 15*(4), 34–45.

Hollebeek, L., Glynn, M., & Brodie, R. (2014). Consumer brand engagement in social media: Conceptualization, scale development and validation. *Journal of Interactive Marketing, 28*(2), 149–165.

Houman Andersen, P. (2001). Relationship development and marketing communication: An integrative model. *Journal of Business & Industrial Marketing, 16*(3), 167–183.

Howe, N., & Strauss, W. (2000). *Millennials rising: The next great generation*. New York: Vintage Books.

Hoyer, W., & Brown, S. (1990). Effects of brand awareness on choice for a common, repeat-purchase product. *Journal of Consumer Research, 17*(2), 141–148.

Huang, W., Schrank, H., & Dubinsky, A. (2004). Effect of brand name on consumers' risk perceptions of online shopping. *Journal of Consumer Behaviour, 4*(1), 40–50.

Hudson, S., Huang, L., Roth, M., & Madden, T. (2016). The influence of social media interactions on consumer–brand relationships: A three-country study of brand perceptions and marketing behaviors. *International Journal of Research in Marketing, 33*(1), 27–41.

Hunt, S., & Madhavaram, S. (2015). The service-dominant logic of marketing: Theoretical foundations, pedagogy, and resource-advantage theory. In R. Lusch & S. Vargo (Eds.), *The Service-dominant Logic of Marketing: Dialog, Debate, and Directions* (2nd ed., pp. 67–84). New York: Routledge.

Hutter, K., Hautz, J., Dennhardt, S., & Füller, J. (2013). The impact of user interactions in social media on brand awareness and purchase intention: the case of MINI on Facebook. *Journal of Product & Brand Management, 22*(5/6), 342–351.

Huy, Q., & Shipilov, A. (2012). The key to social media success within organisations. *Sloan Management Review, 54*(1), 73–81.

Iacobucci, D. (1994). Analysis of experimental data. In R. P. Bagozzi (Ed.), *Principles of Marketing Research.* Blackwell Publishing, Cambridge, MA.

Jayachandran, S., Gimeno, J., & Varadarajan, P. (1999). The theory of multimarket competition: A synthesis and implications for marketing strategy. *Journal of Marketing, 63*(3), 49.

Jenkins, R. (2008). *Social identity (Key Ideas)* (3rd ed.). London: Routledge.

Kane, G., Alavi, M., Labianca, G., & Borgatti, S. (2014). What's different about social media networks? A framework and research agenda. *MIS Quarterly, 38*(1), 274–304.

Kaplan, A., & Haenlein, M. (2010). Users of the world, unite! The challenges and opportunities of social media. *Business Horizons, 53*(1), 59–68.

Kaplan, A., & Haenlein, M. (2010). Users of the world, unite! The challenges and opportunities of Social Media. *Business Horizons, 53*(1), 61.

Karpinski, R. (2005). The next phase: Bottom-up marketing. *BtoB Magazine, 90*(5), 38.

Keller, K. (1993). Conceptualizing, measuring, and managing customer-based brand equity. *Journal of Marketing, 57*(1), 1.

Keller, K. (2001). Building customer-based brand equity: A blueprint for creating strong brands. *Marketing Science Institute*, 3–23.

Keller, K. (2009). Building strong brands in a modern marketing communications environment. *Journal of Marketing Communications, 15*(2–3), 139–155.

Kietzmann, J., Hermkens, K., McCarthy, I., & Silvestre, B. (2011). Social media? Get serious! Understanding the functional building blocks of social media. *Business Horizons, 54*(3), 241–251.

Kilian, T., Hennigs, N., & Langner, S. (2012). Do millennials read books or blogs? Introducing a media usage typology of the Internet generation. *Journal of Consumer Marketing, 29*(2), 114–124.

Kim, M., Chung, N., & Lee, C. (2011). The effect of perceived trust on electronic commerce: Shopping online for tourism products and services in South Korea. *Tourism Management, 32*(2), 256–265.

Kim, A., & Ko, E. (2012). Do social media marketing activities enhance customer equity? An empirical study of luxury fashion brand. *Journal of Business Research, 65*(10), 1480–1486.

Kleine, R., Kleine, S., & Kernan, J. (1993). Mundane consumption and the self: A social-identity perspective. *Journal of Consumer Psychology, 2*(3), 209–235.

Koh, J., & Kim, Y. (2004). Knowledge sharing in virtual communities: An e-business perspective. *Expert Systems With Applications, 26*(2), 155–166.

Kozinets, R. (1999). E-tribalized marketing? The strategic implications of virtual communities of consumption. *European Management Journal, 17*(3), 252–264.

Kozinets, R. (2002). The field behind the screen: Using netnography for marketing research in online communities. *Journal of Marketing Research, 39*(1), 61–72.

Kozinets, R., de Valck, K., Wojnicki, A., & Wilner, S. (2010). Networked narratives: Understanding word-of-mouth marketing in online communities. *Journal of Marketing, 74*(2), 71–89.

Kulmala, M., Mesiranta, N., & Tuominen, P. (2013). Organic and amplified eWOM in consumer fashion blogs. *Journal of Fashion Marketing and Management: An International Journal, 17*(1), 20–37.

Kumar, V., & George, M. (2007). Measuring and maximizing customer equity: A critical analysis. *Journal of The Academy of Marketing Science, 35*(2), 157–171.

Kumar, N., Hibbard, J., & Stern, L. (1994). *The nature and consequences of marketing channel intermediary commitment* (pp. 94–115). Cambridge: Marketing Science Institute.

Lam, S., Ahearne, M., Hu, Y., & Schillewaert, N. (2010). Resistance to Brand switching when a radically new brand is introduced: A social identity theory perspective. *Journal of Marketing, 74*(6), 128–146.

Laroche, M., Habibi, M., Richard, M., & Sankaranarayanan, R. (2012). The effects of social media based brand communities on brand community markers, value creation practices, brand trust and brand loyalty. *Computers In Human Behavior, 28*(5), 1755–1767.

Lemon, K., Rust, R., & Zeithaml, V. (2001). What drives customer equity. *Marketing Management, 10*(1), 20–25.

Liu, Y. (2006). Word of mouth for movies: Its dynamics and impact on box office revenue. *Journal of Marketing, 70*(3), 74–89.

Luhtanen, R., & Crocker, J. (1992). A collective self-esteem scale: Self-evaluation of one's social identity. *Personality and Social Psychology Bulletin, 18*(3), 302–318.

Lusch, R. (2007). Marketing's evolving identity: Defining our future. *Journal of Public Policy & Marketing, 26*(2), 261–268.

Ma, M., & Agarwal, R. (2007). Through a glass darkly: Information technology design, identity verification, and knowledge contribution in online communities. *Information Systems Research, 18*(1), 42–67.

Mangold, W., & Faulds, D. (2009). Social media: The new hybrid element of the promotion mix. *Business Horizons, 52*(4), 357–365.

Manville, B. (2004). Building customer communities of practice for business value: Success factors profiled from saba software and other case studies. In P. Hildreth & C. Kimble (Eds.), *Knowledge Networks: Innovation through Communities of Practices* (pp. 106–123). Hershey, PA: Idea Group Publishing.

McAlexander, J., Koenig, H., & Schouten, J. (2006). Building relationships of brand community in higher education: A strategic framework for university advancement. *International Journal of Educational Advancement, 6*(2), 107–118.

McAlexander, J., Schouten, J., & Koening, H. (2002). Building brand community. *Journal of Marketing, 66*(1), 38–54.

McKinsey. (2016). The state of fashion. Retrieved from https://www.mckinsey.com/industries/retail/our-insights/the-state-of-fashion

Moore, M. (2012). Interactive media usage among millennial consumers. *Journal of Consumer Marketing, 29*(6), 436–444.

Morgan, R., & Hunt, S. (1994). The commitment-trust theory of relationship marketing. *Journal of Marketing, 58*(3), 20.

Muniz, A., & O'Guinn, T. (2001). Brand community. *Journal of Consumer Research, 27*(4), 412–432.

Murugesan, S. (2007). Understanding Web 2.0. *IT Professional, 9*(4), 34–41.

Naylor, R., Lamberton, C., & West, P. (2012). Beyond the "Like" button: The impact of mere virtual presence on brand evaluations and purchase intentions in social media settings. *Journal of Marketing, 76*(6), 105–120.

Newcomb, T. (1953). An approach to the study of communicative acts. *Psychological Review, 60*(6), 393–404.

Ng, E., Schweitzer, L., & Lyons, S. (2010). New generation, great expectations: A field study of the millennial generation. *Journal of Business and Psychology, 25*(2), 281–292.

Nowak, A., Szamrej, J., & Latané, B. (1990). From private attitude to public opinion: A dynamic theory of social impact. *Psychological Review, 97*(3), 362–376.

O'Reilly, T. (2005). Web 2.0: Compact Definition?—O'Reilly Radar. Radar.oreilly.com. Retrieved from http://radar.oreilly.com/2005/10/web-20-compact-definition.html

O'Reilly, T., & Battelle, J. (2009). *Web squared: Web 2.0 five years on.* Sebastopol, California: O'Reilly Media.

Onorato, R., & Turner, J. (2004). Fluidity in the self-concept: The shift from personal to social identity. *European Journal of Social Psychology, 34*(3), 257–278.

Ozuem, W., Howell, K., & Lancaster, G. (2008). Communicating in the new interactive marketspace. *European Journal of Marketing, 42*(9/10), 1059–1083.

Ozuem, W., Patel, A, Howell, K., & Lancaster, G. (2017). An exploration of consumers' response to online service recovery initiatives. *International Journal of Market Research, 59*(1), 97–115.

Ozuem, W., Thomas, T., & Lancaster, G. (2016). The influence of customer loyalty on small island economies: An empirical and exploratory study. *Journal of Strategic Marketing, 24*(6), 447–469.

Parameswaran, M., & Whinston, A. (2007). Research Issues in Social Computing. *Journal of the Association for Information Systems, 8*(6), 336–350.

Park, D., Lee, J., & Han, I. (2007). The effect of on-line consumer reviews on consumer purchasing intention: The moderating role of involvement. *International Journal of Electronic Commerce, 11*(4), 125–148.

Paroutis, S., & Al Saleh, A. (2009). Determinants of knowledge sharing using Web 2.0 technologies. *Journal of Knowledge Management, 13*(4), 52–63.

Pentina, I., Gammoh, B., Zhang, L., & Mallin, M. (2013). Drivers and outcomes of brand relationship quality in the context of online social networks. *International Journal of Electronic Commerce, 17*(3), 63–86.

Pentina, I., Prybutok, V., & Zhang, X. (2008). The role of virtual communities as shopping reference groups. *Journal of Electronic Commerce Research, 9*(2), 114–136.

Phan, M., Thomas, R., & Heine, K. (2011). Social media and luxury brand management: The case of burberry. *Journal of Global Fashion Marketing, 2*(4), 213–222.

Pitta, D., & Fowler, D. (2005). Internet community forums: An untapped resource for consumer marketers. *Journal of Consumer Marketing, 22*(5), 265–274.

Pongsakornrungsilp, S., & Schroeder, J. (2011). Understanding value co-creation in a co-consuming brand community. *Marketing Theory, 11*(3), 303–324.

Prahalad, C., & Ramaswamy, V. (2000). Co-opting customer competence. *Harvard Business Review, 78*(1), 79–87.

Prahalad, C., & Ramaswamy, V. (2004). Co-creating unique value with customers. *Strategy & Leadership, 32*(3), 4–9.

Qualman, E. (2013). *Socialnomics.* Hoboken, NJ: John Wiley & Sons.

Rainer, T., & Rainer, J. (2011). *The millennials.* Nashville, Tennessee: B & H Publishing Group.

Ramaswamy, V. (2008). Co-creating value through customers' experiences: The Nike case. *Strategy & Leadership, 36*(5), 9–14.

Ren, Y., Harper, M., Drenner, S., Terveen, L., Kiesler, S., Riedl, J., & Kraut, R. (2012). Building member attachment in online communities: Applying theories of group identity and interpersonal bonds. *MIS Quarterly, 36*(3), 841–864.

Rheingold, H. (2002). *Smart mobs.* Cambridge, Mass.: Perseus Books Group.

Richards, K., & Jones, E. (2008). Customer relationship management: Finding value drivers. *Industrial Marketing Management, 37*(2), 120–130.

Romero, D., & Molina, A. (2011). Collaborative networked organisations and customer communities: Value co-creation and co-innovation in the networking era. *Production Planning & Control, 22*(5–6), 447–472.

Ross, C., Orr, E., Sisic, M., Arseneault, J., Simmering, M., & Orr, R. (2009). Personality and motivations associated with Facebook use. *Computers In Human Behavior, 25*(2), 578–586.

Rossiter, J., & Percy, L. (1978). *Advertising and promotion management.* New York: McGraw Hill.

Royo-Vela, M., & Casamassima, P. (2011). The influence of belonging to virtual brand communities on consumers' affective commitment, satisfaction and word-of-mouth advertising. *Online Information Review, 35*(4), 517–542.

Rust, R., Lemon, K., & Zeithaml, V. (2000). *Driving customer equity: How customer lifetime value is reshaping corporate strategy.* New York: The Free Pree.

Rust, R., Lemon, K., & Zeithaml, V. (2004). Return on marketing: Using customer equity to focus marketing strategy. *Journal of Marketing, 68*(1), 109–127.

Sashi, C. (2012). Customer engagement, buyer-seller relationships, and social media. *Management Decision, 50*(2), 253–272.

Schau, H., Muñiz, A., & Arnould, E. (2009). How brand community practices create value. *Journal of Marketing, 73*(5), 30–51.

Schembri, S., Merrilees, B., & Kristiansen, S. (2010). Brand consumption and narrative of the self. *Psychology and Marketing, 27*(6), 623–637.

Schewe, C., & Meredith, G. (2004). Segmenting global markets by generational cohorts: Determining motivations by age. *Journal of Consumer Behaviour, 4*(1), 51–63.

Schivinski, B., & Dabrowski, D. (2016). The impact of brand communication on brand equity through Facebook. *Journal of Marketing Communications, 22*(2), 189–214.

Schouten, J., & McAlexander, J. (1995). Subcultures of consumption: An ethnography of the new bikers. *Journal of Consumer Research, 22*(1), 43.

Sheth, J. (2011). Impact of emerging markets on marketing: Rethinking existing perspectives and practices. *Journal of Marketing, 75*(4), 166–182.

Sheth, J., & Sisodia, R. (1999). Revisiting marketing's lawlike generalizations. *Journal of The Academy of Marketing Science, 27*(1), 71–87.

Shang, R., Chen, Y., & Liao, H. (2006). The value of participation in virtual consumer communities on brand loyalty. *Internet Research, 16*(4), 398–418.

Simmons, G. (2008). Marketing to postmodern consumers: Introducing the internet chameleon. *European Journal of Marketing, 42*(3/4), 299–310.

Smith, A., & Anderson, M. (2018). *Social media use in 2018* (pp. 2–7). PewResearch Center. Retrieved from http://assets.pewresearch.org/wp-content/uploads/sites/14/2018/03/01105133/PI_2018.03.01_Social-Media_FINAL.pdf

Solomon, G., & Schrum, L. (2007). *Web 2.0: New tools, new schools.* Eugene, Oregon: International Society for Technology in Education.

Statista. (2016). *Global daily social media usage by age 2016.* Retrieved from https://www.statista.com/statistics/613456/daily-social-media-usage-worldwide-age/

Statista. (2016). *Fashion brands: Social visibility score on social networks 2016 | Statistic.* Retrieved from https://www.statista.com/statistics/729691/fashion-brands-social-visibility-score-social-networks-world/

Statista. (2016). *Instagram: Global brand adoption rate 2016.* Retrieved from https://www.statista.com/statistics/305292/worldwide-instagram-brand-adoption-rate-category/

Statista. (2016). *Instagram usage during MFW by action Italy 2016.* Retrieved from https://www.statista.com/statistics/676023/instagram-usage-during-mfw-by-action-italy/

Statista. (2017). *Luxury brands discovery sources among Millennials worldwide 2017 | Statistic.* Retrieved from https://www.statista.com/statistics/441758/sources-for-hearing-about-new-luxury-brands-worldwide/

Statista. (2017). *Number of worldwide social network users 2010–2021 | Statistic.* Retrieved from https://www.statista.com/statistics/278414/number-of-worldwide-social-network-users/

Statista. (2017). *Snapchat brand stories by media type and industry 2017 | Statistic.* Retrieved from https://www.statista.com/statistics/753645/snapchat-brand-stories-media-type-industry/

Statista. (2017). *Social network penetration worldwide 2021.* Retrieved from https://www.statista.com/statistics/260811/social-network-penetration-worldwide/

Statista. (2018). *Social media: Worldwide penetration rate 2018.* Retrieved from https://www.statista.com/statistics/269615/social-network-penetration-by-region/

Stokburger-Sauer, N. (2010). *Brand community: Drivers and outcomes. Psychology and Marketing, 27*(4), 347–368.

Stokburger-Sauer, N., & Teichmann, K. (2013). Is luxury just a female thing? The role of gender in luxury brand consumption. *Journal of Business Research, 66*(7), 889–896.

Susarla, A., Oh, J., & Tan, Y. (2012). Social networks and the diffusion of user-generated content: Evidence from YouTube. *Information Systems Research, 23*(1), 23–41.

Taken Smith, K. (2012). Longitudinal study of digital marketing strategies targeting Millennials. *Journal of Consumer Marketing, 29*(2), 86–92.

Tajfel, H. (1959). Quantitative judgement in social perception. *British Journal of Psychology, 50*(1), 16–29.

Tajfel, H. (1969). Cognitive aspects of prejudice. *Journal of Social Issues, 25*(4), 79–97.

Tajfel, H. (1972). Social categorization. English manuscript of 'La catégorisation sociale.' In S. Moscovici (Ed.), *Introduction à la Psychologie Sociale* (Vol. 1, pp. 272–302). Paris: Larousse.

Tajfel, H. (1978). The achievement of intergroup differentiation. In H. Tajfel (Ed.), *Differentiation between social groups* (pp. 77–100). London: Academic Press.

Tajfel, H. (1978). The achievement of intergroup differentiation. In H. Tajfel (Ed.), *Differentiation between social groups* (pp. 62). London: Academic Press.

Tajfel, H. (1982). Social psychology of intergroup relations. *Annual Review of Psychology, 33*(1), 1–39.

Tajfel, H., & Turner, J. (1985). The social identity theory of intergroup behaviour. In S. Worchel & W. Austen (Eds.), *Psychology of Intergroup Relations* (2nd ed., pp. 7–24). Chicago: Nelson-Hall.

Tiago, M., & Veríssimo, J. (2014). Digital marketing and social media: Why bother? *Business Horizons, 57*(6), 703–708.

Tikkanen, H., Hietanen, J., Henttonen, T., & Rokka, J. (2009). Exploring virtual worlds: Success factors in virtual world marketing. *Management Decision, 47*(8), 1357–1381.

Tolman, E. (1943). Identification and the postwar world. *The Journal of Abnormal and Social Psychology, 38*(2), 141–148.

Trepte, S. (2008). Social identity theory. In J. Bryant & P. Vorderer (Eds.), *Psychology of Entertainment* (2nd ed., pp. 255–271). New York: Routledge.

Trusov, M., Bucklin, R., & Pauwels, K. (2009). Effects of word-of-mouth versus traditional marketing: Findings from an internet social networking site. *Journal of Marketing, 73*(5), 90–102.

Turner, J. (1982). Towards a cognitive redefinition of the social group. In H. Tajfel (Ed.), *Social Identity and Intergroup Relations* (pp. 15–40). Cambridge: Cambridge University Press.

Turner, J. (1985). Social categorization and self-concept: A social cognitive theory of group behavior. In E. Lawler (Ed.), *Advances in Group Process: Theory and Research* (pp. 77–121). Greenwich, Connecticut: JAI Press.

Van Dijck, J. (2013). *The culture of connectivity*. Oxford: Oxford University Press.

Van Dijck, J., & Poell, T. (2013). Understanding social media logic. *Media and Communication, 1*(1), 2–14.

Vargo, S., & Lusch, R. (2004). Evolving to a new dominant logic for marketing. *Journal of Marketing, 68*(1), 1–17.

Vargo, S., Lusch, R., & Morgan, F. (2015). Historical perspectives on service-dominant logic. In R. Lusch & S. Vargo (Eds.), *The Service-dominant Logic of Marketing: Dialog, Debate, and Directions* (2nd ed., pp. 29–42). New York: Routledge.

Veletsianos, G. (2013). Open practices and identity: Evidence from researchers and educators' social media participation. *British Journal of Educational Technology, 44*(4), 639–651.

Veloutsou, C., & Moutinho, L. (2009). Brand relationships through brand reputation and brand tribalism. *Journal of Business Research, 62*(3), 314–322.

Vogel, V., Evanschitzky, H., & Ramaseshan, B. (2008). Customer equity drivers and future sales. *Journal of Marketing, 72*(6), 98–108.

Walden, E. (2000). Some value propositions of online communities. *Electronic Markets, 10*(4), 244–249.

Wattanasuwan, K. (2005). The self and symbolic consumption. *Journal of American Academy of Business, 6*(1), 179–184.

Weber, M. (1978). *Economy and society: An outline of interpretive sociology* (2nd ed.). California: University of California Press.

Whiting, A., & Williams, D. (2013). Why people use social media: A uses and gratifications approach. *Qualitative Market Research: An International Journal, 16*(4), 362–369.

Williams, D., Crittenden, V., Keo, T., & McCarty, P. (2012). The use of social media: An exploratory study of usage among digital natives. *Journal of Public Affairs, 12*(2), 127–136.

Wirtz, J., den Ambtman, A., Bloemer, J., Horváth, C., Ramaseshan, B., & van de Klundert, J. et al. (2013). Managing brands and customer engagement in online brand communities. *Journal of Service Management, 24*(3), 223–24.

Woisetschläger, D., Hartleb, V., & Blut, M. (2008). How to make brand communities work: Antecedents and consequences of consumer participation. *Journal of Relationship Marketing, 7*(3), 237–256.

Wolny, J., & Mueller, C. (2013). Analysis of fashion consumers' motives to engage in electronic word-of-mouth communication through social media platforms. *Journal of Marketing Management, 29*(5–6), 562–583.

Zaglia, M. (2013). Brand Communities embedded in social networks. *Journal of Business Research, 66*(2), 216–223.

Zhang, K., Benyoucef, M., & Zhao, S. (2016). Building brand loyalty in social commerce: The case of brand microblogs. *Electronic Commerce Research and Applications, 15*, 14–25.

Zheng, X., Cheung, C., Lee, M., & Liang, L. (2015). Building brand loyalty through user engagement in online brand communities in social networking sites. *Information Technology & People, 28*(1), 90–106.

Zhu, Y., & Chen, H. (2015). Social media and human need satisfaction: Implications for social media marketing. *Business Horizons, 58*(3), 335–345.

Zinkhan, G., & Hirschheim, R. (1992). Truth in marketing theory and research: An alternative perspective. *Journal of Marketing, 56*(2), 80–88.

Chapter 7

Omni-Channel Purchasing Behaviour: Issues and Insights

Elena Patten

Macromedia University of Applied Sciences, Germany

ABSTRACT

In omni-channel retailing, the combination of different retail channels along the various customer touchpoints has become the predominant purchasing pattern for customers. The so-called "research shopper phenomenon" describes a common tendency amongst customers to use one channel to search and another to purchase. This paper suggests that four different types of German omni-channel fashion customers exist and therefore presents an omni-channel customer typology.

KEYWORDS

Channel Integration, Consumer Behaviour, Customer Typology, Omni-channel Retailing, Shopping Experience

INTRODUCTION

Nowadays, the customer primarily knows what product they want before choosing the final retail channel. The "point of decision" is, nowadays, often relocated to the online environment, while the store is only perceived as the "point of sale" (Heinemann, 2013; Reinartz, Wiegand, & Imschloss, 2019; Shankar, 2011). However, previous literature has studied these omni-channel customers as a relatively homogeneous group (Verhoef, Neslin, & Vroomen, 2007). The current paper considers omni-channel customers as a heterogeneous group of customers, consisting of four distinctive customer types. The drivers of heterogeneity can be considered to be rational/ emotional involvement and income level. The investigated customer groups of the current paper are (1) hedonistic shoppers and (2) connoisseurs for emotionally involved customers and (3) smart shoppers and (4) phlegmatic shoppers for rationally involved customers. These customer types have not been discovered in previous studies.

FROM MULTICHANNEL TO OMNICHANNEL RETAILING

In recent years, strategies for retailers that operate more than one channel have developed at some pace (Beck & Rygl, 2015; Heinemann, 2019; Hult, Tomas, & Zhang, 2019; Verhoef, Kannan, & Inman, 2015). Retailers aim to offer their customers a seamless shopping experience by integrating their different retail channels. As a consequence, switching between channels during the process of performing a purchase has become easier for customers (KPMG, 2018; Mahrdt, Lessing, Wagner, & Geissler, 2013).

Customers interface with different formats and media, such as stores, computers, mobile devices, tablets and social media during the purchasing process and they use these media as sources of inspiration and communication (Cao, Liu, & Cao, 2018; Verhoef et al., 2015; Ozuem et al., 2017). The borders between the different channels have consequently become blurred (Ozuem, Howell, & Lancaster, 2008; Brynjolfsson, Hu, & Rahman, 2013; Saghiri, Wilding, Mena, & Bourlakis, 2017).

The complexity of retail channel strategies has led to confusion regarding a coherent terminology for both professional classes and practitioners. There are different terminologies that refer to the processes of retailing that operate across more than one retail channel. These have been variously called "multichannel", "cross-channel" and "omni-channel" retailing. To date, these terminologies are used indistinctly (Beck & Rygl, 2015).

The initial perception of multichannel retailing was of a system that administered two or more parallel channels (Berman, 1996; Pelton, Strutton, & Lumpkin, 2002). During the next phase, the concept of integration became a topic of major interest for both practitioners and academia (Neslin et al., 2006; Ozuem, Thomas, & Lancaster, 2016). In this context, the terms "cross-channel" and "omni-channel" augmented the terminology of "multichannel" retailing. Yet there has been no obvious attempt to conceptualise these new terms (Heinemann, 2019; Verhoef et al., 2015), although Beck and Rygl (2015) published some initial research on the topic. The following image illustrates their arguments succinctly:

Figure 1. Terminology of multi-, cross-, and omni-channel retailing

	Multichannel	Cross-channel			Omni-Channel		
		I	II Hybrid	III Hybrid	I	II Hybrid	III Hybrid
Customer Interaction	◯	◖	◯	◖	●	●	◖
Company Integration	◯	◖	◖	◯	●	◗	●

◯ = No   ◖ = Partial   ● = Full

As the image illustrates, Beck and Rygl (2015) categorised multichannel, cross-channel and omni-channel retailing according to the degree to which they enable customer interactions and the degree to which they facilitate company integration. They defined multichannel retailing as "the set of activities involved in selling merchandise or services through more than one channel, or all widespread channels, whereby the customer cannot trigger channel interaction and the retailer does not control channel interaction" (Beck & Rygl, 2015, p. 175). The term "cross-channel retailing" developed from multichannel retailing. In this context, the multiple channels of a retailer are integrated to a higher degree. Thus, such a concept can be considered to represent an evolution in retail. Cross-channel retailing means "the customer can trigger partial channel interaction and/or the retailer controls partial channel integration" (Beck & Rygl, 2015, p. 176). The term "omni-channel" ultimately refers to the most advanced stage of a multichannel retailing system. Hence, omni-channel retailing means full customer interaction and/or retailer integration (Beck & Rygl, 2015). Furthermore, Beck and Rygl (2015) suggested a third form: If just one party—customer or retailer—fulfils the criterion of interaction/integration this is known as the "hybrid form" (Beck & Rygl, 2015, p. 174). For several reasons, this framework is a valuable contribution to retailing research in this context, particularly in instances when retailers operate more than one channel. It helps to set clear boundaries for the classification of each of the three connected, albeit different concepts. This conceptualisation considers both perspectives: the customer's interaction with different channels and the retailer's level of integration. Moreover, it provides guidelines for both researchers and practitioners to use when approaching the different terms more distinctively.

THE OMNI-CHANNEL CUSTOMER JOURNEY

In omni-channel retailing, the combination of different retail channels along the different customer touchpoints has become the predominant purchasing pattern for customers (Mahrdt et al., 2013; Patten, 2014; Saghiri et al., 2017).

The so-called "research-shopper" phenomenon is described as a common tendency among customers to use one channel for search and another for purchase (Gensler, Neslin, & Verhoef, 2017; Verhoef et al., 2007).

Shankar (2011) and Heinemann (2013) call the switch between different channels "ropo", which basically has two meanings:

(1) "Research online and purchase offline" means that Internet users research online before making any purchase decision. They compare prices online, obtain information from the producer's webpage or read comments of other users of the same product. This trend is called "web-rooming", a wordplay of "show-rooming", where customers shop online, but use the store before they physically interact with the product (Verhoef et al., 2015). This purchase pattern has an important impact on the overall purchase process: In the past, a customer first decided about the retailer and then decided about the product that he wanted to buy from this retailer. Then, he went to the store to get information about different products in the assortment of this retailer. Most probably, he also frequented other retailers in order to compare the offer and afterwards made their purchase decision. Nowadays, the customer primarily decides about the product and then chooses an adequate retailer. Thus, when the customer—after the initial phase of product decision—frequents a retail store, he has already collected several information, such as product features, prices, online availability and opinions from other users (Patten & Ozuem, 2017; Verhoef et al.,

2007). The customer increasingly trusts the opinions of other product users more than the recommendations made by in-store sales people or advertisements. When the customer enters a retail store, he already possesses high knowledge about products and feature. Hence, the customer nowadays has high expectations regarding product availability, immediate accessibility to information, products and service delivery.

(2) Customers can also "research offline and purchase online". In this context, the store can be seen as a "show-room", where customers can physically touch their product, interact with sales people, gather information and enjoy a shopping experience (Verhoef et al., 2015). A survey reveals that over 50% of non-food online customers use stores as the pre-purchase channel. Customers try a product in-store, especially when high "mispurchase risks" are associated with buying the product (Heinemann, 2013).

Verhoef et al. (2007) explain that there are three reasons for this phenomenon: First, customers prefer the channel that offers them the most advantages in each part of the purchase process- and they switch among channels during the purchase process if another channel offers more advantages ("Attribute-based decision-making"). Second, it is seen as unlikely that customers generally purchase via the channel with the most research advantages ("Lack of channel lock-in"). Third, customers carry out research shopping when a channel switch increases their overall shopping experience ("Cross-channel synergy").

Another study focussed on retention and free-riding behaviour: Customers search at one channel from a certain retailer and buy at a different channel but stay with the same retailer ("cross-channel retention") or they search at a channel at one retailer, but then purchase at a different channel of another retailer ("cross-channel free-riding") (Heitz-Spahn, 2013). Chiu et al. (2011) identified two major reasons for cross-channel free riding: Customers who have a high level of self-efficacy tend to switch channels and retailers during their purchasing process. Second, customers will buy at the retailer who offers good quality and a low risk. Furthermore they investigated, that within-firm lock-in decreases cross-channel free-riding. This means, that retailers can install switching barriers, which reduce the customers' intention to switch channels. Heitz-Spahn (2013) however elaborated shopping convenience, flexibility and price comparisons as the three major cross-channel free-riding motives. It is arguable, if these motives are similar in any industry or if there are major differences regarding the purchasing pattern. Regarding that, Heitz-Spahn (2013) argued, that for products, which customers buy in a low frequency but have a high financial value, cross-channel free-riding behaviour is more likely than for other product categories. Kushwaha and Shankar (2013) also found out, that customer behaviour is different among product categories. They clustered these different product categories in hedonic and utilitarian ones. Kushwaha and Shankar investigated, that customers of hedonic products, such as apparel, tend more towards impulse purchase and variety-seeking behaviour and switch the channel more often than customers of utilitarian products (Kushwaha & Shankar, 2013). Besides a different purchasing behaviour across product categories, the degree of maturity plays an important role in omni-channel purchasing behaviour: Melis et al. (2015) conducted research in the UK grocery omni-channel market. They found out, that at the beginning of purchasing online, customers tend to buy at the retailer first, which they prefer when purchasing offline. When they become more convenient with purchasing online, they start switching channels (Ailawadi & Farris, 2017; Melis, 2015).

RESEARCH DESIGN

Extant literature conceptualizes omni-channel customers as a homogeneous group of customers. Therefore, extant conceptual frameworks of omni-channel customers suggest a dualistic ontology and objectivistic epistemology. In contrast with the dominant existence of dualistic and objectivistic studies, this chapter acknowledges the apparent characteristics of the omni-channel customer from a threefold perspective: (1) It represents a pluralistic ideology, which permits diverse customer perceptions, (2) it considers the dynamic nature of shopping experiences and thus perceptions, and (3) it considers "different income level" and "different involvement" as important drivers of heterogeneity for omnichannel customers.

Such arguments are associated with an interpretivist ontological worldview, as they postulate the existence of "multiple realities" (Golafshani, 2003). Interpretivism places emphasis on *Verstehen*—understanding something in its context (Tucker, 1965). The researcher's way of understanding and explaining knowledge is central to research (Crotty, 1998), thus the epistemological choice for this study emphasises that potential meaning can exist, but that actual meaning emerges only when it engages with consciousness (Merleau-Ponty, 1962). This way of seeing the world is in line with social constructivism, which was selected as the basic paradigmatic choice for this paper.

As in any research study, the coherent selection of cases is essential for the outcome of this research. The technique applied to the sample selection was *purposeful sampling* (Patton, 1990). Patton (1990) emphasises that the value of a sample in a qualitative study lies in the richness of information about the selected sample. He lists several different strategies for purposefully selecting information-rich cases.

For this chapter, "combination, or mixed purposeful sampling" was applied, as participants were selected (1) on the basis of their experience of purchasing fashion products by using different channels of one retailer ("homogeneous sampling"). (2) Furthermore, sales people and managers of a German fashion department store chain in three different cities were asked to suggest customers who might participate in the study ("snowball sampling"), and (3) people were chosen based on predetermined criteria ("criterion sampling").

These criteria were defined to ensure that the selected participants could provide "information-richness" (Patton, 1990).

Hence, four inclusion and exclusion criteria were set, as illustrated in the following table:

Table 1. Inclusion and exclusion criteria for purposeful sampling

Criteria	Inclusion	Exclusion
Full capacity to contract	18 years and above	People below 18 years old
Experienced omni-channel customers	At least 3 omni-channel purchases within the last 12 months	Fewer than 3 omni-channel purchases within the last 12 months
Experiences with different omni-channel retailers	Purchases from at least 2 different omni-channel retailers	Purchases at fewer than 2 different omni-channel retailers
Fashion enthusiasm	High fashion enthusiasm	Low fashion enthusiasm

First, only the people who had obtained full capacity to contract were included in this study. In Germany, people receive full capacity to contract at the age of 18. Therefore, people younger than 18 were excluded from the study.

Second, customers were included who were experienced in searching for and purchasing clothing through different channels during one purchase. This is in keeping with Verhoef's (2007) definition of multichannel customers, as those that use different channels for searching and for purchasing. The inclusion of "experienced" omni-channel customers who had made at least three purchases in the last 12 months enhances the information-richness of the selected customers. Less experienced omni-channel customers who had made fewer than three omni-channel purchases in the last 12 months were excluded from this study.

Third, it was crucial for the outcome of this study that the participating customers had had omni-channel experiences with at least two omni-channel retailers. This is important because the concept of service quality is widely based on expectations, which are to some extent based on previous experiences (Parasuraman, Zeithaml, & Berry, 1985). Simply by including the customers who had experiences of more than two omni-channel retailers enhances the significance of the data.

Fourth, as it turned out during the pilot study, interview participants with little enthusiasm regarding fashion were also excluded from the study. Two out of three pilot participants considered themselves to be "fashion grouches", although they met the other inclusion criteria. These pilot participants could be considered less valuable for the purposes of further analysis, since they tended to digress from the topic of omni-channel fashion purchases to discuss omni-channel purchases of other items, such as house appliances, CDs or books. Moreover, these participants did not provide valuable insights into the fashion industry and could not be considered to enhance the current study.

In any research, the number of participants is one criterion that determines the extent to which a study is valuable enough to generate theory. In quantitative terminology, interview participants are referred to as sample size. Various published resources provide standard statistical methods to guide sample size selection in order to represent a population (Bartlett & Kotrlik, 2001). In qualitative research, the case is different and more complex. Patton argues that, in qualitative enquiry, "there are purposeful strategies instead of methodological rules" (Patton, 1990, p. 183). Literature on research methods that speaks to interview selection in qualitative studies suggests that sample selection will depend on the nature of each enquiry. "There are no rules for sample size in qualitative inquiry. Sample size depends on what you want to know, the purpose of the inquiry, what's at stake, what will be useful, what will have credibility, and what can be done with available time and resources" (Patton, 1990, p. 184). Others claim that the deeper and broader the unit of analysis is, the smaller the sample size can be to generate a new theory (Leavy, 2014). Charmaz (2011) points out that numerous researchers have legitimised studies with small data. She argues that a researcher can finish off by obtaining data when the different categories become "saturated". "Categories are saturated when gathering fresh data no longer illuminates new theoretical insights or new properties to the core theoretical categories" (Charmaz, 2011, p. 113). Thus, it is not possible to determine the final number of interviews beforehand. The interviews need to proceed until saturation is reached. Saunders et al. (2016) analysed a number of participants in several qualitative research enquiries and concluded that, on average, 32 participants were interrogated. They concluded that this number of participants could be considered sufficient (Saunders & Townsed, 2016). Creswell (1998) recommends conducting at least 10 in-depth interviews for a phenomenological study. He claims that he has observed a large range of sample sizes in different research projects. For this study, it is therefore worth analysing the sample sizes in analogous studies. Previous qualitative research studies focusing on service quality were based on between 15 and 58 in-depth interviews.

Accordingly, the sample size for this study consists of 24 in-depth interviews and two focus groups including nine focus group participants. This accounts for 33 participants in total. Omni-channel service quality in general, and in a German fashion retailing setting in particular, has not yet been fully conceptualised (Verhoef et al., 2015). This limited understanding of omni-channel customers justifies the selection of a relatively small sample. The focus of the current chapter was to understand the researched phenomenon in some depth.

In-depth interviews and focus groups were executed iteratively. First, the 24 in-depth interviews were conducted and analysed. Their focus was to receive the lived purchase experiences of several participants in depth. For the study's outcome it was valuable to gather these individual service quality perceptions from experienced omni-channel customers. The major outcome from the in-depth interviews was the six themes representing the vivid perceptions of the empirical reality of German omni-channel fashion customers.

After completing the in-depth interviews and carrying out some preliminary data analysis, two focus group interviews took place with a total of nine participants. The aim of the focus groups was to discuss relevant in-depth interview statements and emerging concepts in order to receive further insights. During the focus groups, a lively debate arose. The most valuable outcome of the focus groups was the finding that participants had different perceptions and thus omni-channel customers cannot be considered a "homogeneous group of customers" as the extant literature suggests (Verhoef et al., 2007). This built the foundation for the omni-channel customer typology.

The following omni-channel customers participated in the survey:

Table 2. Interview participants

No.	Age	Gender	Income level	Occupation
1	18–24	F	Low	Marketing student
2	25–30	F	Medium/high	Department manager in fashion retail
3	18–24	F	Low	Apprentice in fashion retail
4	25–30	F	Medium/high	Department manager in fashion retail
5	18–24	M	Low	Student
6	25–30	F	High	Mother
7	25–30	F	Low	Fashion management student
8	25–30	F	Medium	Fashion management trainee
9	18–24	M	Low	Apprentice in fashion retail
10	31–35	M	Medium/high	Department manager in fashion retail
11	18–24	F	Low	Apprentice in fashion retail
12	18–24	F	Low	Apprentice in fashion retail
13	25–30	M	Medium/ high	Project manager
14	41–46	M	High	Store manager
15	18–24	F	Low	Fashion management student
16	36–40	F	High	Brand director
17	25–30	F	Low	Fashion student

(Continued)

Table 2. Interview participants (Continued)

No.	Age	Gender	Income level	Occupation
18	31–35	F	High	Senior project manager
19	25–30	F	High	Sales manager
20	25–30	M	High	Senior project manager
21	25–30	F	Low/medium	Deputy department manager in fashion retail
22	31–35	M	High	Store manager
23	25–30	M	High	Senior project manager
24	31–35	F	High	Senior purchaser
25	41–46	F	High	Purchasing director
26	25–30	F	High	Sales director
27	18–24	F	Low	Design student
28	31–35	M	Low	Sales assistant
29	41–46	F	High	Brand director
30	31–35	F	High	Senior project manager
31	31–35	M	High	Logistics manager
32	31–35	F	Medium/high	Project manager
33	36–40	F	High	Mother

The income classification was conducted according to the following criteria:

Table 3. Income clusters

	Available gross income p.a. in EUR
Low	<= 30,000
Low/medium	> 30,000 <= 50,000
Medium	> 50,000 <= 70,000
Medium/high	> 70,000 <= 90,000
High	> 90,000

The in-depth and focus group interviews were conducted in three major German cities.

The interviews lasted between 30 and 60 minutes each. The average duration time was 42 minutes. This corresponds with the recommended duration of interviews as more than 30 minutes but less than one hour, in order to capitalise on concentration level (Robson, 2007).

As participants consented to take part, they were asked about a preferred location where the interview should take place. The choice of interview location is an important decision since it has a certain impact on the interview outcomes. The literature suggests that it is important to choose a location where the participant feels comfortable (Saunders, Lewis, & Thornhill, 2009). Participants mostly selected their favourite canteens and time-out areas or their offices as interview locations.

The interviews were recorded. Furthermore, notes were taken to summarise key statements. The body language of participants was also observed during the undertaking of interviews. Verbal and non-verbal communications can be considered valuable in order to understand the perceptions of participants and the meaning they give to the investigated phenomenon (Robson, 2007).

The interview questions were designed for "an analytic use" with the aim of answering the research questions of the study (Robson, 2007, p. 242). A direct involvement in this process enhanced the experiential knowledge about the topic under investigation. Moreover, due to the semi-structured nature of interviews, questions could be adjusted and new questions could be added in the course of the interviews, where it was felt beneficial in order to enhance the quality of discussion.

The interviews took around 50 minutes each, which Robson (2011) considers an appropriate length of time in which to receive sufficient information.

DATA ANALYSIS

The interview and focus group findings suggest that four different types of German omni-channel fashion customers exist within the sample. Based on these findings, the current study was able to develop a customer typology. "The appeal of such typologies is their potential to improve retail strategy decision-making by enabling retailers to differentiate and target their offerings, locations, and promotional efforts according to the varying patronage responses of the basic shopper types. In addition, shopper typologies are of interest for the insights they lend into the determinants of consumer shopping behaviour and the development of theories thereof" (Westbrook & Black, 1985, p. 78).

"Each type of customer is distinguished by a specific pattern of social characteristics reflecting his position in the social structure" (Stone, 1954, p. 36). The generators of heterogeneity amongst German omni-channel fashion customers can be considered to be "available income level" and "involvement".

Omni-channel customers with a lower available income level pay close attention to savings and costs. Among the respondents, apprentices, students, young professionals and non-academics represent this group. For students and young professionals, in particular, the income level is likely to increase in future, as a 22-year-old student from Stuttgart noted:

I'm convinced that when I have more money to spend in future, I'll pay attention to other things. For example, I'll pay less attention to the method of payment.

This statement suggests that the customer typology is a dynamic construct. Purchase behaviour changes over time, when certain living conditions such as income levels change.

Other respondents with higher available income are generally not as price-conscious as those with a lower available income. A 40-year-old brand director from Düsseldorf stated:

My awareness of price/performance has been changing during the last few years. I don't care about the price when I like an item. I'd buy it anyway.

This respondent demonstrated a keen awareness of her altering tastes with regard to price/performance ratio. She admitted that she now paid more attention to the hedonic value of an item.

Generally, interview participants were selected based on their high level of involvement in fashion products. Yet, as the interviews suggest, some respondents showed a higher emotional involvement, while others evinced a higher rational involvement. Emotionally concerned customers are highly involved in sensory, emotive, and/or hedonic stimuli. Rationally involved customers, on the contrary, are highly involved in cognitive and/or utilitarian stimuli.

Figure 2. Customer typology matrix

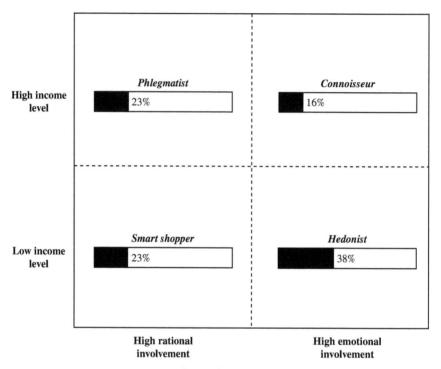

Hedonists were the largest customer segment (38 per cent of the respondents). They have a low or medium available income and they show high emotional involvement. Their principal drivers are shopping experience and amusement. The following statement from a 19-year-old apprentice in fashion retail illustrates the typical purchasing pattern of a hedonist:

I'm permanently checking Instagram to be up-to-date with what's new. You can choose the 'like to know' option and then get immediately informed to which brand the item belongs. It's too expensive most of the time. That's why I go to Store X and check if they have something similar. But most of the time, these are just inspirations and I end up buying something else.

As this statement supports, hedonist customers seek inspiration from Instagram and fashion blogs. For these customers, it is important to remain well informed about the latest fashion trends. They are price-sensitive due to their low available income. That is why they prefer to purchase from fast fashion discounters. Strong reference to affiliation and emotive stimulation are indicators of high emotional involvement amongst this customer segment. Hedonists value omni-channel retailing for efficiency reasons. Since fashion trends are very short-lived nowadays, they mainly use channel integration for availability checks across channels and they value fast delivery and an effortless purchasing process.

The connoisseur customer segment also demonstrates high emotional involvement in fashion purchases, but has a medium/high or high income. This segment accounts for 16 per cent of the respondents. The connoisseur looks for indulgence when purchasing a fashion product, as the following statement from a 46-year-old purchasing director in fashion illustrates:

I go shopping when I want to reward myself. I always know where to shop. There are certain brands and shops I prefer. It can be online or in-store—always after my fancy. I need an appealing atmosphere. It's the whole sideshow: the colours and the lighting. That's what really matters.

Connoisseurs can be considered the most demanding customer segment. They tend to have a clear idea of what they want. They are not dependent on the lower-priced retailing segment and they have high expectations concerning service quality. Generally, connoisseurs can be considered loyal customers, but if they migrate due to unsatisfying experiences it is hard for retailers to win them back. This customer segment seeks inspiration online and offline. They are receptive to aesthetic store design and visual merchandising. Furthermore, they follow lifestyle bloggers. However, in contrast to hedonists, who are influenced by bloggers and their fashion styles, connoisseurs look for bloggers who share a similar attitude and lifestyle. This segment seeks to appreciate competent personal advice and they avoid visiting stores with poor personal advice. When purchasing online, they value visual stories and editorials as well as aesthetic web design and sophisticated packaging. Connoisseurs have limited time and so they carry out omni-channel shopping to be efficient. They seek availability checks across channels and prefer the option to reserve items online and try them on in-store.

In contrast, smart shoppers (23 per cent of the respondents) have a low or medium available income and show a higher rational involvement. They are principally driven by savings. Smart shoppers can be considered the least loyal segment because they show opportunistic buying behaviour at the retailer that offers them the cheapest price. A 22-year-old student from Stuttgart argued:

I can understand that retailers with online shops and stores sometimes offer a cheaper price online. Normally, the online shops have opened more recently, and they want to push them. For me, it's not a problem, since I always compare prices before buying.

A 23-year-old marketing student stated, with reference to payment:

When I can purchase somewhere and have the option to pay later, I'll always buy from there. I even buy more items by thinking that I might like them!

These two statements illustrate the price-orientation of smart shoppers. In the first statement, the respondent claimed that he did not necessarily need price-consistency among channels, since he compared different channels before purchasing. The second statement referred to the payment-after-receiving option. Smart shoppers show a preference towards online shopping, since price comparison is easier online than offline. Furthermore, smart shoppers generally perceive prices to be lower online. They value integration quality for a more efficient comparison of prices across channels.

Phlegmatic shoppers are the second segment of higher rationally involved omni-channel customers (23 per cent of the respondents). These shoppers are mainly driven by convenience. They can be considered loyal customers, except when they experience failure of service at a retailer. Once they migrate, recovery is challenging for the retailer. The behavioural characteristics of the phlegmatic customer segment are illustrated in the following statement from a 29-year-old senior project manager of a business development department:

Well... in my case, it depends very much on what I need. For example, if I buy office clothes, I tend to buy online from X. I don't like to drive to the city especially for that purpose, and, you know, I know the sizes I need for shirts and suits. This is what I basically need. Anyway, I find that X has a very large assortment. But nevertheless, the layout of their site is very clear. And what I find also good is that they inform you with a newsletter about novelties and other interesting topics. Recently, they wrote about smart grids. But thankfully they do not send me a standardised newsletter. That would have made me nuts! Their newsletter is customised and considers which brands or products I have bought recently. Sometimes I buy new items from there which I didn't want to buy, just because of their newsletter.

Phlegmatic shoppers tend to have high expectations regarding the services they are offered. They value efficiency, convenience, practicability, and competence above all. These shoppers have a clear channel preference when it comes to purchasing fashion products. Switching barriers can be a helpful tool for omni-channel retailers to hinder phlegmatic shoppers from cross-channel free- riding. This segment has a positive perception of channel integration because they value choice optimisation for effort, availability, price and support.

The following table presents a summary of the four different customer types, as discussed in the previous section; specifically, their drivers of heterogeneity, their principal drivers, their special behavioural characteristics, and their perceptions of the three different omni-channel service quality dimensions.

Table 4. Customer typology

	Smart shopper	Phlegmatic shopper	Hedonist	Connoisseur
Generator: Available income level	Low and medium	Medium/high and high	Low and medium	Medium/high and high
Generator: Involvement	High degree of rational involvement	High degree of rational involvement	Higher degree of emotional involvement	Higher degree of emotional involvement
Principal driver	Savings	Convenience	Experience, amusement	Indulgence
Special behavioural characteristics	• Least loyal customer segment • Most opportunistic customer segment • Little importance of price consistency among channels when personally gaining an advantage • Frequent channel and retailer switching during purchase • Well-informed about prices before purchasing • Look for a retailer with a high level of goodwill policy	• Loyal customer segment: 'Creatures of habit'	• Social media affinity • See fashion blogs as an important source of inspiration • Continually in search of upcoming brands and new retail formats • Well-informed about fashion trends before purchasing	• Read editorials as a source of inspiration • Follow like-minded lifestyle bloggers • Well-informed about fashion trends and brands before purchasing • Expect a high level of goodwill policy • Generally loyal customer segment, but if they experience bad service, these customers are likely to migrate to other retailers with a better perceived service

(Continued)

Table 4. Customer typology (Continued)

	Smart shopper	Phlegmatic shopper	Hedonist	Connoisseur
Perception of physical service quality	• Personal advice is not a decisive factor • Keen on discount clearing points	• Value efficiency of in-store purchases (i.e. no long queues, low availability of sales people, long waiting time) • Value clarity of store design and visual merchandising in order to find items quickly • Value tidiness of items • Attach importance to competent personal advice in-store	• Strong reference to affiliation (look for like-minded people in-store, spend leisure time with friends and family) • Customer segment with the most negative perception of sales people (competence, friendliness and honesty) • Tend to accept poor personal advice when purchasing a product that has high desirability and limited accessibility • Seek physical stimulation through visual merchandising ('new looks', outfit combinations)	• Seek affiliation with other people, who have the same high status • Value an exclusive retail environment • Tendency to prefer in-store shopping, due to better perceived shopping experience • High degree of value-orientation in relation to brand/retailer image and personal interaction • Competent and appreciative personal advice when needed • Look for sensuality as well as for aesthetic store design and visual merchandising • Haptics plays a predominant role for choosing physical channels

Perception of electronic service quality			
• Tendency to prefer online shopping because of easier price comparison and perceived lower price • Prefer instalment payments • Pay attention to free shipping and free returns online • Favour a wide range of products	• Value practical aspects of web design when purchasing online (e.g. clear layout, filter options) • Value efficiency and convenience • Delivery and return options need to be convenient; if too complicated these customers tend to reject purchase	• Tendency to switch online shop after a short time when they do not find what they are looking for • Importance of practicability, clear structure and filter options • Pay attention to packaging of online purchases • Attractiveness of web design • Favour large assortments • Value free shipping and free returns • Tendency to order many items and have high return rates	• Seek electronic stimulation • Attractiveness of web design • Value visual stories and editorials • Value sophisticated packaging • Favour a smaller and customer-individual assortment • Look for personal contact when having a query

(Continued)

Table 4. Customer typology (Continued)

	Smart shopper	Phlegmatic shopper	Hedonist	Connoisseur
Perception of integration quality	• Positive impact of channel integration by means of price comparison option between channels	• Switching barriers can help to avoid cross-channel free-riding for this customer segment • Customer segment with the strongest positive impact of channel integration by means of effort, availability, price and support optimisation • Value availability check for both channels and also across channels • Value options of receiving and returning items in both channels	• Value effort optimisation since they intend to make as little effort as possible with non-emotional purchasing process elements (transaction, pick-up, return) • Demand for receiving the item as fast as possible; value different delivery options (same day, delivery in-store or at home) • Pay attention to availability check across channels	• Limited available time, seek the channel with least effort and the ability to check availability across channels • Use the Internet as the research channel, but prefer to shop in-store (preference to click-and-reserve) • When purchasing online, still request personal contact in-store, if needed

CONCLUSION AND MANAGERIAL IMPLICATIONS

In the context of omni-channel retailing, customer behaviour has developed into a complex construct. Omni-channel customers constantly adjust their decisions about vendor and retail channels during the purchase process. They tend to switch retail channels several times during their purchasing process.

A major shortcoming of the majority of extant studies in this area is their adoption of a positivist epistemological paradigm. Therefore, extant conceptual frameworks of omni-channel customers suggest a dualistic ontology and objectivistic epistemology. This chapter acknowledges the apparent characteristics of the omni-channel customer from a threefold perspective: (1) It represents a pluralistic ideology, which permits diverse customer perceptions, (2) it considers the dynamic nature of shopping experiences and thus perceptions, and (3) it considers "different income level" and "different involvement" as important drivers of heterogeneity for omni-channel customers.

Whereas previous studies have studied omni-channel customers as a relatively homogeneous group, this paper identifies four different customer types, based on two generators of heterogeneity: "available income level" and "involvement". Each customer type has a different principal driver and distinctive behavioural characteristics.

Consequently, omni-channel fashion retailers could prospectively analyse their customer base by means of the four Omni-channel customer types proposed by this paper, namely (1) phlegmatic, (2) smart, (3) hedonist, and (4) connoisseur shoppers. There is no "one-size-fits-all" solution, since each customer group has distinctive drivers, behavioural characteristics and perceptions. Thus, the fundamental question retailers that operate more than one retail channel should be able to answer is: "Which specific customer type do we want to target?" in order to be able to set up an effective and successful strategy.

REFERENCES

Ailawadi, K. L., & Farris, P. (2017). Managing multi- and omni-channel distribution: Metrics and research directions. *Journal of Retailing, 93*(1), 120–135.

Bartlett, J., & Kotrlik, J. (2001). Organizational research: Determining appropriate sample size in survey research. *Information Technology, Learning, and Performance Journal, 19*(1), 43–50.

Beck, N., & Rygl, D. (2015). Categorization of multiple channel retailing in multi-, cross-, and omni-channel for retailers and retailing. *Journal of Retailing and Consumer Services, 27*, 170–178.

Berman, B. (1996). *Marketing channels.* New York: John Wiley & Sons.

Brynjolfsson, E., Hu, Y. J., & Rahman, M. S. (2013). Competing in the age of omnichannel retailing. *MIT Sloan Management Review, 54*(4), 23–29.

Cao, L., Liu, X., & Cao, W. (2018). The effects of search-related and purchase-related mobile app additions on retailers' shareholder wealth: The roles of firm size, product category, and customer segment. *Journal of Retailing, 94*(4), 343–351.

Charmaz, K. (2011). *Constructing grounded theory. A practical guide through qualitative analysis* (Vol. 3). London: Sage.

Crotty, M. (1998). *The foundations of social research.* London: Sage.

Gensler, S., Neslin, S. A., & Verhoef, P. C. (2017). The showrooming phenomenon. *Journal of Interactive Marketing, 38*, 29–43.

Golafshani, N. (2003). Understanding reliability and validity in qualitative research. *The Qualitative Report, 8*, 597–607.

Heinemann, G. (2013). *No-Line-Handel.* Wiesbaden: Gabler Verlag.

Heinemann, G. (2019). *Handel mit Mehrwert.* Wiesbaden: Springer Gabler.

Heitz-Spahn, S. (2013). Cross-channel free-riding consumer behavior in a multichannel environment: An investigation of shopping motives, sociodemographics and product categories. *Journal of Retailing and Consumer Services, 20*, 570–578.

Hult, G., Tomas, M., & Zhang, Y. (2019). Antecedents and consequences of customer satisfaction: Do they differ across online and offline purchases? *Journal of Retailing, 95*(1), 10–23.

KPMG. (2018). Studie zum Einzelhandel 2025.

Kushwaha, T., & Shankar, V. (2013). Are multichannel customers really more valuable? The moderating role of product category characteristics. *Journal of Marketing, 77*(4), 67–102.

Leavy, P. (2014). Writing up qualitative research. In J. Gilgun (Ed.), *The Oxford Handbook of Qualitative Research*. Oxford: Oxford University Press.

Mahrdt, N., Lessing, M., Wagner, W., & Geissler, H. (2013). *Herausforderung Multi - Channel - Neue Wege zum Markterfolg*. Bad Homburg:Gemini.

Melis, K., Campo, K., & Breugelmans, L. (2015). The impact of the multuchannel retail mix on online store choice: Does online experience matter? *Journal of Retailing, 91*, 272–288.

Merleau-Ponty, M. (1962). *Phenomenology of perception*. London: Routledge & Kegan Paul.

Neslin, S., Grewal, D., Leghorn, R., Shankar, V., Teerlin, M., Thomas, J., & Verhoef, P. (2006). Challenges and opportunities in multichannel customer management. *Journal of Service Research, 9*(2), 95–112.

Ozuem, W., Howell, K., & Lancaster, G. (2008). Communicating in the new interactive marketspace. *European Journal of Marketing, 42*(9/10), 1059–1083.

Ozuem, W., Thomas, T., & Lancaster, G. (2016). The influence of customer loyalty on small island economies: An empirical and exploratory study. *Journal of Strategic Marketing, 24*(6), 447–469.

Ozuem, W., Patel, A., Howell, K., & Lancaster, G. (2017). An exploration of consumers' response to online service recovery initiatives. *International Journal of Market Research, 59*(1), 97–115.

Parasuraman, A., Zeithaml, V., & Berry, L. (1985). A conceptual model of service quality and its implications for future research. *Journal of Marketing, 49*, 41–50.

Patten, E. (2014). *The process is the product: Investigating, measuring, and evaluating service quality as source of value creation for multichannel retailers*. Paper presented at the International CIRCLE conference, Manchester.

Patten, E., & Ozuem, W. (2017). *The notion of omni-channel retailing in the fashion industry*. Paper presented at the Global Business and Technology Association-Conference, Vienna.

Patton, M. (1990). *Qualitative evaluation and research methods*. Beverly Hills: Sage.

Pelton, L., Strutton, D., & Lumpkin, J. (2002). *Marketing channels- a relationship management approach* (2nd ed.). Chicago: Irwin/McGraw-Hill.

Reinartz, W., Wiegand, N., & Imschloss, M. (2019). *The impact of digital transformation on the retailing value chain*. International Journal of Research in Marketing.

Robson, C. (2007). *Real world research* (Vol. 2). Chichester: Blackwell.

Saghiri, S., Wilding, R., Mena, C., & Bourlakis, M. (2017). Toward a three-dimensional framework for omni-channel. *Journal of Business Research, 77*, 53–67.

Saunders, M., Lewis, P., & Thornhill, A. (2009). *Research methods for business students* (5th ed., Vol. 5). Harlow: Pearson.

Saunders, M., & Townsed, K. (2016). Reporting and justifying the number of interview participants in organization and workplace research. *British Journal of Management, 27*(4), 1–17.

Shankar, V. (2011). Innovations in shopper marketing: Current insights and future research issues. *Journal of Retailing, 87*(1), 29–43.

Stone, G. (1954). City shoppers and urban identifications. Observation on the psychology of city life. *American Journal of Sociology, 60*, 36–45.

Tucker, W. (1965). Max Weber's 'Verstehen'. *The Sociological Quarterly, 6*(2), 157–165.

Verhoef, P., Kannan, P. K., & Inman, J. J. (2015). From multi-channel retailing to omni-channel retailing: Introduction to the special issue on multi-channel retailing. *Journal of Retailing, 91*(2), 174–181.

Verhoef, P., Neslin, S., & Vroomen, B. (2007). Multichannel customer management: Understanding the research shopper phenomenon. *International Journal of Research in Marketing, 24*(2), 129–148.

Westbrook, R. A., & Black, W. C. (1985). A motivation-based shopper typology. *Journal of Retailing, 61*(1), 78–103.

KEYTERMS

Cross-channel retailing: A retailing system consisting of more than one channel with partial channel integration and/or customer interaction across different retail channels.

Customer typology: A construct, where each type of customer is distinguished by a specific pattern of social characteristics reflecting his position in the social structure.

Omni-channel retailing: A retailing system consisting of more than one channel with full channel integration and/or customer interaction across different retail channels.

Chapter 8

Online Service Failure, Recovery Strategy and Customer Retention

Dipen Rai
University of the West of Scotland, UK

Kenneth Appiah
University of Cumbria, UK

ABSTRACT

This book chapter assesses the relationships between perceived justice and online service failure and recovery strategies in the fashion industry for customer retention. The existing literature has examined three-way and two-way interactions between procedural, distributive and interactional justice. The outcomes vary in terms of which combinations of justice create substantial interaction effects on customer recovery assessment. It recommends that for fashion brand providers to be competitive, they must combine both immersive technology and dimension metrics that comprise of subjective assessments. Both of these are critical to improve online service failure-recovery experiences which can have a significant impact on customer satisfaction and post-recovery behaviour. Furthermore, such a combination can mediate the relationship between satisfaction variables and justice dimensions.

INTRODUCTION AND CONTEXT

Online service failure is defined as *"the gap that occurs when customers' perceived quality of service delivery does not match their service expectations"* (Tate et al., 2014. p. 2). Similarly, service failures have been defined as *"service performances that fall below customer expectation"* (Hoffman & Bateson, 2010, p. 327). Others have described service failure as any service associated calamity or trouble that occurs during the experience of a consumer in their dealings with a company (Maxham, 2001; Ozuem et al., 2017). Some researchers have argued that it can be expensive for service providers to negect to tackle service failures. Such failures can also lead to consumer refusals (Liu et al., 2000; Maxham, 2001; Kotler & Keller, 2011). The idea of online service failures is based on Expectation Confirmation Theory (ECT) and can be defined on the basis of the conventional "gap" framework of service quality (Oliver, 1980; Parasuraman et al., 2005). E-tail consumers experience various online service failures as compared with their conventional retail counterparts (Kelley et al., 2005). Consequently, novel failure recovery strategies are essential in order to deal with online service failures.

The literature on service failures and recovery strategies emphasises understanding the clients' perspective excelling explanations from the provider's view (Parasuraman et al., 2005; Zhu et al., 2013). The provider's outlook is often anticipated and can be approached from the perspective of two different types of performers which are enacted in order to enrich the experiences of customers (Grewal et al., 2008; Huang et al., 2013). It has been argued that consumers have entirely similar experiences of service failures and recovery strategies but there are limited exceptions that affect subjective fact in the occurrence (Maxham & Netemeyer, 2002). Further, it has been suggested that failure severity and critical failure have a substantial impact on consumer satisfaction. These can lead to adverse word-of-mouth communications and reduced levels of consumer loyalty. Previous research (see Jones et al., 2004; Azemi & Ozuem, 2016) has investigated the effect of service failure severity on trust, loyalty, consumer satisfaction and negative word-of-mouth. Research has found that service failure severity has a substantial effect on consumer trust, loyalty and adverse word-of-mouth (Maxham, 2001). Kim and Ulgado (2012) investigated the perspectives of consumers in relation to service failure severity, repurchase behaviour and recovery satisfaction in hospitality services. Moreover, they concluded that service failure severity has a substantial adverse effect on consumer repurchasing behaviour.

CONTEXTUALISATION: ONLINE SERVICE FAILURES

A complete outline of the literature ascribes service failure-recovery experience to a five-stage procedure; i.e. service failure occurs, recovery expectations arise, the provision of recovery strategies occurs, an evaluation of recovery takes place and post-recovery behaviour emerges. Though, consumers' perception is significantly related with particular process stages (Grewal et al., 2008), overwhelming descriptions heritable to the missing stage. According to Mohr et al. (2006) understanding the consumer is about appreciating the above stages. Therefore, consumers' experience accounts for particular backgrounds, exceeding the possibility of other descriptive factors (Rio-Lanza et al., 2009; Mattila & Choi, 2008). The literature has established a context-free method based on a positivist ontological view to measure the responses of consumers, and these are typically highly concentrated and organised. It indicates that service failures and recovery strategies are related to an iterative experience. Moreover, the experience of the customer is anticipated during the service failure-recovery. Consequently, Miller et al. (2000) illustrated that the literature on service failures and recovery strategies recognises the attempts of academics to assign customer perceptions to service failures and recovery to objective facts.

Nevertheless, the literature sets out some contrasting and contradictory outcomes. It advises that consumers are heterogeneous and need to be managed subjectively (Diaz-Martin et al., 2008; Wang et al., 2011; Azemi & Ozuem, 2016). The existing literature on service failure and recovery strategies sets out a number of advantages associated with service recovery. Rust and Oliver (2000) argue that suggestive outcomes affirm that acceptable recoveries might be harmful to the service provider. This provides an indication of how distinctive consumers are from a realist persepctive. The author suggests a contextual method for understanding of service failure and recovery strategies which places the consumer at the heart of analysis. The literature on service recovery also follows a particular espistemological orientation (McCarthy et al., 2011). Electronic media literature has established some knowledge in terms of service failure and recovery strategies, while the evolution of the internet has exposed offline service failures and recovery strategies from the persepctive of traditional offline practices (Salle et al., 2015; Ozuem et al., 2016). It has been suggested that

Computer-Mediated Marketing Environments (CMMEs) have empowered society and have allowed consumers to develop insights and highly individualised orientations to the world of consumerism (Ellis-Chadwick & Chaffey, 2012). This underscores the subjectivity of the insights of consumers and relates service failure and recovery strategies to experiences of impulsive results. Moreover, the practice of providers observing consumers has also been highlighted and authors have related service failure-recovery occurrences to the combined experience created between the customer and the provider.

Ozuem and Lancaster (2013) attributed service failure-recovery experiences to interactions between consumers and others as part of the process of social constructivitism. The present research study suggests that service failure, recovery expectancy and appraisal, as well as after-recovery actions are formed through interactions between consumers and providers. This suggests that individuals constantly accept the latest information that matches and substitutes inherited characteristics. This contrasts with work undertaken by Ringberg et al. (2007) since the present research does not separate out the inherited characteristics of customers before service failure occurs. This study views service failure and recovery strategies as combined initiatives that are carried out in concert between providers and consumers. It evaluates service failure-recovery from the perspectives of both customers and providers in order to develop an understanding of the topic. The study presents a contextual and inclusive conceptualisation of consumers during service failure-recovery procedures. This study is not isolated from previous research because a social constructivist approach is used. Strauss (1988) states that such an approach links data enrichment to the empirical data of the researcher. Maxwell (2012) illustrated that empirical data can include the personal and professional experiences of the researcher as part of the studied phenomenon. The personal and professional experiences, and the background of the researcher have therefore directed the current study which is produced in the conext of online service failures and recovery strategies in the fashion industry. Such an investigation represents a timely addition to the existing literature.

Academics have identified descriptions of service failure- recovery occurrences based on feedback from customers (Wirtz & Mattila, 2004; Vazquez-Casielles et al., 2008). Similar approaches and comprehensions of service failure and recovery strategies have been developed in the literature (Cheng et al., 2012; Huang et al., 2014). This type of positivist orientation creates limited explanations as to the specific antecedents and process phases associated with service recovery (Chou & Lai, 2015). Furthermore, such arguments are related occurrences that are part of an iterative experience. They view the behaviours and reactions of consumers as predictable. Positivistic approaches to understanding consumers seem to have obstructed the clarifications inherited to the main theory. Regardless, academics have attempted to understand service failure and recovery strategy occurrences from various theoretical approaches such as justice and appraisal theory (Azemi & Ozuem, 2016; Mohr et al., 2006; Zhang et al., 2013). These varied arguments have perhaps over-complicated issues relating to service (Choi & Choi, 2014). The literature has keenly focussed on the customer's perspective and descriptions of the realities that consumers experience in the context of service failures and recovery. Studies have also looked at post-recovery behaviour and purchase decisions. Therefore, the present research paper approaches consumers as heterogeneous and relates customer perspectives of service failure-recovery to their state of their mind.

SERVICE RECOVERY IN FASHION INDUSTRY

It is essential to address the problems inherent to service failures in the fashion industry on account of the costs associated with gaining new clients. Such costs are five times higher than the costs associated with the retention of current clients (Maxham, 2001; Gitomer, 2013). Such high costs are associated with the expensive nature of marketing activities required to attain new clients. Furthermore, service providers could conceivably harm the long-term success of their business if they are unable to recover service failure properly (Magnini & Ford, 2004). Accordingly, Tschohl (2013) stated that an effective recovery strategy can reduce negative feelings and increase positive sentiments amongst customers.

Consumers are likely to switch fashion brand service providers if the service recovery they experience does not fulfil their expectations (Zeithaml et al., 2012). However, it has been argued that customers are likely to publicize more intense negative sentiments if they no not perceive of a sufficient level of service recovery following service failure (Neira et al., 2010; Ayertey & Ozuem, 2017). Therefore, service recovery can be approched as a second opportunity for the service provider to address failings as soon as they occur (Bowen & Johnston, 1999). The eficient management of failure has an effect on the satisfaction of customers and their intentions to switch service providers (Ahmed & Amir, 2011). Service failure recovery is considered a key factor behind the customer's decision to switch service provider (Azemi & Ozuem, 2016).

JUSTICE THEORY: THE INTERMEDIARY OF THE FASHION BRANDS PROVIDER

This research study is based on justice theory which is used to investigate service recovery in fashion brands by figuring out the impact of efficient service recovery processes. This theory looks at the perceptions of customers regarding the fairness of service recovery attempts and the impact of these on consumer satisfaction and potential behavioural intentions (McColl-Kennedy & Sparks, 2003). The consumer's verdict of service justice emerges when deviations between their perceptions of fairness and their intelligence occur with the result that they feel they have been treated unfairly (Berry & Seiders, 2008). Service fairness is the level of justice perceived by the customer in reviewing the behaviour of the service provider.

Extensive literature in service failure and recovery has produced substantial evidence to support the notion of justice based on understanding the procedures of service recovery and its consequences (Goodwin & Ross, 1992; Tax et al., 1998; Smith et al., 1999; Blodgett & Li, 2007; Knox & Oest, 2014). Consumers determine the fairness concerning service recovery according to three dimensions of justice:

1. distributive justice, which concerntrates on the perceived fairness of the procedural outcome,
2. procedural justice which focuses on the perceived fairness of procedures in order to resolve problems and
3. interactional justice which emphasises the methods by which consumers are treated during the process (Ruyter & Wetzels, 2000; Liao & Chuang, 2007).

However, it has been argued that a four-dimensional model is better than a two or three-dimensional framework (Colquitt, 2001). Therefore, informational justice has been added into these justice dimensions.

Hence, this paper follows the four-dimensional justice framework proposed by Colquitt (2001) in order to investigate online service failures and recovery strategies in the fasion industry.

DISTRIBUTIVE JUSTICE

Distributive justice signifies an agreement or decision implicating two or more alliances. It measures the perceived fairness of the substantial outcome of a disagreement (Lin et al., 2011; Nikbin et al., 2012). Distributive justice is *"the allocation of costs and benefits in achieving equitable exchange relationships"* (Smith et al., 1999, p. 359). Similarly, it is described as the deployment of tangible resources held by the organisation in order to resolve and recompense customers for a service failure (Río-Lanza et al., 2009).

Distributive justice concerns the outcome provided during service recovery in fashion industry. This might include recompense such as discounts, rewards, vouchers and the provision of products/services after service failures (McColl-Kennedy & Sparks, 2003; Mattila et al., 2011). The perception of distributive justice may be influenced by tangible recompenses which are expected from service providers to offer solutions after the occurance of service failure. The fairness of recompense may be influenced by the prior experiences of consumers with the organisation, and their insight into the magnitude of the loss that has occurred through service failure (Tax et al., 1998).

The extent of recompense may be different, and it relies on the level of failure severity. A customer who experiences service failure might expect a fair-fix and some value-added compensation (Hocutt et al., 2007; Bell & Ridge, 1992 cited in Koc, 2017). A customer might be disappointed with an unjust relationship with fashion brands and this could lead to adverse word-of-mouth. Therefore, distributive justice from the perspective of customers can impact on their satisfaction (Colquitt et al., 2005). For customers, the outcome of service recovery has a positive influence on their satisfaction after service failure occurs and this can mitigate adverse word-of-mouth. It has been identified that tangible recompense can lead to greater insight in terms of distributive justice (Hocutt et al., 2007).

Distributive justice is recompense which the consumer obtains for inconvenience and loss due to service failure (Rashid et al., 2014).

Recompense can be an efficient tool for justifying customer disappointment with service failure, and several consumers expect such justice for losses that they experience (Noone, 2012; Bambauer-Sachse & Rabeson, 2015). Recompense can be financial or non-financial and can include reimbursements, exchanges, maintenance and store credit (Lin et al., 2011; Choi & Choi, 2014). In addition, recompense escalates positive behavioural intentions like positive word-of-mouth (Grewal et al., 2008). Distributive justice creates a positive impact on customer satisfaction as well as on switching and repurchase intentions (Nikbin et al., 2012; Lopes & Silva, 2015).

PROCEDURAL JUSTICE

According to Kelley et al. (2005), Procedural justice is the perceived level of fairness for attaining suitable recovery results. Service recovery might include factors like time, how quick the provider recovers the failure, and the effectiveness and flexibility of recovery. Procedural justice is the perceived fairness of procedures, guidelines, and criteria implemented in order to reach the result of a disagreement or negotiation (Blodgett & Li, 2007). Moreover, it indicates that customer's perception of justice for the various stages of processes required to recover the service failure for the effective service recovery (Choi & Choi, 2014). Additionally, it seeks to deliver specific outcomes like 'time to receive refund (timing)' and 'refund policies' to arrive at a positive result from the negotiation (Tyler & Lind, 1988). Furthermore, timing is the core idea of procedural justice in terms of customer complaint conditions (Wagner et al., 1999).

Procedural justice is the assessment of customers in terms of decision making, and the policies and procedures of organisations in order to resolve disagreements (Maxham & Netemeyer, 2002). Such justice is assessed according to the methods by which organisations endure the responsibility for service failure, the speed of how complaints are tackled and the nature of how service failure is fixed (Chi & Wen, 2013). Speed/timing, flexibility, decision and process control are the components of procedural justice (Tax et al., 1998). Previous studies revealed only subjective evidence as to the possible effects of procedural justice on consumer assessments of service recovery (Bitner et al., 1994).

According to Nikbin et al. (2012), various policies and systems are used to tackle service failures as well as to respond to complaints.

Service providers must accept error and make some effort to rectify faults on time in order to achieve procedural justice (Chang et al., 2011; Kuo & Wu, 2012). It reveals that the fast response of fashion brands can reduce the adverse affects of negative WOM and can impact positively on customer intentions. Moreover, research shows that procedural justice has a substantial positive impact on post-recovery satisfaction (Nikbin et al., 2012; Yau et al., 2013). Furthermore, service providers can increase consumer satisfaction with service recovery due to the development of their awareness concerning procedural justice (Rio-Lanza et al., 2009). It is evident that perceived procedural justice influences customer satisfaction significantly through effective complaint handling (Huang & Wu, 2015).

INTERACTIONAL JUSTICE

Interactional justice is about customer's feelings in terms of how they were treated by those involved with recovering service failure (Kuo & Wu, 2012; Cheng et al., 2014). Interactional justice necessitates that the service provider exhibits concern, courtesy and sympathy during service failures (Choi & Choi, 2014). It has been observed that higher interactional justice levels lead to higher customer satisfaction levels (Kuo & Wu, 2012). On the other hand, lower levels of interactional justice escalate adverse WOM from dissatisfied customers (Chang et al., 2011). Additionally, interactional justice has a substantial impact on post-recovery satisfaction in fashion industry. There is a substantial positive association between repurchase intentions and interactional justice (Nikbin et al., 2012).

Interactional justice focuses on the interactions between customers and employees based on communications that occur within a complaint period (Fernandes & Santos, 2008). Service recovery is the method customers engage with in failed service. It provides an indication of the extent to which consumers have experienced justice in human interactions with staff during the recovery process (McColl-Kennedy & Sparks, 2003). Scholars believe that interactional justice has the most substantial impact on customer satisfaction throughout service recovery (Maxham & Netemeyer, 2002; Fürst & Homburg, 2005). In addition, there is a positive relationship between customer satisfaction and interactional justice throughout service recovery (Zhang et al., 2013).

INFORMATIONAL JUSTICE

According to Colquitt (2001, p. 390), *"informational justice comprises justification (e.g., explaining the basis for decisions), truthfulness (e.g., an authority figure being candid and not engaging in deception), respect (e.g., being polite rather than rude), and propriety (e.g., refraining from improper remarks or prejudicial statement)"*. It emphases the equity of the descriptions and justifications presented regarding the decisions and causes behind things (Ambrose et al., 2007). A four-dimensional justice model is thus proposed to describe justice more effectively than a three-dimensional justice model (Colquitt, 2001). Informational justice is vulnerable from the customer's perspective due to the lack of descriptions offered to people regarding why processes are used in specific ways, or why results are distributed in a specific way (Colquitt, 2001; Nikbin et al., 2012). Informational justice does much to underscore the credibility of a firm by diminishing dishonesty and confidentiality (Colquitt, 2001).

Service scholars have studied procedural, distributive and interactional justice in some detail, although informational justice has been given very little attention in fashion industry. Very few studies have been conducted to look at complaint handling in terms of informational justice. A study carried out by Cranage and Mattila (2005) in the hospitality sector related service information to customer decisions so that the customer's perspective of informational justice was influenced despite the result of the service recovery. Moreover, it increases the consumer's self-responsibility whilst concurrently decreasing the probability of accusing the fashion brands. Informational justice considerably impacts on customer satisfaction through complaint handling in the financial sector (Iglesias et al., 2010). However, very few studies have sought to find the impact of informational justice on overall organizational satisfaction in fashion industry, especially in online setting firms.

INTERACTION AMONG PERCEIVED JUSTICE EXTENTS

It has been argued that distributive and interactional justice have an interaction impact on service recovery assessments in fashion industry. This indicates that a higher level of interactional justice can recompense for a lower level of distributive justice, although other probable three-way and two-way interactions are not essential for fashion brands. Nevertheless,

Tax et al. (1998) stated that two-way interactions between procedural-distributive and procedural-interactional justice are essential in service recovery assessment. After incorporating informational justice into the justice dimensions, it has been shown that a combination of informational and procedural justice has the most direct impact on customer satisfaction (Cranage & Mattila, 2005).

Some contradictory findings have been reported from studies in online fashion brands concerning the interactions between variables in the justice framework. According to Chang et al. (2011), both the interaction between procedural and distributive justice as well as interactions between interactional and distributive justice have positive substantial impacts on complaint handling evaluation. Similarly, the interactions between distributive and procedural justice have only a partial impact on customer satisfaction. Interactional justice has no significant impact on it (Siu et al., 2013). Nevertheless, Fan et al. (2010) stated that interactions between procedural and ditributive justice have no substantial effect. Thus, it is difficult to predict which interactions between the justice elements create the greatest effect on customer satisfaction in fashion industry. Studies suggest there may be a probable interaction amongst all of the justice elements in terms of customer satisfaction after service recovery.

SATISFACTION WITH RECOVERY

This book chapter concerns overall customer satisfaction with fashion brands after they have taken action to recover service failures. Service recovery satisfaction make consumers more likely to spread positive WOM regarding the service provider (Henrique et al., 2013; Choi & Choi, 2014). In addition, satisfaction after service recovery increases customer loyalty (Osarenkhoe & Komunda, 2012). Failure in terms of service recovery results in dissatisfaction in customers and leads to greater switching intentions (Lin et al., 2011).

Boshoff (1997) stated that recovery satisfaction indicates the extent to which a consumer is satisfied with the service recovery efforts of the provider following a service failure. Moreover, recovery satisfaction is an analysis of the possibility of spreading positive WOM and this accords with previous studies (Tax & Brown, 1998; Maxham & Netemeyer, 2002). Not only does recovery satisfaction improve the assessment of a service experience (Estelami, 2000) but it also develops post-recovery commitment amongst customers to a long-standing association with the fashion brands. It also leads to better customer retention rates (Miller et al., 2000). Furthermore, complaint handling is an intermediary intervention that associates the perceptions of the fairness dimensions to mindsets after recovery and customer loyalty behaviours (Miller et al., 2000; Parasuraman et al., 2005).

According to Spreng et al. (1995), service recovery is an action performed by firms to recover failures following complaints by customers. To prohibit anger and motivate customers, effective service recovery is useful for customer retention (Hart et al., 1990). Thus, satisfaction with recovery has a positive impact on trust (Nadiri, 2016). In addition, trust can be developed from fashion brands amongst consumers by letting them feel they are valued and their complaints matter. Organisational service recovery can be converted into recovery satisfaction by eliciting the customer's trust.

Earlier studies on justice theory have suggested that the three dimensions of justice comprising distributive, procedural and interactional justice impact on recovery satisfaction (Bolton et al., 1999; Maxham & Netemeyer, 2002). Normally, perceived justice is postulated as an antecedent of cognition that impacts directly on recovery satisfaction (Tax et al., 1998; Bolton & Smith, 2002). Beginning with consumer complaint behaviour, the justice perspectives are a strong predictor of customer satisfaction (Siu et al., 2013; Ding et al., 2015). Efficient service recovery efforts can fix consumer dissatisfaction (Kuo & Wu, 2012). Service providers have an opportunity throigh recovery to maintain a strong relationship with customers when provided the chance to right a perceived wrong (Migacz et al., 2017).

However, the effect of justice dimensions on customer satisfaction is less clear in fashion industry. Distributive justice is the most essential determinant of service recovery in relation to recovery satisfaction (Tax & Brown, 1998). Other studies have revealed that distributive justice is the most essential aspect of post-recovery satisfaction (Bolton & Smith, 2002; Cranage & Mattila, 2005). Previos research has advised that distributive justice is the most basic determinant of recovery satisfaction (Shanklin et al., 2005). Nevertheless, Karatepe (2006) found procedural justice to be the most important factor of customer satisfaction. Many scholars agree that procedural justice has the least effect on recovery satisfaction (Kim et al., 2009).

MANAGERIAL IMPLICATIONS

The implications for managers are significant, particularly for profitability, customer satisfaction and market share in the fashion industry. Studies of online service failure and recovery strategies first emerged earlier this century and so the topic has not been fully and adequately conceptualized (Boroumand et al., 2008; Fan et al., 2010). Researchers have attempted to transfer some of the conventional wisdom associated with offline failure recovery literature to online settings with mixed success (Ozuem & Lancaster, 2013). Descriptions of service failure and recovery strategies illuminate some of the risks and opportunities associated with digital settings (Piercy & Archer-Brown, 2014). The existing literature on service failure and recovery strategies shows that failing to understand the consumer is the main reason for the ambiguity and complications that have been identified by academics and specialists (Netemeyer & Maxham, 2002; Lo & Wu, 2012; Zhu et al., 2013). This would suggest that comprehending service failure and recovery experiences from an online perspective is essential to create positive recovery platforms for fashion brands. The above discussion emphasizes the need to comprehend service failures and recovery to hypothetical situations, leading the researcher to explore the phenomenon comprehensively.

This research study delivers substantial indicators for managers in the fashion industry. Apologizing, compensation, confirming a speedy response to the consumers and following-up have been acknowledged as effective recovery strategies in order to increase consumer satisfaction (Smith et al., 1999; Gelbrich & Roschk, 2011). The findings advise that businesses should have in place practical recovery strategies that they may implement in order to resolve service failures. Service failure is common, and consumers may experience disappointment with services after failure occurs. Therefore, it is essential that managers should train employees to respond to disappointed consumers with a recovery strategy in a way that expresses sincere regret for the service failure (Lastner et al., 2016).

Other managerial implications that have emerged from this research study include the use of apologies, which are not just anticipated by affected consumers, but are also advantageous in reinstating organizational reputation particularly in the context of service failure. Such gratitude may enhance and enable the process of managerial decision-making involving communication choices aimed at strengthening relationships with consumers (Salvador et al., 2012). Moreover, the impact of recovery strategies on the revenue of the firm can be important for maintaining a relationship with existing customers as a crucial strategy (Ozuem et al., 2017).

Finally, the ultimate aim is not only to impede the loss of customers but to sustain a long-term supportive relationship with them. These outcomes have valuable implications for fashion brand managers who are concerned with developing measures that can maximize customer satisfaction through service recovery to successively enrich long-term customer relationships.

REFERENCES

Ahmed, I., & Amir, M. (2011). Service quality; service features; and customer complaint handling as the major drivers of customer satisfaction in banking sector of Pakistan. *International Review of Business Research Papers, 7*(1), 313–318.

Ambrose, M., Hess, R. L., & Ganesan, S. (2007). The relationship between justice and attitudes: An examination of justice effects on event and system-related attitudes. *Organizational Behavior and Human Decision Processes, 103*(1), 21–36.

Ayertey, S., & Ozuem, W. (2017). Developing compelling online recovery strategies: Implications for the fashion clothing industry. In *Digital Marketing Strategies for Fashion and Luxury Brands* (pp. 264–288). Hershey: IGI Global.

Azemi, Y., & Ozuem, W. (2016). *Online service failure and recovery strategy: The mediating role of social media.* Hershey: IGI Global.

Bambauer-Sachse, S., & Rabeson, L. E. (2015). Service recovery for moderate and high involvement services. *Journal of Services Marketing, 29*(29), 331–343.

Berry, L. L., & Seiders, K. (2008). Serving unfair customers. *Business Horizons, 51*(1), 29–37.

Blodgett, J. G., & Li, H. (2007). Assessing the effects of post-purchase dissatisfaction and complaint behavior on profitability: A monte carlo simulation. *Journal of Consumer Satisfaction, Dissatisfaction and Complaining Behavior, 20*(1), 3–14.

Boroumand, L., et al. (2008). Service failure-recovery in online shops in Iran. *International Journal of Information Science and Technology, 6*(2), 61–75.

Boshoff, C. (1997). An experimental study of service recovery options. *International Journal of Service Industry Management, 8*(2), 110–130.

Brown, S. W., Fisk, R. P., & Bitner, M. J. (1994). The development and emergence of services marketing thought. *International Journal of Service Industry Management, 54*(1), 21–48.

Chang, D. S., & Wang, T. H. (2012). Consumer preferences for service recovery options after delivery delay when shopping online. *Social Behavior and Personality: An International Journal, 40*(6), 1033–1044.

Cheng, Y. H., Chuang, S. C., Chang, C. J., & Shun-Wen, Y. (2012). The effect of service failure types and service recovery on customer satisfaction: A mental accounting perspective. *The Service Industries Journal, 32*(2), 257–271.

Chi, C. G., & Wen, B. (2013). Examine the cognitive and affective antecedents to service recovery satisfaction: A field study of delayed airline passengers. *International Journal of Contemporary Hospitality Management, 25*(3), 306–327.

Choi, B., & Choi, B. J. (2014). The effects of perceived service recovery justice on customer affection, loyalty, and word-of-mouth. *European Journal of Marketing, 48*(1/2), 108–131.

Chou, F. S., & Lai, M. C. (2015). The relationships among involvement level, service failure, service recovery disconfirmation and customer lifetime value. *Journal of Economics, Business and Management, 3*(4), 452–456.

Colquitt, J. A. (2001). On the dimensionality of organizational justice: A construct validation of a measure. *Journal of Applied Psychology, 86*(3), 386–400.

Colquitt, J. A., Greenberg, J., & Zapata-Phelan, C. P. (2005). What is organizational justice? A historical overview. *Organizational Behavior and Human Decision Processes, 100*(1), 110–127.

Cranage, D., & Mattila, A. S. (2005). The impact of choice on fairness in the context of service recovery. *Journal of Services Marketing, 19*(5), 271–279.

Ding, M. C., Ho, C. W., & Lii, Y. S. (2015). Is corporate reputation a double-edged sword? Relative effects of perceived justice in airline service recovery. *International Journal of Economics and Business Research, 10*(1), 1–17.

Ellis-Chadwick, F., & Chaffey, D. (2012). *Digital marketing: Strategy, implementation and practice* (5th ed.). London: Pearson Education Ltd.

Estelami, H. (2000). Competitive and procedural determinants of delight and disappointment in consumer complaint outcomes. *Journal of Service Research, 2*(3), 285–300.

Fan, Y. W., Wu, C. C., & Wu, W. T. (2010). The impacts of online retailing service failure recovery and perceived justice on consumer loyalty. *International Journal of Electronic Business Management, 8*(3), 239–249.

Fernandes, D. v. d. H., & Santos, C. P. d. (2008). The antecedents of the consumer complaining behavior. *Advances in Consumer Research, 35*, 584–592.

Gelbrich, K., & Roschk, H. (2011). A meta-analysis of organizational complaint handling and customer responses. *Journal of Service Research, 14*(1), 24–43.

Gitomer, J. (2013). *Customer satisfaction is worthless customer loyalty is priceless* (7th ed.). Texas: Bard Press.

Goodwin, C., & Ross, I. (1992). Consumer responses to service failures: influence of procedural and interactional fairness perceptions. *Journal of Business Research, 25*(2), 149–163.

Grewal, D., Roggeveen, A. L., & Tsiros, M. (2008). The effect of compensation on repurchase intentions in service recovery. *Journal of Retailing, 84*(4), 424–434.

Hart, C. W., Heskett, J. L., & Sasser, W. E. (1990). The profitable art of service recovery. *Harvard Business Review*, 148–156.

Henrique, J. L., Rosa, F., & Matos, C. A. (2013). Customer reactions to service failure and recovery in the banking industry: The influence of switching costs. *Journal of Services Marketing, 27*(7), 526–538.

Hocutt, M. A., Bowers, M. R., & Donavan, T. (2007). The art of service recovery: Fact or fction? *Journal of Service Marketing, 20*(3), 199–207.

Hoffman, K. D., & Bateson, J. E. (2010). *Services marketing: Concepts, strategies, & cases.* Mason: Cengage Learning.

Huang, M., Zhou, Y., Tsang, A. S. L., & Zhou, N. (2014). Group service recovery strategies effectiveness: The moderating effects of group size and relational distance. *Journal of Business Research, 67*(11), 2480–2485.

Karatepe, O. M. (2006). Customer complaints and organizational responses: The effects of complainants' perceptions of justice on satisfaction and loyalty. *International Journal of Hospitality Management, 25*(1), 69–90.

Kelley, S. W., Forbes, L. P., & Hoffman, K. D. (2005). Typologies of e-commerce retail failures and recovery strategies. *Journal of Services Marketing, 19*(5), 280–292.

Kim, N., & Ulgado, F. M. (2012). The effect of on-the-spot versus delayed compensation: The moderating role of failure severity. *Journal of Services Marketing, 26*(3), 158–167.

Knox, G., & Oest, R. V. (2014). Customer complaints and recovery effectiveness: A customer base approach. *Journal of Marketing, 78*(5), 42–57.

Kotler, P., & Keller, K. L. (2011). *Marketing management* (14th ed.). New Jersey: Pearson Education.

Kuo, Y. F., & Wu, C. M. (2012). Satisfaction and post-purchase intentions with service recovery of online shopping websites: Perspectives on perceived justice and emotions. *International Journal of Information Management, 32*(2), 127–138.

Lastner, M. M., Folse, J. A. G., Mangus, S. M., & Fennell, P. (2016). The road to recovery: Overcoming service failures through positive emotions. *Journal of Business Research, 69*(10), 4278–4286.

Liao, H. (2007). Do it right this time: The role of employee service recovery performance in customer-perceived justice and customer loyalty after service failures. *J Appl Psychol, 92*(2), 475–489.

Liao, H., & Chuang, A. (2007). Transforming service employees and climate: A multilevel, multisource examination of transformational leadership in building long-term service relationships. *Journal of Applied Psychology, 92*(4), 1006–1019.

Lin, S. C., Chang, H. T., Chen, F. S., & Lin, Y. M. (2011). Study on the effects of transformational leadership by managers and organizational justice consciousness on organizational citizenship behaviour of high-tech electronics industry in Taiwan. *African Journal of Business Management, 5*(7), 2930–2941.

Liu, B. S., Sudharshan, D., & Hamer, L. O. (2000). After-service response in service quality assessment: A real-time updating model approach. *Journal of Services Marketing, 14*(2), 160–177.

Lopes, E. L., & Silva, M. A. (2015). The effect of justice in the history of loyalty: A study in failure recovery in the retail context. *Journal of Retailing and Consumer Services, 24*(1), 110–120.

Magnini, V. P., & Ford, J. B. (2004). Service failure recovery in China. *International Journal of Contemporary Hospitality Management, 16*(5), 279–286.

Mattila, A., & Choi, S. (2008). Perceived controllability and service expectations: Influences on customer reactions following service failure. *Journal of Business Research, 61*(1), 24–30.

Maxham, J. (2001). Service recovery's influence on consumer satisfaction, positive word-of-mouth, and purchase intentions. *Journal of Business Research, 54*(1), 11–24.

Maxham, J. G., & Netemeyer, R. G. (2002). A longitudinal study of complaining customers' evaluations of multiple service failures and recovery efforts. *Journal of Marketing, 66*(4), 57–71.

Maxwell, J. A. (2012). *Qualitative research design: An interactive approach* (3rd ed.). London: SAGE Publications, Inc.

McColl-Kennedy, J. R., Daus, C. S., & Sparks, B. A. (2003). The role of gender in reactions to service failure and recovery. *Journal of Service Research, 6*(1), 66–82.

McColl-Kennedy, J. R., & Sparks, B. A. (2003). Application of fairness theory to service failures and service recovery. *Journal of Service Research, 5*(3), 251–266.

Migacz, S. J., Zou, S., & Petrick, J. F. (2017). The "Terminal" effects of service failure on airlines: Examining service recovery with justice theory. *Journal of Travel Research*, 1–16.

Miller, J. L., Craighead, C. W., & Karwan, K. R. (2000). Service recovery: A framework and empirical investigation. *Journal of Operations Management, 18*(4), 387–400.

Mohr, L. A., Harris, K. E., & Bernhardt, K. L. (2006). Online service failure, consumer attributions and expectations. *Journal of Services Marketing, 20*(7), 453–458.

Nadiri, H. (2016). Diagnosing the impact of retail bank customers' perceived justice on their service recovery satisfaction and post-purchase behaviours. *Economic Research, 29*(1), 193–216.

Neira, C. V., Casielles, R. V., & Iglesias, V. (2010). The effects of customer age and recovery strategies in a service failure setting. *Journal of Financial Services Marketing, 15*(1), 32–48.

Nikbin, D., Ismail, I., Marimuthu, M., & Salarzehi, H. (2012). The relationship of service failure attributions, service recovery justice and recovery satisfactionin the context of airlines. *Scandinavian Journal of Hospitality and Tourism, 12*(3), 232–254.

Noone, B. M. (2012). Overcompensating for severe service failure: Perceived fairness and effect on negative word-of-mouth intent. *Journal of Services Marketing, 26*(5), 342–351.

Oliver, R. L. (1980). A cognitive model of the antecedents and consequences of satisfaction decisions. *Journal of Marketing Research, 17*(4), 460–469.

Osarenkhoe, A., & Komunda, M. (2012). Remedy or cure for service failure?: Effects of service recovery on customer satisfaction and loyalty. *Business Process Management Journal, 18*(1), 82–103.

Ozuem, W., & Azemi, Y. (2017). Online service failure and recovery strategies in luxury brands: A view from justice theory. *IGI Global*, 108–120.

Ozuem, W., Howell, K. E., & Lancaster, G. (2008). Communicating in the new interactive marketspace. *European Journal of Marketing, 42*(9), 1059–1083.

Ozuem, W., & Lancaster, G. (2013). Recovery strategies in on-line service failure. *Marketing in the Cyber Era: Strategies and Emerging Trends,* 143–159.

Ozuem, W., & Lancaster, G. (2013). *Recovery Strategies in On-Line Service Failure.* Hershey: IGI Global.

Ozuem, W., Patel, A., Howell, K., & Lancaster, G. (2017). An exploration of consumers' response to online service recovery initiatives. *International Journal of Market Research, 59*(1), 97–115.

Parasuraman, A., Zeithaml, V. A., & Malhotra, A. (2005). A multiple-item scale for assessing electronic service quality. *Journal of Service Research, 7*, 1–21.

Piercy, N., & Archer-Brown, C. (2014). Online service failure and propensity to suspend offline consumption. *The Service Industries Journal, 34*(8), 659–676.

Rashid, M. H. A., Ahmad, F. S., & Othman, A. K. (2014). Does service recovery affect customer satisfaction? A study on co-created retail industry. *Procedia—Social and Behavioral Sciences, 130*, 455–460.

Ringberg, T., Odekerken-Schröder, G., & Christensen, G. L. (2007). A cultural models approach to service recovery. *Journal of Marketing, 71*(3), 194–214.

Río-Lanza, A. B. D., Vázquez-Casielles, R., & Díaz-Martín, A. M. (2009). Satisfaction with service recovery: Perceived justice and emotional responses. *Journal of Business Research, 62*(8), 775–781.

Rust, R. T., & Oliver, R. L. (2000). Should we delight the customer? *Journal of the Academy of Marketing Science, 28*(1), 86–94.

Ruyter, K. D., & Wetzels, M. (2000). Customer equity considerations in service recovery: A cross-industry perspective. *International Journal of Service Industry Management, 11*(1), 91–108.

Salle, A., Tripp, T. M., & Grégoire, Y. (2015). Managing social media crises with your customers: The good, the bad, and the ugly. *Business Horizons, 58*(2), 173–182.

Salvador, R. O., Folger, R., & Priesemuth, M. (2012). Organizational apology and defense: Effects of guilt and managerial status. *Journal of Managerial, 24*(2), 124–139.

Shanklin, C. W., Back, K. J., & Ok, C. (2005). Modeling roles of service recovery strategy: A relationship-focused view. *Journal of Hospitality & Tourism Research, 29*(4), 484–507.

Smith, A. K., Bolton, R. N., & Wagner, J. (1999). A model of customer satisfaction with service encounters involving failure and recovery. *Journal of Marketing Research, 36*(3), 356–372.

Strauss, A. L. (1988). Qualitative analysis for social scientists. *European Sociological Review, 4*(3), 276–277.

Spreng, R. A., Harrell, G. D., & Mackoy, R. D. (1995). Service recovery: Impact on satisfaction and intentions. *Journal of Services Marketing, 9*(1), 15–23.

Tate, M., Nili, A., & Gable, G. G. (2014). *A typology of technological enablers of website service failure prevention.* Wellington, PACIS 2014 Proceedings, p. Paper 78.

Tax, S. S., & Brown, S. W. (1998). Recovering and learning from service failure. *Sloan Management Review, 40*(1), 70.

Tax, S. S., Brown, S. W., & Chandrashekaran, M. (1998). Customer evaluations of service complaint experiences: Implications for relationship marketing. *Journal of Marketing, 62*(1), 60–76.

Tschohl, J. (2013). *Loyal for life: How to take unhappy customers from hell to heaven in 60 seconds or less* (5th ed.). Pasadena: Best Sellers Publishing.

Tyler, T. R., & Lind, E. A. (1988). *The social psychology of procedural justice.* New York: Springer US.

Vazquez-Casielles, R., Rio-Lanza, A. B. D., & Diaz-Martin, A. M. (2008). Satisfaction with service recovery: Perceived justice and emotional responses. *Journal of Business Research, 62,* 775–781.

Wang, Y. S., Wu, S. C., Lin, H. H., & Wang, Y. Y. (2011). The relationship of service failure severity, service recovery justice and perceived switching costs with customer loyalty in the context of e-tailing. *International Journal of Information Management, 31*(4), 350–359.

Wirtz, J., & Mattila, A. S. (2004). Consumer responses to compensation, speed of recovery and apology after a service failure. *International Journal of Service Industry Management, 15*(2), 150–166.

Zeithaml, V. A., Bitner, M. J., & Gremler, D. D. (2012). *Services marketing* (6th ed.). s.l.: McGraw-Hill Education.

Zhang, T. J. F., Siu, N. Y. M., & Yau, C. Y. J. (2013). The roles of justice and customer satisfaction in customer retention: A lesson from service recovery. *Journal of Business Ethics, 114*(4), 675–686.

Zhu, Z., Nakata, C., Sivakumar, K., & Grewal, D. (2013). Fix it or leave it? Customer recovery from self-service technology failures. *Journal of Retailing, 89*(1), 15–29.

Chapter 9

Social Media Marketing in Fashion Brands: Communication and Consumption Trajectories

Md Nazmul Islam
University of the West of Scotland, UK

Vivek Chitran
University of Cumbria, UK

ABSTRACT

Given the increasing focus on the practice of social media publicity in the context of fashion brands, this chapter discusses the key features associated with social media marketing approaches. The chapter reflects on varied approaches amongst the brands in terms of brand equity, value equity, affiliation equity, buyer equity, and buying behaviour. This study presents a critical review of the literature that overtly discusses the acceptance of practices associated with and influences of social media amongst the fashion brands. The literature review presents an assessment of recently published material on the context of social media standards amongst fashion brands. Various types of social networking sites are discussed along with the recognised advantages of using such sites from the perspective of public relations practitioners. Consumer power and the role of design are also discussed, and a literature gap is identified.

INTRODUCTION

Fashion is a value-added industry defined by its high brand assets (Nash, 2018). The industry is undergoing a modification on account of the proliferation of the use of social media. Instagram, Twitter, Facebook and Snapchat are the leading social media platforms that fashion communities engage with. Together with the steady development of the market and fast growth in the number of customers, the fashion industry has achieved maturity over recent years (Kim & Ko, 2012; Helal, Ozuem, & Lancaster, 2018). As a consequence of the augmented demand for fashion in emergent markets such as the Middle East, India and China there is considerable scope to expand the industry into new markets. Discussions regarding the direction the fashion industry is moving in are increasingly common (Kim et al., 2016; Godart, 2014). Previously fashion firms have undergone vicissitudes, but under the present set of circumstances, attracting customers has become more challenging (Ki & Kim, 2016). Fast development in electronic commerce has brought about a phenomenal revaluation in the traditional management and marketing of fashion businesses (Esteban-Santos, García Medina, Carey, & Bellido-Pérez, 2018; Zhenxiang & Lijie, 2011). Over recent years, the fashion industry has undergone significant modifications with the arrival of fast fashion (Hyunsook, Choo, & Namhee, 2013). This trend takes the latest trends to the marketplace quickly, efficiently and at a reduced cost (Hyunsook, Choo, & Namhee, 2013).

Developments in the contemporary economy have influenced the nature of the fashion industry (Barkha Ravi Shende, 2017). Currently, generic, top-level Internet domain (dot.com) based firms advertise online (Ki & Kim, 2016). However, they also create potential threats to sellers in terms of bringing new channels to market. In many cases, this type of business offers discounts for exclusive products. The appearance of brick and mortar vendors has also forced traditional retailers to take their offers online (Nash, 2018; Godart, 2014; Ozuem, Thomas, & Lancaster, 2016). This phenomenon has motivated more consumers to shop online. Consequently, the gap between manufacturers, sellers, and web-based companies is becoming increasingly hazy (Godart, 2014; Guercini, Bernal, & Prentice, 2018).

Traditionally, fashion products have depended on sturdy brand resources and loyal customers to succeed (Ki & Kim, 2016; Jayasuriya et al., 2018; Ozuem et al., 2017). Yet, the current appearance of many new fashion brands in the marketplace and the ensuing intense competition have created an unpredicted rivalry in the market. The cost of branded products is higher than non-branded products, and people are happy to pay for them. Sometimes this popularity is considered to be an indication of quality. Yet brand name mark-ups are predominantly distinct in the fashion industry when functionality is less significant than evidence of style and brand uniqueness (Kort et al., 2006). Conversely, the fashion industry is growing more than ever before (Kim et al., 2016). This intensity of competition is the consequence of the use of digital marketing in cooperation with branding and regular practice (Rathnayaka, 2018; Godart, 2014). With such widespread expansion, social media has turned out to be very popular with the public due to the ease of access to retailers that is facilitated by the Internet. Fashion industry products have a very brief lifespan (Ko et al., 2016) and success is entirely contingent on shifting cultures. Marketers should be sufficiently talented to be able to examine and anticipate new style ideas before consumers are alerted. Thus, fashion providers have become trendsetters and social media converts who are prepared to try out new methods to obtain and adapt to clients. To maintain this process, fashion providers increasingly use digital media with the aim of sustaining clients to ensure satisfaction and longer-term loyalty (Rathnayaka, 2018).

To create brand uniqueness, brands should deliver customers messages via marketing in a way that links brand identity with originality. Currently, such promotions have extended to social media (Ozuem, Howell, & Lancaster, 2008; Lee, Hur, & Watkins, 2018). According to Christopher, Lowson, and Peck. (2004), competitive pressure amongst fashion brands requires some to revise their product series continually. This suggests that there is an unavoidable passage that is followed by many fashion sellers to organise products carefully across the year to coincide with seasons.

Innovation, responding to current trends and ensuring quality are imperative to the success of any fashion company (Kim et al., 2016). Declines in sales in light of economic recession can force fashion firms to modify their strategy and approaches (Guercini et al., 2018). Such firms can no longer depend on the uniqueness of their brand representation. They need to emphasise brand inheritance, eminence, aesthetic value, and strong consumer service in order to survive (Rupik, 2015; Park, 2017). A vital component of the fashion industry is maintaining high standards in every possible way.

Fashion companies are establishing a customer base via effective methods of interaction and by turning their attention to social media (Nekmat et al., 2015; Kim & Ko, 2012). Marketing through social media networking sites has already proven very successful for brands. In this manner, companies and consumers can create innovative products, facilities, corporate structures and principles. In addition, brands can develop strong experiences and fortify their relations with clientele. Marketing via social media is a shared communications tool based on establishing a level of understanding when it comes to young consumers (Ozuem, Howell, & Lancaster, 2008; Nash, 2018). It is also increasingly important to understand how older age groups engage with social media (Kim & Ko, 2012; Esteban-Santos et al., 2018). In addition, brand activities on social media can establish some clarity as to the brand message, and ideas and concepts can be shared between online users. For fashion brands, social media platforms are a vital part of public relations. However, it took a while for the brands, particularly luxury brands, to acclimatise to the intensity of social media. Many firms have been hesitant to adopt social media such as Facebook, which became increasingly popular in the late-2000s (Ki & Kim, 2016).

Conventionally, popular brands can benefit from word-of-mouth recommendations and can carve out a substantial position in the fashion world by forming a deluxe brand image (Godart, 2014; Nekmat et al., 2015; Esteban-Santos et al., 2018). Yet this involves much effort and a drive to become associated with big names. Huge sums of capital are also required to build stores and participate in exhibitions. Although the requirements for setting up a strong brand image remain relatively constant, social media has offered smaller companies a chance to grow brand awareness (Godart, 2014). The appearance of online-based marketing has curtailed the gap between new fashion brands and recognised stylish brands (Guercini et al., 2018). Social media makes it easier for new fashion inventors to win attention and admiration. In addition, it is now more comfortable for them to find their place in the international field. Traditionally, the fashion markets have tended to show the perceptions of insufficiency. However, present-day markets function well based on the perceptions of profusion (Islam & Chitran, 2019). As a consequence of online prospects, physical shelf space is no longer a vital consideration (Islam & Chitran, 2019) and this reduces the cost of matching demand with supply (Nekmat et al., 2015).

As the popularity of social media continues to increase and to become a fixed aspect of daily activity, society is becoming more influenced by online content than ever before (Ozuem, Howell, & Lancaster, 2014; Henninger, Alevizou, & Oates, 2017), and fashion is no exception. Through active and common social media platforms like Facebook and Twitter, fashion brands can advertise their own personal styles with potentially millions of users (Ozuem et al., 2016). Social media is very efficient at exposing product trends, and it has replaced traditional print publications such as Vogue as a source of intelligence. Through social media, fashionistas can identify the products that retailers are pushing in particular seasons. Individuals can identify which fashion trends are popular by looking at the social media posts of friends or contacts. Therefore, it can be argued that people depend less on traditional forms of marketing which frequently appear to be over-planned and confusing. In the present fashion territory, this suggests that conventional promotion formats (such as campaigns, magazines, leaflets) do not exert as powerful an influence as they used to (Nash, 2018). With such intense levels of social media usage and advertising by fashion industries, the effects of social media are becoming increasingly apparent.

THEORETICAL CONTEXT

Social media manifest as online platforms which offer interactive ways to communicate, to form relationships and to share content (Park, 2017; Calderon, 2019). The notion of social media is linked with the use of computer-generated societies and systems to share ideas, views, evidence, interests and many other types of expression (Kadam & Ayarekar, 2014; Armstrong et al., 2015). Social media platforms exhibit a diverse range of approaches, comprising blogs, wikis, podcasts, pictures, video files, ratings and social bookmarking. As they become increasingly popular, individuals as well as businesses and governmental organisations are joining in and harnessing social media as interactive tools. Unlike distinct social networkers, organisations use social media for the purpose of advertising and marketing (Calderon, 2019). According to Leberecht (2009), social media symbolises an arrangement of 'owned' media that lets businesses generate and share their own content which represents their brands and products. Social media is a collaboration of various types of digital platforms that offers marketers and brand managers tools to meet precise branding aims.

It is difficult to provide a comprehensive description of the perceptions of social media (Calderon, 2019; Kadam & Ayarekar, 2014). This complexity has arisen because the terms social media and Web 2.0 are increasingly used reciprocally. Kaplan and Haenlein (2010, p. 61) note that social media are 'a group of Internet-based applications that build on the ideological and technological foundations of Web 2.0 and that allow the creation and exchange of user-generated content'. Previous studies have provided many complex technical explanations as well as descriptions of social media. These emphasise the key practices associated with social media usage (Rupik, 2015; Park, 2017). Thus, defining social media is not an easy endeavour. According to O'Reilly (2007), Web 2.0 is a networked platform that allows the user to create, design, improve, and share content and services. Shared aptitude is one of Web 2.0's ultimate features. Thus, Chu and Xu (2009, p. 717) explain that Web 2.0 'is of the user, by the user, and, more importantly, for the user'. Web 2.0 encompasses technologies such as blogs, wikis, mashups, RSS feeds, podcasts, blogs, tagging, social bookmarking, and social networking sites.

Consumers are becoming increasingly discerning in the face of the range of products and the choices that they face. The continuous progression of technology and the all-access approach of social media has empowered customers more than ever before (Calderon, 2019). Gamboa and Goncalves (2014) suggest that 'buying in' to social media involves a smaller investment than other forms of communications used in marketing. Extant literature on social media characteristics can be summarised diagrammatically as follows:

Figure 1. Characteristics of social media
Adapted from Chan-Olmsted, Cho and Lee (2013)

Participatory nature is one of the most idiosyncratic features of social media, which presents a prospect to become involved in a communication (Chan-Olmsted et al., 2013; Pulido et al., 2018). Social media is a collective term denoting a great number of applications that aid users to connect, relate, and share contents. Social media blurs the line between media and audience by inspiring contributions and response from many participants. In order to enable a participative principle in the operational territory, social media has been employed by several organisations (Islam & Chitran, 2019). As a key constituent of interactivity, participation can be demarcated as the extent to which correspondents and receivers are dynamically involved in the interaction. On the other hand, participation can be understood as action-based interactivity (Calderon, 2019).

Another noticeable distinction of social media is its openness to user response and involvement by partaking in few barriers to retrieving information or making remarks (Chan-Olmsted et al., 2013). Most social media comprise limited barriers in transferability of both applications and technology. Thus, information can be sent or received without trouble between sources and operators as well as to the users (Ariel & Avidar, 2015; Pulido et al., 2018). This idiosyncratic openness is heightened by the interacting viewpoints and comprehensible mechanisms of social media for generating and distributing content. In the era of information, it is more significant than before to highlight the vital part that people play in conveying information and giving sense to it (Chan-Olmsted et al., 2013; Nekmat et al., 2015). New media technologies empower people to obtain, create, and distribute information online and to become co-makers of connotation (Ariel & Avidar, 2015).

Social media allows reciprocal discussions rather than one-directional shows or deliveries of evidence to a purely receptive audience such as television, radio, newspapers and magazines (Chan-Olmsted et al., 2013). While participation is behaviour- or action-oriented interactivity, the communicator is entrenched in the communicational characteristic of interactivity. Social bonds can be continued by an interceding interface via communication technologies alongside corporeal presence communication. Social media permits users to recognise and link with the individuals with whom they want to communicate (Chan-Olmsted et al., 2013; Pulido et al., 2018). This way of interaction creates a mode of communication for people and businesses to collaborate quickly with people and to form associations. Indeed, social media have been observed as an active mechanism of evolving societies. Although social media supports serving communities, its significance is not just in constructing societies which are more incessant and systematic in nature and designed with a notion or shared goal, as divergent from an assortment of content (Ariel & Avidar, 2015). Social media lets individuals interchange from one site to others in the World Wide Web and offers connectedness to its users by delivering Web links to other sites, resources, and people (Chan-Olmsted et al., 2013).

Although social scientists initiated studies into social media in previous years, fashion as a research context is still relatively untested. Cho and

Workman (2011) and Workman and Studak (2006) identified that women tend to buy their fashion products in social surroundings where they can connect with their peers. Moreover, women buy fashion products out of desire rather than necessity or utility. In other studies, Bakewell et al. (2006), Seock and Bailey (2008), Workman and Cho (2012) and Jackson et al. (2011) found that prior to making a purchase, a woman spends more time gathering information than men. Studies such as, for example, that of Shephard et al. (2016) suggest that men's shopping behaviour may be shifting to integrate personalities that have been hitherto linked with females. According to Brosdahl and Carpenter (2011), millennial men show higher echelons of shopping delight than older men do. Men are increasingly challenging gender stereotypes, and are more exposed to and enthusiastic about shopping (Otnes & McGrath, 2001; Guercini et al., 2018). As a result of shifting tastes, shopping activities that would have otherwise been well-thought-out and 'womanly' have become appealing to male sensibilities.

As shopping behaviours transform, it becomes increasingly vital to comprehend the mechanisms of modification (Shephard et al., 2016; Ozuem, Limb, & Lancaster, 2016). Perceptions of fashion awareness and fashion management which have traditionally been connected to feminine shopping activities are now being observed in men (Workman & Cho, 2012; Bakewell et al., 2006). Furthermore, advertising media messages are embryonic with new scenes together with digital media. This digital media has not been thoroughly discussed in the current literature.

From the earlier literature it can be established that creativity, desire and aspiration are the three key elements that drive the fashion industry (Barkha Ravi Shende, 2017). Customers like to obtain an expensive product that is expressive and special, and which imitates their taste and status (Kim et al., 2016). Fashion designers and shops have to offer apparel that meets these ever-shifting desires. These have to be available at a reasonable price (Nash, 2018). Correspondingly, they outline and replicate trends (Barkha Ravi Shende, 2017; Kim et al., 2016). O'Cass (2004) describes fashion product connection as 'the extent to which a consumer views the related fashion activities as a central part of their life'. Further, Goldsmith et al. (1999) identified affiliation with fashion brands linked to consumer awareness and eagerness to own many types of product. Therefore, the grade of engrossment in a product category has become a significant factor pertinent to organisational advertising tactics (Kim et al., 2001), predominantly with respect to fashion choices. Earlier studies sought to establish the method by which clients engage with brands to create new fashion products and to understand the outcome of their involvement (Rupik, 2015; Park, 2017). Sen (2008) tried to identify common characteristics of fashion products in his study and those are shown in the following diagram.

Figure 2. Characteristics of fashion products

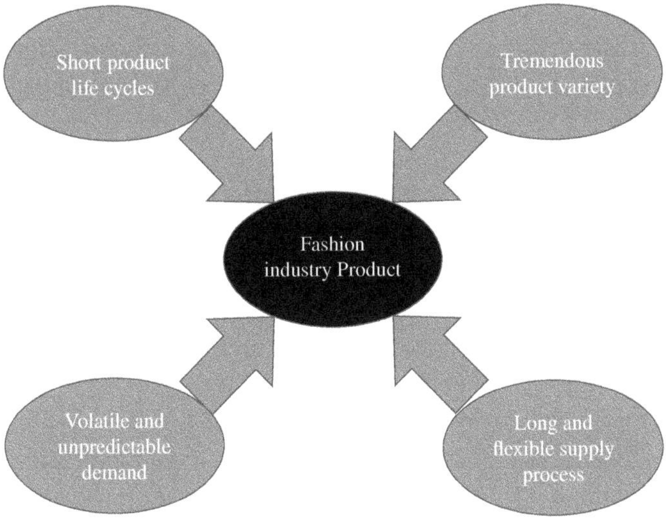

Source: Sen, 2008

According to McCormick and Livett (2012), online buyers adopting different features can appeal to online consumers with which they are directly interacting. This feature distils a number of risk factors associated with buying online. Studies by, for example, Kapferer and Bastien (2012), Chevalier and Gutsatz (2012), and Okonkwo (2010) suggest that although the diffusion and adoption of social media have been seen in most industries, luxury firms have long been immune to the effects of social media. In the last few years, the luxury segment of the fashion industry has begun to harness social media to meet the increasing pervasiveness of social networks and communities in the lives of customers (Esteban-Santos et al., 2018; Arrigo, 2018).

Customers now have admittance to information pertaining to fashion and products across a variety of media platforms outside of the parameters of 'old' mass media formats (Bailey & Seock, 2010; Esteban-Santos et al., 2018; Lee, Hur, & Watkins 2018). The primary goal of Bailey and Seock's (2010) study was to observe the effects of fashion magazine content on customer constancy behaviour. The investigation was conducted using exploratory factor analysis, multiple regression, multivariate analysis of variance, analysis of variance, and descriptive statistics including means, frequencies, and percentiles (Bailey & Seock, 2010). The outcomes of the research revealed that fashion magazine content was expressly interrelated to the tendency of reliability. The study also found that limited research had been undertaken to study fashion magazine content and its effect on loyalty tendencies, although fashion magazines are a vital source of information in the context of fashion. Visual intricacy is the extent to which the elements of a visual image have an impact on users' likings and insights in relation to brands and products (Hall & Hanna, 2004). Kim and Ko (2010) conducted studies on the use of social media marketing for luxury fashion brands. Their research context was Korea, and they performed a self-directed inquiry with visual stimuli to gather data from consumers of luxury fashion brands. Their quantitative data analysis illuminated the importance of adopting social media as a publicising option for luxury fashion brands to enhance customer affairs and buying intentions. Additionally, they recommended an approach to advance the performance of luxury fashion brands. They suggested that social media marketing is an appropriate technique to maintain retentive regular buyers and to entice new customers. Later, using a structural equation modelling approach Kim and Ko (2012) acknowledged the critical traits of social media advertising for fashion branding. They found that brand equity has an expressively adverse consequence for customer equity. They argued that value equity and relationship equity do not have any statistically substantial outcome. On the other hand, they also demonstrated that the connection between purchase intention and customer equity is significant.

Conversely, Lee, Hur, and Watkins (2018) found that sellers of luxury brands had incorporated innovative tactics to take their products to customers using visual communication through social media. The study also found that, although social media posts have the potential to progress promotional content for luxury brands, there is a lack of literature on the outcome of visual communication approaches when it comes to luxury brands. The study mainly examined the consequences of the visual intricacy of social media images on consumer brand insights in a luxury fashion setting. They conducted two tests which exposed that selection of luxury products is higher in less intricate image settings when respondents are familiar with the luxury brand. Yet when the brand is not familiar, and unknown to the participants, a complex image setting is more effective than a simple one. Lee, Hur, and Watkins (2018) recommended that to increase positive insights into luxury brands, suppliers should control the visual intricacy of social media images they use by determining the customers' degree of understanding of the brand.

However, studies of visual intricacy have generated mixed results. Peracchio and Meyers-Levy (2005) identified a positive relationship between image complexity and buying intention, stating that high visual involvedness drives customers to select a style. A negative relationship such as low visual complexity encouraged better predilection than high intricacy, as was the case with earlier research findings (e.g. Tuch et al., 2009; Pieters et al., 2010). Van Mulken, van Hooft, and Nederstigt (2014) suggested a modest visual density, which is based on an overturned U-shape relationship. Therefore, in previous studies the outcomes of visual complexity are inconsistent. The absence of research into luxury brands leaves much clarity to be achieved in terms of the degree of visual complexity that is appropriate for marketing.

McCormick and Livett (2012) conducted qualitative research and studied the effect of the exhibition of fashion garments on the online behaviour of young consumers. The main aim of their investigation was to find the elements of Web experience that encouraged an interface between the buyer and the online fashion retailer. By implementing photo-elicitation and projective techniques they identified two main factors: 'product viewing and fashion information online'. In order to determine how the signs affect consumer communications and encourage shopping behaviour, an investigation of the elements is essential (McCormick & Livett, 2012). Based on semi-structured interviews, the study revealed that the two aforementioned elements produce very diverse effects for customers with regard to online fashion observance. The initial stage of the study found that practical product observing opportunities permit the buyer to personalise their assessment. This finding is very similar to that of the study of Aragoncillo and Orus (2018), where they discoursed that offline businesses are able to generate buying compulsion to a better level than online sellers. This product observing opportunity also creates an interrelationship with attire products. The research of McCormick and Livett (2012) further identified that artistic fashion updates controlled by the seller provide information and recommendations about the inspiring hedonic effects of fashion. As such, online vendors must adequately link hedonic interaction with practical utilitarianism to deliver a substantial online shopping experience.

Hyunsook, Choo, and Namhee (2013) carried out research in Korea, funded by the National Research Foundation of Korea, with the aim of examining the theoretical structure of fast fashion circumvention amongst young consumers. By analysing literature and blogs, the first phase of the study proposed and tested a conceptual model of fast fashion. During the second phase of the research, factor analysis and hierarchical regression models were used to identify the impact of adverse conception on the behavioural intention of fast fashion consumers. The statistical analysis found eight negative beliefs. Fast fashion avoidance, antagonistic beliefs, poor presentation and similarity have constructive effects. Contrary inauthenticity has an adverse impact. On the other hand, larger store distress and foreignness have a collaborating effect.

Ko et al. (2016) asserted that young luxury-purchasing consumers who use social media had motivated well-known luxury companies to develop pioneering approaches in order to hold their positions in what is a backdrop of dynamic and unstable competition. Additionally, Phan et al. (2011) note that luxury fashion companies must adopt a pragmatic understanding regarding the perceived advantages of social media. They also outlined a vibrant tactic to advance clients' involvement with products through social media. Meadows (2009) and Jones and Livingstone (2017) noted that with the appearance of fast-fashion and strong online-only sellers it is now mandatory for high street fashion sellers to adapt their communication approaches appropriately. This approach means they can flexibly respond quickly to shifting demands. As a continually growing market, the spread of customer demand and moving consumer expectations have exaggerated this procedure (Jones & Livingstone, 2017). Consequently, retailers are forced to operate outside of traditional approaches (Burt & Sparks, 2003; Esteban-Santos et al., 2018) in order to meet ever-changing customer demand.

Kamal and Chu (2013) conducted a study on American and Arab young social media users. Their investigation, based on the question of whether materialism is an outcome of social media practice, found that, in the case of luxury fashion products, a positive association exists between materialism and consumer purchase intention in terms of both groups of participants. Their study also found that Arab social media users have a more sophisticated level of materialism and social media practices than American users. On the other hand, the Cross-National Study (of the USA and South Korea) of Thoumrungroje (2018) found that social media concentration more sturdily inspires shopper spending in the American context than South Korea.

Nash (2018) studied social media platforms in order to find their levels of influence on consumer decisions. He adopted qualitative methods with an interpretivist philosophy and exploratory approach in this study. It found different kinds of motivational factors which, aided and facilitated by social media platforms, influence customer behaviour. At the same time, the study concluded with the opinion that social media is not only the source of these motivational factors, but the expectation from social media is increasing day by day.

It is not surprising to note that much of the literature on fashion branding concentrates on China (Liu et al., 2011; Gao et al., 2009; Choi et al., 2008) as the Chinese brands are one of the most significant target groups of consumers (Rovai, 2018). Gao et al. (2009) investigated market segmentation structures in the context of wealthy Chinese customers. They methodically outlined and recognised various sections for luxury fashion products, discovered that there are five different market sectors and claimed that luxury fashion products could engage these market subdivisions in order to formulate their branding approaches more effectively.

Jung and Shen (2011) conducted research into women from universities in China and the USA to observe brand equity amongst luxury fashion brands and their social alignment. They noted a degree of collectivism, and power distance, which was higher in the group of women in China than the USA. Remarkably, they found that US participants expressed a higher grade of uncertainty avoidance. Additionally, they identified cultural transformations in which the American sample had a higher score in perceived eminence, brand cognizance, and brand connotation than their Chinese counterparts did. Conversely, Li et al. (2012) found that fashion lifestyles, the apparent value of social and emotional variables, professed practical values, and assumed monetary values were all expressly persuading the inclinations of Chinese customers to invest in luxury fashion. The findings of the study of Wei, Lee, and Shen (2018) indicates that perceived benefits have a noteworthy effect on buyers' intention to spend on clothing online. Moreover, perceived expediency, money-saving, and time-saving elements have a constructive influence on buying intention (Wei, Lee, & Shen, 2018).

Zhenxiang and Lijie (2011) conducted a study on the Chinese fast fashion industry and analysed the performance of a recently merged online retailing company. In their study, they provided recommendations in relation to the Chinese fast fashion industry to remain competitive in the future. The study investigated unusual value conceptions, competent supply chain management approaches, low-cost marketing and positioning approaches. The study was strengthened by carrying out an empirical inquiry into several unique fashion brand elements. It showed that there is the capacity to explore online retailing fast fashion brands further. Then again, the researchers noted that there is 'a far way to catch up with the leading enterprises in the world in terms of e-commerce scales'. The studies of Zhenxiang and Lijie (2011) and Wu and Lo (2017) agree with the statement that online sellers are frequently ignored if product otherness or added value is not provided.

Chen and Kim (2013) examined how effectively customers' individual values and the attitudes of customers influence their procurement intentions towards luxury fashion products. They framed individual values as a measurement standard which involved acquisitiveness, self-indulgence, face-saving, and social construction. By conducting regression analyses on the collected data of 201 Chinese consumers, they demonstrated that self-indulgence positively impacts on customer intentions to buy luxury fashion brands, while they also found that face-saving and social construction do not have a substantial influence of this kind. On the other hand, Zhang and Kim (2013) explored the various aspects that inspire Chinese buyers' attitudes towards obtaining luxury fashion goods and their procuring intent. Their statistical investigation showed that brand awareness, social evaluation, and fashion innovativeness all have far-reaching influences on user attitudes in terms of acquiring luxury fashion goods. Nonetheless, the findings of the study of Voorveld et al. (2018) demonstrate that engagement is decidedly situation-specific. They mentioned that the engagement contains many forms of involvements on each social media site; thus each platform is practised in an exclusive mode. Additionally, on each site, a diverse set of involvements is associated with publicising valuations (Voorveld et al., 2018). This study also exposed that assignation with social media marketing itself is crucial in demonstrating in what way social media engagement is connected to marketing assessments (Voorveld et al., 2018).

However, Koufaris and Hampton-Sosa (2004) found that the less confidence and trust that the consumer has in online stores, the more likely they are to be unsuccessful. This issue has been supported by Ogonowski, Montandon, Botha, and Reyneke (2014) and Liu et al. (2018). They suggest

that the custom of online buying has increased, and the number of businesses that have an online platform to sell their products has risen at the
same time. However, trust is the chief reason why customers fail to engage
in online purchasing (Liu et al., 2018; Ogonowski et al., 2014). According
to Wang and Emurian (2005), any means that can develop customer trust
levels is therefore vital for the success of an online store. As a remedy, they
suggest increasing the level of social presence. According to Ogonowski
et al. (2014), social presence brings about consumer confidence, satisfaction and professed usefulness as regards the adopted online platforms of
businesses. This statement has been supported by others (for example Cyr
et al., 2007; Gefen and Straub, 2004; Siebenaler et al., 2019).

Chui, Tzeng, and Li (2013) stated that as a result of what is a convenient and fast shopping environment it has become progressively common
for consumers to buy merchandise and adapt services from online platforms. Thus, online sellers are becoming one of the main retailing channels,
and they continue to spread their operations internationally. Chui, Tzeng,
and Li (2013) also suggested that because of proliferation, managers of
online retailers should adopt new and proper management skills and strategies since online platforms heavily depend on these.

On the other hand, Henninger et al. (2017) investigated micro-businesses
operating in the UK fashion industry through qualitative research design
and found that micro-companies in the UK have inadequate consideration
of integrated marketing communication. The findings of the study exposed
that the time expended on social media platforms is considered as waste
from the manufacture and designing time for micro-businesses. Proper
time utilisation for production is vital for the survival of fashion micro-
organisations. Additionally, these micro-organisations are incapable of
posting messages in a consistent manner in social media platforms, which
makes them unsuccessful in social media marketing.

CONCLUSION AND MANAGERIAL IMPLICATION

Fashion clothing brands have appeared over recent decades since many
sellers are drawn towards the possibility of conducting business on a worldwide scale. This tendency has established a shifting dynamic in trade. For
example, there is an increasing demand for a lower price (Turker & Altunas,
2014; Ozuem et al., 2016). In addition, the market has witnessed the

disappearance of mass manufacturing and improved organisational features in the supply chain. Other consequences include increased flexibility in customisation (Burt & Sparks, 2003) and design and delivery (Mo, 2015; Zhenxiang & Lijie, 2011). According to Turker and Altunas (2014), the purpose of fashion industry companies is to entice customers into stores as often as possible in order to adopt the capability to elevate the rate at which individuals purchase fashionable styles. Their goal can be achieved by maintaining lower costs and offering cheaper clothing that stays in the shop for a shorter period than is the case with conventional attire retailers. This means that product rotation becomes briefer and various logistics associated with buying requirements become simpler. Companies that harness social media as a business promotion tactic are making use of the Web and have transformed their selling strategies to online trading (Öztamur & Karakadılar, 2014; Guercini et al., 2018).

The Internet has become one of the most effective and efficient tools for businesses to publicise their products and services with the aim of enticing target customers (Islam & Chitran, 2019). Nowadays, the concept of social media marketing is a feature of many business plans. Decision-makers continue to find options through which industries can utilise applications in a profitable way. It has been found that businesses appear to perform efficiently where the option to give opinions freely exists. According to Kaplan and Haenlein (2010), companies are losing control over their own information which is available on online platforms. Moreover, social media provides enterprises with efficient ways to engage with limitless consumers. This engagement ability allows data to be rapidly collected in the form of consumer comments. Consequently, the rising rate of social media adoption in fashion industries provides the opportunity for users to interact with brands. Users can recommend and suggest trends and styles which help to make brands and designers more popular. The comments and feedback have a long-lasting impact on the formation of long-term affairs. Thus, fashion customers are passionate about their ideas and feel that online shopping and not physical fashion stores is the best way to buy garments (Esteban-Santos et al., 2018).

It has been suggested that social media supports collaboration between consumers and fashion garments online (McCormick & Livett, 2012; Guercini et al., 2018), and this communication is vital in persuading customer conduct, cognizance and attitudes (Mangold & Faulds, 2009). Hence, it is mandatory for fashion vendors to update and advance their concept of the impact of social media platforms on fashion customers, and to review their decision-making processes regularly. Many scholars have suggested that age is a vital influencer in fashion decision-making (Rocha et al., 2005; Ogonowski et al., 2014), yet there is limited academic research concerning how social media can affect age demographics in this process (Rupik, 2015; Park, 2017). Trends continually come and go, and fashion is mercurial by nature (Guercini et al., 2018). The adaptation to shifting technologies is essential for all types of sellers, and thus fashion vendors should receive special consideration. From the buyer's viewpoint, it is easy to understand that social media could be a vehicle to accelerate transactions. Yet, from a seller's perception, it is significant to stay not only entirely conversant but also very connected, in order to better oblige customers' desires.

Social media has not been recognised as a useful public relations tool for fashion stakeholders (Ogonowski et al., 2014; Esteban-Santos et al., 2018). The content makers who have engaged in social media have yet to change and improve their social media approaches to keep up to speed with industry standards (Guercini et al., 2018). Conventionally, the fashion industry has been restricted in terms of its public relations tools and has focused on those that act as an interface between designers and brands. This limitation creates inadequate exposure to the fashion market and confines the spread of knowledge about forthcoming collections, styles or promotions. From the analysis of literature, it is clear that there is limited research into the use and growth of social media as a public relations tactic in the fashion business. As a potential and useful gadget in the public relations approach, social media can develop relationships between consumers and brands. Public relations practitioners and content creators must form an effective structure for the practice of social media channels to create better performance.

REFERENCES

Aragoncillo, L., & Orus, C. (2018). Impulse buying behaviour: An online-offline comparative and the impact of social media. *Spanish Journal of Marketing – ESIC, 22*(1), 42–62. doi:10.1108/SJME-03-2018-007

Ariel, Y., & Avidar, R. (2015). Information, interactivity, and social media. *Atlantic Journal of Communication, 23*(1), 19–30. doi:10.1080/154 56870.2015.972404

Armstrong, G., Kotler, P., Harker, M., & Brennan, R. (2015). *Marketing.* Harlow, England: Pearson.

Bailey, L. R., & Seock, Y. (2010). The relationship of fashion leadership, fashion magazine content and loyalty tendency. *Journal of Fashion Marketing and Management, 14*(1), 39–57. doi:10.1108/13612021011025429

Bakewell, C., Mitchell, V. W., & Rothwell, M. (2006). UK generation Y male fashion consciousness. *Journal of Fashion Marketing and Management, 10*(2), 169–180. doi:10.1108/13612020610667487

Barkha Ravi Shende, B. (2017). Fashion trends and its impact on society: A case study on apparel trends of Indian society. *International Journal of Researches in Biosciences and Agriculture Technology.*

Brosdahl, D. J. C., & Carpenter, J. M. (2011). Shopping orientations of US males: A generational "cohort comparison". *Journal of Retailing and Consumer Services, 18*(6), 548–554. doi:10.1016/j.jretconser.2011.07.005

Burt, S., & Sparks, L. (2003). *Competitive analysis of the retail sector in the UK.* London: Institute for Retail Studies, Department of Trade and Industry.

Calderon, C. (2019). The importance of shared beliefs for social marketing programmes. *Journal of Social Marketing, 9*(1), 26–39. doi:10.1108/JSOCM-01-2018-0013

Chan-Olmsted, S., Cho, M., & Lee, S. (2013). User perceptions of social media: A comparative study of perceived characteristics and user profiles by social media. *Online Journal of Communication and Media Technologies, 3*(4), 149–178.

Chen, J., & Kim, S. (2013). A comparison of Chinese consumers' intentions to purchase luxury fashion brands for self-use and for gifts. *Journal of International Consumer Marketing, 25*(1), 29–44. doi:10.1080/0896153 0.2013.751796

Chevalier, M., & Gutsatz, M. (2012). *Luxury retail management: How the world's top brands provide quality product and service support.* Singapore: John Wiley & Son.

Cho, S., & Workman, J. (2011). Gender, fashion innovativeness and opinion leadership, and need for touch: Effects on multi-channel choice and touch/non-touch preferences in clothing shopping. *Journal of Fashion Marketing and Management, 15*(3), 363–382. doi:10.1108/13612021111151941

Choi, T. M., Liu, S. C., Pang, K. M., & Chow, P. S. (2008). A study of the shopping behaviour of individual travellers from the mainland China. *Tourism Management, 29*, 811–820. doi:10.1016/j.tourman.2007.07.009

Christopher, M., Lowson, R., & Peck, H. (2004). Creating agile supply chains in the fashion industry. *International Journal of Retail and Distribution Management, 32*(8), 367–376. doi:10.1108/09590550410546188

Chu, H., & Xu, C. (2009). Web 2.0 and its dimensions in the scholarly world. *Scientometrics, 80*(3), 717–729. doi:10.1007/s11192-008-2103-y

Chui, W. Y., Tzeng, G. H., & Li, H. L. (2013). A new hybrid MCDM model combining DANP with VIKOR to improve e-store business. *Knowledge-Based System, 37*(4), 48–61. doi:10.1016/j.knosys.2012.06.017

Cyr, D., Hassanein, K., Head, M., & Ivanov, A. (2007). The role of social presence in establishing loyalty in e-Service environments. *Interacting with Computers, 19*(1), 43–56. doi:10.1016/j.intcom.2006.07.010

Elisa, A. (2018). Social media marketing in luxury brands: A systematic literature review and implications for management research. *Management Research Review, 41*(6), 657–679. doi:org/10.1108/MRR-04-2017-0134

Esteban-Santos, L., García Medina, I., Carey, L., & Bellido-Pérez, E. (2018). Fashion bloggers: Communication tools for the fashion industry. *Journal of Fashion Marketing and Management: An International Journal, 22*(3), 420–437. doi:10.1108/JFMM-10-2017-0101

Gamboa, A. M., & Goncalves, H. M. (2014). Customer loyalty through social networks: Lessons from Zara on Facebook. *Business Horizons, 57*(6), 709–717. doi:10.1016/j.bushor.2014.07.003

Gao, L., Norton, M. J. T., Zhang, Z. M., & To, C. K. (2009). Potential niche markets for luxury fashion goods in China. *Journal of Fashion Marketing and Management, 13*(4), 514–526. doi:10.1108/13612020910991376

Godart, F. (2014). The power structure of the fashion industry: Fashion capitals, globalization and creativity. *International Journal of Fashion Studies, 1*(1), 39–55. doi:10.1386/infs.1.1.39_1

Goldsmith, R. E., Moore, M. A., & Beaudoin, P. (1999). Fashion innovativeness and self-concept: A replication. *Journal of Product & Brand Management, 8*(1), 7–18. doi:10.1108/10610429910257904

Griffith, D., Hu, M., & Ryans, J. (2000). Process standardization across intra- and inter-cultural relationships. *Journal of International Business Studies, 31*(2), 303–324. doi:10.1057/palgrave.jibs.8490908

Guercini, S., Bernal, P., & Prentice, C. (2018). New marketing in fashion e-commerce. *Journal of Global Fashion Marketing, 9*(1), 1–8. doi.org/10.1080/20932685.2018.1407018

Hall, R., & Hanna, P. (2004). The impact of web page text-background colour combinations on readability, retention, aesthetics and behavioural intention. *Behaviour & Information Technology, 23*(3), 183–195. doi:10.1080/01449290410001669932

Helal, G., Ozuem, W., & Lancaster, G. (2018). Social media brand perceptions of millennials. *International Journal of Retail & Distribution Management, 46*(10), 977–998. doi:10.1108/IJRDM-03-2018-0066

Henninger, C., Alevizou, P., & Oates, C. (2017). IMC, social media and UK fashion micro-organisations. *European Journal of Marketing, 51*(3), 668–691. doi:10.1108/EJM-08-2015-0599

Hyunsook, K., Choo, H. J., & Namhee, N. (2013). Motivational drivers of fast fashion avoidance. *Journal of Fashion Marketing and Management: An International Journal, 17*(2), 243–260. doi:10.1108/JFMM-10-2011-0070

Islam, M. N., & Chitran, V. (2019). Social media and social entrepreneurship. In G. Bowen & W. Ozuem (Eds.), *Leveraging Computer-Mediated Marketing Environments* [online] (pp. 104–1230). Hershey, PA: IGI Global. Retrieved February 20, 2019, from https://www.igi-global.com/chapter/social-media-and-social-entrepreneurship/221505

Jackson, V., Stoel, L., & Brantley, A. (2011). Mall attributes and shopping value: Differences by gender and generational cohort. *Journal of Retailing and Consumer Services, 18*(1), 1–9. doi:10.1016/j.jretconser.2010.08.002

Jayasuriya, N., Azam, D., Khatibi, D., Atan, D., & Dharmaratne, D. (2018). The role of facebook marketing on customer-based brand equity and purchase intention in fashion-wear retail industry, Sri Lanka. *Global Journal of Management and Business Research: E Marketing, 18*(7), 1–11.

Jung, J., & Shen, D. (2011). Brand equity of luxury fashion brands among Chinese and U.S. young female consumers. *Journal of East-West Business, 17*(1), 48–69. doi:org/10.1080/10669868.2011.598756

Kadam, A., & Ayarekar, S. (2014). Impact of social media on entrepreneurship and entrepreneurial performance: Special reference to small and medium scale enterprises. *SIES Journal of Management, 10*(1), 3–11.

Kamal, S., & Chu, S. C. (2013). Materialism, attitudes, and social media usage and their impact on purchase intention of luxury fashion goods among American and Arab young generations. *Journal of Interactive Advertising, 13*(1), 27–40. doi:org/10.1080/15252019.2013.768052

Kapferer, J. N., & Bastien, V. (2012). *The luxury strategy: Break the rules of marketing to build luxury brands*. London: Kogan Page Publishers.

Kaplan, A. M., & Haenlein, M. (2010). Users of the world, unite! The challenges and opportunities of social media. *Business Horizons, 53*, 59–68. doi:10.1016/j.bushor.2009.09.003

Ki, C., & Kim, Y. (2016). Sustainable luxury fashion consumption and the moderating role of guilt. *Fashion, Industry and Education, 14*(1), 18–30. doi:10.7741/fie.2016.14.1.018

Kim, A., & Ko, E. (2012). Do social media marketing activities enhance customer equity? An empirical study of luxury fashion brand. *Journal of Business Research, 65*(10), 1480–1486. doi:10.1016/j.jbusres.2011.10.014

Kim, A. J., & Ko, E. (2010). Impacts of luxury fashion brand's social media marketing on customer relationship and purchase intention. *Journal of Global Fashion Marketing, 1*(3), 164–171. doi:10.1080/20932685.2010.10593068

Kim, C. K., Han, D., & Park, S. B. (2001). The effect of brand personality and brand identification on brand loyalty: Applying the theory of social identification. *Japanese Psychological Research, 43*(4), 195–206. doi:10.1111/1468-5884.00177

Kim, H., Byun, S., Choi, S., & Lee, K. (2016). The use of Facebook in international multi-course collaborative projects in fashion merchandising curriculums. *Fashion, Industry and Education, 14*(1), 40–49. doi:10.18848/1447-9494/CGP/v17i11/47356

Kort, P., Caulkins, J., Hartl, R., & Feichtinger, G. (2006). Brand image and brand dilution in the fashion industry. *Automatica, 42*(8), 1363–1370. doi:10.1016/j.automatica.2005.10.002

Koufaris, M., & Hampton-Sosa, W. (2004). The development of initial trust in an online company by new customers. *Information & Management, 41*(3), 377–397. doi:10.1016/j.im.2003.08.004

Lee, J. E., Hur, S., & Watkins, B. (2018). Visual communication of luxury fashion brands on social media: Effects of visual complexity and brand familiarity. *Journal of Brand Management, 25*(5), 449–462. doi:10.1057/s41262-018-0092-6

Li, G., Li, G., & Kambele, Z. (2012). Luxury fashion brand consumers in China: Perceived value, fashion lifestyle, and willingness to pay. *Journal of Business Research, 65*(10), 1516–1522. doi:10.1016/j.jbusres.2011.10.019

Liu, L., Lee, M., Liu, R., & Chen, J. (2018). Trust transfer in social media brand communities: The role of consumer engagement. *International Journal of Information Management, 41*, 1–13. doi:10.1016/j.ijinfomgt.2018.02.006

Liu, S. C., Choi, T. M., Au, R., & Hui, C. L. (2011). A study on individual tourists from the Chinese mainland to Hongkong: Implications for tourism marketing in fashion. *Tourism Economics, 17*, 1287–1309. doi:10.5367/te.2011.0090

Mangold, W., & Faulds, D. (2009). Social media: The new hybrid element of the promotion mix. *Business Horizons, 52*(4), 357–365. doi:10.1016/j.bushor.2009.03.002

McCormick, H., & Livett, C. (2012). Analysing the influence of the presentation of fashion garments on young consumers' online behaviour. *Journal of Fashion Marketing and Management: An International Journal, 16*(1), 21–41. doi:10.1108/13612021211203014

Meadows, T. (2009). *How to set up and run a fashion label*. London: Laurence King Publishing.

Mo, Z. (2015). Internationalisation process of fast fashion retailers: Evidence of H&M and Zara. *International Journal of Business and Management, 10*(3), 217–236. doi:10.5539/ijbm.v10n3p217

Nash, J. (2018). Exploring how social media platforms influence fashion consumer decisions in the UK retail sector. *Journal of Fashion Marketing and Management: An International Journal*. doi:10.1108/JFMM-01-2018-0012

Nekmat, E., Gower, K., Zhou, S., & Metzger, M. (2015). Connective-collective action on social media: Moderated mediation of cognitive elaboration and perceived source credibility on personalness of source. *Communication Research, 46*(1), 62–87.

O'Cass, A. (2004). Fashion clothing consumption: Antecedents and consequences of fashion clothing involvement. *European Journal of Marketing, 38*(7), 869–882. doi:10.1108/03090560410539294

Ogonowski, A., Montandon, A., Botha, E., & Reyneke, M. (2014). Should new online stores invest in social presence elements? The effect of social presence on initial trust formation. *Journal of Retailing and Consumer Services, 21*(4), 482–491. doi:10.1016/j.jretconser.2014.03.004

Okonkwo, U. (2010). *Luxury online: Styles, systems, strategies*. New York, NY: Springer.

O'Reilly, T. (2007). What Is web 2.0: Design patterns and business models for the next generation of software. *International Journal of Digital Economics, 65*, 17–37.

Otnes, C., & McGrath, M. A. (2001). Perceptions and realities of male shopping behaviour. *Journal of Retailing, 77*(1), 111–137. doi:10.1016/S0022-4359(00)00047-6

Öztamur, D., & Karakadılar, I. B. (2014). Exploring the role of social media for SMEs: As a new marketing strategy tool for the firm performance perspective. *Procedia—Social and Behavioural Sciences, 150*(56), 511–520. doi:10.1016/j.sbspro.2014.09.067

Ozuem, W., Howell, K., & Lancaster, G. (2008). Communicating in the new interactive marketspace. *European Journal of Marketing, 42*(9/10), 1059–1083. doi:10.1108/03090560810891145

Ozuem, W., Howell, K., & Lancaster, G. (2014). Corporate social responsibility: Towards a context-specific perspective in developing countries. *Social Responsibility Journal, 10*(3), 399–415. doi:10.1108/SRJ-04-2012-0086

Ozuem, W., Limb, N., & Lancaster, G. (2016). Exploring the locus of internal marketing. *Journal of Strategic Marketing, 26*(4), 356–372. doi:10.1080/0965254X.2016.1211729

Ozuem, W., Thomas, T., & Lancaster, G. (2016). The influence of customer loyalty on small island economies: An empirical and exploratory study. *Journal of Strategic Marketing, 24*(6), 447–469. doi:10.1080/09652 54X.2015.1011205

Ozuem, W., Patel, A., Howell, K., & Lancaster, G. (2017). An exploration of consumers' response to online service recovery initiatives. *International Journal of Market Research, 59*(1), 97–115.

Park, H. (2017). How social media is transforming the fashion consumers: The effects of "social" consumer attributes on brand engagement in social networking sites. *Fashion, Industry and Education, 15*(1), 1–11. doi:10.10 80/13527266.2013.871323

Peracchio, L., & Meyers-Levy, J. (2005). Using stylistic properties of ad pictures to communicate with consumers. *Journal of Consumer Research, 32*(1), 29–40.

Phan, M., & Park, S. Y. (2014). Introduction: Social media marketing and luxury brands. *Journal of Global Fashion Marketing, 5*(3), 195–196. doi.org/10.1080/20932685.2014.908528

Pieters, R., Wedel, M., & Batra, R. (2010). The stopping power of advertising: Measures and effects of visual complexity. *Journal of Marketing, 74*(5), 48–60. doi:10.1509/jmkg.74.5.48

Pulido, C., Redondo-Sama, G., Sordé-Martí, T., & Flecha, R. (2018). Social impact in social media: A new method to evaluate the social impact of research. *PLOS ONE, 13*(8). doi:10.1371/journal.pone.0203117

Rathnayaka, U. (2018). Role of digital marketing in retail fashion industry: A synthesis of the theory and the practice. *Journal of Accounting & Marketing, 07*(02). doi:10.4172/2168-9601.1000279

Rovai, S. (2018). Digitalisation, luxury fashion and "Chineseness": The influence of the Chinese context for luxury brands and the online luxury consumers experience. *Journal of Global Fashion Marketing, 9*(2), 116–128.

Rupik, K. (2015). Applying the customer engagement concept in the fashion industry. *Zeszyty Naukowe Uniwersytetu Szczecińskiego. Problemy Zarządzania, Finansów i Marketingu, 41*, 141–154.

Şen, A. (2008). The US fashion industry: A supply chain review. *International Journal of Production Economics, 114*(2), 571–593. doi:10.1016/j.ijpe.2007.05.022

Seock, Y. K., & Bailey, L. R. (2008). The influence of college students' shopping orientations and gender differences on online information searches and purchase behaviours. *International Journal of Consumer Studies, 32*(2), 113–121. doi:10.1111/j.1470-6431.2007.00647.x

Shephard, A., Pookulangara, S., Kinley, T., & Josiam, B. (2016). Media influence, fashion, and shopping: A gender perspective. *Journal of Fashion Marketing and Management: An International Journal, 20*(1), 4–18. doi:10.1108/JFMM-09-2014-0068

Siebenaler, S., Szymkowiak, A., Robertson, P., Johnson, G., Law, J., & Fee, K. (2019). Honesty, social presence and self-service in retail. *Interacting with Computers.* doi:10.1093/iwc/iwz010

Thoumrungroje, A. (2018). A Cross-national study of consumer spending behavior: The impact of social media intensity and materialism. *Journal of International Consumer Marketing, 30*(4), 276–286.

Tuch, A., Bargas-Avila, J., Opwis, K., & Wilhelm, F. (2009). Visual complexity of websites: Effects on users' experience, physiology, performance, and memory. *International Journal of Human-Computer Studies, 67*(9), 703–715. doi:10.1016/j.ijhcs.2009.04.002

Turker, D., & Altunas, C. (2014). Sustainable supply chain management in the fast fashion industry: An analysis of corporate reports. *European Management Journal, 32*(5), 837–849. doi:10.1016/j.emj.2014.02.001

van Mulken, M., van Hooft, A., & Nederstigt, U. (2014). Finding the tipping point: Visual metaphor and conceptual complexity in advertising. *Journal of Advertising, 43*(4), 333–343. doi:10.1080/00913367.2014.920283

Wei, Z., Lee, M., & Shen, H. (2018). What drives consumers in China to buy clothing online? Application of the technology acceptance model. *Journal of Textiles and Fibrous Materials, 1*, 251522111875679. doi:10.1177/2515221118756791

Workman, J. E., & Cho, S. (2012). Gender, fashion consumer groups, and shopping orientation. *Family and Consumer Sciences Research Journal, 40*(3), 267–283. doi.org/10.1111/j.1552-3934.2011.02110.x

Workman, J. E., & Studak, C. M. (2006). Fashion consumers and fashion problem recognition style. *International Journal of Consumer Studies, 30*(1), 75–84. doi:10.1111/j.1470-6431.2005.00451.x

Zhenxiang, W., & Lijie, Z. (2011). Case study of online retailing fast fashion industry. *International Journal of e-Education, e-Business, e-Management and e-Learning, 1*(3), 196–200. doi:10.7763/IJEEEE.2011.V1.31

Chapter 10

Navigating Luxury Brands Ecosystems: Evidence from Conceptual Marketing

Yllka Azemi
Indiana University Northwest, USA

Wilson Ozuem
University of Cumbria, UK

Ana Hobson
The American Chamber of Commerce Resources, USA

ABSTRACT

Online luxury brands are uniformly recognizing the practical advantages of electronic commerce. The existing literature provides conceptual elucidation that focuses on utilization of specific online marketing strategies. However, digital platforms invite holistic marketing applications—an all-embracing approach that nullifies the risk of potentially overlooked online marketing practices. This chapter provides conceptual insight into the overarching existing marketing literature, extending beyond the discourse of unconventional marketing utilization. The chapter also discerns insights fundamental to luxury customers with disabilities, as a customer group with increased potential to appraise a comprehensive marketing strategy. The chapter presents a model that provides four consequently driven marketing steps, which lead to customer attention grasp, customer zero-error perception, customer luxury brand online engagement, and monitoring of customers.

KEYWORDS

Online luxury brands, holistic online marketing, online customers with disabilities, customer attention, customer engagement

INTRODUCTION

The advent of the Internet invites an all-embracing participation in the online environment, risking companies losing customers isolated in the conventional brick-and-mortar marketing domain. Luxury brands are unique in facing this challenge, primarily due to the inherited inferences encapsulated by their definition. Ferrel and Hartline (2014) define luxury brands as 'unique, one-of-a kind products that consumers will spend considerable time, effort, and money to acquire' (p. 152). Kapferer (2015) signifies luxury as a 'made up of a mix of high-quality product, brand heritage, unique knowledge, exclusivity, personalization of service, and bespoke communications fused with long term relationships with selected clientele and categorized by high prices and prestigious physical stores' (p. 716). This implies that luxury brands in the online environment are at a greater risk of failing to meet customers' expectations, revealing the potential of losing customers upon online exposure. According to Hennings et al. (2012), luxury consumers are mainly 'risk-averse' and 'prefer the "touch and feel" experience in luxury stores while being afraid of the product deception risk associated with an online shopping environment' (pp. 34–35). Recently, Azemi et al. (2019) recognized the presence of two other customer groups in addition to the 'risk-averse' one: solutionist customers and impulsive customers. The former exploits online brands when online purchase supports their overall job-related behavior, whereas impulsive customers utilize the online environment to fulfill a personal void for unique products. Azemi et al.'s (2019) study reflects customers' stance within online banking, asserting that impulsive customers as less sensitive to banks' failure to meet their expectations. Kapferer and Bastien (2009) suggest that in luxury branding, the product 'should have a very strong personal and hedonistic component, otherwise it is no longer luxury but simple snobbery' (p. 314). This highlights a potentially equal increased sensitivity across all luxury customer types.

A stream of researchers talk about usage of online platforms, such as social media as conventional mediums to ease the process of provider-customer communication—a prerequisite to meet customer expectations (Abney et al., 2017; Kietzmann et al., 2011; Lima et al., 2019; Ozuem et al., 2017). Other scholars emphasize the integration of websites as a prime marketing tool (Luo et al., 2012; Ong et al., 2015; Ye et al., 2019). They accentuate user experience (UX) as essential to satisfactory company-clientele collaboration. Marketing literature has traditionally recognized the concept of service failure to encapsulate customer dissatisfaction with the brand experience (Choi & Mattila, 2008; Ozuem & Lancaster, 2014; Herhausen et al., 2019). Scholars' efforts to find recovery strategies following service failure are evident (Forbes et al., 2005; Harris et al., 2006; Chuang et al., 2012). In online services marketing, compensation, product replacement and response speed are the recommended recovery strategies (Forbes et al., 2005; Ozuem & Azemi, 2018). While these studies provide rich insight into constituents of marketing, the present literature lacks discussion of a holistic approach to online marketing. Recently, Felix et al. (2017) revealed the strategic social media marketing framework, divulging four potential continuums of the company-provider communication. The authors elucidate these in the context of four constituents: scope, culture, structure, and governance. According to them, the scope comprises explorers or defenders—the former refers to company-customer two-way communication, whereas the latter alludes to a company's centralized way to conveying information. The culture of companies is interpreted through conservative usage of 'an encapsulated, traditional, mass advertising', whereas a modernistic social media culture is one that is 'more permeable, open, and flexible' (p. 120). Social media structure alludes to the hierarchy (i.e., a company's single representative versus networks (i.e., all-employee embracement of communication with customers). Governance is examined in the context of autocracy and anarchy—the former implying companies' usage of social media based on a set of policies, the latter suggesting open policy criteria to determine social media usage.

Felix et al.'s (2017) study enlightens marketing literature with insight into the means of provider-customer communication. However, they seem to have isolated conceptualization of a company's stance after an established customer's request to communicate. Their study also provides no distinction between customers' peculiarities, nullifying the potential for particular online marketing strategies per customer type. The present chapter suggests that online marketing strategies should be inclusive of means that start well before an established customer-provider interaction—suggesting online marketing platforms consisting of strategies that capture potential customers, and support a satisfactory cooperation with dissatisfied ones. This is particularly important for online luxury brands as the industry with increased customer delicacy within the online environment. Further, this chapter is centered within the disabled customer target group with its extended demands resulting from impairment. Notably, disabled customers remain one of the groups with the least attention from marketing scholars.

This chapter provides a twofold contribution to luxury online marketing literature. Firstly, it introduces conceptual insight into a holistic online marketing strategy platform—imperative to conceptualize and develop satisfactory online luxury provider-customer collaboration. Secondly, it addresses persons with disabilities, enlightening existing marketing literature with specific strategies that pertain to the idiosyncrasies of a particular customer group. The developed conceptual model provides guidelines for how online luxury brands should apply online marketing strategies that lead to mutual satisfaction for the company and the customer.

LITERATURE REVIEW

Luxury branding remains a powerful industry in the global economy. According to a Deloitte (2018) report, 'the world's 100 largest luxury goods companies generated personal luxury goods sales of US$217 billion' (p. 3). However, market positioning of luxury brands no longer seems to be secure in depending upon conventional marketing strategies. As quoted in the Deloitte's (2018) report, 'rapid digital transformation and evolving consumer preferences and tastes are creating a new competitive landscape where traditional corporate strategies are under threat' (p. 5). Websites are the main online medium of communication with customers. However, the challenge remains as to how to turn website visitors into actual customers. The technical aspects of websites have traditionally been analyzed as foundational to meeting customer expectations. For example, Donthu (2001) examined processing speed, revealing potential customer confrontation with the companies over slow websites. Wolfinbarger and Gilly (2003) posit protection of customer privacy as directing customer choice of one brand over another. Parasuraman et al. (2005) question websites that do not ensure a constant presence, arguing that a company's unavailable website alters customers' preferences towards other available retailers. Tshin et al. (2014) assert a website that is easy to navigate as a prerequisite to customer satisfaction. This indicates that a website that hinders customers' usage of the platform translates into a loss of customers. Recently, authors have extended analysis beyond the technology incorporated in the website construct, highlighting the significance of a website outline that accords well with the customers' emotional stance. This information is imperative for industries with emotionally attached customers such as those of fashion and luxury brands. Ong et al. (2015) developed the WebHApp model which consists of six features that lead to customer happiness, namely 'website satisfaction, website reliability, information support, connection, and self-growth' (p. 596). The authors explain the customers' happy stance across the customer expectation-perception continuum. McDowell et al. (2016) suggest that only 'one out of every twenty-five unique [website] visitors makes a purchase' (p. 4839). Luxury industry was not the focus of the study, providing implication for a lower number of conversions across luxury customers. They reveal visitor greeting, catalog, shopping cart, and checkout as prerequisites to turn visitors into actual customers.

Social media is introduced as the medium to support the company's performance in general and the website medium in particular. Oberoi et al. (2017) suggest that a website that meets customers' expectations takes over the effort of internal (e.g., employees) and external expertise, further enhancing companies' positioning in the social media environment. This invites the inclusion of employees from the department of marketing into the website construct. However, contemporary marketing ideology suggests that any employee within the organization is an important stakeholder of the marketing department. This implies that employees in other departments should be drawn into online luxury provider-customer communication. This is particularly important for luxury brands' marketing strategies that are based in the usage of diverse social media. Ozuem and Azemi (2018) favor a multiple social media usage suggesting that the company's presence across diverse social media enhances company-customer communication. Their discussion provides implication for how luxury companies regardless of the life cycle would gain higher customer trust from being present across multiple online platforms. Further, these authors highlight employees' representation of the luxury brands in real customer settings such as, for example, demonstrating how the he/she purchased a product from the company and the benefits/value encountered from the purchase—reifying the inclusion of the marketing practice of all employees in online marketing. Not all the companies would be able to afford utilizing paid social media across multiple platforms. Hence, luxury brands should choose the social media that is determined by its customers' preference. For example, according to a Pew Research Center report, '78% of 18-24 years olds use Snapchat ... 71% of Americans in this age group now use Instagram and close to half (45%) are Twitter users' (Smith & Andreson, 2018). This provides a rationale for how companies that target 18-24-year-old customers should choose Snapchat and Instagram over Twitter. All three should be utilized upon availability of resources. In this case, the company's presence on Twitter is important in particular if its main customers are on Twitter more than on Snapchat and Instagram.

The company's appearance across diverse social media ensures its enhanced usage of practices in occurrences of customers' online complaints. The marketing strategy literature defines practices utilized to address customers' complaints with recovery strategies (Kuo et al., 2011; Ozuem et al., 2016; Azemi & Ozuem, 2016). The consensus in services marketing literature assigns the speed of response to a customer's complaint with a satisfactory recovery strategy (Miller et al., 2000; Wirtz & Mattila, 2004). The speed of response is even more important for online complaints, which are visible to millions of people. Limited evidence suggests that online customers assign themselves rather than the provider responsible for an issue and/or complaint, suggesting that these customers disagree with others' online negative complaints (Harris et al., 2006). They seem to take an epithetical stance towards the company. Many scholars have discussed the increased impact online complaints have on other customers' negative perception of a company (Duan et al., 2008; Piercy & Archer-Brown, 2014; Gu & Ye, 2014). So the practice of going over others' reviews before making a purchase decision is a common one. This is particularly evident across luxury branding customers, for many of whom the luxury product purchase is a psychological utility-based choice. As Ferrell and Hartline (2014) explain, psychological utility is reached upon customers' psychological satisfaction with the product/service purchased. For online luxury customers psychological satisfaction is primarily driven from the conception that the product supports the customer's social status, social belonging especially within the influencer group, and prestige.

Mate et al. (2019) invite providers' apology as the first recovery strategy to manage online complaints—asserting that 'the act of apologizing is seen as representing a caring attitude and shows compassion for the negative event experienced by the customer' (p. 639). These authors acknowledge defensive recovery, i.e., 'the acts of dismissing or denying responsibility for the service failure identified in a customer review' (p. 640), as a strategy with a satisfactory potency. Defensive recovery strategies might be appropriate for industries such as a luxury one embedded within a prestige business environment. However, they could be criticized when dealing with disabled customers—assuming that these are customers with an increased need for support rather than justifications from luxury brands. Hence, recognizing recovery strategies that support luxury-branding identity irrespective of the customer type is imperative.

Regardless of the nature of the customer, they require instant support (Ott & Theunissen, 2015; Lastner et al., 2016; Ozuem et al., 2018). Instant support takes many forms with live chat being a dominant one, which could be delivered as either a written and a speaking live chat. Services marketing literature highlights the inclusion of customers or stakeholders in the other customers' online questions to a company (Weitzl & Hutzinger, 2017). Gruber et al.'s (2015) study provides implications for how online customers experience an increased trust in the company when exposed to other customers' online threads. Further, Baker and Meyer (2014) talk about the customers' trust following conversations with highly positioned company representatives compared to the frontline ones. Companies should constantly monitor customers to understand their expectations and perceptions. Research methodologists have successfully set the stage for numerous research techniques that marketers could use to conceptualize customers, with some of those techniques being interviews and surveys (Fontana & Frey, 2000; Howell, 2013; Maxwell, 2013). Services marketing has traditionally appreciated monetary value customers receive from the company (Bonifield & Cole, 2008; Sharifi & Aghazadeh, 2016). This advocates for luxury brands to provide financial rewards to customers upon completion of offline and/or online interviews and/or surveys. The explanation of the means of contemporary customer monitoring has roots in online customer behavior. This in practice could be achieved through a company's monitoring of customers' step-by-step usage of its website and social media. Such an approach deciphers detailed information on issues that would hinder customers' usage of the online platform, and the transition process of the customer from a visitor to an actual purchaser.

While these studies individually provide imperative explanation for contemporary marketing, the information they decipher pertains to specific components of marketing applications. The risk of customer dissatisfaction inherited in e-commerce in particular within the luxury branding industry invites holistic marketing practices. Recently, Felix et al. (2017) provided an overarching explanation of social media usage, revealing four scenarios of providers' stance in online platforms. These are (1) explorer/defender, (2) conservatism/modernism, (3) autocracy/anarchy, and (4) hierarchy/networks. The explorer/defender refers to the continuum of two-way vs. one-way communication between the company and the customer. Conservatism/modernism alludes to the company's usage of traditional vs. social media. Autocracy/anarchy suggests providers' organization of social media usage based on rules/policies vs. no order, whereas hierarchy/networks reveal a company's single social media representative vs. the all-embracing inclusion of employees. These authors alter traditional marketing into an overarching social media application. They reveal insight that would support companies recognize potential market positioning across different social media utilization scenarios. However, this study appraises services marketing literature across customer-company communication in social media after an established customer-provider relationship. Critical assessment of extant theoretical insight into the phenomena implies that social media communication should be a single step within the online marketing strategy practices. This invites holistic marketing programs inclusive of detailed information that begins with the customers' recognition of luxury companies in the online competitive market and extends to practices that support forever-lasting company-customer collaboration. Such an approach is even more important when dealing with disabled customers, as a customer group that has received the least attention from online marketing scholars.

DISCUSSION

The review of extant knowledge resulted in the construct of a fourfold holistic conceptual online marketing model (see Figure 1). While this conceptual model does not constitute empirically based insight, it enlightens marketing literature with a new perspective of an all-embracing marketing approach with potential to improve luxury branding online marketing performance. The components of the model are (1) attention, (2) zero-error, (3) engagement, and (4) monitoring impact. An all-embracing perspective to direct the step-by-step collaboration of online providers-customers is particularly imperative due to the increased sensitivity of disabled online customers in the online luxury markets, whose expectation is to acquire an exclusive product which meets their psychological and societal needs (Kapferer & Bastien, 2009; Hennings et al., 2012; Ferrel & Hartline, 2014). Marketing literature has traditionally acknowledged the presence of different types of customers, implying the potentials of online luxury customers' definitions of exclusivity differently (Schoefer & Diamanatapolous, 2009; Azemi et al., 2019).

Attention refers to the successful marketing strategies a company utilizes to make itself recognizable to customers and to increase the customers' desire to make an online purchase (Ozuem et al., 2008). The highly competitive market in the online environment positions the grasp of customer

Figure 1. The azem holistic online marketing model of luxury brands

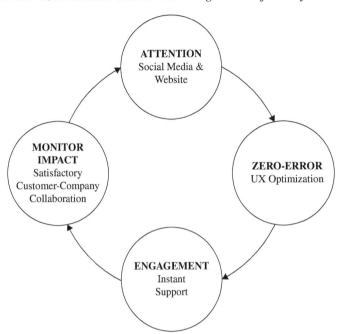

attention to be the central problem of practitioners (Kotler & Keller, 2016; Ozuem & Azemi, 2018). The existing literature has acknowledged the website as the main online platform to support a company's visibility in the online market, setting social media as an underlying means to assist provider-customer collaboration (Luo et al., 2012; Ye et al., 2019). However, for luxury brands, website and social media are apprehended to be mutually inclusive in the company's online positioning over other competitors. Multiple social media platforms are imposed to enlarge the online presence of luxury brands. Customers with disabilities could identify the most lucrative social media platform for them, even though marketing requires identical usage of practices across all online platforms (Ferrell & Hartline, 2014). This nullifies customers' potential confusion with the company. The emotional stance of customers has been assigned as the mediator for how they evaluate a company's website and social media (Ong et al., 2015; McDowell et al., 2016). The antecedents to drive customers' emotional construct are: a company's 24-hour online presence, the processing speed of the online platform, ease of use of the online platform, and the safety of the customers' data upon entrance into the online platform (Donthu, 2001; Wolfinbarger & Gilly, 2003; Parasuraman et al., 2005). The absence of any foretasted criteria would lead to the customer assembling negative emotions, and his/her dissatisfactory perception of the user experience respectively.

Zero-error refers to the luxury company's utilization of marketing techniques that ensure satisfactory user experience (Azemi & Ozuem, 2016). User experience is reached upon utilization of marketing techniques in line with the disabled customers' expectations posited to be the controller of one's satisfaction with a brand (Choi & Mattila, 2008; Abney et al., 2017; Herhausen et al., 2019). A zero-error experience leads to customer-provider engagement. *Engagement* is identified with online luxury marketing strategies that ensure a satisfactory provider-customer experience (Ott & Theunissen, 2015). The literature on online customer engagement is primarily focused on the service failure-recovery continuum (Ringberg et al., 2007; Roggeveen et al., 2012; Siu et al., 2013). Online luxury company-customer engagement should support customer utilization of the online platform regardless of the presence of incidents. This would refine failure occurrences, enhancing the market positioning of luxury companies in online tapestries. Website live chat is a pivotal tool utilized for customer engagement. The engagement of existing customers in supporting complainants has proved to be satisfactory (Duan et al., 2008; Gu & Ye, 2014). Customer engagement in assisting others overcomes even the most severe incidents. Email, video and/or phone calls and scripts with the most frequent questions/answers are the other potential company-customer engagement mediums. These strategies depict prompt customer support (Ozuem & Lancaster, 2014; Gruber et al., 2015). Further, the involvement of employees from multiple organizational levels are acknowledged as an imperative source in supporting complainants. This requires the luxury companies to construct policies that would control employees' representation of the company without intrusion.

Monitoring impact refers to marketing techniques utilized for conceptualization of customers' expectations and evaluations of the online luxury experience with intent to improve performance (Harris et al., 2006). The monitoring anticipates utilization of both offline and online means of data collection regarding customers' perception of the luxury online experience. It advocates data collection across multiple formats such as paid, rewarded, and unpaid online and mailed surveys. This aligns well with many customers who perceive paid surveys as a conventional promotional strategy (Kotler & Keller, 2016).

MANAGERIAL IMPLICATIONS

The advent of the Internet posed the urge for the luxury companies' shift from bricks-and-mortar to online business (Ozuem & Azemi, 2018). For the luxury brands, the online environment presents an opportunity for customer augmentation upon successful utilization of marketing practices. This invites contemporary marketing strategies with foregrounds in holistic online marketing programs. The exclusion of any marketing practice would lead to a lost or dissatisfied customer (Wang et al., 2011; Zhang et al., 2018). Such an approach is imperative in particular for customers' with an increased need for support, even though the sensitive nature of the online environment does not allow usage of marketing strategies that differ much across customers. The online environment leads to the construct of a marketing department integrative of the digital marketing unit with specialists in the targeted customers' behavior and expectation construct. To optimize their online presence, companies exploit diverse online platforms including websites and multiple social media mediums such as Facebook, Twitter, and Instagram (Abney et al., 2017; Felix et al., 2017). This facilitates customers' process of conceptualizing the platform that aligns best with their expectations. Also, being visible across numerous platforms supports the companies to communicate better with customers, ensuring that they would not switch to the other brands available because of lack of communication (Harris et al., 2006; Ozuem & Lancaster, 2014).

Digital marketing departments or external experts are assigned to run user experience tests for a company's website. This enables brands to set website and social media design and content that are within customers' domain of expectations. While it is impossible to be a zero-error online brand for all, digital marketing departments set guidelines that emphasize instant support for all customer types (Forbes et al., 2005; Choi & Mattila, 2008; Herhausen et al., 2019). The foreground of satisfactory support policies lies within customers' assemblies of expectations and evaluations (Ringberg et al., 2007). Website live chat is the dominant instant support mechanism, which when displayed across both the typing and speaking options enhances company-customer communication. Rather than the employees from the digital marketing department alone, other employees in the company are also encouraged to support online customers. Training all the employees in delivering instant online support to customers has been well recognized (Azemi et al., 2019). Marketing and digital marketing representatives stimulate online customers to support other customers—recognizing that an enhanced trust in the company is evident upon other customers' inclusion in answering each other's questions (Weitzl & Hutzinger, 2017). A growing body of companies also place videos that would answer the most frequent questions from all customers on their websites and social media pages. The videos contain captions that are accessible to all customer types.

Company support of the customer experience goes beyond the online environment (Harris et al., 2006). The online tapestries are still subject to technical limitations that hinder satisfactory support for specific customer requests (Wolfinbarger & Gilly, 2003; Parasuraman et al., 2005; Luo et al., 2012). Hence, digital marketing representatives invite online complainants into an email, video and or phone call conversation. If none of the three works, the customer-company communication moves to a face-to-face setting. It is paramount for the company to train employees in how to communicate with customers across all the communication modes—email, video, phone, and face-to-face (Ozuem & Lancaster, 2014). The foundations of the training program should be set based on the data collected as part of the monitoring of customers. Digital marketing representatives consistently monitor online customers' behavior to address questions and complaints (Gu & Ye, 2014; Vaerenbergh & Holmqvist, 2014; Gruber et al., 2015). This assists the company's decision-making for delivering satisfactory recovery strategies upon customers' dissatisfaction. Recognizing that customers in general do not convey their complaints, companies employ methods that would stimulate customers to reveal their true perception of the online service (Kau & Loh, 2006; Casado-Diaz & Nicolau-Gonzalbez, 2009). Some of the monitoring methods that companies utilize are: paid, rewarded and unpaid online surveys; paid, rewarded and unpaid mail surveys; monitoring of social media and website customers' usage steps, i.e., the time that customers spend to move from one activity to another, the amount of time customers spend on the website or social media before making a purchase, the number of times customers visit the website/social media before making a purchase, and customers' involvement in website reviews and/or social media activities through likes/shares/tweets. The representatives of the marketing/digital marketing department work closely with the customer service department, as the latter is often the first to be reached out to by dissatisfied customers (Ozuem et al., 2018; Azemi et al., 2019). This entails integration of the marketing department as a function of the company's overall operation—an operational convention that evolved with the advent of digital marketing.

LIMITATIONS AND FUTURE RESEARCH

The present conceptual explanation provides rich insight into the online mass marketing strategies that luxury brands could utilize to ensure a comprehensive environment for all customer types. However, the emerged elucidation reflects a conceptual approach, inviting empirical research to confirm the comfort of its application. A future mixed methods study embracing qualitative and quantitative research could reveal in-depth contextual findings to support the generalizability of the insight. It is also suggested that future research utilizes an embedded case study as a research strategy. This would support comprehension of both the provider's and the customers' perception of the online luxury experience, ensuring diverse yet trustworthy information. Further, examining the emerged knowledge across distinct luxury products would deploy imperative discernment to enable the construction of a model for a mutually inclusive experience across both the provider and the customer. Finally, comprehension of the model across distinct disabilities would support luxury companies' performance beyond specific customer groups.

REFERENCES

Abney, A. K., Pelletier, M. J., Ford, T. R. S., & Horky, A. B. (2017). #IHateYourBrand: Adaptive service recovery strategies on Twitter. *Journal of Services Marketing, 31*(3), 281–294.

Azemi, Y., & Ozuem, W. (2016). Online service failure and recovery strategy: The mediating role of social media. In Ozuem & Bowen (Eds.), *Competitive Social Media Marketing Strategies* (pp. 112–136). Hershey: IGI Global.

Azemi, Y., Ozuem, W., Howell, K. E., & Lancaster, G. (2019). An exploration into the practice of online service failure and recovery strategies in the Balkans. *Journal of Business Research, 94*, 420–431.

Baker, T., & Meyer, T. (2014). Explanation information and source in service recovery initiatives. *Journal of Services Marketing, 28*(4), 311–318.

Bonifield, C., & Cole, C. A. (2008). Better him than me: Social comparison theory and service recovery. *Journal of the Academy of Marketing Science, 36*(4), 565–577.

Casado-Diaz, A. B., & Nicolau-Gonzalbez, J. L. (2009). Explaining consumer complaining behaviour in double deviation scenarios: The banking services. *The Service Industries Journal, 29*(12), 1659–1668.

Chuang, S. C., Cheng, Y. H., Chang, C. J., & Yang, S. W. (2012). The effect of service failure types and service recovery on customer satisfaction: A mental accounting perspective. *The Service Industries Journal, 32*(2), 257–271.

Choi, S., & Mattila, A. S. (2008). Perceived controllability and service expectations: Influences on customer reactions following service failure. *Journal of Business Research, 61*(1), 24–30.

Deloitte. (2018). *The global powers of luxury goods: Shaping the future of the luxury industry.*

Donthu, N. (2001). Does your web site measure up? *Marketing Management, 10*(4), 29–32.

Duan, W., Gu, B., & Whinston, A. B. (2008). Do online reviews matter?—An empirical investigation of panel data. *Decision Support Systems, 45*(4), 1007–1016.

Felix, R., Rauschnabel, P. A., & Hinsch, C. (2017). Elements of strategic social media marketing: A holistic framework. *Journal of Business Research, 70*, 118–126.

Ferrell, O. C., & Hartline, M. D. (2014). *Marketing strategy* (6th ed.). Boston: Cengage Learning.

Fontana, A., & Frey, J. H. (2000). The interview: From structured questions to negotiated text. In N. K. Denzin & Y. S. Lincoln (Eds.), *Handbook of Qualitative Research* (2nd ed., pp. 645–672). Thousand Oaks: Sage Publications.

Forbes, L. P., Kelley, S. W., & Hoffman, K. D. (2005). Typologies of e-commerce retail failures and recovery strategies. *Journal of Services Marketing, 19*(5), 280–292.

Gruber, D. A., Smerek, R. E., Thomas-Hunt, M. C., & James, E. H. (2015). The real-time power of twitter: Crises management and leadership in an age of social media. *Business Horizons, 58*(2), 163–172.

Gu, B., & Ye, Q. (2014). First step in social media: Measuring the influence of online management responses on customer satisfaction. *Production and Operations Management, 23*(4), 570–582.

Harris, K. E., Grewal, D., Mohr, L. A., & Bernhardt, K. L. (2006). Consumer responses to service recovery strategies: The moderating role of online versus offline environment. *Journal of Business Research, 59*(4), 425–431.

Hennings, N., Wiedmann, K. P., & Klarmann, C. (2012). Luxury brands in the digital age—exclusivity versus ubiquity. St. Gallen: *Marketing Review*, 30–35.

Herhausen, D., Ludwig, S., Grewal, D., Wulf, J., & Schoegel, M. (2019). Detecting, preventing, and mitigating online firestorms in brand communities. *Journal of Marketing, 83*(3), 1–21.

Howell, K. E. (2013). *An introduction to the philosophy of methodology.* London: Sage Publications.

Kapferer, J. N. (2015). The future of luxury: Challenges and opportunities. *Journal of Brand Management, 21*(9), 716–726.

Kapferer, J. N., & Bastien, V. (2009). The specificity of luxury management: Turning marketing upside down. *Journal of Brand Management, 16*, 311–322.

Kau, A., & Loh, E. W. (2006). The effects of service recovery on consumer satisfaction: A comparison between complainants and non-complainants. *Journal of Services Marketing, 20*(2), 101–111.

Kietzmann, J. H., Hermkens, K., McCarthy, I. P., & Silvestre, B. S. (2011). Social media? Get serious! Understanding the functional building blocks of social media. *Business Horizons, 54*(3), 241–251.

Kotler, P., & Keller, K. L. (2016). *A framework for marketing management* (6th ed.). Boston: Pearson Education.

Kuo, Y., Yen, S., & Chen, L. (2011). Online auction service failures in Taiwan: Typologies and recovery strategies. *Electronic Commerce Research and Applications, 10*(2), 183–193.

Lastner, M. M., Folse, J. A. G., Mangus, S. M., & Fennell, P. (2016). The road to recovery: Overcoming service failures through positive emotions. *Journal of Business Research, 69*(10), 4278–4286.

Lima, V. M., Irigaray, H. A. R., & Lourenco, C. (2019). Consumer engagement on social media: Insights from a virtual brand community. *Qualitative Market Research: An International Journal, 22*(1), 14–32.

Luo, J., Ba, S., & Zhang, H. (2012). The effectiveness of online shopping characteristics and well-designed websites on satisfaction. *MIS Quarterly, 36*(4), 1131–1144.

Mate, M. J., Trupp, A., & Pratt, S. (2019). Managing negative online accommodation reviews: Evidence from the Cook Islands. *Journal of Travel & Tourism Marketing, 36*(5), 627–644.

Maxwell, J. A. (2013). *Qualitative research design: An interactive approach* (3rd ed.). Thousand Oaks: Sage Publications.

McDowell, W. C., Wilson, R. C., & Kile Jr., C. O. (2016). An examination of retail website design and conversion rate. *Journal of Business Research, 69*, 4837–4842.

Miller, J. L., Craighead, C. W., & Karwan, K. R. (2000). Service recovery: A framework and empirical investigation. *Journal of Operations Management, 18*(4), 387–400.

Oberoi, P., Patel, C., & Haon, C. (2017). Technology sourcing for website personalization and social media marketing: A study of e-retailing industry. *Journal of Business Research, 80*, 10–23.

Ong, C. S., Chang, S. C., & Lee, S. M. (2015). Development of webhapp: Factors in predicting user perceptions of website-related happiness. *Journal of Business Research, 68*, 591–598.

Ott, L., & Theunissen, P. (2015). Reputations at risk: Engagement during social media crises. *Public Relations Review, 41*(1), 97–102.

Ozuem, W., & Azemi, Y. (2018). *Digital marketing strategies for fashion and luxury brands*. Hershey: IGI Global.

Ozuem, W., & Azemi, Y. (2018). Online service failure and recovery strategies in luxury brands: A view from justice theory. In W. Ozuem & Y. Azemi (Eds.), *Digital Marketing Strategies for Fashion and Luxury Brands* (pp. 108–125). Hershey: IGI Global.

Ozuem, W., Howell, K. E., & Lancaster, G. (2008). Communicating in the new interactive marketspace. *European Journal of Marketing, 42*(9/10), 1059–1083.

Ozuem, W., Howell, K. E., & Lancaster, G. (2018). Developing technologically induced environments: The case of the Nigerian banking sector. *Journal of Financial Services Marketing, 23*(1), 50–61.

Ozuem, W., Patel, A., Howell, K., & Lancaster, G. (2017). An exploration of consumers' response to online service recovery initiatives. *International Journal of Market Research, 59*(1), 97–115.

Ozuem, W., Howell, K. E., & Lancaster, G. (2016). Understanding technologically-induced customer services in the Nigerian banking sector: The internet as a post-modern phenomenon. *International Journal of Information Technology and Management, 15*(3), 272–290.

Ozuem, W., & Lancaster, G. (2014). Recovery strategies in on-line service failure. In A. Ghorbani (Ed.), *Marketing in the Cyber Era: Strategies and Emerging Trends* (pp. 143–159). Hershey: IGI Global.

Parasuraman, A., Zeithaml, V. A., & Malhotra, A. (2005). E-S-QUAL: A multiple-item scale for assessing electronic service quality. *Journal of Service Research, 7*(3), 213–233.

Piercy, N., & Archer-Brown, C. (2014). Online service failure and propensity to suspend offline consumption. *The Service Industries Journal, 34*(8), 659–676.

Ringberg, T., Odekerken-Schroder, G., & Christensen, G. L. (2007). A cultural models approach to service recovery. *Journal of Marketing, 71*(3), 194–214.

Roggeveen, A. L., Tsiros, M., & Grewal, D. (2012). Understanding the co-creation effect: When does collaborating with customers provide a lift to service recovery? *Journal of the Academy of Marketing Science, 40*(6), 771–790.

Schoefer, K., & Diamantopoulos, A. (2009). A typology of consumers' emotional response style during service recovery encounters. *British Journal of Management, 20*(3), 292–308.

Siu, N. Y., Zhang, T. J., & Yau, C. J. (2013). The roles of justice and customer satisfaction in customer retention: A lesson from service recovery. *Journal of Business Ethics, 114*(4), 675–686.

Sharifi, S. S., & Aghazadeh, H. (2016). Discount reference moderates customers' reactions to discount frames after online service failure. *Journal of Business Research, 69*(10), 4074–4080.

Smith, A., & Anderson, M. (2018). *Social media use in 2018: A majority of Americans use Facebook and YouTube, but young adults are especially heavy users of Snapchat and Instagram.* Pew Research Center. Retrieved from https://www.pewinternet.org/2018/03/01/social-media-use-in-2018/

Tshin, E. Y. H., Tanakinjal, G. H., & Sondoh Jr., S. L. (2014). The key dimensions of online service quality: A study of consumer perceptions. *IUP Journal of Marketing Management, 13*(2), 7–18.

Vaerenbergh, Y. V., & Holmqvist, J. (2014). Examining the relationship between language divergence and word-of-mouth intentions. *Journal of Business Research, 67*, 1601–1608.

Wang, Y., Wu, S., Lin, H., & Wang, Y. (2011). The relationship of service failure severity, service recovery justice and perceived switching costs with customer loyalty in the context of e-tailing. *International Journal of Information Management, 31*(4), 350–359.

Weitzl, W., & Hutzinger, C. (2017). The effects of marketer- and advocate-initiated online service recovery responses on silent bystanders. *Journal of Business Research, 80*, 164–175.

Wirtz, J., & Mattila, A. S. (2004). Consumer responses to compensation, speed of recovery and apology after a service failure. *International Journal of Service Industry Management, 15*(2), 150–166.

Wolfinbarger, M., & Gilly, M. C. (2003). eTailQ: Dimensionalizing, measuring and predicting etail quality. *Journal of Retailing, 79*(3), 183–198.

Ye, B. H., Barreda, A. A., Okumus, F., & Nusair, K. (2019). Website interactivity and brand development of online travel agencies in China: The moderating role of age. *Journal of Business Research, 99*, 382–389.

Zhang, T., Lu, C., Torres, E., & Chen, P. J. (2018). Engaging customers in value co-creation or co-destruction online. *Journal of Services Marketing, 32*(1), 57–69.

Chapter 11

Understanding Brand Loyalty in the Luxury Smartphones Industry: Some Antecedents and the Moderating Role of Switching Behaviour

Dominic Appiah
Arden University, United Kingdom

Kerry Howell
University of Plymouth, United Kingdom

Geoff Lancaster
London School of Commerce

ABSTRACT

The smartphone is increasingly redefining our identities, and reshaping our perspectives about shopping, socialising, teaching and learning. With current developments and the shift towards luxury smartphones, the expectation of luxury smartphone manufacturers is ultimately to consolidate customer loyalty through improved user experiences. Nevertheless, luxury is considered as an experience that adds value to consumer-brand relationships, and emphasizes that luxury brands enable consumers to derive, to some extent, intangible benefits beyond their functional utility. Loyalty to a luxury smartphone brand occurs as a consequence of positive attitudes which motivate consumers to repeatedly demand a particular brand, or a limited number of brands within a suitably defined period of time. The management of these luxury smartphones is a key marketing function. A strong and healthy brand is instrumental in creating sustainable competitive advantage and the transition to a relationship marketing para-digm places brand loyalty at the heart of customer relational strength. It is widely accepted that brand loyalty has traditionally been perceived as a behavioural construct relating to intentions towards repeat purchases. This chapter aims to provide some insights into brand switching in the smart-phone industry and offers opportunities for marketers and scholars in the development of related marketing plans.

KEYWORDS

Luxury Brands, Luxury Smartphones, Brand Loyalty, Attitudinal Loyalty, Behavioural Loyalty, Consumer Behaviour

INTRODUCTION AND CONTEXT

Luxury brands rely on strong brand identities to establish loyalty amongst consumers. Loyalty and luxury consumption is built on the meanings that the relationships consumers establish with luxury brands. The power of strong brands is increasing and is absolutely critical in the high-tech luxury industry. Appiah et al. (2019) share the view that a brand is a name, design, symbol or major feature that helps to identify one or more products or ser-vices of a particular organization from others within the same product cat-egory. Hence, branding remains a powerful tool as consumers recognize that brands provide them focused information such as identity and value, as well as some unique features of branded products or services. Broadly, research on brand loyalty focuses on two main schools of thought; behav-ioural loyalty and attitudinal loyalty (e.g., Dick & Basu, 1994; Ball, Coelho & Macha, 2004; Ringberg & Gupta, 2003). Nam, Ekinci & Whyatt (2011) confirm that brand loyalty has traditionally been perceived as a behavioural construct relating to intentions towards repeat purchases. Indeed, consumer behavior tends to be based on repeat purchase of particular products or services (Hallowell, 1996; Homburg & Giering, 2001; Yi, 1990). However, this chapter considers attitudinal loyalty as a form of long-term and emo-tional commitment to a brand (Bennett & Rundle-Thiele, 2002; Shankar, Smith & Rangaswamy, 2003). This is why attitudinal loyalty is referred to as 'emotional loyalty' and is regarded as 'much stronger and longer lasting' (Hofmeyr & Rice, 2000). This paper reviews the literature on brand loyalty and then presents a discussion on brand switching based on two contrasting perspectives. An evaluation of both behavioural and attitudinal loyalty is carried out to establish the latter as more of a sustainable choice. Finally, the paper concludes with a discussion of managerial implications.

CONCEPTUAL CLARIFICATION OF LUXURY BRANDS

Branding is important in the hyper-competitive luxury industry because the brand is a significant factor that influences product loyalty (Ozuem et al., 2016; Ahn, Park & Hyun, 2018; Appiah et al., 2019). Luxury brands are often associated with high-income consumers, and this category of consumers are typically willing to pay larger premiums compared to middle-income consumers. The emergence of new technologies has given luxury brands higher visibility and such technologies continue to attract more attention amongst consumers all over the world (Appiah and Ozuem, 2018). Luxury brands are characterized as one of the fastest-growing brand segments generating high profits in various markets. Luxury brands are defined and categorised based on different perspectives. Vickers and Renand (2003) described luxury brands as symbols of personal identity, and emphasise that consumer luxury consumption is dependent on personal, social and individual attachments. For the purposes of this chapter, and in line with the above clarification, luxury brands are described as the outward expression of a consumer's own identity. However, consumer's intensions to purchase luxury brands are complex and multifaceted (Giovannini, Xu, & Thomas, 2015). Luxury brands are considered as conspicuous possessions categorized by exclusivity, prestige, and premium pricing (Berthon, Pitt, and Campbell 2008; Miller and Mills, 2012). They possess distinct brand identities and meanings distinguished by specific associations (Tynan, McKechnie, and Chhuon 2010; Ozuem et al., 2017). Luxury brands benefit from associations utilized by firms in developing strong brand identities which typically include (a) authenticity, (b) stylistic consistency; (c) quality commitment; (d) unique aesthetic symbolism; and (e) hedonic and emotional promotional appeals (Okonkwo, 2009).

Aaker, (2004) argues that luxury brands have a deeper and richer extended form of brand identity compared to more mundane brands. Luxury branding is, in many ways one of the purest examples of branding that exists within the realm of strategic marketing as the brand and its image often provide key competitive advantages, creating enormous value and wealth for organizations (Keller, 2009). Crucially, academics and marketers seek to understand consumer intentions in the context of the purchasing of luxury goods and services. They also seek to understand what consumers believe luxury stands for, and how their perceptions of luxury value affect their buying behaviour (Wiedmann, Hennings, & Siebels, 2009). Traditionally the meaning of luxury has been linked to excellence, creativity and exclusivity (Okonkwo, 2009) as well as premium pricing (Nuemo & Quelch, 1998). Based on these attributes, luxury brands help to develop and form the consumer's identity by connecting the consumer's inner self with the external world (Belk, 1988; Jenkins, 2004). Nevertheless, luxury is considered an experience that adds value to consumer-brand relationships, and emphasizes the possibility to derive particular intangible benefits beyond the functional utility of luxury goods and services (Bastien & Kapferer, 2013; Vickers & Renand, 2003; Vigneron & Johnson, 2004). Again, consumers may also buy luxury brands for symbolic reasons in order to reflect their individual or social goals (Wilcox et al., 2009).

SYMBOLIC BENEFITS OF LUXURY BRANDS

Luxury Brands serve as symbolic resources which users may employ to construct social identities in order to assign meaning to themselves and, further, to signal meaning to others (Elliott and Wattanasuwan, 1998; McCracken, 1988). The more 'symbolic' the luxury brand, the more likely the brand is to enable the user to communicate their self-concept (Escalas and Bettman, 2005). The symbolic nature of brands, specifically the range of distinctive images they reflect (Chaplin and John, 2005) has meant that they are particularly useful as a means of satisfying the self-definitional needs of consumers (Bhattacharya and Sen, 2003; Fournier, 1998). In some cases, consumers derive symbolic meaning from the associations they make between the brand and typical users of the brand (Muniz and O'Guinn, 2001; Kumar and Shah, 2004; Ozuem et al., 2016). The symbolic benefits of luxury brands allow consumers to construct their self-identity and to signal this identity to others. Individuals select luxury brands that bear unique personalities and images, which they use to express a self-image or an idealised self-image which can serve a self-enhancing or self-consistency role (Aaker, 1997; Sirgy, 1982; He et al., 2012; Yeh et al., 2016). The idea of the signalling component of the luxury brand resonates with Ligas and Cotte's (1999) holistic framework in which the process of brand meaning negotiation is explained using symbolic interactionism. It is suggested that consumers do not always necessarily act independently when interpreting marketer-induced brand meaning in the cultural system since social forces also exert influence (Appiah et al., 2019).

Earlier work by Belk (1980) suggests that consumers elicit symbolic meaning from brands which they then use to "extend and bolster a consumer's self-concept". More specifically, by owning brands that they perceive to possess symbolic images which are congruent with certain elements of their own self-concept, consumers maintain or strengthen their self-concept (Dolich, 1969). As an extension of this ownership, consumers are also able to express their own identities, in that the brands they choose project images similar to their own self-image (Aaker, 1996; Sirgy, 1982; Appiah et al., 2019), this view suggests that symbolic benefits correspond with the need for socially approval, self-expressive and outer-directed self-esteem.

Consumers may value the exclusive nature of a brand because of the way in which it relates to their self-concept (Solomon, 1983; Orth and De Marchi, 2007; Da Siveira et al., 2013). Self-congruity is driven by self-consistency motives such that idea that the greater the similarity between the brand image or brand personality and the consumer's self-concept, the higher the self-congruity. Since self-consistency is a means of self-expression, the greater the self-congruity, the more likely consumers are to identify with the brand to uphold their self-consistency (Kressman et al., 2006; Da Siveira et al., 2013). Symbolic needs are internally generated and are motivated by social meaning (Solomon, 1983). For example, self-enhancement, group membership and ego-identification are described as symbolic needs (Park et al., 1986). A symbolic need helps the consumer to be defined as a member of a specific group (He et al., 2012).

The branding literature exploring the role of brands in the lives of consumers reveals that brands can provide self-definitional benefits beyond utilitarian benefits (Aaker, 1999; Escalas and Bettman, 2005; Fournier, 1998; Keller, 1993; Keller and Lehmann, 2006; Farhana, 2014; Leckie et al., 2016). The idea of luxury brands as a means of self-expression has come to the fore because brand consumption allows consumers to express their identities by choosing brands whose images are perceived to be similar to their own self-images (Aaker, 1996). Since consumers by nature seek to reaffirm their self-image, brands allow consumers to not only express their identities, but to also reaffirm their principles or beliefs (Kleine et al., 1993; Solomon, 1983; Chernev et al., 2011). As implied earlier by Hoyer and MacInnis (1997), consumers may choose brands to form a particular association with other stereotypical brand users (Escalas and Bettman, 2003, 2005; He et al., 2012).

Consumer choices about luxury brands may be used to send social signals to other consumers, as is particularly the case with luxury brands (Han et al., 2010). In some instances, consumers extract meaning from the brand by assessing its personality, such that the signalling effect may be based not only on a stereotypical user of the luxury brand but also on the brand's personality (Lee, 2009). The symbolic values of luxury brands extend deeper than their role as a signalling device in that they help consumers to retain a sense of the past, to categorise themselves in society, and to communicate cultural meanings such as social status and group identity (Belk, 1988). Consistent with this view, it is apparent that the symbolic consumption of brands enables consumers to communicate some of their cultural categories such as age, gender, social status and other cultural values such as family and tradition (McCracken, 1993). In an attempt to explain the symbolic nature of the brand, Menneaghan (1995) suggests that the luxury brand is separate from the product. The product performs the function and the brand is grafted on by advertising. Since products are easy to replicate, the emergent symbolic meanings form the basis for the positioning and differentiation of brands. According to Appiah et al. (2019), consumer purchasing behaviour is influenced by the symbolic meaning of the brand in the form of shared values (Sirgy et al., 1997, 2000; He et al., 2012; Da Siveira et al., 2013). Zhang and Bloemer (2008), share the view that consumer–brand value congruence describes the similarity between a consumer's own personal values and his or her perceptions of the luxury brand's values.

THE SYMBOLIC NATURE OF LUXURY BRANDS AND SELF-CONGRUITY

Individuals are driven by a need to feel good about themselves and to try to maintain as well as to enhance their own self-esteem (Malär et al., 2011). One way towards achieving this is to consume brands that are congruent with the subject's view of the self as an ideal (Sirgy, 1982). Indeed, luxury brands may be viewed as a system of signs in construction of the self (Schembri et al., 2010). Consumers evaluate the symbolism of the luxury brand and determine whether it is appropriate for their 'selves' (Ahuvia, 2005; Belk, 1988). According to Levy (1999) the sign is appropriate for a consumer if it reinforces or enhances the self. Self-congruity, according to Helgeson and Supphellen (2004) is viewed as the extent to which "...a consumer's self-concept matches the personality of a typical user of a luxury brand".

Self-congruity also refers to the extent to which a consumer compares the image of him/herself and the image of the luxury brand. That is defined in accordance with a stereotypical user of the luxury brand, which influences consumer behaviour. The concept of 'self' is of great importance to individuals and by nature individual behaviours reflects the desire to both protect and, at the same time enhance their self-concept (Kleine et al., 1993; Sirgy, 1982; Underwood, 2003). Aaker (1999) proposed that the self-concept encompasses all aspects of self, including readily accessible or "schematic traits and those that are not necessarily schematic". Schematic traits are those that are very descriptive of and important to an individual. The need to express a self-schema stems from the need for consistency and positivity, which in turn improves self-esteem and maintains self-presentation (Aaker, 1999). By owning luxury brands which they perceive to possess symbolic images that are congruent with certain elements of their own self-concept, consumers maintain or strengthen their self-concept (Dolich, 1969). As an extension of this ownership, consumers are also able to express their own identities in that the luxury brands they choose bear images similar to their own self-image (Aaker, 1999; Sirgy, 1982). Consistent with this view, such ownership leads to strong relationships with those brands that have values and personality associations that are congruent with their self-concept (Sirgy, 1982). The subsequent brand relationships can therefore be viewed as expressions of consumer identity (Swaminathan et al., 2007).

Consumers psychologically compare their self-images with those of the stereotypical user of a luxury brand. The psychological comparison involving the interaction between the product-user image and consumer's self-concept creates a subjective experience called self-image congruence and this is considered an important predictor of consumer behaviour. According to Sirgy et al. (1997), luxury brands also possess personal image attributes which are themselves reflective of the stereotypical user of the luxury brand, e.g. young, hip or cool. Consumers draw not only on the perceived stereotypical user of the luxury brand to form congruity judgments, but also on the brand personality itself. The greater the congruence between brand personality and self-concept, the more likely the consumer is to exhibit a favourable attitude towards the bransd (Kuenzel and Halliday, 2010). It is widely held that self-congruity explains consumer preferences in respect of the fact that they seek products and brands that have higher self-congruity than lower self-congruity (Helgeson and Supphellen, 2004; Kettle and Hauble, 2011; Da Silveira et al., 2013). According to Puzakova et al. (2009), self-concept/brand image congruity is described as the level of congruity that exists between key elements of a person's own self-concept and that of brand image. This means that when consumers evaluate luxury brands such that their perception of the brand is at a level of congruence between the brand image and their self-concept, they are more likely to exhibit higher levels of both brand preference and brand loyalty (He et al., 2012; Yeh et al., 2016). Sirgy et al. (1997) validate this idea, suggesting that customer behaviours, in the form of positive word-of-mouth and brand attitudes, also develop as a result of self-concept/brand image congruency. Moreover, self-image congruence has been shown to influence brand satisfaction (Sirgy et al., 1997).

LUXURY SMARTPHONES AND BRAND LOYALTY

The emergence of a networked world, of which the smartphone plays a significant part, has changed the definition of the basic necessity of the smartphone; shifting towards a focus on high-end luxury smartphones. For instance, Apple appear to be evolving from egalitarian providers of mass market technology to gadgets for the wealthy. Other luxury smartphones operating within the Smartphone market include the Solarin smartphone. The Solarin smartphone stands out because of its sleek surface, leather and titanium exterior. Again, the luxury device boasts technology that provides protection to thwart cyber-attacks and military grade chip-to-chip 256-bit encryption. By flicking a unique security switch on the back of the device, the smartphone enters a special shielded mode which allows end-to-end encrypted calls and messages. These unique features of the phone are actually physically different from other phones (http://www.solarin.com). Another Luxury Smartphone is the Fantome Arcane. It is a high-performance, designed luxury smartphone built to satisfy the increasing demands of consumers seeking security and privacy features. It has very unique features and functions including a secure space to enrich the mobile user experience that allows multiple virtual phones to co-exist on the device. Each virtual phone created on the device can be paired to one of the two SIMs available on the Arcane. Each virtual phone isolates the accounts and data from other virtual phones on the device. This allows device owners to use the same app with different accounts in each virtual phone making it easy to maintain personal, public and work accounts and identities all on a single premium device (http://www.fantom3.com/arcane).

In line with the above developments and shift towards luxury smartphones, the expectation of these luxury smartphone firms is to ultimately consolidate customer loyalty through improved user experience. Loyalty to a brand is expressed due to a positive attitude, which makes a consumer repeatedly demand goods or services of a particular brand or a limited number of brands within a suitably defined period of time. Consistent with this view, Appiah (2019) suggests that consumers can have a positive attitude which may have a strong effect on their behaviour towards a particular brand. Brand loyalty is a "deeply held commitment to rebuy or re-patronise a preferred product or service consistently in the future, causing repetitive same-brand or same-brand-set purchasing, despite situational influence and marketing efforts having the potential to cause switching behaviour" (Oliver 1999, p. 34). Dimitriades (2006) shares a similar view in noting that it is widely accepted that satisfied consumers are less sensitive to price changes, less influenced by competitor attacks and increasingly more loyal to firms than dissatisfied customers.

SWITCHING BRANDS TO MAXIMISE FUNCTIONAL UTILITY

Switching occurs when a customer is motivated to review their available alternatives in a marketplace due to a change in competitive activity in the marketplace' (Seiders & Tigert, 1997; Appiah et al., 2019). Similarly, Hogan and Armstrong (2001) posited that brand switching is about replacing an incumbent resource with a more valuable one to achieve competitive advantage. Sathish, Kumar, Naveen and Jeevanantham (2011) posit that brand switching is a form of consumer behaviour whereby the behaviour of the consumer differs based on their satisfaction with providers or companies. Switching behaviour can be enunciated as the process of being loyal to one service and switching to another, due to dissatisfaction or any other problems. Even if a consumer is loyal to a particular brand, if the brand does not satisfy his/her needs, the consumer will switch to a competitor brand. As noted earlier, consumer loyalty is defined as "the degree to which a Consumer exhibits repeat purchasing behaviour from a service provider, possesses a positive attitudinal disposition toward the provider, and considers using only this provider when a need for this service arises" (Gremler & Brown, 1996, p. 6). Losing a consumer is a serious setback for the firm in terms of its present and future earnings. In addition to losing the benefits discussed above, the firm needs to invest resources in attracting new consumers to replace the ones it has lost (advertising, promotion, initial discounts). Peters (1987) shows that it can cost five times more to acquire a new customer than to retain an existing one. Consequently, retaining the current customer base is much more attractive and viable than searching for new customers. There are different factors and determinants which affect consumers in switching from one product to another. Two of these main switching behaviours for the purpose of this chapter are elaborated below.

First, in terms of switching as functional utility maximization occurs when a customer is motivated to review their available alternatives in the marketplace due to a change in competitive activities in the market (Seiders & Tigerts, 1997). Economists view consumer choices as a means to achieve maximization of functional utility (McFadden, 1986). In addition, a common practice among marketing researchers is to model consumer brand switching as choices based on product attributes and the marketing mix (Guadagni & Little, 1983; Ozuem, Limb & Lancaster, 2016). However, according to the original text on multi attribute utility theory (Lancaster, 1966), consumer utility includes not only a brand's functional attributes but also its socio psychological attributes. Correspondingly, McFadden (1986, p. 284) contends that "it is necessary to incorporate psychometric data in choice models because these factors also shape the utility function". Surprisingly, it is not until recently that research on choice models has revived the need to incorporate softer, non-product related attributes, such as customer attitudes and perceptions, into models of brand choice and brand switching (Swait & Erdem, 2007). These researchers posit that these attributes also play an important role in predicting brand choice, and brand preference. Secondly, brand switching occurs as social mobility, in line with recent developments in choice modelling. Social identity theory suggests that brand switching also serves socio psychological purposes besides functional utility maximization (Rao, Davis & Ward, 2000; Tajfel & Turner, 1979). This theory posits that people derive an identity from their affiliations with social groups. They value such membership and distinguish themselves from those who did not share such affiliations, forming the in-group and the out-group. According to Lam, Ahearn, Hu, and Schillewaert (2010), when a social identity is threatened, that is, negatively perceived, in-group members will likely respond by resorting to three basic strategies: social mobility, social creativity, and social change. Social mobility refers to a person's attempt to leave or dissociate his or herself from the group. Moving from a lower-status group to a higher status one is an example (ibid). Social creativity describes a person's attempt to "seek positive distinctiveness for the in-group by redefining or altering the elements of the comparative situation" (Tajfel & Turner, 1979, p. 43). For example, a business school that does not compare favourably with other schools in terms of overall evaluation may seek out specific dimensions of comparison that grant it superiority over these other schools (Elsbach & Kramer, 1996). Finally, social change refers to direct competition with the out-group to retrieve higher status. In a marketing context, social change can be initiated either by competitors or by customers who identify with a brand. Market disruptions that are externally caused by competitors (e.g., radically innovative brands) can be viewed as attempts to initiate social change between competitors to vie for favour amongst customers. When a radically new brand is introduced, some customers may perceive the new brand as having a more attractive identity than the incumbent's identity.

IDENTITY THEORY AND BRAND SWITCHING

In practice, brands reflect a dynamic and ongoing dialogue between companies and customers (Appiah et al., 2018). According to de Chernatony (2010), brands are complex entities that can be simplified to the level of functional and emotional value. In view of this, it can be said that customers develop a strong relationship with brands to form a unique identity (Fournier, 1998). This complexity requires an in-depth review of the impact of identities on brand loyalty and switching behaviour. Identity theory and self-concept literature are interlinked as both examine the relationship that exists between the self and social entities (Belk, 1988; Sirgy, 1982). Both theories are introduced into marketing because they have common concepts, and the current chapter therefore draws upon this theory to conceptualise brand switching resistance. In so doing, a brand is perceived as a relationship partner that is significant to the private self. Thus, the consumer relies on a preferred brand as a definition of what they are in society or part of a wider group that identifies with the brand (the social self). From the above discussions, it can be said that shoppers re-purchase specific brands that convey meaning which transcends simple product utility. Before offering a detailed review of identity theory, this section of the chapter initially explores various definitions and perspectives of identity. An identity is a collection of meanings which defines a person, as an occupant of a certain role in a social setting, affiliated to a group, or with certain acceptable features identifying a person as unique (Burke and Stets, 2009; Yeh et al., 2016; He et al., 2012). Identity is used in two ways, as either social or personal identity. 'Identity' in this context denotes a social category; thus, a group of people particularly labelled and distinguished as members with similar features or attributes. In the latter sense of identity, upon which this chapter focuses, an identity consists of distinctive features or characteristics which an individual accepts with pride, or opinions that are socially consequential but unalterable. Identity involves seeing oneself as a unique and distinct individual who is different from others (Burke and Stets, 2009; Yeh et al., 2016; He et al., 2012; Da Silveira, 2013). Drawing from the above, it is striking that the definitions of 'identity' appear to make reference to a fundamental concept, thus a sense of recognition, despite the diversity.

EFFECTS OF IDENTITY THEORY ON SOCIETY AND THE 'SELF'

Identity theory is principally a micro-sociological theory that sets out to explain individual role-related behaviour. The theory places major theoretical emphasis on a multifaceted and dynamic self that mediates the relationship between social structure and individual behaviour. Identity theory (Stryker, 1968, 1980, 1987; Stryker and Serpe, 1982; Burke, 1980; Turner, 1978; Yeh et al., 2016; Stokburger-Sauer et al., 2012; Da Silveira, 2013; He et al., 2012) explains social behaviour in terms of the reciprocal relations between self and society. Consistently, Turner (2007) posits that identity theory seeks to explain why, where choice is possible, one role-related behavioural choice is made rather than another (Yeh et al., 2016; Stokburger-Sauer et al., 2012; Da Silveira, 2013; He et al., 2012). Identity theory traces its roots to Mead (1934) who presented a framework underwriting analyses of numerous sociological and social psychological issues. Mead's (1934) Framework asserted a formula: "Society shapes self, which in turn shapes social behaviour". Identity theory then began to attempt to specify and make researchable the concepts of "society" and "self". In line with the above, identity theory began with questions about the differential salience of identities in an individual's self-structures and the reasons why identity salience might change over time (Stryker, 1968; Wells and Stryker, 1988). These inquiries have resulted in the development of theory regarding ways in which people are tied to social structures and the consequences of these ties for their identities. Stryker and Burke (2000) claim that identity theory evolved along two different but closely related directions. Both are instantiations of a theoretical and research programme termed "*structural symbolic interactionism*" (Stryker, 1980), which aims to understand and explain how social structures affect self and how self affects social behaviours.

Historically, identity theory grew out of Symbolic Interaction (SI), particularly structural symbolic interaction (Stryker, 1980). Specifically, structural symbolic interaction is a version of symbolic interaction that stands in stark contrast to the traditional approach to symbolic interactions. Both versions of symbolic interactions have the same intellectual heritage since they draw on the seminal work of Mead (1934) and earlier intellectuals such as James (1890) and Cooley (1902). Blumer (1969) coined the term "symbolic interactionism", and his ideas led to the development of what we refer to as traditional symbolic interaction. The first aspect (structural symbolic interaction) concentrates on examining how social structures affect the structure of self and how the structure of the self, influences social behaviour. The second of his ideas concentrates on the internal dynamics of self-processes as these affect social behaviour. Identity theory is strongly associated with the symbolic interactionist view which holds that society affects social behaviour through its influence on self (Mead, 1934; Blumer, 1969). Identity theory, however, rejects the symbolic interactionist view of society as a "relatively undifferentiated, co-operative whole", arguing instead that society is "complexly differentiated but nevertheless organised" (Stryker and Serpe, 1982, p. 206). This vision of society forms the basis for the central proposition on which identity theory is predicated: that as a reflection of society, the self should be regarded as a multifaceted and organised construct. Identity theorists refer to the multiple components of self as identities (or, more specifically, role identities). The notions of identity salience and commitment are used in turn to account for the impact of role identities on social behaviour. Although identity theory was originally formulated by Stryker (Stryker, 1968, 1980, 1987; Stryker and Serpe, 1982), the term is now used more widely to refer to related theoretical work that acknowledges links between a multifaceted notion of self and the wider social structure (Burke, 1980; McCall and Simmons, 1978; Turner, 1978). This wider perspective, although still clearly grounded in symbolic interactionism, is not homogeneous. There are differences in emphasis and interpretation. Stryker, for instance, views identities as more stable than some other identity theorists, and he tends to place less emphasis on the key symbolic interactionist mechanism of "taking the role of the other". In general, identity theory is perceived as the foundation of a relatively huge body of micro-sociological literature concerned with predicting role-related behaviour (Simon, 1992; Thoits, 1991). Accordingly, identity theorists have tended to focus on the individualistic consequences of identity-related processes (Rosenberg, 1981).

BUILDING RESISTANCE THROUGH IDENTITY SALIENCE AND COMMITMENT

Consumer loyalty is broadly viewed from two perspectives; behavioural loyalty and attitudinal loyalty (Bandyopadhyay & Martell, 2007; Dick & Basu, 1994; Ball et al., 2004). Customer loyalty, initially has been perceived in a behavioural way, measuring the concept as behaviour based on the repeat purchase of a particular product or service, evaluated by the sequence in which it is purchased (Hallowell, 1996; Homburg & Giering, 2001; Yi, 1990). Nam et al, (2011) confirmed the above-mentioned perception by asserting that loyalty has traditionally been conceived as a behavioural construct relating to intentions towards repeat purchase. Kuusik and Varblane (2009) clarified three sub-segmented reasons for behaviourally loyal customers. The authors suggest they may be variously (i) forced to be loyal (e.g. monopoly or high exit costs); (ii) loyal due to inertia and (iii) functionally loyal. The above clarification from a marketing perspective, suggests that without any particular 'triggers' to compel behaviorally loyal customers to switch brands, consumers remain passively loyal (Roos, 1999). According to Liu, Wu and Hung (2007) even when presented with more attractive alternatives, consumers who have high inertia will be reluctant to change.

The behavioral view above, has been heavily criticized by Day (1969) as one-dimensional and therefore not useful for distinguishing true loyalty from 'spurious loyalty'. This has triggered the need to add an attitudinal component to the behavioural one (Berne, Mugica & Yague, 2001; Dick & Basu, 1994; Jacoby & Kyner, 1973; Oliver, 1997). Dick and Basu (1994) contend that a favourable attitude and repeat purchase are indicators of loyalty. They suggest that loyalty as an attitude-behaviour relationship. Attitudinal loyalty on the other hand can be defined as capturing emotional and cognitive components of consumer loyalty (Kumar & Shah, 2004; Appiah et al., 2018). Oliver (1999) aligns his view with this perspective by emphasizing that loyalty is a deeply held commitment to rebuy or re-patronise preferred products or services consistently, irrespective of changes in the marketing environment and the efforts of competitors. This type of loyalty represents a more long-term and emotional commitment to a brand (Bennett & Rundle-Thiele, 2002; Shankar et al., 2003), which is why attitudinal loyalty is referred to as 'emotional loyalty' that is regarded as being much stronger and long lasting (Hofmeyr & Rice, 2000; Ozuem, Thomas, & Lancaster, 2016; Albert & Merunka, 2013).

Drawing from the above, attitudinal loyalty is commonly preferred to behavioural loyalty (Day, 1969; Dick & Basu, 1994) for the following reasons. i) A behaviourally loyal customer may be spuriously loyal, that is, they may remain loyal to a brand, an organization or service provider until a better alternative in the marketplace is available (Dick & Basu, 1994; Appiah et al., 2018). Attitudinally loyal customers on the other hand have some attachment or commitment to an organization, service or brand and are not easily swayed by a slightly more attractive alternative. ii) Attitudinal loyalty not only indicates higher repurchase intent, but also resistance to counter-persuasion, resistance to adverse expert opinion, a willingness to pay a price premium, and a willingness to recommend the service provider or brand to others. From the above discussion, it is evident that consumer behavioural and attitudinal loyalty are linked to identity salience and commitment. As explained by Stryker and Burke (2000), identity salience is conceptualised and operationalised as the likelihood that an identity will be invoked in diverse situations. The direct and explicit implication of this behavioural notion of identity salience is that identities positioned higher in the salience hierarchy are tied more closely to behaviour. Thus, people with the same role identities may behave differently in a given context because of variations to identity salience (e.g. Callero, 1985; Thoits, 1991). For example, one person may work over the weekend, while another may spend time with the children, although both may have a "parent" role identity. The difference in behaviour is due to variation in identity salience.

Nuttbrock and Freudiger (1991) insist that people may also enact role-congruent behaviours even in situations that are not role-relevant. For instance, people with salient "parent" identity may, at work, engage inappropriately in behaviours related to their roles as parents. As well as affecting behaviour, salient identities have affective outcomes. Their enactment should exert more influence than the identities lower in the hierarchy over a person's sense of self-meaning, feeling of self-worth, and level of psychological well-being (Callero, 1985; Thoits, 1991). In addition to behavioural and affective outcomes, identity salience influences people's relationships, particularly their perceptions and evaluations of others (Callero, 1985; McCall and Simmons, 1978). Identity theory proposes that the salience of a particular identity will be determined by the person's commitment to that role. Commitment, defined as the "degree to which the individual's relationships to others are dependent on being a given kind of person", reflects the extent to which important significant others want the person to occupy a particular role position (Stryker and Stratham, 1985, p. 345). Commitment to a particular role identity is high if people perceive that many of their important social relationships are predicated based on their occupancy of that role. The consequence of vacating such a role is loss of a social network that is psychologically important, for example for the self-concept and for self-esteem (Hoelter, 1983). Stryker (1980) identified two types of commitment. First, interactional commitment which reflects the number of roles associated with a particular identity (the extensivity of commitment) and second, affective commitment which refers to the importance of the relationships associated with the identity; in other words, the level of effect associated with the potential loss of these social relationships. The more strongly committed a person is to an identity in terms of both interactional and affective commitment, the higher the level of identity salience. In terms of network relationships, the more fully a person's important social relationships are based on occupancy of a particular identity, in comparison with other identities, the more salient that identity will be. Similarly, the larger the number of people included in such a set of social relationships, the more salient the identity (Stryker and Serpe, 1982).

Callero (1985) shows that the salience of a brand identity predicts the frequency of repeat purchase of the brand. He also presents evidence that commitment to others in that specific brand community affects the salience of that brand identity. For instance, Nuttbrock and Freudiger (1991) provide evidence that the salience of the mother identity among first-time mothers explains (albeit to a limited degree) the extent to which they accept the burdens of motherhood and the necessity to make sacrifices for their child. Stryker and Serpe (1982) demonstrate that the salience of religious identities predicts time spent in religious activities, and the salience of religious identities is predicted by commitment to role relationships based on religion. By acknowledging the impact of social networks on people's self-concepts, identity theory links the wider social structure, in terms of role positions, and the person's more intimate social networks (through levels of commitment to different role positions) to the self-concept. It also connects social structure to the development and maintenance of social relationships (Serpe, 1987).

MARKETING IMPLICATIONS OF IDENTITY THEORY ON BRANDS

As indicated above, identity theory (Stryker, 1968) focuses on the social roles of people in various social settings. Hence, marketing research based on identity theory focuses on how individual customers perceive a product as "me" or "not me" (Kliene et al., 1995) and how they behave in agreement with the most salient identity (Arnet, German and Hunt, 2003; Bolton and Reed, 2004; Oyserman, 2009). Burke and Stets (2009) affirm that one of the early views of identity that grew out of the symbolic interaction framework, with its emphasis on symbols and meanings, is that identities provide "meaning" for individuals' lives. They stress that a life without meaning has no purpose, no structure, and no framework. Consistent with this view, Thoits (1983) suggests that identities provide a sense of purpose and meaning in life, defining who we are, as well as why we behave in specified ways in society. Such identities integrate us with the actions and expectations of others. Identities thus increase self-esteem and reduce depression and anxiety (Thoits, 1983).

From an identity point of view, people consume in many ways that are consistent with their sense of self (Levy, 1999; Sirgy, 1982). Successful brands are designed to satisfy not only the functional needs of consumers but also their symbolic needs (Kapferer, 1997). Consumers often use the "self" as a reference category for understanding their surroundings, especially when they judge other people. Customers develop strong relationships with the unique identities of brands for their unique identity (Fournier, 1998). In support of Fournier's view, Tian et al. (2001) insist that individuals have different levels of motivation and needs for distinctiveness in their identities. Identity theory is closely related to the self-concept literature, and both examine the connection between the self and social entities (Belk, 1988; Sirgy, 1982), as such, a brand is perceived as a relationship partner that is significant to the private self. Thus, the individual customer uses the brand to define who they are (including the social self), such that customers consider themselves to be part of a group who identify with a particular brand.

CONCLUSIONS AND MANAGERIAL IMPLICATIONS

This chapter has substantial managerial implications. First, our approach to explore both attitudinal loyalty and behavioural loyalty offers more managerial insights than examining either type of loyalty independently. For example, it can be deduced that users of luxury smartphones re-purchase specific brands that carry meaning for them, as opposed to just offering product utility. Drawing from the above, it can be argued that particular luxury smartphones that possess distinctive identities have the potential to win the attention of consumers and, ultimately, their loyalty. Accordingly, brand managers should develop and maintain a clear and consistent identity, so that brands can serve as stable references for consumers (Aaker, 1996; Kapferer, 2008). A widely-held belief is that a stable brand identity can help firms navigate and adapt to market changes (Collins and Porras, 1994). In practice, and consistent with this principle, companies seek to stabilise the identity of their brands over time. These insights will help managers plan their marketing programs more effectively. Furthermore, attitudinal loyalty provides more insight about the possible reasons a customer demonstrates behavioural loyalty, for example, a customer may be driven by functional attributes, quality attributes or simply by price. Attitudinal loyalty measures will help brand mangers understand (1) why and for what reasons, customers purchase their brands as well as those of their competitors, and (2) what are the strengths and vulnerabilities of their brands.

REFERENCES

Aaker, D. A. (1995). *Building strong brands*. New York: The Free Press.

Aaker, D. A. (1996). Measuring brand equity across products and markets. *California Management Review, 38*(3), 102–20.

Aaker, J. (1997). Dimensions of brand personality. *Journal of Market Research, 34*, 347–56.

Ahuvia, A. C. (2005). Beyond the extended self: Loved objects and consumers' identity narratives. *Journal of Consumer Research, 32*(1), 171–84.

Alang, N. (2015). Make smartphones, not war. *New Republic, 246*(13), 14–16. Retrieved from http://search.ebscohost.com/login.aspx?direct=true&db=a9h&AN=110474502&site=eds-live

Albert, N., & Merunka, D. (2013). The role of Brand love in consumer-brand relationships. *Journal of Consumer Marketing, 30*, 258–266.

Appiah, D., & Ozuem, W. (2019). Brand switching: Background to contestable customer–brand relationships. Global Business and Technology Association, Paris, France.

Appiah, D., Ozuem, W., Howell, E. K., & Lancaster, G. (2019). Building resistance to brand switching during disruptions in a competitive market. *Journal of Retailing & Consumer Services, 50*(9), 249–257.

Appiah, D., Ozuem, W., & Howell, E. K. (2019). Disruptive technology in the smartphone industry: Identity theory perspective. In *Wilson Ozuem and Gordon Bowen (2019) Leveraging Computer-Mediated Marketing Environment*. IGI Global. Hershey.

Appiah, D., & Ozuem, W. (2018). Resistance to brand switching in the smartphone industry. In Nilanjan Ray (Ed.), *Managing Diversity, innovation and Infrastructure in Digital Business*. IGI Global. Hershey.

Appiah, D., & Ozuem, W. (2018). Issues with the importance of branding, brand personality and symbolic meaning of brands in the smartphone industry. In Zuopeng Zhang (Ed.), *Global Information Diffusion and Management in Contemporary Society*. IGI Global. Hershey.

Ahn. J., Park, J. K., & Hyun, H. (2018). Luxury product to service brand extension and brand equity transfer. *Journal of Retailing and Consumer Services, 42*, 22–28.

Arnett, D. B., German, S. D., & Hunt, S. D. (2003). The identity salience model of relationship marketing success: The case of Non-profit Marketing. *Journal of Marketing, 67*(4), 89–105.

Associated Press. (2016). The $13,000 smartphone for security conscious celebrities [Streaming video]. Retrieved from Associated Press Video Collection database.

Ball, D., Coelho, P. S., & Macha, S. A. (2004). The role of communication and trust in explaining customer loyalty: An extension to the ECSI model. *European Journal of Marketing, 38*, 1272–1293.

Bandyopadhyay, S., & Martell, M. (2007). Does attitudinal loyalty influence behavioural loyalty? A theoretical and empirical study. *Journal of Retailing and Consumer Services, 14*(1), 35–44.

Bastien, V., & Kapferer, J. N. (2013). More on luxury anti-laws of marketing. In K. P. Wiedmann & N. Hennigs (Eds.), *Luxury Marketing: A Challenge for Theory and Practice* (pp. 19–34). Wiesbaden: Gabler, Verlag.

Belk, R. W. (1988). Possessions and the extended self. *Journal of Consumer Research, 15*(2), 139–168.

Bennett, R., & Rundle-Thiele, S. (2002). A comparison of attitudinal loyalty measurement approaches. *Journal of Brand Management, 9*, 193–209.

Berne, C., Mugica, J. M., & Yague, M. J. (2001). The effect of variety-seeking on customer retention in services. *Journal of Retailing and Consumer Services, 8*, 335–345.

Berthon, P., Pitt, L., Parent, M., & Berthon, J. P. (2009). Aesthetics and ephemerality: Observing and preserving the luxury brand. *California Management Review, 52*(1), 45–66.

Bhattacharya, C. B., & Lordish, L. (2000). Towards a system for monitoring brand health from store scanner data. MSI working Paper, Report No. 00-111.

Bhattacharya, C. B., & Sanker S. (2005). Consumer-company identification: A framework for understanding consumers' relationship with companies. *Journal of Marketing, 67*(4), 76–88.

Bolton, L. E., & Reed, A. (2004). Sticky priors: The perseverance of identity effects on judgements. *Journal of Marketing Research, 41*(11), 397–410.

Burke, P. J. (1980). The self: Measurement implications from a symbolic interactionist perspective. *Social Psychology Quarterly, 43*:18–29.

Bulmer, M. (1979). Concepts in the analysis of qualitative data. *Sociological Review, 27*, 651–677.

Burke, P., & Stets, J. E. (2009). *Identity theory.* Oxford: Oxford University Press.

Callero, P. (1985). Role identity salience. *Social Psychology Quarterly, 48*, 203–15.

Collins, J. C., & Porras J. L. (1994). *Built to last: Successful habits of visionary companies.* New York: Harper Collins.

Copeland, M. T. (1923). Relation of consumers' buying habits to marketing methods. *Harvard Business Review, I*, 282–289.

Crouch, G. I., Perdue, R. R., Timmermans, H. J. P., & Uysal, M. (2004). *Consumer psychology of tourism, hospitality and leisure* (pp. 275–277). Oxon: CABI.

Chaplin, L. N., & Roedder, D. J. (2005). The development of self-brand connections in children and adolescents. *Journal of Consumer Research, 32*(1), 119–29.

Chernev, A., Hamilton, R., & Gal, D. (2011). Competing for consumer identity: Limits to self-expression and the perils of lifestyle branding. *Journal of Marketing, 75*(3), 66–82.

de Chernatony, L. (2010). *From Brand vision to brand evaluation* (3rd ed.). Oxford: Butterworth Heinemann.

Day, G. S. (1969). A two-dimensional concept of brand loyalty. *Journal of Advertising Research, 9*, 29–35.

Da Silveira, C., Lages, C., & Simões, C. (2013). Reconceptualizing brand identity in a dynamic environment. *Journal of Business Research, 66*(1), 28–36.

Dick, A., & Basu, K. (1994). Customer loyalty: Towards an integrated conceptual framework. *Journal of the Academy of Marketing Science, 22*, 99–113.

Dimitriades, Z. S. (2006). Customer satisfaction, loyalty and commitment in service organisations: Some evidence from Greece. *Management Research News, 29*(12), 782–800.

Dolich, I. J. (1969). Congruence relationships between self images and product brands. *Journal of Marketing Research, 6*(1), 80–84.

Dwyer, F. R., Schurr, P. H., & Oh, S. (1987). Developing buyer-seller relationships. *Journal of Marketing, 51*, 11–27.

Escalas, J. E., & Bettman, J. R. (2003). You are what you eat: The influence of reference groups on consumers' connections to brands. *Journal of Consumer Psychology, 13*(3), 339.

Escalas, J. E., & Bettman, J. R. (2005). Self construal, reference groups, and brand meaning. *Journal of Consumer Research, 32*(12), 378–89.

Elliott, R., & Wattanasuwan, K. (1998). Brand as symbolic resources for the construction of identity. *International Journal of Advertising, 17*(2), 131–44.

Elsbach, K. D., & Kramer R. M. (1996). Members' responses to organizational identity threats: Encountering and countering the business week rankings. *Administrative Science Quarterly, 41*(3), 442–76.

Ehrenberg, A. S. C., & Goodhardt, G. J. (1970). A model of multi-brand buying. *Journal of Marketing Research, 7*, 77–84.

Farhana, M. (2014). Implication of brand identity facets on marketing communication of lifestyle magazine: Case study of a Swedish brand. *Journal of Applied Economics and Business Research, 4*(1), 23–4.

Frick, W., & Berinato, S. (2014). Apple: Luxury brand or mass marketer? *Harvard Business Review Digital Articles*, 2–7. Retrieved from http://search.ebscohost.com/login.aspx?direct=true&db=bth&AN=118647762&site=eds-live

Fournier, S. (1998). Consumers and their brands: Developing relationship theory in consumer research. *Journal of Consumer Research, 24*(3), 343–73.

Giovannini, S., Xu, Y., & Thomas, J. (2015). Luxury fashion consumption and generation Y consumers: self, brand consciousness, and consumption motivations. *Journal of Fashion Marketing and Management, 19*(1), 22–40.

Gremler, D. D., & Brown, S. W. (1996). Service loyalty; its nature, importance and implications. In B. Edvardsson, S. W. Brown, R. Johnston, & E. Scheuing (Eds), *QUIS V:* Advancing Service Quality: A Global Perspective, ISQA, New York, NY, 171–81.

Guadagni, P. M., & Little, J. D. C. (1983). A logit model of brand choice calibrated on scanner data: A logit model of brand choice calibrated on scanner data. *Marketing Science, 2*(3), 203–238.

Han, Y. J., Joseph, C. N., & Drèze, X. (2010). Signaling status with luxury goods: The role of brand prominence. *Journal of Marketing, 74*(4), 15–30.

Hallowell, R. (1996). The relationships of customer satisfaction, customer loyalty, and profitability: An empirical study. *International Journal of Service Industry Management, 7*(4), 27–42.

He, H., Yan, L., & Lloyd, H. (2012). Social identity perspective on brand Loyalty. *Journal of Business Research, 65*(5), 648–57.

Helgeson, J. G., & Supphellen, M. (2004). A conceptual and measurement comparison of self-congruity and brand personality. *International Journal of Market Research, 46*(2), 205–33.

Hoelter, J. W. (1983). The effects of role evaluation and commitment on identity salience. *Social Psychology Quarterly, 46*, 140–47.

Hofmeyr, J., & Rice, B. (2000). *Commitment-led marketing.* Chichester: Wiley.

Hogan, E. J., & Armstrong, G. (2001). Toward a resource based theory of business exchange relationships: The role of relational asset value. *Journal of Business to Business Marketing, 8*(4), 3–28.

Homburg, C., & Giering, A. (2001). Personal characteristics as moderators of the relationship between customer satisfaction and loyalty—an empirical analysis. *Psychology and Marketing, 18*(1), 43–66.

Hoyer, W. D., & MacInnis, D. J. (1997). *Consumer behaviour.* Boston: Houghton Mifflin Publishers.

Jacoby, J. (1971). A model of multi-brand loyalty. *Journal of Advertising Research, 11*(3), 25–31.

Jacoby, J., & Kyner, D. B. (1973). Brand loyalty vs. Repeat purchasing behaviour. *Journal of Marketing Research, 10*, 1–9.

James, W. (1890). *The principles of psychology.* New York: Holt Rinehart and Winston.

Jenkins, R. (2004). *Social identity* (2nd ed.). London: Routledge.

Kapferer, J. N. (1997). *Strategic brand management: Creating and sustaining brand equity long term.* London: Kogan Page Ltd.

Keller, K. L. (1993). Conceptualizing, measuring and managing customer-based brand equity. *Journal of Marketing, 57*(1), 1–22.

Keller, K. L. (2009). Managing the growth trade off: Challenges and opportunities in luxury branding. *Journal of Brand Management, 16*(5–6), 290–301.

Keller, K. L., & Lehmann, D. R. (2006). Brands and branding: Research findings and future priorities. *Journal of Marketing Science, 25*(6), 740–59.

Kettle, K. L., & Hauble, G. (2011). The Signature effect: Signing influences consumption-related behavior by priming self-identity. *Journal of Consumer Research*, (38).

Kleine, S. S., Kleine III, R. E., & Allen, C. T. (1995). How is a possession 'me' or 'not me'? Characterizing types and antecedents of material possession attachment. *Journal of Consumer Research, 22*(12), 327–43.

Kim, C. K., Han, D. C., & Park, S. B. (2001). The effect of brand personality and brand identification on brand loyalty: Applying the theory of social identification. *Japanese Psychological Research, 43* (4), 195–206.

Kressman, F., Sirgy, M. J., Hermmann, A., Hubber, F., Hubber, S., & Lee, D. J. (2006). Direct and indirect effects of self-image congruence on brand loyalty. *Journal of Business Research, 59*(9), 955–64.

Kuenzel, S., & Halliday, S. V. (2008). Investigating antecedents and consequences of brand identification. *Journal of Product and Brand Management, 17*(5), 293–304.

Kumar, V., & Shah, D. (2004). Building and sustaining profitable customer loyalty for 21st century. *Journal of Retailing, 80*, 317–330.

Kuusik, A., & Varblane, U. (2009). How to avoid customers leaving: The case of the Estonian telecommunication industry. *Baltic Journal of Management, 4*, 66–79.

Lam, S. K., Ahearn M., Hu Y., & Schillewaert, N. (2010). Resistance to brand switching when a radically new brand is introduced: A social identity theory perspective. *Journal of Marketing, 74* (6), 128–46.

Lancaster, K. J. (1966). A new approach to consumer theory. *Journal of Political Economy, 74*(2), 132–57.

Levy, S. J. (1999). Symbols for sale. In Dennis W. Rook (Compiler), *Brand Consumers Symbols and Research*. London: Sage Publications.

Liu, T. C., Wu, L. W., & Hung, C. T. (2007). The effects of inertia and switching barriers on satisfaction-retention relationship: A case of financial service industries. *Journal of Management, 24*, 671–687.

Ligas, M., & Cotte, J. (1999). The process of negotiating brand meaning: A symbolic interactionist perspective. *Advances in Consumer Research, 26*(1), 609–14.

Malär, L., Krohmer, H., Hoyer, W. D., & Nyffenegger, B. (2011). Emotional brand attachment and brand personality: The relative importance of the actual and the ideal self. *Journal of Marketing, 75*(4), 35–52.

Mead, G. H. (1934). *Mind, self and society*. Chicago: University of Chicago Press.

McCall, G. J., & Simmons, J. L. (1978). *Identities and interactions* (Rev. ed.). New York: Free Press.

McFadden, D. (1986). The choice theory approach to market research. *Marketing Science, 5*(4), 275–97.

McCracken, G. (1988). *The long interview*. London: Sage.

Meenaghan, T. (1995). The role of advertising in brand image development. *Journal of Product and Brand Management, 4*(4), 23–34.

Miller, K. W., & Mills, M. K. (2012). Contributing clarity by examining brand luxury in the fashion market. *Journal of Business Research, 65*(10), 1471–1479.

Muniz Jr, A. M., & O'Guinn, T. C (2001). Brand community. *Journal of Consumer Research, 27*(4), 412–32.

Nam, J., Ekinci, Y., & Whyatt, G. (2011). Brand equity, brand loyalty and consumer satisfaction. *Annals of Tourism Research, 38*(3), 1009–30.

Nuttbrock, L., & Freudiger, P. (1991). Identity salience and motherhood: A test of stryker's theory. *Social Psychology Quarterly, 54*, 146–57.

Nuemo, J. L., & Quelch, J. A. (1998). The mass marketing of luxury. *Business Horizons, 41*(6), 61–68. doi:10.1016/S0007-6813(98)90023-4

Okonkwo, U. (2009). Sustaining the luxury brand on the Internet. *Journal of Brand Management, 16*(5–6), 302–310.

Oliver, R. L. (1980). A cognitive model of the antecedents and consequences of satisfaction decisions. *Journal of Marketing Research, 17*, 460–469.

Oliver, R. L. (1981). Measurement and evaluation of satisfaction processes in retail settings. *Journal of Retailing, 57*(3), 25–48.

Oliver, R. L. (1993). Cognitive, affective and attribute bases of the satisfaction response. *Journal of Consumer Research, 20*(3), 418–430.

Oliver, R. L. (1997). *Satisfaction: A behavioural perspective on the consumer.* New York: Irwin/McGraw-Hill.

Oliver, R. L. (1999). Whence consumer loyalty? *Journal of Marketing, 63*, 33–44.

Orth, U. R., & Renata de Marchi (2007). Understanding the relationships between functional, symbolic, and experiential brand beliefs, product experiential attributes, and product schema advertising-trial interactions revisited. *Journal of Marketing Theory and Practice, 15*(3), 219–33.

Oyserman, D. (2009). Identity-based motivation: Implications for action-readiness, procedural readiness and consumer behaviour. *Journal of Consumer Psychology, 19*(3), 250–60.

Ozuem, W., Limb, N., & Lancaster, G. (2016). Exploring the locus of internal marketing. *Journal of Strategic Marketing, 26*(4), 356–372.

Ozuem, W., & Lancaster, G. (2012). Technology-induced customer services in developing countries. Delener Nick (2012), Service Science Research, Strategy and Innovation: Dynamic Knowledge Management Methods, vols. 185–201 IGI Global, Hershey, PA.

Ozuem, W., Thomas, T., & Lancaster, G. (2016). The influence of customer loyalty on small island economies: An empirical and exploratory study. *Journal Strategic Marketing, 24*(6), 447–469.

Ozuem, W., Patel, A., Howell, K., & Lancaster, G. (2017). An exploration of consumers' response to online service recovery initiatives. *International Journal of Market Research, 59*(1), 97–115.

Park, C. W., B., Jaworski, J., & MacInnis, D. J. (1986). Strategic Brand Concept-Image Management. *Journal of Marketing, 50*(4), 135–45.

Peters, T. (1987). *Thriving on chaos*. Alfred A. Knopf, New York.

Peter, J., Paul, J., Olson, C., & Grunert, K. G. (1999). *Consumer behaviour and marketing strategy: European Edition*. London: McGraw Hill.

PR Newswire. (2015). Secure Spaces incorporated with Fantome Arcane luxury smartphones. PR Newswire US. Retrieved from http://search.ebsco-host.com/login.aspx?

Puzakova, M., Hyokjin, K., & Rocereto, J. F. (2009). Pushing the envelope of brand and personality: Antecedents and moderators of anthropomorphized brands. *Advances in Consumer Research—North American Conference Proceedings, 36*, 413–20.

Rao, H., Davis, F. G., & Ward, A. (2000). Embeddedness, social identity and mobility: Why firms leave the NASDAQ and Join the New York Stock Exchange. *Administrative Science Quarterly, 45*(2), 268–92.

Ringberg, T., & Gupta, S. F. (2003). The importance of understanding the symbolic world of customers in asymmetric business-to-business relationships. *Journal of Business and Industrial Marketing, 18*, 607–626.

Roos, I. (1999). Switching processes in customer relationships. *Journal of Service Research, 2*, 376–393.

Rosenberg, M. (1981). The self-concept: social product and social force. Pp. 562–92 in Social Psychology: Sociological Perspectives, edited by Morris Rosenberg and Ralph H. Turner. New York: Basic Books.

Sathish, M., Kumar, K. S., Naveen, K. J., & Jeevanantham, V. (2011). A study on consumer switching behaviour in cellular service provider: A study with reference to Chennai. Far East. *Journal of Psychology and Business, 2*(2), 72.

Schembri, S., Merrilees, B., & Kristiansen, S. (2010). Brand consumption and narrative of the self. *Journal of Psychology and Marketing, 27*(6), 623–37.

Seiders, K., & Tigert, D. J. (1997). Impact of market entry and competitive structure on store switching/store loylalty. *International Review of Retail, Distribution & Consumer Research, 7*(3), 227–247.

Shankar, V., Smith, A. K., & Rangaswamy, A. (2003). Customer satisfaction and loyalty in online and offline environments. *International Journal of Research in Marketing, 20*(2), 153–75.

Simon, R. W. (1992). Parental role strains, salience of parental identity, and gender differences in psychological distress. *Journal of Health and Social Behaviour, 33*, 25–35.

Sirgy, J. M. (1982). Self-concept in consumer behaviour: A critical review. *Journal of Consumer Research, 9*(12), 287–300.

Solomon, M. R. (1983). The role of products as social stimuli: A symbolic interactionism perspective. *Journal of Consumer Research, 10*(10), 319–29.

Solomon, M. (2002). *Consumer behaviour: Buying, having and being.* (5th ed.). Upper Saddle River, New Jersey: Prentice Hall.

Stokburger-Sauer, N., Ratneshwar, S., & Sen, S. (2012). Drivers of Consumer-brand identification. *International Journal of Research in Marketing, 29*(4), 406–18.

Stryker, S. (1968). Identity salience and role performance: The relevance of symbolic interaction theory for family research. *Journal of Marriage and Family, 30*(40), 558–64.

Stryker, S. (1980). *Symbolic interactionism: A social structural version.* Menlo Park, CA: Benjamin Cummings.

Stryker, S. (1987). The interplay of affect and identity: Exploring the relationships of social structure, social interaction, self, and emotion." Presented at the annual meetings of the American Sociological Association, Chicago.

Stryker, S., & Serpe, R. T. (1982). Commitment, identity salience, and role behavior: a theory and research example. Pp. 199–218 in Personality, Roles, and Social Behavior, edited by William Ickes and Eric S. Knowles. New York: Springer-Verlag.

Stryker, S., & Burke, P. J. (2000). The past, present and future of an identity theory. *Social Psychology Quarterly, 63*(4), 284–297.

Stryker, S., & Statham, A. (1985). Symbolic interaction and role theory. In The Handbook of Social Psychology, 3rd ed., edited by G. Lindzey and E. Aronson. New York: Random House.

Swait, J., & Erdem, T. (2007). Brand effects on choice and choice Set formation under uncertainty. *Marketing Science, 26*(5), 679–97.

Swaminathan, V., Karen L. Page, & Gürhan-Canli, Z. (2007). "My" brand or "Our" brand: The effects of brand relationship dimensions and selfconstrual on brand evaluations. *Journal of Consumer Research, 34*(2), 248–59.

Tajfel, H., & Turner, J. C. (1979). The social identity theory of intergroup behaviour, in Psychology of Intergroup Relations, Stephen Worchel & William, G. Austin, eds. Chicargo: Nelson-Hall, 33–47.

Tian, K. T., Bearden, W. O., & Hunter, G. L. (2001). Consumers need for uniqueness: Scale development and validation. *Journal of Consumer Research, 28*(1), 50–56.

Thoits, P. A. (1983). Multiple identities and psychological well-being: A reformulation and test of the social isolation hypothesis. *American Sociological Review, 49*, 174–87.

Turner, H. J. (2007). *Handbook of sociological theory*. New York: Springer.

Tynan, C., McKechnie, S., & Chhuon, C. (2010). Co-creating value for luxury brands. *Journal of Business Research, 63*(11), 1156–1163.

Uncles, M. D., & Laurent, G. (1997). Editorial: Special issue on loyalty. *International Journal of Research in Marketing, 14*, 399–404.

Underwood, R. L. (2003). The communicative power of product packaging: Creating brand identity via lived and mediated experience. *Journal of Marketing Theory and Practice, 11*(1).

Vella, M. (2013). The Ultra-Luxe Phone. *Fortune, 167*(6), 10. Retrieved from http://search.ebscohost.com/login.aspx?direct=true&db=bth&AN=87076006&site=eds-live

Vickers, J. S., & Renand, F. (2003). The marketing of luxury goods: An exploratory study—three conceptual dimensions. *The Marketing Review, 3*(4), 459–478. doi:10.1362/146934703771910071

Vigneron, F., & Johnson, L. W. (1999). A review and a conceptual framework of prestige seeking consumer behavior. *Academy of Marketing Science Review, 1*(1), 1–15.

Wells, L. E., & Stryker, S. (1988). Stability and Change in Self over the Life Course. Pp. 191–229 in Life-Span Development and Behavior, vol. 9, edited by Paul B. Bates, David L. Featherman, and Richard M. Lerner. Hillsdale, NJ: Erlbaum.

Wiedmann, K. P., Hennings, N., & Sibels, A. (2007). Measuring consumers' luxury value perceptions: A cross-cultural framework. *Academy of Marketing Science Review, 7*(7), 1–21.

Wilcox, K., Min, K. H., & Sen, S. (2009). Why do consumers buy counterfeit luxury brands? *Journal of Marketing Research, 46*(2), 247–259.

Yi, Y. (1990). A Critical review of consumer satisfaction. In V. Zeithaml (Ed.), *American Marketing Association* (pp. 68–123). Chicago. http://www.solarin.com (accessed on 07/03/2019). http://www.fantom3.com/arcane Accessed on (07/03/2019).

Yeh, C., Wang, Y., & Yieh, K. (2016). Predicting smartphone brand loyalty: Consumer value and consumer-brand identification perspectives. *International Journal of Information Management, 36*(3), 245–257.

Zhang, J., & Bloemer, J. M. M. (2008). The impact of value congruence on consumer-service brand relationships. *Journal of Service Research, 11*(8), 161.

Chapter 12

Building Brands Together: Online Brand Community and Commitment in the Luxury Fashion Industry

Jianqiong Xu
University of Gloucestershire, UK

Wilson Ozuem
Arden University, UK

ABSTRACT

Extant studies have illustrated that online brand communities (OBCs) are an important platform for customer participation in, and engagement with, brands. It is essential for OBC practitioners to focus on self-brand image congruity, and value congruity, to develop consumer engagement, which in turn, generates heightened brand loyalty. This chapter suggests that, in OBCs, consumer engagement is driven by OBC self-brand image congruity and value congruity. The current chapter makes a theoretical contribution in explaining brand loyalty through user engagement in OBCs. In addition, the chapter identifies that perceived benefits and perceived costs are key antecedents of user engagement, whilst user engagement influences brand loyalty both directly and indirectly through online community commitment. Therefore, the research results suggests that marketers are encouraged to demonstrate the benefits to their online brand community users to encourage customer participation and engagement.

INTRODUCTION AND BACKGROUND

The introduction of Web 2.0 has transformed content generation on the World Wide Web (Stokinger & Ozuem, 2016). The advancement of social media in recent years has changed the nature of consumer buying behaviour from searching for and sharing product information to purchasing channels (Kim & Ko, 2012). Customers are accordingly more behaviourally and perceptually engaged with the major social media platforms (Kim & Kim, 2018; Shareef et al., 2017). In comparison with traditional mass media advertising or online ads, businesses are able to have more informative and interactive (two-way) communication with their customers through social media (Barreda et al., 2016; Swani et al., 2017). The interactions with friends or with the public in general has been changed. Social media platforms are the new place where consumers and organisations can commercially, socially, and politically interact with people and exchange information (Rathore, Ilavarasan, & Dwivedi, 2016). Therefore, marketers have started thinking about understanding how to effectively communicate their brand values through these platforms. It is important for them to successfully manage their brand communities and build a profitable marketing relationship with customers on these platforms in the face of an everchanging social media environment (Chi, 2012; Jung & Kim, 2016). Over the last decade, OBCs have seen a thriving research interest (Habibi et al., 2014; Zhang & Luo, 2016; Ozuem et al., 2008). The role of OBCs in engaging customers, developing and strengthening customer relationships has also been of significant academic interest (Dessart et al., 2015). Many of the world's biggest brands have developed brand communities on Facebook to advertise, promote, and communicate their offerings to their customers, as well as to engage them so as to build long-term customer-firm relationships (Zaglia, 2013).

The world of luxury cosmetic products is ever-growing. The demand for such products is booming, especially within the Asian Markets including China and Japan. The success of the beauty sector plays a crucial role in the survival of the luxury market. Commonly, cosmetics and fragrances are the first luxury investments made by young consumers; thus, through beauty acquisitions, premium brands can subtly influence customer loyalty (Deloitte, 2017). The market for luxury and prestige cosmetics was valued at $116 billion in 2017 and is expected to grow to about $126 billion by 2019 (Statista, 2019). The majority of the sales value of prestige cosmetics is attributed to premium skincare products. South America is currently experiencing the highest level of annual growth in the global prestige beauty industry, with the Argentinean prestige beauty market growing by 32 percent in 2017 compared to the previous year (Statista, 2019). According to Zion Market Research (2018), the global beauty market is projected to reach an estimated $863 billion by 2024 and China is set to become the biggest global market for cosmetics, thus driving consumer trends. Personal care and beauty product sales are on the rise and are projected to register a growth from 3.5 to 4.5% between 2015 and 2020. It is anticipated to reach $500 billion by 2020. The Asia Pacific accounts for a major share in the global personal care industry; increasing demand in the region is attributed to its bulging population. In the U.S, the growing Hispanic population is propelling demand for luxurious personal care brands and will escalate during the forecast years.

Luxury cosmetic brands, such as Lancôme and Estée Lauder, are among some of the most valuable personal care brands in the world. Estée Lauder saw a substantial increase in sales between 2017 and 2018, growing from just under $12 billion to just under $14 billion over the course of a year (Statista, 2019). About 25 per cent of Estée Lauder's revenue is generated by makeup sales, making it the largest product category for the company. The luxury sector has changed significantly in the last decade with the growing of the use of social media as a way to market and communicate with customers. Understanding the use of social media is an important and effective marketing strategy for businesses. Luxury brands have turned their attention to luxury consumers on social media platforms devoted to their brands (Ko & Megehee, 2012). Luxury consumption is therefore multidimensional and embraces financial, functional, individual and social values (Hennigs et al., 2013). As a result, luxury brand managers recognise that complex and psychological motivations drive consumers to purchase their items.

THEORETICAL CONTEXT

Communities can be defined as places where individuals have a mutual understanding and they can comfortably discuss all topics with members (Bauman, 2003). Muniz and O'Guinn (2001) defined brand community as "a specialized, non-geographically bound community, based on a structured set of social relationships among users of a brand". Brand communities are social groups characterised by a shared culture in which the brand identity is collectively implemented, negotiated and co-created by the consumption meanings, rituals and practices (Muniz & O'Guinn, 2001). The members in these brand communities are the brand admirers, who possess a social identification with others and are willing to express their perceptions in the brand community (Merz et al., 2009). Muniz & O'Guinn (2001) stated three particular dimensions of brand communities: (1) consciousness of kind; (2) evidence of the rituals and traditions; and (3) a sense of obligation to the community and its members. These kinds of communities present themselves as specialised because, among others, they are connected to particular characteristics such as a brand, a ritual, a set of beliefs.

The technological capabilities of this environment allow consumers to become active participants, supporting different interaction possibilities with the community, and over time, more and more consumers interact, generating different types of participation (Gong, 2018). Dessart et al. (2015) presented a scale of engagement in brand communities on social networks based on three dimensions: cognition, affect and behaviour. Baldus et al. (2015) adopted a psychologically based customer perspective, claiming that customer brand engagement in OBCs is the intrinsic motivation to continue interacting with OBCs.

Li et al. (2018) explored the effect of consumer visiting behaviour on the two identified online intermediaries (online communities and product channels). An online community contains communication contents, such as product reviews and online discussions. A product channel, on the other hand, is a venue for marketers to convey information unidirectionally to consumers. A product channel is a website showing and exhibiting information, such as product descriptions and marketing activities. It was interesting to note that the research results indicated that the integration of online communities and product channels may have a negative impact on sales. However, both of them individually are effective in driving sales.

Millán and Díaz (2014) examined the importance of the creation of a brand community in brand management. Relationship marketing is one of the important ways to keep customers motivated and committed to the brand. It seeks to build and sustain long-term customer relationships and is regarded as a strategic resource for a company (Laroche et al., 2012). A brand community is a powerful tool to strengthen these relationships. These communities have been implemented as a solution to integrate and serve customers in their brand relationship management.

As noted by Zhou et al. (2012), there are two main dimensions of a brand community; brand community identification and brand community commitment. With regard to brand community identification, Dholakia et al. (2004) claim that identification is related to individuals' assessments of belonging to a brand community. In their opinion, belonging to a brand community has a unique meaning for the person, as this indicates the participation in an emotional group resulting in the individual having a commitment to the community or the brand (Bagozzi & Dholakia, 2002). Brand community identification refers to a person's self-concept that renders him/her equal to other in-group members and distinct from outsiders. This type of definition and identification enables an individual to actively participate as a member of the brand community and maintain positive relationships with other members (Hung, 2014). Social identity theory (Tajfel, 1978) is the theoretical support to the value of individuals' identification with the community. The study by Helal et al. (2018) focused on how evolving social media platforms have influenced brand perceptions in the fashion apparel and accessories sector based on social identity theory.

The research by Kornum et al. (2017) reveals that brand communities play a powerful role in brand identity co-creation. It noted that the interplay between brand identities and community identities creates synergy and tensions. Essamri et al. (2018) regard brand identity as an appropriate context for examining company-led processes intended to take part in the wider process of co-creating brand identity with other stakeholders. For brand managers, it is important to provide an environment of trust (Ramaswamy & Ozcan, 2016) to enable dialogue, and exchange resources with brand community members such that they feel part of a larger family. It is vital that firm-owned platforms are available as they allow for interactional co-creation to occur (Ramaswamy & Ozcan, 2018).

Popp and Woratsches' (2017) study extends our understanding of identification and satisfaction for consumer-brand relationships in different contexts. The research reveals that the brand and community follow various patterns of the formation of loyalty, while, in the case of the brand community, identification mainly has a direct effect on customer loyalty (or positive WOM); this relationship is strongly mediated by customer satisfaction if the brand is the target of identification. These findings contribute to previous studies on the effectiveness of identification and satisfaction in producing favourable relationship outcomes (Haumann et al., 2014). The study by Coelho et al. (2018) proposed a conceptual model in the mass-market focused on understanding consumers' engagement in a social media brand community, brand identity and consumer-brand identification. It can be found that consumer-brand identification has a significant role in reinforcing the possibility of transforming consumer-brand interactions into consumer-brand relationships.

On the other hand, Kim et al. (2008) defined brand community commitment as members' psychological attachment to a community and their belief in the value of the relationship. As mentioned by Li and Chang (2016), commitment is a significant construct in relationship marketing as consumers commit to only connections that they trust. In the online context, Chen et al. (2013) noted that commitment can capture a wider perspective of forces that drive the participants' behaviour. Kang et al. (2014) further stated that in the context of online communities, commitment could be described as the "member's willingness to continue relationship with the brand through participation in online communities". The research by Vohra and Bhardwaj (2019) focuses on the customer engagement literature by comparing alternative frameworks. It outlines three antecedents of customer engagement: active participation, community trust, and community commitment. The research results indicate that a more active involvement in the brand communities infuses trust and commitment to the community and this further increases customer engagement in the community. The results also support Hanshim and Tan's (2015) research, in which they proposed a more pronounced role of affective commitment compared to that of trust in the context of online communities. According to Zhou et al. (2012), when people think the brand can represent their own personality and enhance their social status, a brand commitment will be developed. Individuals will have a strong sense of brand identification with the brand if there is a strong bond with the brand and the community. Members' commitment to a brand community usually leads to commitment to the brand. Therefore, committed consumers tend to purchase the same brand consistently and create a unique relationship similar to love (Zhou et al., 2012). For Jang et al. (2008), committed participation and interactions with other members of the community help strengthen consumers' brand experience and value, leading to enhanced brand and community commitment, so as to promote greater loyalty to the brand and the community.

MEMBERS BRAND COMMUNITY COMMITMENT

Cruz and Mendelsohn (2010) suggested that members of brand communities are more engaging and more likely to buy and recommend the brands to others as compared to non-members. This is supported by the study of Becerra and Badrinarayanan (2013) in which they found that members who demonstrate high brand identification towards their brand community would contribute to brand evangelism (positive referral or oppositional brand referral). These two studies attempted to examine how committed members of OBCs determined their brand satisfaction, loyalty and repurchase intention. However, Shaari and Ahmad (2016) proposed to extend the understanding of how members' brand community commitment influenced brand evangelism. This study conceptualised brand evangelism into two constructs, namely positive brand referral and oppositional brand referral. It illustrated that individuals who have a common interest and high self-brand identification tend to actively participate in the brand community in different ways, like producing brand evangelism and referral (Shaari & Ahmad, 2016).

An OBC is a collection of individuals who are active and interact online and they have their common interest in a particular brand. In such a community, consumers not only share an interest in the brand, but also abide by common rules. OBCs will exist because of the brands, and the interaction between each party all revolves around the brands. OBCs constitute a space where consumers share a particular brand-related content. The technological development of Web 2.0 provided the social media platforms which enable real-time communication in different formats such as text, voice, photos or videos without any location limitation. Web 20.0 has enabled the development of important platforms for facilitating communication and interaction between customers and business, which help to develop the OBCs (Brodie, Ilic, Juric, & Hollebeek, 2013; Zhou et al., 2013).

The online community is a significant platform for customer participation to brand co-create in the internet environment (Brodie et al., 2013). Customers are involved in the brand design and development, sharing experiences with the OBCs. From the enterprise perspective, they can communicate and interact with customers on these platforms, collecting customer feedback and suggestions. This creates new opportunities for businesses to develop their brand identities. Customers share their experiences on these platforms and create shared meanings for brands (Muniz & O'Guinn, 2000). Academia has a long-standing consensus on the important role of consumers in brand creation, such as the study by Keller (1993) in which he proposed that the brand creation should take the customer as the starting point based on the customer brand equity theory. Merz et al. (2009) defined brand co-creation as a cooperative process in which stakeholders participate and enhance brand value through interaction based on social relations.

Co-creation of value is a unique opportunity for marketing in the social commerce era. Companies are now using social media and digital marketing to co-create brand images with their customers in OBCs (Dessart & Morgan, 2015). Hatch and Schultz (2010) believe that brand co-creation is the result of network interaction of the dynamic stakeholders, which jointly creates the meaning and value of the brand. From the perspective of scholars' definition of brand co-creation, brand is jointly created by enterprises (brand managers) and stakeholders, and relationship interaction is the basic method of brand creation. The interaction between enterprises and stakeholders forms the meaning and value of the brand, and ultimately builds and improves brand assets. Co-creation is always related to an OBCs, where people can play as providers and beneficiaries. This creates value for users and communities as well as companies (Pongsakornrungsilp & Schroeder, 2011). Companies are motivated to take part in OBCs by the benefits. In addition to enhancing the brand's core value and stimulating creativity (Ind, Iglesias, & Schultz, 2013) to enable the innovation in products (Gyrd-Jones & Kornum, 2013), one of the important things is that they can co-create brand identity with community members (Vallaster & von Wallpach, 2013). On the other hand, the customers are motivated to participate in the OBCs as they can share and express themselves in creating. Therefore, this is an opportunity for them to fulfil their thoughts and exchange experiences (Vallaster & von Wallpach, 2013).

The characteristic of involvement and participation of online communities is an important part of branding co-creation. Due to the participatory culture, branding has shifted from a firm-based activity providing products to customers with little feedback to branding as a collaborative, value co-creation activity (Merz, He, & Vargo, 2009). In turn, co-creation is a process of engaging customers in creating value (Prahalad & Ramaswamy, 2004) as here customers are transformed from passive customers to active players (Vargo & Lusch, 2004). Co-creation of value represents a participatory culture in which individuals seek the opportunity to contribute to their worlds and the firm's search for customer insights on brands (Ind, Iglesias, & Schultz, 2013; Ozuem, Howell, & Lancaster, 2018). For instance, Parmentier (2015) has shown that a business can innovate with users by developing co-creation activities within a brand community, generating valuable innovations by bringing together leads, creativity, and other users to generate ideas and new functions, uses, and contents pertaining to innovation.

CONCLUSION AND MANAGERIAL IMPLICATIONS

OBCs exist because of the brands, and the interaction between enterprises and their customers and the interactions among customers which all revolve around the brands. With these interactions, the meaning and value of the brands are created and enhanced. Hence, in virtual brand communities, customer engagement in value co-creation should be regarded as co-creation of brand value. It is more appropriate to understand and explain the behaviour of customer engagement in co-creation in OBCs from an integrated perspective of brand co-creation (Essamri et al., 2018; Ozuem & Azemi, 2018). In addition, customer engagement in brand co-creation in OBCs contains both enterprise-initiated brand co-creation such as brand development, evaluation and promotion, and customer-spontaneous brand co-creation such as brand use, communication and experience sharing.

Coelho et al. (2018) believe that brand loyalty is a promise that consumers will repeat purchase decisions of their preferred brands or products in the future. Zheng et al. (2015) highlight the importance of user engagement in brand loyalty directly and indirectly through online community commitment. With the expansion of the social range of consumers from the real world to the online network, enterprises are increasingly establishing relationships with customers through social media platforms. An OBC has become a new way for enterprises to cultivate customer brand loyalty. As for the influence of co-creation of brands initiated by customers in OBCs. on brand loyalty, according to the research conducted by Grissemann and Stokburger-sauer (2012) on co-creation behaviour between travel agencies and customers, the degree of customers' participation in making travel plans affects their satisfaction and loyalty with travel agencies as well as their travel expenses. Chan et al. (2010) found that customer participation in service value creation enhanced customer satisfaction with financial services as the background. Ostrom et al. (2010) pointed out that customers' perception of service quality, brand evaluation, repeat purchase and recommendation to others was affected by the co-creation of services. In OBCs, customer participation with enterprise brands to create, such as brand development, assessment and promotion activities, will deepen the understanding of the brand and customer perception, and establish the emotional bond between customer and brand, so as to improve customer satisfaction and trust, and promote brand loyalty and brand promise (Brodie et al., 2013). The interconnectivities of customers in OBCs produce relationship marketing and loyalty, which can be a practical strategy of co-creation of value for branding.

REFERENCES

Bagozzi, R., & Dholakia, U. (2002). Intentional social action in virtual communities. *Journal of Interactive Marketing, 16*(2), 2–21.

Baldus, B. J., Voorhees, C., & Calantone, R. (2015). Online brand community engagement: Scale development and validation. *Journal of Business Research, 68*(5), 978–985.

Barreda, A. A., Bilgihan, A., Nusair, K., & Okumus, F. (2016). Online branding: Development of hotel branding through interactivity theory. *Tourism Management, 57*, 180–192.

Bauman, Z. (2003). Comunidade: a busca por segurança no mundo atual, Jorge Zahar Ed, Rio de Janeiro.

Becerra, E. P., & Badrinarayanan, V. (2013). The influence of brand trust and brand identification on brand evangelism. *Journal of Product & Brand Management, 22*(5/6), 371–383. doi:10.1108/JPBM-09-2013-0394

Brodie, R. J., Ilic, A., Juric, B., et al. (2013). Consumer engagement in a virtual brand community: An exploratory analysis. *Journal of Business Research, 66*(1), 105–114.

Chan, K. W., Yim, C. K., & Lam, S. S. K. (2010, May). Is customer participation in value creation a doubleedged sword? Evidence from professional financial services across cultures. *Journal of Marketing, 74*, 48–64.

Chen, A., Lu, Y., Wang, B., Zhao, L., & Li, M. (2013). What drives content creation behavior on SNSs? A commitment perspective. *Journal of Business Research, 66*(12), 2529–2535.

Chi, H. H. (2012). Interactive Digital advertising vs. virtual brand community exploratory study of user motivation and social media marketing responses in Taiwan. *Journal of Global Fashion Marketing, 12*(1), 44–61.

Coelho, P. S., Rita, P., & Santos, Z. R. (2018). On the relationship between consumer-brand identification, brand community, and brand loyalty. *Journal of Retailing and Consumer Services, 43*, 101–110. doi:10.1016/j. jretconser.2018.03.011

Cruz, B., & Mendelsohn, J. (2010). *Why social media matters to your business.* Retrieved July 30, 2019, from http://www.cmbinfo.com/cmb-cms/ wp-content/uploads/2010/04/Why_Social_Media_Matters_2010.pdf

Deloitte. (2017). The Deloitte Consumer Review Customer loyalty: A relationship, not just a scheme. Retrieved June 15, 2019, from https://www2.deloitte.com/content/dam/Deloitte/uk/Documents/consumer-business/deloitte-uk-consumer-review-customer-loyalty.pdf

Dessart, L., Veloutsou, C., & Morgan-Thomas, A. (2015). Consumer engagement in online brand communities: A social media perspective. *Journal of Product & Brand Management, 24*(1), 28–42. doi:10.1108/jpbm-06-2014-0635

Dholakia, U. M., Bagozzia, R. P., & Pearo, L. K. (2004). A social influence model of consumer participation in network and small-group-based virtual communities. *International Journal of Research in Marketing, 21*(3), 241–263.

Essamri, A., McKechnie, S., & Winklhofer, H. (2018). Co-creating corporate brand identity with online brand communities: A managerial perspective. *Journal of Business Research.* doi:10.1016/j.jbusres.2018.07.015

Gong, T. (2018). Customer brand engagement behavior in online brand communities. *Journal of Services Marketing, 32*(3), 286–299. doi:10.1108/jsm-08-2016-0293

Grissemann, U. S., & Stokburger-Sauer, N. E. (2012). Customer co-creation of travel services: The role of company support and customer satisfaction with the co-creation performance. *Tourism Management, 33*(6), 1483–1492.

Gyrd-Jones, R., & Kornum, N. (2013). Managing the co-created brand: Value and cultural complementarity in online and offline multi-stakeholder ecosystems. *Journal of Business Research, 66*(9), 1484–1493.

Habibi, M. R., Laroche, M., & Richard, M. O. (2014). The roles of brand community and community engagement in building brand trust on social media. *Computers in Human Behavior, 37*(1), 152–161.

Hashim, K. F., & Tan, F. B. (2015). The mediating role of trust and commitment on members' continuous knowledge sharing intention: A commitment-trust theory perspective. *International Journal of Information Management, 35*(2), 145–151. doi:10.1016/j.ijinfomgt.2014.11.001

Hatch, M. J., & Schultz, M. (2010). Toward a theory of brand co-creation with implications for brand governance. *Journal of Brand Management, 17*(8), 590–604.

Haumann, T., Quaiser, B., Wieseke, J., & Rese, M. (2014). Footprints in the sands of time: A comparative analysis of the effectiveness of customer satisfaction and customer – Company identification over time. *Journal of Marketing, 78*(6), 78–102.

Hennigs, N., Wiedmann, K. P., Klarmann, C., & Behrens, S. (2013, August). The concept of luxury: Phenomenon of local implications. *The European Financial Review*, 62–64.

Helal, G., Ozuem, W., & Lancaster, G. (2018). Social media brand perceptions of millennials. *International Journal of Retail & Distribution Management*. doi:10.1108/ijrdm-03-2018-0066

Hung, H. (2014). Attachment, identification, and loyalty: Examinating mediating mechanisms across Brand and Brand community contexts. *Journal of Brand Management, 21*(7/8), 594–614.

Ind, N., Iglesias, O., & Schultz, M. (2013). Building brands together: Emergence and outcomes of co-creation. *California Management Review, 55*(3), 5–26.

Jang, H., Olfman, L., Ko, I., Koh, J., & Kim, K. (2008). The influence of on-line brand community characteristics on community commitment and brand loyalty. *International Journal of Electronic Commerce, 12*(3), 57–80.

Jung, Y. J., & Kim, J. (2016). Facebook marketing for fashion apparel brands: Effect of other consumers' postings and type of brand comment on brand trust and purchase intention. *Journal of Global Fashion Marketing, 7*(3), 196–210

Kang, J., Tang, L., & Fiore, A. M. (2014). Enhancing consumer-brand relationships on restaurant facebook fan pages: Maximizing consumer benefits and increasing active participation. *International Journal of Hospitality Management, 36*, 145–155.

Keller, K. L. (1993). Conceptualizing, measuring, and managing customer-based brand equity. *Journal of Marketing, 57*(1), 1–22.

Kim, A. J., & Ko, E. (2012). Do social media marketing activities enhance customer equity? An empirical study of luxury fashion brand. *Journal of Business Research, 65*(10), 1480–1486. doi:10.1016/j.jbusres.2011.10.014

Kim, J., Morris, J. D., & Swait, J. (2008). Antecedents of true Brand loyalty. *Journal of Advertising, 37*(2), 99–117.

Kim, N., & Kim, W. (2018, April). Do your social media lead you to make social deal purchases? Consumer-generated social referrals for sales via social commerce. *International Journal of Information Management, 39*, 38–48.

Ko, E., & Megehee, C. M. (2012). Fashion marketing of luxury brands: Recent research issues and contributions. *Journal of Business Research, 65*(10), 1395–1398. doi:10.1016/j.jbusres.2011.10.004

Kornum, N., Gyrd-Jones, R., Al Zagir, N., & Brandis, K. A. (2017). Interplay between intended brand identity and identities in a Nike related brand community: Co-existing synergies and tensions in a nested system. *Journal of Business Research, 70*, 432–440. doi:10.1016/j.jbusres.2016.06.019

Laroche, M., Habibi, M. R., Richard, M., & Sankaranarayanan, R. (2012). The effects of social media based Brand communities on Brand community markers, value creation practices, brand trust and Brand loyalty. *Computers in Human Behavior, 28*(5), 1755–1767.

Li, C.H., & Chang, C. M. (2016). The influence of trust and percieved playfulness on the relationship commitment of hospitality online social network-moderating effects of gender. *International Journal of Contemporary Hospitality Management, 28*(5), 924–944.

Li, Q., Wang, Q., & Lin, Z. (2018). Effects of consumer visit to online community and product channel on local sales of large consumer goods: Evidence from real estate industry. *The Journal of Strategic Information Systems, 27*(2), 191–204. doi:10.1016/j.jsis.2017.11.001

Merz, M. A., He, Y., & Vargo, S. L. (2009). The evolving brand logic: A service-dominant logicperspective. *Journal of the Academy of Marketing Science, 37*(3), 328–344.

Millán, A., & Díaz, E. (2014). Analysis of consumers' response to Brand community integration and Brand identification. *Journal of Brand Management, 21*(3), 254–272.

Muniz, A. M., & O'Guinn, T. C. (2001). Brand community. *Journal of Consumer Research, 27*(4), 412–432.

Ostrom, A. L., Bitner, M. J., Brown, S. W., et al. (2010). Moving forward and making a difference: Research priorities for the science of service. *Journal of Service Research, 13*(1), 4–36.

Ozuem, W., Howell, K., & Lancaster, G. (2008). Communicating in the new interactive marketspace. *European Journal of Marketing, 42*(9/10), 1059–1083.

Ozuem, W., Thomas, T., & Lancaster, G. (2016). The influence of customer loyalty on small island economies: An empirical and exploratory study. *Journal of Strategic Marketing, 24*(6), 447–469.

Ozuem, W., & Azemi, Y. (2018). Online service failure and recovery strategies in luxury brands: A view from justice theory. In W. Ozuem & Y. Azemi (Eds.), *Digital Marketing Strategies for Fashion and Luxury Brands* (pp. 108–125). Hershey: IGI Global.

Ozuem, W., Howell, K. E., & Lancaster, G. (2018). Developing technologically induced environments: The case of the Nigerian banking sector. *Journal of Financial Services Marketing, 23*(1), 50–61.

Ozuem, W., Howell, K. E., & Lancaster, G. (2016). Understanding technologically-induced customer services in the Nigerian banking sector: The internet as a post-modern phenomenon. *International Journal of Information Technology and Management, 15*(3), 272–290.

Ozuem, W., & Lancaster, G. (2014). Recovery strategies in on-line service failure. In A. Ghorbani (Ed.), *Marketing in the Cyber Era: Strategies and Emerging Trends* (pp. 143–159). Hershey: IGI Global.

Ozuem, W., Patel, A, Howell, K., & Lancaster, G. (2017). An exploration of consumers' response to online service recovery initiatives. *International Journal of Market Research, 59*(1), 97–115.

Parmentier, G. (2015). How to innovate with a brand community. *Journal of Engineering and Technology Management, 37*, 78–89.

Pongsakornrungsilp, S., & Schroeder, J. E. (2011). Understanding value co-creation in a co-consuming brand community. *Marketing Theory, 11*(3), 303–324.

Popp, B., & Woratschek, H. (2017). Consumers' relationships with brands and brand communities – The multifaceted roles of identification and satisfaction. *Journal of Retailing and Consumer Services, 35*, 46–56. doi:10.1016/j.jretconser.2016.11.006

Prahalad, C. K., & Ramaswamy, V. (2004). Co-creation experiences: The next practice in value creation. *Journal of Interactive Marketing, 18*(3), 5–14. doi:10.1002/dir.20015

Ramaswamy, V., & Ozcan, K. (2016). Brand value co-creation in a digitalized world: An integrative framework and research implications. *International Journal of Research in Marketing, 33*(1), 93–106.

Ramaswamy, V., & Ozcan, K. (2018, March). What is co-creation? An interactional creation framework and its implications for value creation. *Journal of Business Research, 84*, 196–205.

Rathore, A. K., Ilavarasan, P. V., & Dwivedi, Y. K. (2016). Social media content and product co-creation: An emerging paradigm. *Journal of Enterprise Information Management, 29*(1), 7–18.

Shaari, H., & Ahmad, I. S. (2016). Brand Evangelism among online Brand community members. *International Review of Management and Business Research, 5*(1), 80.

Shareef, M. A., Mukerji, B., Dwivedi, Y. K., Rana, N. P., & Islam, R. (2017). Social media marketing: Comparative effect of advertisement sources. *Journal of Retailing and Consumer Services*, http://dx.doi.org/10.1016/j.jretconser.2017.11.001

Statista. (2019) Prestige/Luxury Cosmetics Market – Statistics & Facts. Retrieved June 30, 2019, from https://www.statista.com/topics/5073/prestige-luxury-cosmetics/

Stokinger, E., & Ozuem, W. (2016). The intersection of social media and customer retention in the luxury beauty industry. In I. Management Association (Ed.), *Digital Marketing and Consumer Engagement: Concepts, Methodologies, Tools, and Applications* (pp. 1305–1328). Hershey, PA: IGI Global. doi:10.4018/978-1-5225-5187-4.ch066

Swani, K., Milne, G. R., Brown, B. P., Assaf, A. G., & Donthu, N. (2017, April). What messages to post? Evaluating the popularity of social media communications in business versus consumer markets. *Industrial Marketing Management, 62*, 77–87.

Tajfel, H. (1978). Intergroup behavior. *Introducing social psychology. Harmondsworth: Penguin*, 401–422.

Vallaster, C., & von Wallpach, S. (2013). An online discursive inquiry into the social dynamics of multi-stakeholder brand meaning co-creation. *Journal of Business Research, 66*(9), 1505–1515.

Vargo, S. L., & Lusch, R. F. (2004). Evolving to a new dominant logic for marketing. *Journal of Marketing, 68*, 1–17.

Vohra, A., & Bhardwaj, N. (2019). Customer engagement in an e-commerce brand community: An empirical comparison of alternate models. *Journal of Research in Interactive Marketing*, https://doi.org/10.1108/JRIM-01-2018-0003

Zaglia, M. E. (2013). Brand communities embedded in social networks. *Journal of Business Research, 66*(2), 216–223.

Zhang, M., & Luo, N. (2016). Understanding relationship benefits from harmonious brand community on social media. *Internet Research, 26*(4), 809–826.

Zheng, X., Cheung, C. M. K., Lee, M. K. O., & Liang, L. (2015). Building brand loyalty through user engagement in online brand communities in social networking sites. *Information Technology & People, 28*(1), 90–106. doi:10.1108/itp-08-2013-0144

Zhou, Z., Zhang, Q., Su, C., & Zhou, N. (2012). How do Brand communities generate brand relationships? Intermediate mechanisms. *Journal of Business Research, 65*(7), 890–895.

Zhou, Z., Wu, J. P., Zhang, Q., & Xu, S. (2013). Transforming visitors into members in online brand communities: Evidence from China. *Journal of Business Research, 66*, 2438–2443.

Zion Market Research. (2018). Global Cosmetic Products Market Will Reach USD 863 Billion by 2024. Retrieved June 29, 2019, from https://www.globenewswire.com/news-release/2018/06/22/1528369/0/en/Global-Cosmetic-Products-Market-Will-Reach-USD-863-Billion-by-2024-Zion-Market-Research.html

Chapter 13

Online Service Failure and Recovery Strategies: Creative Insights and Strategies

Samuel Ayertey
University of Plymouth, UK

Gordon Bowen
Northumbria University, UK

Maxwell Ayertey Banor
Lakeland University, USA

ABSTRACT

By being able to fill the gap in product knowledge that is totally impossible to provide in a physical shop setting, fashion retailers are now able to merchandise an impressive variety of goods and products online. Yet, the phenomenal growth of online luxury fashion retailing has not occurred without a unique set of issues in terms of service delivery, product defects and website failure. Even though inexhaustible studies have been carried out in relation to service failure and recovery, the extent to which service recovery needs to be explored so that it is deciphered into a satisfactory state remains unresolved. Drawing on the constructivist perspective, this current chapter provides creative insights into failure-recovery strategies as competitive tools for marketing in the digital age. The closing section contributes to extant knowledge and provides some strategic implications and insights for fashion and luxury brands seeking accelerated success in the online marketplace.

KEYWORDS

Service Failure, Recovery Strategy, Justice Theory, Luxury Brands, Online Customer Satisfaction, Fast Fashion, Social Constructivism.

INTRODUCTION AND BACKGROUND

The new digital age has changed customer notions of speed, price, convenience, service and product information (Ozuem, Howell & Lancaster 2008). Thus, the Internet has become an essential part of the buying practices of many groups of buyers and sellers who interact through websites. Every day, some 432,000 collectable items are sold on eBay (Guta, 2018). In the United Kingdom (UK), for example, a typical superstore on the high street lists 80 stock-keeping units or SKUs of shampoo whilst Amazon lists 2,000 (Amed & Berg, 2019). However, since the start of the digital age, luxury brands have faced a key issue when attempting to bring about the same high-end experiences to digital marketplaces as brick-and-mortar retailers have brought to the high street (Weiners, 2017). The problem of acclimatising to an ever-more omnichannel-focussed world is one that luxury brands are currently facing. Online clientele differ in their buying tactics from old-fashioned offline clientele. Luo, Ba and Zhang (2012) concur that product uncertainty has become a particularly important dimension in online-purchasing decision-making. Whilst retailers like Amazon have tried to listen to and engage with users to provide immediacy in the online world, they still recognise the value of human interactions and the desire to shop physically in the ever-connected world of today (Zakowicz, 2017).

Depending on the degree of incomplete information involved, product uncertainty can be an essential dimension within consumer online-purchasing decision-making. This may reflect the need that customers have to see a product before deciding to purchase it. To develop this point, Luo et al. (2012) and Chan and Wong (2012) stress the increased risk of failure at providing online services for luxury brands, which most often leads fashion clientele to doubt the quality of fashion clothing. Such customers are also suspicious of customer services and this can have an impact on buying intentions. This results in a dynamic interaction between customer satisfaction, customer loyalty and customer complaints. Given that customers do not have the opportunity to assess items based on product quality, it has also been predicted that online returns will reach £5.6 billion by 2023. Fashion and luxury brands have been hit hardest by this trend because of the importance of fit, solely for online pureplays (Hughes, 2018). Accordingly, many customers continue to experience service failures. For instance, according to the Fifth Annual CAM 2018 Report from the Ombudsman Services, in 2017 alone, there were a total of 173 million problems with services and products, with 57 percent of the UK's population being affected. In addition, the Report reveals that retail received the largest share with 12.7 million complaints. The Report further reveals that typical complaints were directed at administrative errors, cancellations, delivery delays, failed call-backs, incorrect advice and a failure to respond to correspondence (Ombudsman Services, 2018). Historically, the literature has suggested that service defects and unsuccessful recoveries are a major cause of client switching conduct in service organisations. As a result, effective recovery from service failure is therefore directly related to the company's bottom line. More recently, the Trustee Savings Bank (TSB) paid around £125 million to compensate its customers due to information technology chaos (BBC News, 2019). Fashion consumers are amongst the most uncertain buyers in the world and will most likely use at least one form of social media as a way of buying. Indeed, Pham (2017) points out that four in ten UK Internet users considered smartphones to be the most essential device that they owned and used for accessing the Internet, and that they spent an average of 65.3 hours per month online with their smartphones in 2017. This is greater than the average time of 34 hours per month spent online by Internet users on desktops and laptops in the same year. Life without social media is unthinkable for most online fashion and luxury customers. Obeidat, Xiao, Iyer and Nicholson (2017) add that the Internet provides customers with an instant, easy complaint channel at no significant cost and with little effort. Yet, electronic commerce (e-commerce) clientele often fail to provide a response to firms, even when services/goods failures occur, making it tougher for them to comprehend the needs, expectations and wishes of their clientele. Customers may not be as homogeneous in their assessment and response to attempts to recover services as has been historically supposed. Indeed, recovery strategies can lead to diverse responses from customers (Craighead, Karwan, & Miller, 2004; Smith, Bolton, & Wagner, 1999). The UK Ombudsman Services' Report further reveals that many consumers believe that the effort that it takes to resolve a complaint outweighs the benefits (Ombudsman Services, 2018). At the heart of this issue is the need for an improved understanding of customer evaluations of organisational recovery efforts, which is the central theme of this current chapter.

Research in this field addresses a wide range of issues such as emotional and customer affection in response to service failures, and customer service recovery assessments including the attribution of blame and perceptions of fairness or justice. Some other factors that affect service recovery management include consumer–firm relationships and branding. Thus, an all-inclusive understanding of the research is needed to address the issues of service failure and recovery experiences and to develop the failure-recovery experiences that have been analysed through positivist research further (Choi & Choi, 2014). However, this present chapter seeks to provide a subjective point of view on online luxury fashion customers' service failure-recovery experiences rather than viewing the issue in a completely detached manner, and this chapter also seeks to critically evaluate the related literature. The primary objective of this paper is therefore to examine the participants' opinions on the issue under study and to establish a proper 'fit' between a service failure and the respective recovery efforts. Learning from a service failure depends substantially on the establishment of the causes of the service failure as well as on the identification of the fundamental process (es) that contributed to the issue with the aim of addressing or finding effective solutions to the problem. The next section of this paper discusses the luxury fashion industry, service failures and typologies. Furthermore, the chapter considers how to build service recovery and concludes with a discussion on the implications of the study as well as offering solutions and some conclusions for both professionals and academics.

THE LUXURY FASHION INDUSTRY

With the UK being at the forefront of fashion for the last 36 years, fashion retailing has experienced significant change and has become an innovative, vibrant and challenging sector. Letting go of the old and chasing the new, fashion is changing almost by definition (Rome, 2015). As a consequence, with regard to branding, the fashion industry has attracted widespread scholarly attention (Birtwistle & Freathy, 1998; Fletcher & Grose, 2012). Amongst other things, Bhardwaj and Fairhurst (2010) recently researched customer reactions to the rapid fashion industry and found notable problems with regard to their enhancement. As Bhardwaj and Fairhurst (*ibid.*) claim, during the last 20 years, the fashion clothing sector has significantly altered.

Christopher, Lowson and Peck (2004) recognised difficulties in terms of how fashion is consumed and noted that innovation and quality issues have emerged as the industry has become ever-more competitive. This is evident in the demand for more diversity and more educated styles (Fernie, Maniatakis, & Moore, 2009; Ozuem, Thomas & Lancaster 2016), which are more economically priced than ever before. Furthermore, Mollá-Descals, Frasquet-Deltoro and Ruiz-Molina (2011) also noticed differences in the fashion industry's dynamics and growing complexity. Typical of such modifications is a reduction in demand for high-quantity producers and a greater demand for seasonal fashion. Other characteristics include better supply chain organisation that motivates companies to choose styles that can be transported flexibly and quickly and manufactured at lower prices.

Fashion is the highest ranked category for omnichannel shopping in the UK and the explosion in online retailers selling cheaper clothing has given rise to concerns about 'fast fashion' that results in clothes being discarded in landfills. Fast fashion introduces new lines every three to five weeks and it is driven by major retailers such as Zara, Promod and H&M (Hu, Li, Chen, & Wang, 2014). To elicit a high rate of repeat purchases, this industry aims to entice clients to shop as often as possible (Corbellini & Saviolo, 2014). The practical service life of clothes is short and is well below their technical service life. Rapidly changing trends in fashion have emerged which dictate how long clothes can be worn and even if they are no longer fashionable. In addition, clothing cannot be properly cared for and disposed of without a lot of thought. This makes fast fashion a major environmental driver (Roos, Sandin, Zamani, & Peters, 2015). Since the sector is seen as one of the most polluting in the globe, it is essential to integrate sustainability-related procedures into the business models of the fashion industry. Da Giau, Macchion, Caniato, Caridi, Danese, Rinaldi, and Vinelli, (2016) argue that sustainability practices cannot be part of competitive strategies due to the limited information that fashion businesses provide to clients. The authors point out that fashion firms generally cede external pressure from non-governmental organisations (NGOs), the media, and market demand to implement sustainability policies, while other firms see the importance of incorporating sustainability into their business strategies.

The British capital has lost ground in recent years to the other 'big four' international fashion weeks, giving way to the legacy brands in Paris and Milan. London is no longer considered as commercially feasible as New York is. However, London possibly remains the most outspoken city in terms of its fashion designers, who use fashion as a resistance tool by bringing new perspectives and renegade ideas to the runway and to fashion subcultures (Fraser, 2019). London Fashion Week, a global platform celebrating creativity, business, innovation and art for everyone, takes place in February and September and is an example of such renegade ideas. The London College of Fashion, The British Council and the British Fashion Council (BFC) are also leaders in innovation. The trade event organised by the BFC is a city-wide celebration of luxury brands and global high-end fashion of international and British origin. Brands such as Burberry, Armani, Gucci, Louis Vuitton, Paul Smith and Vivienne Westwood participate. Trend forecasters, buyers and editors make up most of the audience at the event, and with rising figures each year, media coverage at London Fashion Week alone matches viewing figures for major news and worldwide sporting events. As a consequence of this vital event, regular customers have the opportunity to see, wear and purchase products advertised in the press by large brands. The event has also taken the social media world by storm. For example, in February 2019, Instagram stories on the official London Fashion Week account received 2,427 posts and 76.9k followers (www.londonfashionweekfestival.com). Additionally, the unmissable British social and fashion event, Royal Ascot, attracted 1.4 million viewers in June 2019 (Shapland, 2019).

Mintel (2017) reported that a major component of the clothing sector is fashion, as six of the UK's top-ten clothing retailers sell mainly fashion-oriented ranges by turnover. There is no doubt that online fast fashion is booming. Boohoo's social media followers have also soared. The brand now has 6.3 million Instagram followers, a 200 percent increase over the past 12 months. It also has 1.4 million Facebook followers (BBC News, 2018). However, the constant consumption of clothing affects the environment and there is a growing awareness of this amongst young people. The vast majority of clothing ends up in landfills, with only 20 percent of clothes being collected for reuse or recycling at present. The latest figures in the UK alone show that each year 235 million clothing items are sent to landfill (BBC News, 2019). Brooks (2015) also added that rapid marketing and production practices promote the fast consumption and disposal of apparel. More recently, the fashion industry has been struggling across Europe, and with the full impact of Brexit yet to be felt, the fear is that the UK will start to follow suit. The British Chambers of Commerce discovered that a pickup in the services industry was not enough to ease the gloom

(British Chambers of Commerce, 2019). Meanwhile, the UK consumer has fully embraced online shopping, with only 1 in 5 claiming to exclusively shop for fashion in physical stores. As more people are choosing to shop online than to visit shops, more high street retailers are, to a greater extent, under pressure. Clients who shop in-store describe the need for products to be seen, touched and handled as part of the purchasing experience. On-the-spot sales are valued over waiting for delivery. However, what clients like least about shopping in-store is checking out or returning merchandise, as this is seen as too time consuming (Statista, 2017).

Consumers these days prefer to shop online for luxury and fashion products, yet there are significant risks associated with purchasing fashion online. Some of these risks relate to product quality, delivery times and hidden costs. These uncertainties are at the root of worries about the ability of fashion and luxury retailers to be able to trade clothes online (Liu, Burns, & Hou, 2013). Clancy (2016) argues that most online clothing clients send something back, meaning that people like to feel and see clothing before they purchase it. In so doing, one in five online companies have increased their prices to cover customer returns management and processing costs, according to a recent Barclaycard investigation (Hope, 2018). Sender (2017) added that generally, three-quarters (73%) of Internet fashion and luxury shoppers want to see more return alternatives such as home collection or drop-offs at multiple locations. A business is, in fact, accountable for returning customers back to a satisfied state in spite of 'self-service' when shopping online (Ayertey & Howell, 2019). Accordingly, rapid recovery is critical to mitigate against the stress encountered by online shoppers (Azemi, Ozuem, Howell, & Lancaster, 2019). Furthermore, service failure without recovery can be readily transmitted through various social media platforms and pressure organisations such as YouTube, Facebook, Instagram and WhatsApp. Social networks such as Facebook provide a very public platform and the kind of simple access to organisations that contemporary customers are looking for (Causon, 2015).

It is no wonder that social media is rapidly becoming a key element of customer service strategies. Word travels fast about goods/products and the services of effective organisations. In contrast, word travels even faster about goods/products and services that are poor. In addition, many organisations such as eComplaints.com, ConsumerReview.com, consumerreports.org and others have come together to provide a forum for clients to air complaints and share information about service and product experiences.

In order to encourage Internet reviews, businesses should use their social presence and website (McNicholas, 2011). Indeed, 93 percent of clients use reviews to determine whether a company has a negative or positive reputation (BrightLocal, 2018). For this reason, failure to recover from client dissatisfaction may result in other competitors being chosen by customers. Service recovery after a failure can be seen as one of the most essential approaches to certifying a good business reputation. Recovery encourages customers to express positive emotions instead of spreading adverse word-of-mouth encounters to friends and family (McCabe, 2018). After all, this awareness is more evident in the luxury branding sector, where the client is heavily affected by his or her emotional connection to the product (Okonkwo, 2010; Stokinger, & Ozuem, 2018). Research indicates that 70 percent of businesses say that retaining a client is cheaper than obtaining one, while others have indicated that acquiring a fresh client can cost as much as seven times or more (Logie, 2019). A quick, efficient and effective method of service recovery directly drives client perceptions of the service recovery process and impacts positively on future sales.

SERVICE FAILURES AND TYPOLOGIES

Service failures are inevitable despite the best efforts of service companies. Simply defined, a service failure is when a company's service performance or product does not meet the high expectations of a customer. The outcomes include dissatisfaction and customer complaints (Ayertey & Ozuem, 2017; Sengupta, Balaji, & Krishnan, 2015). The business impacts of service failure are best demonstrated by the poor service of Southern Rail, when the company was fined £13.4 million over train delays (Westcott, 2017). Albrecht, Walsh and Beatty (2017) revealed the potential for service failure in different ways. Thus, in traditional brick-and-mortar retail settings, four types of service failures can be categorised using Bitner's (1994) and Chung and Hoffman's (1998) typology. The first type concerns service delivery system failures due to unavailable services and other core service failures. The second relates to customer needs and requests, including cases of customer mistakes and other disruptive actions. The third involves unprompted and unwelcome employee actions, including when the behaviour of employees is intolerable in the eyes of the client. The final category is problematic and uncooperative clients, including those who breach company policies.

Smith and Bolton (2002) also proposed a procedure for categorising service failure in terms of outcome and process failures. Outcome failures happen when the service provider fails to deliver the core service. In the context of the online luxury industry, outcome failures can be associated with a failure to meet explicit or implicit consumer requests (Ford, Sturman, & Heaton, 2011). Examples of outcome failures include tangible defects such as when a customer is not pleased with an online luxury fashion retailer shipping the wrong dress (an example of a service product failure). Moreover, service failures related to processes occur when the manner of the service delivery is somewhat flawed and deficient. Such failures are considered as process failures. Process failures might occur when, for example, a customer calls the customer service department of a fashion store to make a complaint and a call centre employee is rude in response. In the online luxury fashion industry, consumers use websites to find product information, make online payments and complete purchases. This often involves indirect contact with employees, which leads to possible outcome failures at every service encounter. The traditional offline setting of failure recovery was also considered as a means of understanding how the evolution of the digital environment has translated the experience of failure recovery into the online world. Luxury branding is no exception. As with offline service failures, Meuter, Ostrom, Roundtree and Bitner (2000) classify four types of service failures: (1) if the website does not work temporarily then this is a type of technical failure; (2) if goods ordered online do not reach the customer then this is a type of product failure; (3) when customers have difficulty navigating their way through the website then this is a type of poor design failure; and (4) customer-originated failures such as a failure to log in when a password is forgotten (Meuter et al., 2000). A technology failure is the most common type of failure, as identified by research. It also highlights the lack of self-service recovery in online services, which suggests an increased risk of failure. The clientele are strictly online spectators as a consequence, and the service provider must comprehend how the clientele give meaning to service failures to develop effective online recovery strategies. The rise of interest in Internet purchases has driven many researchers to undertake explorations into service failures, as illustrated by the classification of online retail service failures by Holloway and Beatty (2003). The authors proposed six groups: (1) delivery (including issues such as the product arriving later than promised, the delivery of the wrong product and the delivery of the goods to the wrong address); (2) website design (including non-responsive websites, non-user-friendly content and websites in one language only); (3) payment (referring to the perception of the customer being charged more than expected); (4) security (including issues with fraud, for example, falling prey to different forms of online fraud); (5) product quality (a failure to meet the expectations of the customer); and (6) customer service problems (where the provider does not respond to requests from the customer) (Holloway & Beatty, 2003). Delivery problems associated with the six types of failure listed above were the most frequent online shopping service failures, and most online retailers failed to manage their recoveries effectively. Meuter et al's (2000) technical, product and poor design failures are similar to the first two types of Holloway and Beatty's (2003) classification of online retail failures.

The researchers also used the comprehensive collection of categorisations and definitions of Internet service failures created by Tan (2011) to guide their research. There are three types of service failures associated with online services according to this categorisation, specifically: (1) information failures, (2) functional failures, and (3) system failures. Functional failures relate to Internet service failures where the functionalities supplied are inadequate or incapable of supporting clients in carrying out a transaction. This can lead to a failure to meet the functional requirements/expectations of the user. For instance, a banking system that does not provide notifications when a client enters his or her overdraft and accumulates a penalty may work 'as stipulated' but may not satisfy the service expectations of the client. Information failures relate to Internet service failures resulting from clients receiving meaningless, inaccurate or unfinished information that adversely impacts on their service experience. An example of this type of failure might be when a client is advised that an online product is in the inventory, only to discover that it is not accessible once ordered. System failures relate to Internet service failures triggered by poor website functionality leading to a poor customer experience. This includes a broad variety of mistakes in technology, including, for example, hardware, software and network problems. These kinds of failures are not mutually exclusive. Nili, Tate and Gable (2014) argue that functional failures can also arise as a result of system failures and informational failures. Guillory (2016) examined customer complaints regarding leading brands including Gap, American Eagle, Gucci and Louis Vuitton, amongst others, in the online luxury fashion industry. His analysis suggested five common attributions regarding online service failures. The specific dimensions were (1) the provision of an online customer experience (e.g. comprising of problems associated with online transactions that are split into ordering mistakes and delivery complaints); (2) the provision of in-store customer experiences (e.g. relating to factors such as unfair, rude or insufficient attention from sales associates); (3) credit card procedures (e.g. poor communication or a lack of solutions provided for billing questions and issues. This can include errors related to billing and credit card procedural issues); (4) return/refund policies and procedures (e.g. concerns related to unclear returns and refund policies); and (5) product quality (luxury items) (e.g. problems with expensive luxury items such as handbags). The five most frequent complaints relate to online service failures such as those suggested by Meuter et al. (2000) and Holloway and Beauty (2003). Online experience, credit card procedures and problems with product quality can all be identified as technology failures and website design problems, whilst return/refund policies and in-store experiences are identified as service encounter failures.

The insights acquired from the research conducted by Guillory (2016) reveal a multitude of luxury branding online service failures that overshadow those in offline situations, indicating that luxury brand shoppers do transfer their purchasing methods to online platforms. Moreover, when it comes to adjusting to a digital future, the luxury industry has lagged behind the remainder of the fashion world. In the omnichannel setting using Facebook complaints, Rosenmayer, McQuilken, Robertson and Ogden (2018) investigated the different kinds of service failures and recoveries. Their research shows that shipping problems, bricks-and-mortar shopping, marketing operations as well as pricing and communications were all identified as failures. Customer service problems as well as products were the most predominant failures. The authors noted that the dimensions of distributive, procedural, informational and interpersonal justice are valid for Facebook recovery. Developing strategies for online service recovery that can reinforce customer loyalty and satisfaction in case of service failure has become a major challenge for online luxury businesses.

CONSTRUCTING A SERVICE RECOVERY STRATEGY

Service failure occurs, and so recovery from failures such as direct client complaints, social media messages and posts amongst others have become very important (Ozuem & Tan, 2014). Service recovery is essentially a chance to reinforce interactions with customers and the attitudes of customers are influenced by the degree to which they believe they have been handled impartially (Ozuem, Patel, Howell, & Lancaster, 2017). Thus, Lotich (2019) refers to service recovery as a theory that indicates that a client who has had a poor experience and gets a timely and efficient reaction to his or her problems will be a more faithful client than a client who has had no negative experience at all. In every organisation, customers are the income engine and must be acknowledged as such. Therefore, it is essential to manage dissatisfied clients. Service failures and recoveries can be hard to manage. Traditional service failures and recoveries are dissimilar from failures and recoveries in the online environment and digital era. In the interim, a range of recovery activities identified in past research include offering a token apology and compensation, amongst others (Goode, Hoehle, Venkatesh, & Brown, 2017). Recovery strategies are divided into two types; namely, psychological and tangible strategies (Kozub, O'Neill, & Palmer, 2014). Psychological recovery strategies include apologies, explanations, empathy and courtesy, and these are mostly linked to customers who experience process-related service failures. On the other hand, tangible recovery strategies which include discounts, coupons, refunds and gifts, amongst others, are linked to customers who experience outcome-related service failures (Fang, Luo, & Jiang, 2013).

Justice theory can be used to show the relationship between clients and businesses in the context of service failure and recovery. The theory of justice indicates that clients assess a service recovery effort as either reasonable or unfair (Choi & Choi, 2014). Adams (1963) affirms that clients tend to compare inputs with outputs, and if there is an equal balance between them, the exchange is deemed 'fair', but if the outputs do not satisfy the expectations of clients, then the outcome is deemed 'unfair'. Service recovery studies have commonly embraced the theoretical structure of justice (Kumar & Kumar, 2016) for which there are three dimensions: distributive justice, procedural justice and interactional justice. These three dimensions need to be understood by companies for them to develop effective service recovery strategies. Service recovery is critical to companies, particularly in the fashion and luxury business. In the online fashion and luxury industry, recovery is difficult to implement because of the physical absence of the customer. Executing these recovery strategies is very challenging. Other recovery strategies such as co-creation have proven useful (Hazée et al., 2017). In practical terms, clients participate with the service provider in the co-recovery process by explaining what they want from the service provider in the event of a service failure operation. They interact with staff by providing adequate data and responses to service-related issues and they act courteously as a means of creating a powerful relationship with staff. Therefore, the perception of the client is the most useful strategy for an organisation. With this background in mind, the authors agreed to continue with a qualitative inquiry which sought to unravel complexity and contextualisation and that they thought was essential in order to obtain the critical case view of the clientele.

Furthermore, constructivists align with a relativist ontological perspective. Relativism states that because reality is uniquely individual, a person's 'truth' is separately well-defined (Denicolo, Long, & Bradley-Cole, 2016). Social constructivists believe that people develop subjective meanings of their experiences of certain things or objects. These meanings are varied and therefore research is required to examine the intricacy of these varied opinions (Lincoln, Lynham, & Guba, 2011). Solomon (2014) suggests four steps to service recovery with the acronym ARFFD, which stands for: (1) Apologise (a real apology, not a fake one); (2) Review the complaint with your customer (turn your clients into your customer service advisers, in other words, let them clarify what went wrong from the customer's perspective and what you should do to solve it); (3) Fix the problem and then follow up (either solve the problem within the next 20 minutes or follow up within 20 minutes to verify things with the client and clarify your progress); and (4) Document the issue in detail so that the deficiency can be permanently solved by recognising trends. Irrespective of the importance placed on personalising recovery methods, all kinds of clients are subject to a set of golden recovery criteria which include: (1) an apology; (2) an acknowledgement; and (3) a genuine explanation of the problem (Barwise & Meehan, 2010; Goode et al., 2017; Kuo, Yen, & Chen, 2011). Research by Collier, Breazeale and White (2017) also found that if a failure happens in isolation, customers want staff to support a transaction after a breakdown. Customers prefer it when other clients are present when staff solve problems and that they enable them to complete the transaction.

Crisafulli and Singh (2017) indicated that direct human interaction in Internet settings has been replaced by technology and that academics have argued that the use of technology can enhance the effectiveness of restoration services (Ayertey & Ozuem, 2018). Therefore, given this context, gaining an idea of how to efficiently handle online service failures is critical for the success of companies working in Internet settings or the digital age.

However, several online fashion and luxury brands have failed to merge their in-store and online experiences. Weiners (2017) added that omnichannel marketing implies closing the gaps in experiences across channels to offer a continuous, unified brand experience across devices and physical touchpoints. This marketing strategy makes sense for customers who are unlikely, after all, to deliberately distinguish between their experience with the website of a brand and their experience with the same in-store brand. From the consumer's point of view, both experiences are part of the overall brand experience and should not be disjointed.

CONCLUSIONS AND MANAGERIAL IMPLICATIONS

Traditionally, fashion and luxury brands have distinguished themselves from the 'average' retailer by establishing a unique experience for clients in shops. This involves factors such as a striking shop layout, excellent personal service and personnel offering shopping guidance. This quality of service, added to the product quality, offers the finest possible shop experience for prospective clients. Nevertheless, when trying to recreate an in-store customer experience online, or at least generating an online experience that suits the brand image, fashion and luxury brands have encountered difficulties and they have not always been successful (Charlton, 2018). For this very reason, some fashion and luxury brands are unwilling to sell online. Some thought that e-commerce would make the brand cheaper or less exclusive. For instance, Chanel only started selling online in 2015, having earlier mentioned that customers needed to be in the fitting room to try clothes on before being able to wear Chanel (Amed, 2018). Purchasing online is distinct from buying offline. In terms of the online shopping experience, if a company works hard enough and knows its clients, any brand can provide an excellent customer experience. It is difficult, therefore, for luxury brands to stand out, and the task of making a website look luxurious is a hard one. Some luxury brands have failed at this challenge in the past, particularly when trying to distinguish themselves through bold designs. This often implies that sites look great but could be terrible to use, because visual design was seen as more important than usability. Whistles is one example of this oversight. It relaunched its website in 2009 and affirmed that it had been researching the best practices online for a long time: 'Then we threw out all we had learned and intended something that visually pleased us' (Mower, 2009, p. 2). The outcome was a site that looked great but that offered a poor purchasing experience as it had ignored fundamental best practices around key fields such as designing checkouts. Whistles has since redesigned the site to make it more user-friendly and this route has been followed by many luxury brands. Rather than looking to reinvent the wheel with site design, Charlton (2018) suggests that luxury retailers should concentrate on variables that contribute to an excellent customer experience such as: (1) the user experience (sites that are easy to purchase from); (2) the image of the product (pictures can be used to demonstrate products in the most favourable possible light. Pictures should be of high quality for luxury products, enabling shoppers to zoom in to see information); (3) great copywriting (the product copy must operate to express the product's quality and luxury. The tone of voice must match the product and cost); (4) excellent service (returns should be trouble-free and individuals will expect better service after spending lots of money on a product); (5) delivery and packaging (fashion and luxury companies need to provide the brand's pledge the next day and identify particular time slots, and even same-day delivery, as appropriate); and (6) customer journeys (online, including mobile) must operate with the offline journey to generate the finest experiences for clients, whatever channel is used.

Subjectivity leads to various realities, as qualitative researchers clarify (Banor, 2017; Maxwell, 2013). This again underlines the significance of various recovery programmes being developed. Consequently, the authors of this paper profess that luxury and fashion retailers should therefore use strategies that can be tailored to satisfy each customer's demands. This chapter highlights some important managerial implications which include the following: Service providers should participate with customers to offer elevated levels of service, process and product technology capabilities in co-recovery. Fashion and luxury brands should get their feet wet in social terms and start harnessing the power of social media as part of an omnichannel style to sharpen their marketing strategies, as luxury marketing is all about storytelling, and luxury retailers should realise that social media is a natural place for storytelling. Social media is a word-of-mouth amplifier. United Airlines discovered this the hard way when one dissatisfied client 'sang' his complaint and got over 15 million hits on YouTube (Ramshaw, 2018). Fashion and luxury brands should use social media monitoring tools to alert them to issues. Ramshaw (2018) added that it helps companies to identify trends, track competitors and comprehend the feelings of clients. It is critical for luxury brands that the level of customer service online matches the level of service that the clientele expect to receive in-store. It is also crucial that digital customer services comprise a personal touch.

For luxury retailers, digital marketing poses distinctive difficulties. Making the online experience feel similar to a high-end offline experience takes planning and significant customer know-how. Luxury and fashion retailers should take up the challenge and adopt the power of omnichannel marketing to deliver a seamless, high-end experience that is present throughout the client journey. Luxury brands should increasingly concentrate on the strengths of mobile and social systems as tools for studies and education. By providing in-store pickup and increased digital customer service that drives clients back to shops, they should also marry the offline to the online world.

REFERENCES

Adams, J. S. (1963). Towards an understanding of inequity. *The Journal of Abnormal and Social Psychology, 67*(5), 422.

Albrecht, A. K., Walsh, G., & Beatty, S. E. (2017). Perceptions of group versus individual service failures and their effects on customer outcomes: The role of attributions and customer entitlement. *Journal of Service Research, 20*(2), 188–203.

Amed, I. (2018). *CEO Talk | Bruno Pavlovsky, President of Fashion, Chanel* [Online]. Retrieved July 17, 2019, from https://www.businessoffashion.com/articles/ceo-talk/ceo-talk-bruno-pavlovsky-president-of-fashion-chanel

Amed, I., & Berg, A. (2019). *The State of Fashion 2019* [Online]. Retrieved July 11, 2019, from https://cdn.businessoffashion.com/reports/The_State_of_Fashion_2019.pdf

Ayertey, S., & Ozuem, W. (2017). *Linking Service Failures to Customer Satisfaction.* 19th Annual International Conference. Global Business and Technology Association. Vienna, Austria.

Ayertey, S., & Ozuem, W. (2018). Developing compelling online recovery strategies: Implications for the fashion clothing industry. In *Digital Marketing Strategies for Fashion and Luxury Brands* (pp. 264–288). IGI Global.

Ayertey, S., & Howell, K. (2019). Service failure and recovery strategy in computer-mediated marketing environments (CMMEs). In *Leveraging Computer-Mediated Marketing Environments* (pp. 173–192). IGI Global.

Azemi, Y., Ozuem, W., Howell, K. E., & Lancaster, G. (2019). An exploration into the practice of online service failure and recovery strategies in the Balkans. *Journal of Business Research, 94*, 420–431.

Banor, M. A. (2017). *Exploring Financial Literacy as a Means to Improving the Ghanaian Economy: A Qualitative Study* (Doctoral dissertation, Northcentral University).

Barwise, P., & Meehan, S. (2010). The one thing you must get right when building a brand. *Harvard Business Review, 88*(12), 80–84.

BBC News. (2018). *Can you be sustainable if you're into fast fashion online?* [Online]. Retrieved January 30, 2019, from https://www.bbc.co.uk/news/newsbeat-45766366

BBC News. (2019). *Fast fashion: How to make clothes last longer and save the planet* [Online]. Retrieved February 20, 2019, from https://www.bbc.co.uk/news/newsbeat-47292087

BBC News. (2019). *TSB suffers £105m loss after computer chaos* [Online]. Retrieved February 2, 2019, from https://www.bbc.co.uk/news/business-47085474

Bhardwaj, V., & Fairhurst, A. (2010). Fast fashion: Response to changes in the fashion industry. *The International Review of Retail, Distribution and Consumer Research, 20*(1), 165–173.

Birtwistle, G., & Freathy, P. (1998). More than just a name above the shop: A comparison of the branding strategies of two UK fashion retailers. *International Journal of Retail & Distribution Management, 26*(8), 318–323.

Bitner, M. J., Booms, B. H., & Mohr, L. A. (1994). Critical service encounters: The employee's viewpoint. *The Journal of Marketing, 58*(4), 95–106.

Bright Local. (2018). *Local Consumer Review Survey* [Online]. Retrieved July 14, 2019, from https://www.brightlocal.com/research/local-consumer-review-survey/

British Chambers of Commerce. (2019). *BCC Quarterly Economic Survey Q2 2019: UK growth stalling amid manufacturing slowdown* [Online]. Retrieved July 16, 2019, from https://www.britishchambers.org.uk/news/2019/07bcc-quarterly-economic-survey-q2-2019-uk-growth-stalling-amid-manufacturing-slowdown

Brooks, A. (2015). *Clothing poverty: The hidden world of fast fashion and secondhand clothes*. London: Zed Books.

Causon, J. (2015). *Customer complaints made via social media on the rise—The Guardian,* May 21 [Online]. Retrieved July 13, 2019, from https://www.theguardian.com/media-network/2015/may/21/customer-complaints-social-media-rise

Chan, T. Y., & Wong, C. W. (2012). The consumption side of sustainable fashion supply chain: Understanding fashion consumer eco-fashion consumption decision. *Journal of Fashion Marketing and Management, 16*(2), 193–215.

Charlton, G. (2018). *How can luxury retailers recreate the in-store experience online?* [Online]. Retrieved July 14, 2019, from https://blog.salecycle.com/featured/how-can-luxury-retailers-recreate-the-in-store-experience-online/

Choi, B., & Choi, B. J. (2014). The effects of perceived service recovery justice on customer affection, loyalty, and word-of-mouth. *European Journal of Marketing, 48*(1/2), 108–131.

Christopher, M., Lowson, R., & Peck, H. (2004). Creating agile supply chains in the fashion industry. *International Journal of Retail & Distribution Management, 32*(8), 367–376.

Chung, B., & Hoffman, K. D. (1998). Critical incidents: Service failures that matter most. *Cornell Hotel and Restaurant Administration Quarterly, 39*(3), 66–71.

Clancy, O. (2016). *Most online clothes shoppers send something back* [Online]. Retrieved January 30, 2019, from http://www.bbc.co.uk/news/business-36395719

Collier, J. E., Breazeale, M., & White, A. (2017). Giving back the "self" in self service: Customer preferences in self-service failure recovery. *Journal of Services Marketing, 31*(6), 604–617.

Corbellini, E., & Saviolo, S. (2014). *Managing fashion and luxury companies*. Milan: Rizzoli Etas.

Craighead, C. W., Karwan, K. R., & Miller, J. L. (2004). The effects of severity of failure and customer loyalty on service recovery strategies. *Production and Operations Management, 13*(4), 307–321.

Crisafulli, B., & Singh, J. (2017). Service failures in e-retailing: Examining the effects of response time, compensation, and service criticality. *Computers in Human Behaviour, 77*, 413–424.

Da Giau, A., Macchion, L., Caniato, F., Caridi, M., Danese, P., Rinaldi, R., & Vinelli, A. (2016). Sustainability practices and web-based communication: An analysis of the Italian fashion industry. *Journal of Fashion Marketing and Management, 20*(1), 72–88.

Denicolo, P., Long, T., & Bradley-Cole, K. (2016). *Constructivist approaches and research methods. A practical guide to exploring personal meanings.* London: Sage Publications.

Fang, Z., Luo, X., & Jiang, M. (2013). Quantifying the dynamic effects of service recovery on customer satisfaction: Evidence from Chinese mobile phone markets. *Journal of Service Research, 16*(3), 341–355.

Fernie, J., Maniatakis, P. A., & Moore, C. M. (2009). The role of international hubs in a fashion retailer's sourcing strategy. *The International Review of Retail, Distribution and Consumer Research, 19*(4), 421–436.

Fletcher, K., & Grose, L. (2012). *Fashion and sustainability: Design for change.* London: Laurence King.

Ford, R., Sturman, M., & Heaton, C. (2011). *Managing quality service in hospitality: How organizations achieve excellence in the guest experience.* Nelson Education. Clifton Park, NY.

Fraser, H. (2019). *London Fashion Week: Brexit, protest and a new femininity* [Online]. Retrieved February 20, 2019, from https://edition.cnn.com/style/article/london-fashion-week-highlights-autumn-winter-2019/index.html

Goode, S., Hoehle, H., Venkatesh, V., & Brown, S. A. (2017). User compensation as a data breach recovery action: An investigation of the Sony PlayStation Network breach. *MIS Quarterly, 41*(3), 703–727.

Guillory, S. (2016). *Top five customer complaints with fashion retailers* [Online]. Retrieved July 10, 2019, from http://apparel.edgl.com/news/Top-Five-Customer-Complaints-With-Fashion-Retailers105498

Guta, M. (2018). *There Are 168 Million Active Buyers on eBay Right Now (INFOGRAPHIC)* [Online]. Retrieved July 13, 2019, from https://smallbiztrends.com/2018/03/ebay-statistics-march-2018.html

Hazée, S., Van Vaerenbergh, Y., & Armirotto, V. (2017). Co-creating service recovery after service failure: The role of brand equity. *Journal of Business Research, 74*, 101–109.

Holloway, B. B., & Beatty, S. E. (2003). Service failure in online retailing: A recovery opportunity. *Journal of Service Research, 6*(1), 92–105.

Hope, K. (2018). *The people who return most of what they buy* [Online]. Retrieved July 29, 2019, from https://www.bbc.co.uk/news/business-46279638

Hu, Z. H., Li, Q., Chen, X. J., & Wang, Y. F. (2014). Sustainable rent-based closed-loop supply chain for fashion products. *Sustainability, 6*(10), 7063–7088.

Hughes, H. (2018). *Online returns to reach 5.6 billion pounds by 2023, fashion hit hardest* [Online]. Retrieved February 9, 2019, from https://fashionunited.uk/news/retail/online-returns-to-reach-5-6-billion-pounds-by-2023/2018121740591

Kozub, K. R., O'Neill, M. A., & Palmer, A. A. (2014). Emotional antecedents and outcomes of service recovery: An exploratory study in the luxury hotel industry. *Journal of Services Marketing, 28*(3), 233–243.

Kumar, M., & Kumar, N. (2016). Three dimensions of service recovery: Examining relationship and impact. *Supply Chain Management: An International Journal, 21*(2), 273–286.

Kuo, Y., Yen, S., & Chen, L. (2011). Online auction service failures in Taiwan: Typologies and recovery strategies. *Electronic Commerce Research and Applications, 10*(2), 183–193.

Lincoln, Y. S., Lynham, S. A., & Guba, E. G. (2011). Paradigmatic controversies, contradictions, and emerging confluences revisited. In N. K. Denzin & Y. S. Lincoln (Eds.), *The SAGE Handbook of Qualitative Research* (4th ed., 97–128). Thousand Oaks, CA: Sage.

Liu, X., Burns, A. C., & Hou, Y. (2013). Comparing online and in-store shopping behavior towards luxury goods. *International Journal of Retail & Distribution Management, 41*(11/12), 885.

Logie, S. (2019). *The price of loyalty* [Online]. Retrieved July 14, 2019, from https://readgroup.co.uk/news/the-price-of-loyalty/

London Fashion week festival (2019). *London Fashion week festival 16–17 February 2019* [Online]. Retrieved July 11, 2019, from https://www.instagram.com/lfw_festival/?hl=en

Lotich, P. (2019). *Service Recovery – 5 Tips For Successful Service Recovery* [Online]. Retrieved July 6, 2019, from https://thethrivingsmallbusiness.com/service-recovery-theory/

Luo, J., Ba, S., & Zhang, H. (2012). The effectiveness of online shopping characteristics and well-designed websites on satisfaction. *Management Information Systems Quarterly, 36*(4), 1131–1144.

Maxwell, J. A. (2013). *Qualitative research design: An Interactive approach* (3rd ed.). Thousands Oaks: Sage Publications, Inc.

McCabe, K. (2018). *50+ Statistics Proving the Power of Customer Reviews* [Online]. Retrieved July 14, 2019, from https://learn.g2.com/customer-reviews-statistics

McNicholas, K. (2011). *How to use social media to promote your small business* [Online]. Retrieved July 29, 2019, from https://www.forbes.com/sites/kymmcnicholas/2011/09/19/how-to-use-social-media-to-promote-your-small-business/#3dba0cb03c50

Meuter, M. L., Ostrom, A. L., Roundtree, R. I., & Bitner, M. J. (2000). Self-service technologies: understanding customer satisfaction with technology-based service encounters. *Journal of Marketing, 64*(3), 50–64.

Mintel (2017). *Clothing retailing—UK—October 2017. London Mintel.* [Online]. Retrieved February 6, 2019, from http://academic.mintel.com/

Mollá-Descals, A., Frasquet-Deltoro, M., & Ruiz-Molina, M. E. (2011). Internationalization patterns in fashion retail distribution: Implications for firm results. *The Service Industries Journal, 31*(12), 1979–1993.

Mower, S. (2009). *Fashion guru who brings fresh hope to the high street* [Online]. Retrieved July 17, 2019, from https://www.theguardian.com/lifeandstyle/2009/feb/15/whistles-jane-shepherdson-fashion

Nili, A., Tate, M., & Gable, G. G. (2014). A typology of techno-logical enablers of website service failure prevention. *PACIS 2014 Proceedings*, 78.

Obeidat, Z. M. I., Xiao, S. H., Iyer, G. R., & Nicholson, M. (2017). Consumer revenge using the internet and social media: An examination of the role of service failure types and cognitive appraisal processes. *Psychology & Marketing, 34*(4), 496–515.

Okonkwo, U. (2010). *Luxury online: styles, systems, strategies.* Basingstoke: Palgrave Macmillan.

Ombudsman Services (2018). *Consumer action monitor—March 2018* [Online]. Retrieved October 13, 2018, from https://www.ombudsman-services.org/docs/default-source/downloads/cam-2018-report.pdf?sfvrsn=0

Ozuem, W., Howell, K., & Lancaster, G. (2008). Communicating in the new interactive marketspace. *European Journal of Marketing, 42*(9/10), 1059–1083.

Ozuem, W., Patel, A., Howell, K. E., & Lancaster, G. (2017). An exploration of consumers' response to online service recovery initiatives. *International Journal of Market Research, 59*(1), 97–115.

Ozuem, W., & Tan, K. (2014). Reconciling social media with luxury fashion brands: An exploratory study. In *Digital Arts and Entertainment: Concepts, Methodologies, Tools, and Applications* (pp. 1546–1574). IGI Global.

Ozuem, W., Thomas, T., & Lancaster, G. (2016). The influence of customer loyalty on small island economies: An empirical and exploratory study. *Journal of Strategic Marketing, 24*(6), 447–469.

Pham, M. (2017). *Communications market report* [Online]. Retrieved February 8, 2019, from https://www.ofcom.org.uk/__data/assets/pdf_file/0017/105074/cmr-2017-uk.pdf

Ramshaw, A. (2018). *The ultimate service recovery implementation guide* [Online]. Retrieved July 13, 2019, from https://www.genroe.com/blog/service-recovery-guide/11189

Rome, A. (2015). Fashion Forward? The Environmental History of Style, from Beaver Hats to IPhones

Roos, S., Sandin, G., Zamani, B., & Peters, G. (2015). *Environmental assessment of Swedish fashion consumption: Five Garments-sustainable futures. A Mistra Future Fashion report, Gothenburg* [Online]. Retrieved January 29, 2019, from http://www.mistrafuturefashion.com

Rosenmayer, A., McQuilken, L., Robertson, N., & Ogden, S. (2018). Omni-channel service failures and recoveries: Refined typologies using Facebook complaints. *Journal of Services Marketing, 32*(3), 269–285.

Sender, T. (2017). *Brits hung up on online fashion: Online sales of clothing, fashion accessories and footwear grow by 17% in 2017* [Online]. Retrieved October 5, 2018, from http://www.mintel.com/press-centre/fashion/uk-online-sales-of-clothing-fashion-accessories-and-footwear-grow-by-17-in-2017

Sengupta, A. S., Balaji, M. S., & Krishnan, B. C. (2015). How customers cope with service failure? A study of brand reputation and customer satisfaction. *Journal of Business Research, 68*(3), 665–674.

Shapland, M. (2019). *Asos on the ropes as City fears US expansion is a step too far* [Online]. Retrieved July 10, 2019, from https://www.pressreader.com/

Smith, A. K., Bolton, R. N., & Wagner, J. (1999). A model of customer satisfaction with service encounters involving failure and recovery. *Journal of Marketing Research, 36*(3), 356–372.

Smith, A. K., & Bolton, R. N. (2002). The effect of customers' emotional responses to service failures on their recovery effort evaluations and satisfaction judgments. *Journal of the Academy of Marketing Science, 30*(1), 5–23.

Solomon, M. (2014). *4 Steps From Customer Anger To Customer Loyalty: The Expert Customer Service Recovery Method* [Online]. Retrieved from https://www.forbes.com/sites/micahsolomon/2014/07/16/customer-service-recovery/#b469fd145fc6

Statista (2017). *Apparel market in the United Kingdom (UK) – Statistics & fact* [Online]. Retrieved October 5, 2018, from https://www.statista.com/topics/3348/apparel-market-in-the-uk/

Stokinger, E., & Ozuem, W. (2018). Social media and customer retention: Implications for the luxury beauty industry. In *Social Media Marketing: Breakthroughs in Research and Practice* (pp. 733–755). IGI Global.

Tan, C. W. (2011). *Understanding e-Service failures: Formation, impact and recovery* (Doctoral dissertation, University of British Columbia).

Weiners, P. (2017). *How Luxury Brands Are Adapting To An Omnichannel World* [Online]. Retrieved February 7, 2019, from https://www.forbes.com/sites/forbescommunicationscouncil/2017/06/02/how-luxury-brands-are-adapting-to-an-omnichannel-world/#7bba44131958

Westcott, R. (2017). *Southern rail: Government fines owners over train delays* [Online]. Retrieved April 23, 2019, from https://www.bbc.co.uk/news/uk-england-40591938

Zakowicz, G. (2017). *Why Brick-and-Mortar is Better Than Ever—for Online Retailers* [Online]. Retrieved April 26, 2019, from https://apparel-mag.com/why-brick-and-mortar-better-ever-online-retailers

KEY TERMS AND DEFINITIONS

Service Failure: Service failure is service performance or product that does not meet the high expectations of a customer by a company.

Recovery Strategy: Is a theory that indicates that a client who has a poor experience and gets a timely and efficient reaction to their problems will be a more faithful client than a client who has had no bad experience at all.

Theory: A major philosophical framework in service marketing literature from academia to service recovery based on social and organisational psychology theory.

Online Customer Satisfaction: The operation or practices used online by the company to satisfy the client after an occurrence of service breakdown.

Fast Fashion: An increasing trend of clients buying inexpensive clothing produced rapidly on a regular basis by mass-market retailers.

Luxury Brands: Luxury brands are seen as pictures in the minds of consumers that include connections about a higher price level, quality, aesthetics, rareness, extraordinariness and a high point of non-functional associations.

Social Constructivism: Social constructivism is an interpretative framework in which people strive to comprehend their world and generate their own precise intellects in line with their own experience.

About the Contributors

Professor Wilson Ozuem teaches and researches communications issues in computer-mediated marketing environments (CMMEs). His research interests include the implications of information technology for decision making by marketers and consumers. The results of his research have been published in scholarly journals, books and international conference papers, including the European Journal of Marketing, Journal of Business Research, Journal of Retailing and Consumer Services. Dr Ozuem was a former Senior Research Fellow (Digital Economy) at the University of Gloucestershire. He was previously an Associate Professor in Digital Marketing at Regents University, London. He currently teaches and supervises both postgraduate and undergraduate students in several universities, including Warwick University (UK), Queens University (Canada), City, University of London, University of Birmingham and Arden University. He is a Senior Fellow of Advance HE and has consulted widely for a variety of firms and public agencies. He received his BA in Business from the University of Portsmouth, MA Marketing from University of West London, MBA from London Metropolitan University, MEd (Educational Leadership and Management) from Open University (UK), PhD in Digital Marketing from Anglia Ruskin University and Postgraduate Degree in Educational Research from University of Cambridge.

Professor Elena Patten's research interests are multichannel retailing and service quality especially in the fashion and luxury field. She has published several papers in these research areas. Currently, Elena Patten works as a Professor of Fashion Management at Macromedia University of Applied Sciences. Before that, Elena Patten worked in the German fashion retail industry for 17 years. Most recently, she was retail director for a major German fashion department store chain.

Yllka Azemi teaches marketing courses to undergraduate and MBA students of the School of Business and Economics, Indiana University Northwest, USA. Her research interests include online service failure and recovery strategies, social media marketing, and consumer behaviour. She received her bachelor degree from Rochester Institute of Technology (USA), Master's degree from University of Wales (UK), and PhD from Cardiff Metropolitan University (UK). She has published research papers in *Journal of Business Research, and Qualitative Market Research: An International Journal.* She has co-authored chapters in textbooks and has written a number of papers and presented at conferences in her specialist area of research.

Professor Geoff Lancaster MSc, PhD, FCIM, FLCC, Professor Lancaster's research interests are customer relations and corporate social responsibility. He has published numerous papers and marketing and research methods textbooks. He was part-time Chairman of a corporate communications group that was in receipt of the Queen's Award for Exporting. He was Senior Examiner to the Chartered Institute of Marketing for 18 years and is in receipt of a Fellowship from the London Chamber of Commerce & Industry for services to business education. He has completed marketing consultancy projects for a number of blue chip international companies.

Dominic Appiah is currently a business lecturer at Arden University, where he leads various modules in the undergraduate level. Dominic holds a PhD in marketing from Plymouth University, an MBA from the University of Wales and a Bachelor of Arts (Politics and Philosophy), from the University Ghana. His expertise lies in offshore business development and marketing. Dominic is actively engaged in academic research. The plethora of his research investigates the dynamics of consumer purchase intentions in digitally disrupted markets and building resistance to brand switching in these competitive markets. He has published extensively in academic books and journals, including International Journal of Consumer Behaviour and International Journal of Retailing & Consumer Services. He also collaborates with leading researchers and has presented papers at reputable international conferences. Dr Appiah also has far-reaching experience in the financial services industry. Prior to joining academia, he worked at State Insurance Company in Ghana; GIA Insurance and Ghana International Bank, both in the UK. Dominic is an associate fellow of the Higher Education Academy (HEA), a member of the Chartered Institute of Marketing

(CIM), Chartered Institute of Insurance (CII) and the British Academy of Management (BAM).

Dipen Rai is a Doctoral candidate at the University of the West of Scotland, UK. He has a masters' degree in Information Technology at Cardiff Metropolitan University, UK. He has also MBA in International Business at Anglia Ruskin University, UK. He has completed the Bachelor honours degree in Business Information Technology at the University of the Wales, Trinity Saint David, UK. His research interest lies on online service failure and recovery strategies and development of effective recovery strategies.

Guida Helal holds a BBA and MA from American University of Beirut and London College of Contemporary Arts, respectively. Her studies in Marketing and Brand Management have led her to explore the current and ensuing relationship between social media marketing and social identity among the millennial generation. Her research interests include social media marketing, consumer behavior, social identity in the digital age among Millennials, luxury and fashion marketing and management. Her research has been published numerous times in conference papers, textbooks and journals including, *The International Journal of Retail & Distribution Management*. She is currently a marketing communications instructor in University of Melbourne and employed in marketing in an Australian retail company. She previously worked as a marketing and public relations consultant in Dubai and London, handling accounts based in the UK and MENA region.

Dr Sebastian Okafor teaches at the University of Cumbria (UK). He undertakes an external MSc Project Supervision at Warwick University. Dr Okafor is a member of the Assessment and Moderation team at the Institute for Professional & Executive Development (IPED) the UK. He is also an Associate Lecturer at the University of West London and Northampton University. Sebastian is a fellow of Higher Education Academy and Chartered Institute of Educational Assessors and holds a doctorate in Business Administration from Newport University. Dr Okafor holds Undergraduate and Masters from Open University (UK). His research interest includes cooperative learning in a multi-cultural environment and digital marketing.

Gordon Bowen has extensive experience in business and academia, with a total of 20 years in business and 17 years in tertiary education. His qualifications include BSc (Physics and Computer Science, Aston University),

PGCE (Postgraduate Certificate in Education, Birmingham University), MBA (specialising in finance, Sheffield Hallam University), DBA (Doctor Business Administration, University of Hull) & Certificate in Corporate Finance (London Business School). Gordon is a visiting lecturer and visiting professor in strategy, marketing & business research. His portfolio of clients include Warwick University, Northumbria University London Campus, Ulster University London Campus, Kingston University Business School, Grenoble Business School, London Campus, Hertfordshire Business School, Hertfordshire University, University of Gloucestershire, Regents University, London, and Plymouth University. Also Gordon is a visiting professor at the University of Central Punjab, UCP Business School, Pakistan. His publications include three edited books, catalogued by Harvard University, with Competitive Social Media Marketing Strategies being listed as a "best seller" by the publisher. He supervises PhD students at Regents University London, University of Central Punjab, Plymouth University, University of Wales Saint David and University of Gloucestershire. Gordon is a PhD International External Examiner for the University of KwaZulu-Natal, South Africa, having examined 3 to date. Gordon has worked in the telecommunications industry with a supplier for 17 years, occupying senior management positions in technical training, sales training, business development and corporate strategy. His roles include considerable international travel in North America, Europe, Middle East, Asia and Australia.

Vivek Chitran is a Senior Lecturer at the University of Cumbria in the UK. He is the programme leader of the Global Business Management course for the university's London campus. His interests lie in the areas of digital marketing and leadership. He is a Chartered Marketer and a member of the Chartered Institute of Marketing.Prior to his involvement in education, Vivek has spent over 14 years in the IT industry working with multinational corporations in the enterprise resource planning (ERP) software sector and supporting IBM systems. He has worked with clients in the capacity of systems advisory and technical training roles. He was an IBM authorised trainer and has conducted various bespoke system workshops for clients in south-east Asia region within the manufacturing and financial sectors. Vivek is an ardent believer in life-long learning and spends much of his time in researching about the role of technology in everyday life. He has a passion for the betterment of human endeavour with the use of technology.

Samuel Ayertey has a PhD in Marketing from the University of Plymouth (UK), an MBA from the University of Wales (UK). Samuel has worked in a number of companies across UK and Africa. He has presented several conference papers in the field of digital marketing, particularly on the impact of emerging technologies on service failure and recovery strategies. Samuel is also a fellow of the Higher Education Academy (HEA) and member of the Chartered Institute of Marketing (CIM).

Silvia Ranfagni PhD, is Associate Professor of Marketing at the Department of Economics and Management at the University of Florence (Italy). Her research interests include innovation, internationalization and brand management with special reference to the fashion and cultural industry. She has participated in international marketing conferences, and has published in national and international journals such as *Journal of Fashion Marketing and Management, Management Decision, European Journal of Marketing, Journal of Consumer Behaviour, Journal of Business Research, Journal of Interactive Marketing*.

Kenneth Appiah PhD is a Lecturer at the University of Cumbria. His research focuses on market entry strategies, internationalisation and competitiveness of SMEs, particularly emerging SMEs and Technology Transfer. Kenneth has published articles in a number of journals such as *Journal of Critical Perspective in International Business, Journal of Business and Retail Management and several other outlets*.

Danio Berti, is Director of Wem Park Research Laboratory. He teaches marketing and digital marketing at the University of Florence. His research interests include digital marketing, internationalization and brand management. He has participated to national and international marketing conferences.

Jianqiong Xu is currently a PhD student at theUniversity of Gloucestershire. Her research interest focuses on luxury fashion brands and social media marketing. She has published several conference papers and book chapters in the field of digital marketing.

Dr. Maxwell Ayertey Banor is the Director of the Hayssen Academic Resource Center (HARC) at Lakeland University, Wisconsin. He holds a PhD in Financial Management from Northcentral University, a Master of Science in Mathematics from Youngstown State University and a Bachelor of Science in Mathematics from University of Cape Coast in Ghana. His primary research interest includes rapid development of microfinance, role of microfinance institutions in the modern finance industry, and understanding of microfinance in developing economies. Prior to being the Director of HARC, he was a Clinical Mathematics Faculty Member at Shepherd University, West Virginia where he taught mathematics to undergraduate students for 10 years.

Md Nazmul Islam completed an MBA and Bachelor of Arts (BA) in Applied Accounting from Anglia Ruskin University (UK). He is currently undertaking a doctoral programme at the University of the West of Scotland His research interest focuses on digital marketing, particularly on the interface between social media marketing and social enterprise.

Ana Hobson manages the marketing department for the American Chamber of Commerce Resources, which is located in downtown Chicago. She received her bachelor degree from Grand Valley State University. Her research interests include marketing to those with disabilities, consumer behavior, and non-profit marketing strategies. She is skilled in advertising, data analysis, and social media. Ana has also worked for numerous organizations including: Indiana University Northwest, Health for Life Grand Rapids, and Hobson Associates. She has also had the honor of presenting at the 2019 International Academy of Business and Public Administration Disciplines Conference.

Ali Usman is a Doctoral Degree candidate in the field of digital marketing at University of the West of Scotland UK. He currently teaches digital marketing at Regent College Higher Education London. His major area of research is social media marketing and consumers' buying behaviour. His recent work includes the role of social media on consumers purchase intentions in luxury fashion industry & Social media and consumers purchase intentions: A social influence perspective.

Dr. Raye Ng is an established academic based in the UK and has research interests in International Business, Cross Cultural Management, and Corporate Culture. He has worked in various UK universities, delivered guest lectures in numerous universities in China, Malaysia, Singapore and Hong Kong, and has vast experience in both taught and research degrees. Raye also has special interests in innovative and creative pedagogical approaches and internationalisation of curriculum. He read BA (Hons)

Financial Economics, MA Geographies of Globalisation and Development, and received his PhD (Corporate Culture) at University of Liverpool (UK). Raye is a Fellow of the Higher Education Academy UK and holds a PGCert in Teaching and Learning, and a PGCert in E-Learning: Theory and Practice.

Michelle Willis is a lecturer in International Business at University of Cumbria (UK) where she is also completing her PhD in e-marketing. She received her MSc in International Business with distinction from the University of Hertfordshire (UK). At the same university she received her BA in Business Studies with First-Class honours and completed a one year study abroad programme in Malaysia. Prior to studying masters' degree, she worked at the Business School Undergraduate Administration department for the University of Hertfordshire as a Student Information Officer. Her research interest focuses on emerging technologies, particularly on the interface between social networking sites (SNS) and the development of marketing programme in the fashion industry.

Professor Kerry Howell holds the Chair of Governance and Leadership at Plymouth Business School (PBS) and through his research generated scholarly expertise in areas relating to methodology, governance, leadership, EU policy and regulation as well as written research texts with Nova Science Press, Palgrave McMillan Press and Sage Publications. He is currently working on a monograph regarding leadership, culture and path-dependency with Cambridge Scholars Publishers. Professor Howell has produced numerous refereed journal articles and managed consultancy and funded research projects for various public and private sector institutions. He was Chair of the Public Administration Committee (PAC) and member of the Joint University Council (JUC) 2014–17. Professor Howell teaches methodology and methods, has supervised over twenty-five research degree completions and is currently Director of Studies for numerous doctoral candidates. Professor Howell developed the PBS Research Assessment Exercise (RAE2008) and (REF2013) submissions for Business and Management; he continues to provide advice for institutions regarding the ongoing development of submissions for (REF2021).

Lightning Source UK Ltd.
Milton Keynes UK
UKHW020610130220
358664UK00006B/548